David Herschell Edwards

Around the ancient city in six circular tours

Historical and descriptive

David Herschell Edwards

Around the ancient city in six circular tours
Historical and descriptive

ISBN/EAN: 9783337270667

Printed in Europe, USA, Canada, Australia, Japan

Cover: Foto ©ninafisch / pixelio.de

More available books at **www.hansebooks.com**

Around the Ancient City

IN SIX CIRCULAR TOURS,

Historical and Descriptive,

WITH NOTES ON THE ANCIENT SUPERSTITIONS, FOLK LORE,
EMINENT MEN, AND CURIOUS CHARACTERS IN VARIOUS
DISTRICTS OF FORFAR AND KINCARDINESHIRES.

A county rich and gay,
Broke into hills, with balmy odours crown'd,
And   .   .   joyous dales ;
Mountains and streams ;
And clust'ring towers, and monuments of fame,
And scenes of glorious deeds in little bounds.

Brechin:
D. H. EDWARDS, "ADVERTISER" OFFICE.

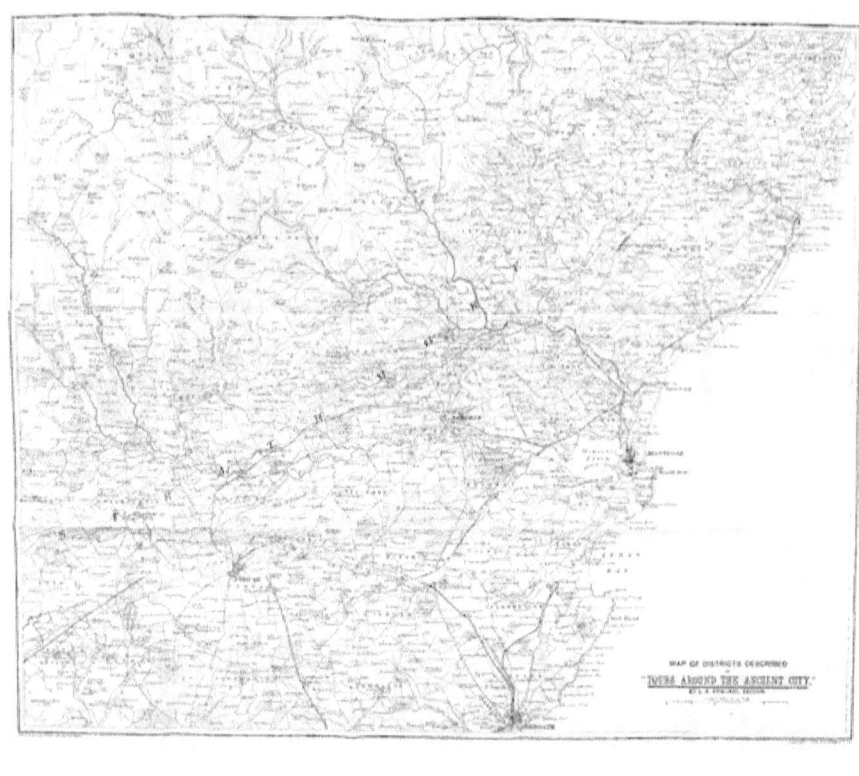

SYNOPSIS OF CONTENTS.

FIRST TOUR.

PAGE.

INTRODUCTION—Approaches to the City—Mechanics' Institution—Dalhousie Memorial Fountain—Bearehill—St Michael's Mount—West Toll—Toll Wood—Maulesden—St Ann's—Kintrockat—Balnabreich—The Noran—Marcus—Finavon Castle—'Earl Beardie'—'The Wicked Master'—Vitrified Fort—Roman Camp—Tannadice—Cortachy Castle—Ogilvys—The Battle of Saughs—'Hawkit Stirk'—Inverquharity Castle—Inverquharity Ogilvys—'It was a' for our richtfu' King'—Glen Clova—Clova—The Peel—Loch Brandy—Glen Ogil—Fentons of Glen Ogil—Castle of Corsens—Castle of Queich—Castle of Wester Ogil—'Loupin' Agne'—Castle of Vane—'Kelpie's Footmark'—Denchar Castle—Fern—Careston Castle—Arms of Carnegy, Balnamoon—Marquis of Montrose—Superstitions, . . . 9-74

Extended Tour.—Cortachy Castle.—The Battle of Saughs.—Inverquharity Castle.—The Ogilvy Family.—Clova.—Loch Brandy.

SECOND TOUR.

'The Kennels'—Aldbar Castle—Sculptured Stones of Angus—Interesting Stone—The Old Chapel—Den o' Aldbar—Ardovie—Cookston—Melgund Castle—Quadrangular Tower—Armorial Bearings—Mysterious Disappearance—Flemington Castle—Church and Parish of Aberlemno—Celebrated Sculptured Stones—Battle at Aberlemno—Forfar—Sutors of Forfar—Public Library—Witches Stone—Forfar Castle—Forfar Loch—Malcolm Canmore—Glamis Castle—Legend—Witchcraft—The Haunted Room—Village of Glamis—Interesting Memorials—Vale of Strathmore'—Glen of Ogilvy—The Nine Maidens—

Kirriemuir — Manufactures — 'Standing Stone' — 'Rocking Stones' — 'Weem's Holes' — The Den — Airlie Castle — Weird Story — Antiquities — Den of Airlie — 'Reekie Linn' — 'Slug of Aucrannie' — Kingoldrum — The Melgund — Castle of Balfour — Angus Hill, ... 70-140

Extended Tour.— Forfar and District.— Royalty at Forfar.— Glamis Castle.— Story of Lady Jane Douglas.— The Haunted Room.— Village of Glamis.— Vale of Strathmore.— Glen of Ogilvy — "The Nine Maidens."— Kirriemuir.— Standing Stone, and Den of Kirriemuir.— Castle of Airlie.— Legend **of** "The Drummer Boy."— Den of Airlie **and** "Reekie Linn.'— Kingoldrum.

THIRD TOUR.

Pittendreich — Willie Mill's Burn — Bridge **of** Blackhall — Glen of Lethnot — West Water — Church **of** Lethnot — Navar — The Arch Fiend — Priest's Road — Menmuir — Lawless Raids — Tragedies — Sepulchral Remains — Witchcraft and other Superstitions — Hill of Wirren — Caterthun — The Work of the Witches and Fairies — Antiquarians Differ — Balnamoon — Interesting Family History — Amusing Anecdotes — 'Bonymune's Cave' — 'Rebel Laird' — Balhall — Little Brechin — Murlingden — The Plague — A Remarkable Family — The 'Cattle Rake' — Cookston Farm — Springfield House, ... 143-178

Extended Tour.— West Water — Glen of Lethnot — Balhall — Hill of Wirren — Craig of Stoneyford, &c., &c.

FOURTH TOUR.

Glencadam — Trinity — Cairnbank — Bridge of Cruick — Inchbare — West Water Bridge — Dalhousie Memorial Arch — Edzell — Suspension Bridge — Mineral Well — The Muir — Edzell Castle — Old Church and Churchyard — Old Lairds of Edzell — Lindsay Vault — Last Laird of Edzell — Bridge of Mooran — The Burn — Bridge of Auchmull — Stone Circles — Shooting Lodge of Millden — The Mason's Tower — Hill of Modloch — Birks of Ardoch — Tarfside — Bridge of Tarf — Rowan Hill — Parish Church and Manse — The Mark — Castle of Invermark — Lochiemore — Invermark Lodge — The Queen's Well — The Old Church — Grave of a Noted Poet — Lochlee — Description of Loch — surrounding Mountains — The Unich and Lee — 'Gryp's Chamber' — Dr Guthrie's Retreat — The Gaberlunzie, ... 180-228

Extended Tour.— Edzell Castle — The Lindsay Vault — Old Churchyard.
Farther Extension.— The Bridge of **Mooran.**

SYNOPSIS OF CONTENTS.

FIFTH TOUR.

The Gannochy—An Old Tradition—Balbegno Castle—Middleton and the Ghost—Fettercairn—The Royal Visit—The Ancient Cross—Witch Burning—Fettercairn House—The House of Fasque and the Gladstones—The Old Town of Kincardine—Murder of Kenneth III.—Legend of Den-Finella—Kincardine Castle—Green Cairn—The Clatterin' Brig—[*Extended Tour*—Cairn o' Mount—Cloch-na-Ben—Forest of Birse—Feughside—The Feuch and the Dee.]—Clatterin' Brig—Whisky and Cockfighting—Glensaugh Lodge—Loch of Glensaugh—Bright's Well—Glen of Drumtochty—**A Picturesque Scene**—Friar's Glen—John o' Fordoun, the Old Historian—**The Priest's Well**—Drumtochty Castle—Castle of Glenfarquhar—Church of St Palladius—Auchinblae—'**A Very Paradise for Retirement**'—Lovely Panorama as viewed from Stra'finla Top—Knock Hill—A Charming View—'The Court Stone'—Drumsleed Woods—An Old Encampment—Pitarrow—George Wishart, the Martyr—Mill of Conveth—Haulkerton—'Brownie's Kettle,' or 'Sheriff's Pot'—**A Gruesome Story**—The Church of Fordoun—The Parish Bier—An Old School—A Tax on Gravestones—Free Church Manse.—[*Extended Tour*: Kincardineshire Villages—Fordoun to Stonemaven—Redhall, Monboddo, Lord Monboddo and Burns, Glenbervie Castle and Churchyard, Tombstones of Burns' Ancestors, Eminent Men of the Mearns, A Small County Rich in Historic Lore—Drumlithie—Stonehaven, Old and New Towns—**Places of** Interest—Cowie—Urie Castle, Fetteresso Castle, Dunnottar Castle, **Prison** for Covenanters, Martyr's Monument, **David** Paterson ('Old Mortality'), and Sir Walter Scott—Church of Kinneff—The Minister's Wife and the Regalia of Scotland—Allardyce House—Arbuthnott House—Bervie—Hallgreen Castle—Benholm Tower—Brotherton Castle—Johnshaven—Lauriston **Castle**—Legend of the Blind Piper—Den Finella—Miltonhaven—**Tanglehaʼ**—Carrying off a Village—Kaim o' Mathers—**Ecclesgreig**—St Cyrus, A Curious Bequest, **A** Poet's Grave, George Beattie, John o' Arnha', the Water Kelpie—Dairnie's Den, Morphie and Canterland, Hill of Garvock, the **Packman's House**—Laurencekirk, Founding a Village, **Lord Gardenstone's** Humours, taking down a 'buck' and sharing his bed with **a** pig, Famous Snuff-boxes, Johnston and **the** Barclays—Thornton and the Thornton Family, 'Men o' the Mearns'—A Historic Vault at Marykirk—Sauchieburn—The Bereans and their Outspoken Pastors—Luthermuir—Balmakewan, **the** First Lindsay of Balcarres—Marykirk, Kirktonhill, Introduction of the Potato—C aigo, a Long-lived Race—Logie-Pert, a picturesque Old Churchyard, the Birthplace of a Famous Historian—The Covenanters of North Water Bridge, John Erskine's Dream—The Gallery—Inglismaldie, the Falconers and Hawkertoun—Dunlappie, Reidhall—The Lands of Luntie, the Rafters of Brechin Kirk—Auchinreoch and Chapelton

—Stracathro, John Baliol's Penance, the Battle of
Stracathro, ... 231-318

Extended Tour.—Redhall—Monboddo—Glenbervie—Drumlithie—Stonehaven—Cowie—Urie—Fetteresso—Dunnottar Castle—Church of Kinneff—Bervie—Benholm—Brotherton—Johnshaven—Den Finella—Kaim o' Mathers—St Cyrus Hill of Garvock.

SIXTH TOUR.

Cairnbank and Bishop Carnott, 'A large white horse,' and leading stones for the building of Brechin Belfry from 1354 to 1884, Huntly Hill, the Battle of Brechin, the Haer Cairn, Keithock Law—The Vicarage of Eglisjohn, Dun House, Superintendent Erskine, Knox preaching at Dun, The Ghost o' Dun, murder of a young priest, the Erskines at Flodden, poisoning 'two zoung boyis'—Bridge of Dun—Langley and Broomley, a great Spanish chestnut—Hillside, a pretty village, Sunnyside—Montrose and its castle, visited by Wallace and Sir James Douglas, its distinguished educational position, the plague, Prince Charles, the Duke of Cumberland, 'The Sea enriches and the Rose adorns,' Montrose visited by Johnson and Burns, its famous men, its beautiful surroundings, a fine health resort, its places of interest, the Basin—Ferryden—Around the coast to Lunan, Usan, fisher superstitions, 'only oor character to depend on,' 'The Cadger's Road,' 'the King's Cadger'—Parish of Craig, Saint Skae, Den of Dunninald, Black Jack's Castle, Castle of Craig, Rossie, 'cheat the wuddy,' Rossie Reformatory—Lunan Bay, Redcastle, a magnificent panorama, the Witches' Pool, a literary dominie, a kirk beadle father-in-law of an Earl's daughter, grandfather of a Marchioness, and great-grandfather of a Marquis and a Duchess, the last Scottish martyr—Inverkeillor, Anniston, Ethie Castle, the ghost of Cardinal Beaton, the Earls of Northesk—Kinblethmont—Auchmithie (Scott's Musselcrag), a quaint old world fishing village, descendants of the 'Mucklebackets,' Sir Walter's bedroom—Seaton House—Arbroath and its Abbey, historical associations, the 'Fairport' of the 'Antiquary,' the 'Round O,' Dr Johnson's visit, the Royal Forest, Legend of the Bell Rock, the Battle of Arbroath, the Cliffs, a scene of great grandeur and wildness, legends and traditions of the Mason's Cove, the Deel's E'e, the Smuggler's Den—Hospitalfield (Monkbarns), a rich art collection—St Vigeans, Celtic memorials, the King's tutor, a remarkable echo—Lethain Grange—Colliston Castle—Friockheim—Gardyne Castle—Braikie and its cantankerous keeper, Castle Jean—Guthrie Castle, Kinnell and the Ogilvy Aisle—Maryton and the Lairds of Baldovie, Andrew Melville's quaint letter, bickering about church stools, curious church collections in the olden time—Old Montrose and its Marquis, the royal forest, Lord

SYNOPSIS OF CONTENTS. vii

Southesk on ancient 'Earth Houses,' 'Cairns,' &c.—the Woods of Bonnyton, a mysterious disappearance, Fullerton and Ananie, the old Montreathmont Moor and substantial 'pin money'—Farnell and its old Castle—Kinnaird Castle and its historic associations, the deer park, the ancient Carnegie family, their brilliant talents and literary gifts, the present Earl as an antiquarian and poet—the Ancient Bridge of Brechin—John Ochterlony on the beautiful surroundings of Brechin in 1682, a picturesque spot 'the keystane o' the Brig'—witchcraft and a branded dog—Brechin Castle, its grounds and gardens, its ancient history, the scene of the homage of King John Baliol and the resignation of the crown and kingdom, besieged by the English in 1303, Sir Thomas Maule's defence, the 'war wolf,' the Maules and their history, the Lords de Brechin, the Earls of Dalhousie—Lord Panmure, his liberality and amusing escapades—Fox Maule, the last Baron Panmure, the Hon. George Ramsay, C.B., 12th Earl, Hon. John William Ramsay, 13th Earl, his bright career and good works, the tragic death of the Earl and Countess—a promising young Earl, ... 319-446

Extended Tour.—Broomley—Montrose—Ferryden—Craig House—Rossie Castle—Lunan, Lunan Bay—Redcastle.

Farther Extension.—Auchmithie—Arbroath—and back by Friockheim—over Montreathmont Muir to Farnell.

Illustrations

	PAGE
Map of District	
Brechin from the Bridge	13
Mechanics' Institute	17
Maulesden	22
Finavon Castle	28
Tannadice	36
,, from the South Esk	36
,, from Railway Viaduct	71
Cortachy Castle	41
Inverquharity Castle	47
On the Noran	62
Castle of Vane	65
Careston Castle	69
,,	71
Brechin Cathedral	75
Aldbar Castle	78
Melgund Castle	88
Glamis Castle	122
Den of Airlie	137
Little Brechin	173
Trinity Muir on Market Day	181
West Water Bridge	183
Dalhousie Memorial Arch	184
Edzell	186

ILLUSTRATIONS.

Edzell Castle	190
Mooran Bridge	200
Woods of the Burn	202
On the Mudloch	208
Tarfside	209
Bridge of Tarf	210
Invermark Castle	214
Invermark Lodge	217
Queen's Well	218
Invermark Churchyard	220
On Lochlee	224
Lochlee	225
Gannochy Bridge	232
Fettercairn	237
Fasque House	240
Den Finella	245
Clatterin' Brig	249
Drumtochty Castle	250
Auchinblae	253
Fordoun Church	260
Monboddo House	263
Urie Castle	270
Dunnottar Castle	270
Johnshaven	278
St Cyrus Churchyard	283
Thornton Castle (from north)	295
,, (from south-west)	295
Marykirk Church	299
Stracathro House	317
Arms of Montrose	336
The Old Windmill	337
Montrose (from Rossie Braes)	340
High Street, Montrose	343
Suspension Bridge	345
Ferryden	346

ILLUSTRATIONS.

Redcastle	357
Lunan Bay	360
Ethie Castle	367
Mussel Craig (Auchmithie)	370
Arbroath Abbey	375
Hospitalfield	384
Maryton Church	398
Farnell Castle	405
Farnell Church	407
Kinnaird Castle	415
Bridge of Brechin	424
View of Brechin	425
Brechin from the Bridge	426
Brechin in 1600	429
Brechin Castle	434

Note

*I have used no gloss, no varnish,
To make fair things fairer look.*

OUR introductory chapter treats of the attractions presented by the many notable things in the counties of Forfar and Kincardine—civil, ecclesiastical, social and architectural, as well as of the richness, beauty, and grandeur they present to the botanist the geologist, and the lover of Nature. Here it is only necessary to express the hope that natives of Angus and Mearns, whether at home or abroad, and who are naturally pleased to know, as concisely as possible, about the numerous facts of interest pertaining to their native counties previous to their own days, will find not a little to entertain them.

We hear a good deal in these times about "the literature of locality." A "National Home Union" was formed in England the other day, with the patriotic intent of specially interesting its members in the history and literature, the physical geography, and the natural history of their country. Throughout this work we again and again refer to the productions of other writers and the sources of our information regarding the traditions, antiquities, old customs, folk-lore, territorial families, eminent men, curious characters, and quaint stories of the districts. Nothing, we think, can be more gratifying than the increasing interest which of late years has sprung up regarding the past annals of our parishes and counties. Many unwritten legends and traditions there are, as well as the already written records and accounts, which in the present transitional and busy age it is advisable to lay hold of and secure in more permanent form than the vicissitudes and chances of traditionary lore can afford. Even more than in the past, says a recent writer, will these be valuable to the future historian. Our rapidly changing customs and modes of living, as well as the exigencies of a highly complex civilization, will soon obliterate from view many picturesque incidents and associations which now invest the different localities with a romantic and enticing charm. The history of the two counties under notice, indeed of a country such as Scotland, naturally divides itself into two sections—the one exhibiting its material progress in the cultivation of the land by the multiplication of its strongholds and baronial residences, and the other displaying the development of civilization by the erection and maintenance of its religious houses. We have, consequently, found it necessary in our rambles to have a good deal to do with these two institutions—the Castle and the Kirk—as affording a safe measure of advancement of a district. For, whilst the Castle was the outcome of physical force and designed to establish territorial rights by the strong hand, the Kirk was the seat of that mental energy which, by the use of letters, could maintain these rights when established, and confirm them to posterity. In early times the province of the ecclesiastic was as much temporal as spiritual, and the history of the most stirring periods was often planned and initiated within the peaceful serenity of the cloister.

Regarding the picturesque scenes we endeavour to describe, we do not require to explain that they can be selected to suit the time and convenience of either tourist or home rambler. The number and *locale* of many of the places referred to may to some extent perplex the visitor, owing to the somewhat zig-zag, switchback style in which, for the sake of connecting history and family details, we have found it necessary to refer to them, but a glance at our route map will be sufficient to make matters clear. A word of thanks is due to the assistance received from friends in our efforts to add interest to the volume by means of illustrations. Particularly are we indebted to Mr D. Waterson, a young and promising local artist now making his way in London, for the design on cover, for the drawing of Lochlee and other places, and also for a number of sketches for our vignettes, etc.

Around our district the journey need not be a long one to afford variety of entertainment and instruction. And as we turn away into the open country we, for the time, leave behind not only the din and the smoke, but also those microscopic cares and worries of daily life, and enjoy the repose and invigoration that mother earth imparts to "her foster child—her inmate, man." Summer strolls leave pleasing pictures in the memory, and when winter's snows and leafless trees are present, these stored-up summer pictures bring summer to the heart.

AROUND THE ANCIENT CITY.

Introductory.

"A district rich and gay,
Broke into hills, with balmy odours crown'd,
And joyous vales,
Mountains and streams,
And clust'ring towers, and monuments of fame,
And scenes of glorious deeds in little bounds"

WHILE far from underrating the value of foreign travel to healthy holiday makers, we entertain considerable doubt as to the restfulness experienced by less fortunate persons in struggling for apartments, and over hotel bills, in what Mr Blenkinsop called "furring parts." For weary mind and body there is better relaxation nearer home. There is no lack in variety of temperature, as well as picturesque and romantic scenery, or of historical and traditional associations within the compass of this island, and there are marvels enough —architectural, archæological, and geographical—to occupy the mind in a genial and holiday-making manner. We know, and we do not forget, that "local" is something of a despised word among certain sunward-soaring folks; but is it not the case that home, which is always local, if seen aright, will be found to comprehend the infinite spirit and the finite form of truth and beauty? Although the district of which Brechin forms the centre presents many glimpses of "the stern and wild"—and the Sovereign herself, in her "Leaves," has testified to some of the charms of our neighbourhood—it will be found by the visitor quite different from those scenes representing the veriest odds and ends of creation, where Nature is seen in what may be called its shreds and patches, gussets and selvedges. Here the eye rests on many a smiling scene and tranquil landscape calculated to charm the lover of rich lowland beauty, and of reminiscences of an historical nature.

> Few frowning steeps, or heaven-defying crags,
> Intrude; but peaceful villages and homes,
> And softly swelling hills and valleys wide,
> And silvery rivers gliding to the sea,
> And placid country seats, from out their wealth
> Of woodland glancing, form a perfect whole,
> Nor wild nor tame, but Harmony itself.

We shall suppose that summer is at its height, and that Nature looks her best, when every walk or drive into the country is full of interest to those who can recognise old friends in the beautiful wayside flowers, and in the voices of the rejoicing birds. The woods have put on the whole of their holiday dress, the green leaves refresh our eyes, and their shade at noon-day is as pleasant as good news from a distant land. Every wayside is now a study of scented beauty, and every dell is a haunt of joyous sounds. Each object is beautiful in its own way to those who love to read the great book that Nature spreads wide open before us.

Now-a-days we hear much about lovers of natural beauty waging warfare against the utilitarian spirit of the age. At one time they are called on to fight against the wanton destruction of time-honoured monuments of the past; and at another against the intrusion of a railway into our most lovely and picturesque districts.

To the tourist and the lover of the romantic anything that would tend to impair the beauty and the historic interest of our most attractive scenes must be guarded with the utmost jealousy.

And here let us say a word about the preservation of ancient monuments, in which our district is so rich. The neglect of public monuments and graveyard memorials has, we are pleased to observe, led to the establishment of a "National Society for Preserving the Memorials of the Dead," a Society in which the Prince of Wales and several of the nobility, including the Earl of Southesk and others, take a warm interest. From the first reports of the local secretaries, it will be seen that great need existed for such a society. A vicar took tombstones from a graveyard to pave his coach-house and cottage floors. At Port-of-Menteith, in Perthshire, gravestones have been used in the construction of the pier for the small boats on the lake. Modern tiles cover curious monumental slabs in scores of churches, and many a churchyard has been "ploughed up." But we need not continue the weary and disgraceful catalogue.

Everyone who is in the least interested in historical or artistic research has been long familiar with examples of gross carelessness—to use no stronger word—displayed towards relics that tell of those who have quitted this world. Opinions will always vary as to the need of such memorials. It will be agreed, however, that if pious associations and the reverence of generations have gathered round such relics, it is hard that now they should run the risk of sheer

Vandalism. We do not refer to the importance which more than once has arisen in cases of disputed succession from the preservation of gravestones and works of art, but we are urging upon the grounds of reverence and common decency, that respect should be shown to the tablets which alone remain to tell us of our fathers. From the fact of our having had in our midst such noted antiquarians as the late Patrick Chalmers of Aldbar and the late Andrew Jervise, this district has been well protected, and their researches have, we shall see, cast much light on many a quaint tradition and richly carved memorial of the past.

As we proceed, it will be our endeavour to speak of the hoary chronicles of the past—give morsels of history and tradition, briefly treated, and so pleasantly flavoured as to tempt the reader and the visitor to more extensive and detailed narrative in such important works as Warden's "Forfarshire," Jervise's "Memorials," Marshall's "Scenes," Carrie's "Ancient Things," &c.

In our "trips" we shall find the eye resting upon many a picturesque landscape and historic scene—the hoary remains of former greatness nestling amid ancestral trees, the homes of great and illustrious families, and modern mansions rearing their graceful towers above much that is naturally romantic as well as artistically beautiful. An intelligent observation of what we see around us will carry with it its own reward, for in such a case we find—

> "Each rock a pulpit, and each stone a book,
> Proclaiming to our fancy numerous teachers,
> From lowliest nook."

First Tour.

MAULESDEN, KINTROCKAT, MARCUS, FINAVON, TANNA-
DICE, GLENOGIL, FERN, CASTLE OF VANE,
CARESTON CASTLE, &c.

We'll awa', we'll awa', to the woods awa',
To the gorsy brae, an' the birken shaw ;
Where the hill burn rows, an' the heather grows,
An' the bricht e'e o' heaven beams bonny owre a'.

THE charming approaches to the Ancient City, and the sylvan beauty by which it is surrounded, are admired by all strangers, and have furnished pleasing themes to the historian as well as the poet. Even at the risk of being censured at the outset for digression, it might be said that we in Brechin are in little danger of ever lacking the largest breathing spaces so long as we have such amplitude of hill and glen. Our landed proprietors, as a rule, allow respectable visitors to feel that their foot is on their "native heath," although their name may not be "Macgregor." It is not so in many districts, where the God-made country is being invaded by the man-made town, and where corn has been seen growing, and where the singing of birds has been heard, now stretch lines of street loud with the hum of a swarming population; and instead of the leafy home of the sweet warblers of the wood is the unsparing march of stone and lime.

However, after all, this lateral extension of human habitation is a sign of progress, and is better than the old extension that was vertical and vicious. Yet if this lateral extension is to go on, what is to become of the bits of green sward and our old friends the buttercups and daisies, and the nooks of wood wherein to retire from the oppression of crowded streets and dream of fairies, if we cannot see them—

"Where the midnight fairies glide."

Although we daresay the green-coated gentry, who are said to be very finical in their tastes, must have long ago taken their departure from such scenes. As a recent writer has said:

"If our great cities continue to expand at the present ratio, and if the towns follow the cities, the villages the towns, and the clachans the villages, the time may at length come when the whole country will be one mass of buildings, with scarcely so much grass left as would sustain a cow, or afford sufficient space for a lark's nest, not to mention the domestic necessities of kindred small birds and many beautiful insects which charm alike the poet and the man of science. Architects, quarrymen, masons, joiners, and other craftsmen may perhaps sneer at this picture as an extravagant fancy, and earnestly wish that there were any chance of its being realised as a hard fact.

We as sincerely hope for our part that anything so deplorable will never happen. But things don't look well. London, for instance, is fast swallowing up one vast region of England, and as it grows with what it feeds upon, its topographical voracity is year by year becoming enormous and almost insatiable. The cattle that at night lie down amid daisies miles outside London find themselves confronted in the morning by an advancing wave of brick. They are herded to fresh fields and new pastures, but the sound of the bricklayer's trowel is ever in their placid ears, as they are driven without pity beyond the circumference of an ever-widening ring."

The late George Gilfillan, whose sun set, and whose eloquent lips became dumb and were sealed by death in Brechin, loved the city and its charming environs as well as the romantic glens and haunted ruins in the district. He wrote—

"I love the town for its beautiful situation, lying so sweetly by the side of the clear and sparkling South Esk, surrounded by rich gardens, overhung by the frowning forehead of its ancient castle, and backed by the stern battlement of the Grampian mountains; for the sake of its kind and intelligent inhabitants; and on account of many pleasing personal associations. It is not only beautiful in itself, but forms the centre to a wide surrounding circle of romantic interest. There are numerous fine old ruins, in which many a gay party, as they dine, feel their laughter deadened by the sound of the wind moaning through the 'rents of ruin' in the hollow windows, or by the sight of the rank grass growing in the dining-rooms where once still gayer parties were convened, and in which everything is in keeping with the spirit of the place—old trees above, old gardens below, and old shadowy hills standing up as grim guardians of the scene behind."

The rivers and streams of the district have been immortalised in verse by Ross of "The Fortunate Shepherdess,", and Laing, whose sweet garland of

"Wayside Flowers" lends a perfume far beyond their place of birth, and who sung so felicitously of the winding Lemno, the limpid Keithock, the silver Noran, the sweet South Esk, the West Water, so dear to anglers, and the romantic North Esk, which has been described by a writer as resembling "in colour a mixture of claret and port wine—a mellow and moving autumnal darkness, finely contrasted with the white bubbles which sparkle on the surface;" the "all-beautiful Burn," too, will yet command our attention and admiration—a place of such impressive grandeur as to make Mr Gilfillan say that if he had the choice of a spot in which to die, and were disembodied spirits permitted to choose some particular scene for an eternal sanctuary, his should be found by the side of these clustering woods.

Having, in our "Pocket History of Brechin," told the visitor what is of interest regarding the story of Brechin, and in imagination conducted him through its streets, it is not necessary to repeat it here. We make our exit from the "west end," which has quite a "select" aspect compared with the air of life and bustle of the principal thoroughfares, and take our way through Castle Street (formerly known as the "West Port").

We make the Mechanics' Institution our starting point. This elegant structure is still the finest specimen of architecture in the city. It was gifted by Lord Panmure (William Maule) along with £1000 in money, and a number of valuable paintings, and feudally vested in the Town Council. There had been previously no proper lecture-room and library for the Mechanics' Institution, which was established in 1835, and increased accommodation was required for the grammar school, parish school, and burgh school.

The foundation stone was laid on 28th June, 1838—the coronation day of Queen Victoria. Shortly after the introduction of the Scottish Education Act the present High School and other schools were built, so that now the schoolrooms are for the accommodation of the City Club reading and billiard rooms, and the attendant's residence.

MECHANICS' INSTITUTE.

The front of the building is in the Tudor style of architecture, with castellated parapet, ornamented with pinnacles. A square tower of fine proportions rises in the centre to a height of eighty feet. From the top of the tower is seen one of the most lovely and variegated prospects imaginable. The Hall, which is open to visitors, is one of the finest sights of the city. It contains many valuable paintings by old and modern artists — including portraits of Wallace, Oliver Cromwell, Charles II., Queen Charlotte, Lord Panmure, Rev. Dr Foote, Alexander Laing, Andrew Jervise, and others. It also contains several of Philip's best productions, including "The Interior of a Cottage," which secured to the artist, then a young man and unknown to fame, the patronage of Lord Panmure, who sent him to study in London, and but for whose generosity and influence Philip might have died unknown. At Brechin Castle he painted several pictures for his Lordship, including "A Group of Cows," probably the best effect of all his pictures, which, with a large historical subject, representing "Bruce receiving the Sacrament from the Abbot of Inchaffry on the Evening of Bannockburn," graces the walls of the Hall. This large painting was exhibited in many towns, but it did not find a purchaser, and as Lord Panmure knew that Philip urgently required money, he gave him "a lordly sum" for it.

    Art and Science own his liberal hand—
    Painters and Poets—all his debtors stand.

Packed together in the most unscientific manner in a corner of the Library, the visitor will find an interesting collection of ancient coins, fragments of pottery, and other relics of antiquity. We trust these form only the nucleus of what will at no distant date become an important museum.

The Dalhousie Memorial Fountain next attracts attention. It was erected by Lady Christian Maule in memory of her brother, Fox, 11th Earl of Dalhousie. He succeeded his father, Lord Panmure, in 1852, and on the death, in 1860, of his cousin, the Marquis of Dalhousie, his Lordship, through the failure of heir-males, became the 11th Earl of Dalhousie, and *Laird o' Cockpen.* Soon after, he resumed the family name of Ramsay in addition to that of Maule. He was long a member of the Privy Council, and held the offices of Vice-President of the Board of Trade, Under-Secretary for the Home Department, Secretary of State for War Department, and President of the Board of Control. As Secretary-at-War, from 1855 to 1858, when the Crimean War and the Indian Mutiny engaged all his energies, the name of Lord Panmure was much before the public.

In 1842 he was elected Lord Rector of Glasgow University. He "came out" in '43, and was ever afterwards an attached elder of the Free Church, and took a leading part in the deliberations of that body. He had a rare combination of business talent, and being naturally of a shrewd and resolute mind, he was frank and outspoken in a remarkable degree. He was a very eloquent speaker, and had an admirable power of controlling public assemblies. Dying in his seventy-third year at Brechin Castle, in July, 1874, he was buried in the family vault at Panbride.

To the right, immediately before entering what might well be termed a grove of great spreading trees, whose branches unite like the roof of a vaulted chamber, we pass the neat lodge at the entrance to the grounds of Bearehill, the beautiful residence of Mr R. Duke, manufacturer. We have seen it stated that the first banking establishment in Brechin was in the house of Bearehill—Alexander Ritchie, Depute City Clerk from 1790 to 1796, being the banker. Mr Ritchie was conjoined to the office of Clerk with John Spence, his brother-in-law, in 1796, and retained it till his death in 1826, when he was succeeded by Mr D. D. Black. The property of Bearehill has passed through many hands. Mr Warden informs us that John Spence, grandson of John Ochterlony of Flemington, and Bishop of Brechin, was in possession towards the end of last century. John Leighton, factor of the estate of Dunninald, who died in 1798, owned the property, and was succeeded by his son, David. After his death the property was acquired by Dr James Don, army surgeon, who died in 1860. Dr Don left £1000 to establish an infirmary in Brechin. In the Edinburgh Almanac for 1821, Alex. Ritchie of Bearehill is among the freeholders in Forfarshire. In the Angus and Mearns Remembrancer for 1858, George Hair Newall of Bearehill is included in the Directory of Brechin. Mr Duke has made tasteful additions to the house, and has greatly beautified the finely-wooded policies.

We are now on the highway between Brechin and Forfar, the handsome entrance to Brechin Castle grounds being on our left. The road is skirted by a wall between the new and old gateway; but as the beautiful policies are described in our "Guide to Brechin," we do not require to linger over them here. It should be noted, however, that a mound within this enclosure is known as "St Michael's Mount," which, strange to say, as we are informed by Jervise, was originally in the Diocese of Dunkeld, and here the Bishop is said to have held consistorial courts.

The hollow adjoining the Mount is called "Michael Den," along which there wimples a pellucid burn as it leaves the wooded recesses, but which becomes turbid and foul by various impurities between the Old Churchyard and the place where it flows into the South Esk below the Castle. The gatekeeper's lodge and the substantial bridge over the burn were erected shortly before the death of Fox Maule, Earl of Dalhousie, and the former is now the principal entrance to the Castle. About twenty years ago there was a continuation of fine old trees and wooded loveliness on the right side of the road, terminating near the West Toll, but now the place has been turned into a market garden, where visitors are supplied in the season with strawberries and cream. The toll-bar has now disappeared also, but the house still stands, just beyond the road striking off to the left, which leads to Stannochy, and Aldbar Castle. Many old Brechiners have still interesting reminiscences of the West Toll. In the olden time tolls, in a measure, were recognised as wayside inns, and here at one time a roaring trade was carried on in the sale of "spirits, porter, and ale." Then the highway between Aberdeen and Edinburgh had a lively traffic, and the "Defiance" and other well-known stage-coaches daily passed through the bar. But the last jingle has been heard of the toll-money as it fell into the tollman's hands.

The abolition of tolls marks also the abolition of a little bit of the social life of the country. Those who have lived long enough to remember the time when railways did not so intersect the country as they now do, must also remember that the toll-bar was a pleasant and convenient resting and refreshment place for "man and beast." In those days nearly every toll-house held a license, and was able with "good cheer" to welcome the traveller, whether on horseback, in carriage, or on foot. But our iron-ways changed all this. The licensed toll became a nuisance—a place, not of refreshment for the necessitous traveller, but of debauch for the people of the neighbouring town. The licenses were gradually withdrawn, and without any inconvenience to the travelling public, who had now found in our extending railway system a speedier and a cheaper means of transit from place to place.

Yet in those times the tollhouse was the place of many happy meetings of friends—of many half-hours of pleasure while the horses bated, and were prepared for another stage of the journey. Here, too, the rollicking carter had his dram in the early morning, and the carrier with his precious load of merchandise from some industrial centre, welcomed the shelter of the tollhouse, and ate his bread and cheese, quaffed his ale, and rejoiced at having made, unmolested, another stage in his journey. All this tollhouse social life has now gone. The railway has spoiled many traditions, and this among the rest. But even now it is possible that many a pleasure-seeker, on horseback or in carriage, will miss the pleasant chat with the toll man, the respectful recognition of his tidy wife, or the modest, smiling face of his daughter when he passes by the old deserted house, and through the dilapidated gates, although he is not required to pull up and produce with humorous chaff the toll money. But we have lingered too long over these "reflections," and must crave the reader's pardon.

We still keep the highway by the side of what Brechin schoolboys know as the "Toll Wood," still the popular recreation ground and favourite walk of young and old. Ay, if these old trees were gifted with tongues, many a tale would they unfold of merry giggling groups, of blushing maids, of harmless words of badinage, and of loving pairs whispering those honeyed nothings which only the initiated can appreciate.

There are not many landscape snatches until we arrive at Finavon. The grounds and imposing mansion of Maulesden demand more than a passing notice. The house occupies a charming site on the banks of the Esk, and within two miles of Brechin, although the dense masses of foliage almost conceal it from view. The policies are extensive, and command rich "bits" of scenery. The walk, amid great overhanging boughs.

MAULESDEN.

along the steep banks of the river, is charming, while rustic bridges span a clear sparkling burn, which, before it enters the South Esk, forms a beautiful cascade. Ornamental terraces and rich flower pots face the river, and a fine lawn slopes smoothly down to the water edge. The mansion is a large and handsome castellated edifice. The original house was built during the last century, and was soon afterwards acquired by Mr Binny. The Hon. Wm. Maule, third son of the Right Hon. William Ramsay Maule, first Lord Panmure, had the western portion of the house built in 1854, and the old or eastern division altered to correspond with the new section. It is in the old Scotch baronial style, after designs by the late Mr Bryce, Edinburgh. After the death of the Hon. Mr Maule, the house was for some time occupied by his widow and family. Mrs Maule sold the estate to George A. Haig, from whom it was purchased in 1871 by Thomas Hunter Cox of Duncarse, Dundee, a partner with his brother in the great firm of Cox Brothers, Lochee and Dundee. Mr Cox, who died in 1892, greatly improved the beautiful surroundings. The view from the grounds is delightful—the stately river, flowing peacefully and disappearing beneath the one-arched Stannochy Bridge, the rich valley and finely-wooded hill, with variegated green fields nestling cheerfully between, the winding foliage-shrouded walks, murmuring rills in the wooded den falling into the river in a miniature cascade of great beauty. The gardens, sloping gently down to the river, are extensive, and are laid out with artistic skill and natural effect. The mansion is altogether a noble and graceful structure, and a very effective view of its general appearance can be had from the Stannochy Bridge. Mr J. B. Don, manufacturer, Forfar, is now proprietor of Maulesden, and resides there.

The next object, on the right, after passing the neat gatehouse of Maulesden is a small group of houses, consisting of smithy, joiner's shop, &c. This was wont to be known as "Chance Inn," where the first halt was made by the famous "Defiance Coach" after leaving Brechin on its way to Edinburgh.

St Ann's Cottage is beautifully situated on our right. Kintrockat House, formerly called Eskmount, is on the left bank of the South Esk, but hidden from our view. In the retour, dated 27th April, 1686, in favour of James, Earl of Panmure, as heir of his brother, Earl George, the town and lands of Kintrockat are included. One of the family of Ochterlony is said to have possessed these lands. He was succeeded by a son, who married Mary Ruperta, daughter of John Skinner, of Brechin, by his wife, who was descended from one of Prince Ruperta's natural children. The Hon. A. Gillies of Kintrockat appears among the list of the freeholders of the county for the year 1821, and ten years later, Hunter of Kintrockat is mentioned. East and West Kintrockat subsequently came into the possession of the laird of Aldbar, and it still forms part of that fine estate—the present proprietor being Patrick Chalmers, Esq.

In the Reg. Ep. Br., Alexander Thome (Thomson) of Kintrockat, Presbytery of Brechin, is twice mentioned—12th Feb., 1435-6, and on 15th and 16th of same month and year.—*See Warden's "Forfarshire," Vol. III. p.* 13. Eskmount was acquired by Alex. Gibson Hunter, who, about 1780, purchased the lands of Blackness. He was succeeded by his son in the lands of Eskmount and Blackness. When Mr Hunter owned Eskmount, as Kintrockat was then called, it was the scene of many exciting frolics. It was one of the meeting-places of the Hon. William Maule, first Lord Panmure, and his jovial companions. Practical jokes were there concocted and perpetrated that have become historical, and illustrate social life in former days.

Balnabreich.

On the left we next pass "Balnabreich Dam," almost covered with "rashies" and other luxuriant vegetation. "Auld Eppie," who writes pithily on many subjects in the *Brechin Advertiser*, says :—

"The woodit glen o' Bonnybreich is ane o' the bonniest, sweetest dells 'at ever ye saw, accreditit, too, in the days o' ither years, as the residence o' a ghaist o' a white wife, like the ghaist o' Thrummy Cap, possessed o' some sad secret which she wis bound to reveal afore she gat leave to enter the abodes o' the faithfu' departit. At onyrate, she wis quite a harmless ghaist—or rather, I wud say, a very usefu' ghaist. She never said a word to naebody, either gude, bad, or indifferent, an' naebody ever daured to speir fat she wantit. But, fan the lassies wis like bidin' ower lang oot wi' the lads, she had a knack o' waggin her lang, thin, white fingers at them, an' sae sendin' them hame as fast's their feet cud carry them. Sae it canna be denied that she was really a guid, usefu' White Wife, an' I houp she's still enjoyin' her lovely sylvan retreat, doin' guid service to mortals as she has opportunity. An' troth, it wid be a guid thing for mony a halliket lassie gin there wis still a white wife wanderin' aboot here and there to raise the warning finger, an' lat them ken that they were treading on dangerous ground. But we're a' ower wise an' ower weel edicatit noo-a-days for puttin' faith in ony sic things."

The Noran.

In our "trips" we will probably view the "Silvery Noran" at various points. Here, with Nether Careston on our left, we cross it for the first time. It is a clear rapid stream, which rises in the Forfarshire Grampians, and has a circuitous course of about twenty miles, passing the modern mansions of Glenogil, Noranside, and the ancient ruins of Vane Castle. Running over for the most part a bed of rock and gravel, it preserves the transparency and purity of its waters throughout. Laing, in his "Wayside Flowers," says:—"The beauties of the district would inspire any poet. The braes of Noran, the banks of the South Esk, into which the former falls below Careston Castle, the Howe o' Angus, and the rich and varied landscape from Ben Dearachie brow to the Bay of Montrose, when seen on a clear summer's day from the burgh hill of Brechin, cannot be better described than in the concise language of Macneill :—

> Frae Grampian heights down to the sea,
> A dazzling view!
> Corn, meadow, mansion, water, tree,
> In varying hue."

Quoting again from "Eppie," who, in this instance, evidently writes in early spring :—

"Ither fouk hae sung the beauties o' Noran and Noranside; but I'll content mysell wi' saying, in plain prose, that the Noran, wi' its finely-wooded banks, its bright sparklin' falls, the auld castle o' the Vane, an' mony a snug farm steadin' an' cantie cozie cottar hoose—wi' its kail yairdie, its flower borders a' buskit wi' lilies, apple-rene, daisies, spinks, an' thyme; an' its windows sae fu' o' fuchias an' geraniums that ye wid winder foo' the licht o' day could ever reach the fireside—is the bonniest bit o' landscape in a' the Braes o' Angus, or, I raither sud say, in a' braid Scotland. Nae doot ye may tell me there are scenes far mair picturesque an' grand—an' I'll nae dispute nor deny but fat ye're richt eneuch—but for sweet sylvan beauty an' loveliness, **Noran** bears the bell. Are not its banks at this present moment bricht wi' the gowden glory o' the **sweet** wild primrose, to be succeeded in a week or twa **by the** tall green stem o' the **cooslip**, bendin' under the **weight** o' its truss o' bonnie wee **bloomlets**? Are not the larch, the elm, the oak, an' the plane burstin' their buds, puttin' on their braw summer claes, an' tellin' a' the world that sweet, smilin' summer is ance mair here. An' dinna ye hear the blackie an' the mavie, the laverock an' the lintie makin' earth an' sky vocal wi' their joyous songs; while, from brown earth, the green blade springs, giving promise o' a bountifu', plentifu' hairst.

Marcus.

Marcus Lodge, the gateway to which we pass on the left, is a fine mansion, in the Elizabethan style, built on the north bank of the South Esk. The late Colonel Swinburn, who died in 1881, purchased the estate of Marcus, or Markhouse, from the representatives of Captain Alex. Skene, R.N., cousin of the late Alex. Skene of Careston. It was previously in the possession of one of the Carnegies of Balnamoon, who was also proprietor of Keithock.

Finavon Castle.

We now reach "The Red Lion Inn," with its old-style swinging sign-board—a distance of six miles from, and half-way house between Brechin and Forfar. We are tempted to linger a little in this neighbourhood. Here we have a fine sample of the pre-historic structures of our remote ancestors—the Hill-fort of Finavon, which is allowed to be the oldest and most considerable vitrified fort in the county of Forfar. Here are also the remains of a famous stronghold, once the property and principal residence of the powerful Earls of Crawford. It is situated in the parish of Oathlaw—anciently called Finavon. The parish church stood near the old castle, at the place now known as Aikenfaulds; but when the church was removed to its present site the parochial designation was changed to Oathlaw. George Shoreswood, who was chosen Bishop of Brechin in 1484, made the incumbent of the church of Finavon a prebendary of his cathedral.

All that now remains of the ancient Castle of Finavon are three sides of the castle-keep or great tower, and some vaults under it; yet, in the magnificent building of which this is only a fragment, the old Earls of Crawford held almost regal state, and royalty itself, with a numerous retinue, has been lodged and entertained there.

The ruins stand upon a small mount at the confluence of the Lemno with the South Esk. It was built in the 14th century, and is considered to have been even a much more extensive structure than Edzell Castle— to which we will yet refer—when occupied by the noble family of Crawford. Ochterlony, in his account of Angus in 1683, calls it "A great old house, but now by the industry of the present laird (Carnegie) is made a most excellent house—fine rooms and good furniture."

In the time of King Robert the Bruce the barony was the property of the Crown; for that monarch before his death, in 1329, granted the barony of Finavon, and the lands of Carsegownie in the neighbouring parish of Aberlemno, to his illegitimate son, Sir Robert Bruce, who fell in the battle of Dupplin, 1332, loyally fighting on behalf of his royal half-brother David II., against the forces of the pretender Edward Baliol. Soon after the barony came into the possession of the noble family of Lindsay, Earls of Crawford. Alexander Lindsay, who became fourth Earl of Crawford, was of a turbulent disposition, and wore an exuberant beard—hence the sobriquets by which he was known—the Tiger Earl, and Earl Beardie. He was generally in trouble with his neighbours, and at one time engaged in rebellion against his sovereign, James II. He contrived eventually to make peace with his sovereign, and to show his gratitude he entertained the King and his Court with great pomp at the Castle of Finavon. Tradition avers that on his return from Spain (where he had fled on being declared the King's enemy and a rebel) the Earl brought with him a sapling chestnut tree, which he planted in the vicinity of the castle, and which ultimately attained a great size. It was unfortunately blown down during a violent storm, about the middle of last century. When Pennant visited Finavon, in the year 1771, the shattered tree still lay in the park. He measured the trunk, and found that at one foot from the ground the girth was 42 feet, at the smallest part of the trunk 33 feet, and at the off-shoot of the branches 35 feet. It was in this castle that the brilliant marriage festivities were held on the celebration, in 1546, of the wedding of Margaret Beaton, daughter of Cardinal Beaton, to David Lindsay, the Master of Crawford.

"Earl Beardie."

Earl Beardie had a strong iron hook projecting from near the top of the south-east wall of his Castle, from which he might conveniently suspend any offending vassal. And it required no great offence to doom one to dangle from that hook. A hapless minstrel, wandering one day into the grounds of the Castle, was overheard crooning some verses which prophesied evil concerning its owner. Brought into his presence and made to repeat the verse, his doom was instantly pronounced by the Tiger.

> The ladie craved pity, but nane wad he gi'e—
> The poor aged minstrel must die ;
> And Crawford's ain hand placed the grey head and lyre,
> On the spikes of the turret sae high.

On another occasion, a gallows was found in the Spanish Chestnut Tree, already referred to, and was commonly called Earl Beardie's Tree. Mr Jervise writes :—

"On a messenger or gillie being sent from Careston to the Castle of Finhaven, he cut a walking stick from it (The Chestnut Tree), and the Earl was so enraged that he had the offender hanged on a branch of it. The ghost of this luckless person still wanders betwixt Finhaven and Careston, and is the constant attendant of benighted travellers, by whom he is minutely described as a lad of about sixteen years of age without bonnet or shoes, and is known as Jock Barefoot. His freaks are curious, and withal inoffensive, and, on reaching a certain burn on the road, he vanishes from view in a blaze of fire! As if to confirm the story of Beardie still living in the secret chamber of Glamis—where he is doomed to play cards until the day of judgment—it is an old prophetic saying that

> Earl Beardie ne'er will dee,
> Nor puir Jock Barefoot be set free,
> As lang's there grows a chestnut tree !"

"The Wicked Master."

In the days of David, son of Earl Beardie, and the fifth Earl of Crawford, Finavon Castle rose in dignity.

In 1448 the Earl was created **Duke of Montrose**, the first dukedom ever conferred on a Scottish family. James III. bestowed on him many royal favours, including the life rent of the Lordship of Brechin and Navar, and the Sheriffship of Angus. He closed his illustrious and honoured career at his Castle of Finavon in 1495; and was succeeded by his second son, John, who, having killed his elder brother, shrunk from assuming the ducal title, and whose death by and by on the fatal field of Flodden foreclosed proceedings against him for his fratricide, and questions springing out of it. The Castle of Finavon was for twelve weeks the prison of his successor. His own son, whom history justly brands as the " Wicked Master " of Crawford, confined him in it for that space of time, and then for fifteen days in Brechin, to which he carried him, during which he broke open and robbed his coffers, and seized his rents. He was the terror and scourge of his generation, and after leading the life of a desperado till 1452, " he was sticked by a soutar of Dundee for taking a stoup of wine from him."

Everything in and about Finavon Castle, in the palmy days of the great Earls of Crawford, showed the princely state which they kept up. Like the monarch himself, they had their Privy Council, and the Councillors were of the oldest and most honourable families of Angus. They had their constables, armour-bearers, chamberlains, &c., the two first being hereditary. In beauty, richness, and costliness, the furniture of their castle was unrivalled, and lacked nothing that could minister to comfort and luxury. The society visiting was the most select and exalted in the land; and for security, the trustiest vassals were located in the immediate neighbourhood, as at Barnyards and Markhouse. If ever earthly greatness and glory promised to be enduring it was here; but they have long since perished utterly.

> "They rose to power, to wealth, to fame;
> They gained a proud, a deathless name—
> First in the field—first in the State—
> But ah! the giddy tide of fate
> Reflowed, and swept them from their throne,
> And thus they came Misfortune's own!"

The Past! How much that word conveys. It takes us back to long centuries ago. "The Poetry of Old Ruins," why, our land is richly dowered with picturesque relics of bygone days—hoary old ruins, whose ivy-mantled walls and moss-wreathed battlements awaken poetic memories, and around whose decay there lingers an exquisite pathos which is almost human. They have a personality about them which we feel to be sacred and awe-inspiring, whether they be the mouldering ruins of monasteries or proud towers which sheltered kings, or of abbeys where queens have died. These old ruins have a fascinating spell about them, whose witchery almost makes us believe them to be the mystic custodians of the secrets of the past.

> There is a charm in footing slow across a silent plain,
> Where patriot battle had been fought, where glory had the gain;
> There is a pleasure on the heath where Druids old have been—
> Where mantles grey have rustled by and swept the nettled green,
> There is a joy in every spot made known in days of old—
> New to the feet, although each tale a hundred times be told.

The castle and barony in course of time passed to James Carnegie, second son of David, second Earl of Northesk. He was succeeded by his eldest son James, who engaged in the rebellion of 1715, but, availing himself of the Act of Grace, he saved his lands from confiscation. It was the younger Mr James Carnegie who "accidentally" killed Charles, Earl of Strathmore, on the High Street of Forfar, on the 9th day of May, 1728. They had been at a *dergie* held at the funeral of a son of Mr Carnegy of Lour in company with Mr Lyon of Brigton and some others. Brigton made some mocking observation concerning Finavon, which aroused his anger, and Lyon afterwards pushed him into the gutter. When Carnegie got up, all covered with mud, he pursued his tormentor, and having nearly overtaken him made a thrust at him with his sword, but, his foot slipping at the time, the lunge aimed at Brigton took effect in the body of his brother, Lord Strathmore, who was then standing with his back to the laird of Finavon, conversing with another person. On discovering the sad consequences of his rash act, Mr Carnegie fled, and was in hiding for a long time; but he was ultimately apprehended and tried for the deed on the charge of murder, but he was acquitted. In 1842 the estate of Finavon was purchased for £75,000. A fine modern mansion has since been erected upon the estate, which is now the property of Colonel Greenhill Gardyne of Finavon,

Vitrified Fort.

Numerous vitrified forts are found in Scotland, and some of them existed in pre-historic times. They are evidently native works, and many had been forts or places of defence, reared by the primeval races. It is said that vitrification was not done during the process of the erection, but was the effect of beacon-fires lighted to warn the neighbourhood of a common danger, or of bonfires kindled on festive occasions, or in connection with religious ceremonies. Angus or Forfarshire possesses several specimens of vitrification, and here we have a famous sample. The hill rises to the height of nearly 600 feet above the Esk at the old fortalice of Finavon. The original fort had occupied the whole of the top of the hill, and had been constructed on military principles, so as to command and protect every point of access. Carrie thus describes it :—

"The fort forms a parallelogram, with the angles rounded off, extending from east to west about 476 feet. At the east end the breadth is about 38 feet ; and as the ascent on that side is easier than at other points it had there been defended by an outwork about 52 feet distant from the rampart-wall. About the middle it widens considerably, and there are vestiges of some inner walls within the enclosure. Towards the west end, which is somewhat lower down the hill, the breadth is about 125 feet, and at that end there are distinct traces of a well which had been dug for the use of the garrison. As the descent is gradual on all sides, the cavity was for a long time mistaken for the crater of an extinct volcano. In many places the stones are covered with a thin coating of soil which supports a luxuriant crop of grasses, but where a large mass of the stones has fallen down the vitrifaction of them is still quite discernible. Mineralogists have ascertained that ten different kinds of stone, not found on the hill itself, have been used in constructing the fort. In the middle there is a considerable admixture of charcoal, which indicates that wood had been piled up amongst the stones, in order to the more perfect vitrifaction of the whole mass. Miss Maclagan remarks that, 'an observant stranger could hardly fail to notice the strange unusual sounds emitted by the stones under the feet ; exactly like that caused by walking over a heap of cinders.' 'Huddlestone thinks that the traces of square fortifications inside the fort are the work of Roman masons— probably belonging to the army of Agricola—and had been constructed by them after they dislodged the Caledonian garrison.' The fortress of Finavon had evidently been the master-fort of a chain of forts erected for the protection of the inhabitants of Strathmore from their foreign and domestic enemies. From its walls could be seen at a glance the two fortresses on the hill of Catterthun ; on the west the fort of Dunoon, about five miles beyond Forfar, and, still onwards towards Perth, the Barry hill at Meigle."

There is a popular legend to the effect that the remains of the fort is the ruin of the first Castle which it was attempted to build at Finavon. The attempt was not allowed to proceed far; not farther than the laying of the foundation. Anything more which the builders raised during the day was always knocked down by some demon-power in the course of the next night. Watchers were set to protect the work, and to frighten away the mischievous spirit; but the result was that the watchers themselves were frightened. At midnight the spirit spoke thus to the watchers, amidst the din of the tumbling wall built the previous day:—

> Found even-down into the bog,
> Where 'twill neither shake nor shog.

They took the hint, left the hill, and set to work in the vale, and their "sticket" work on the hill top remained to exercise the fancy of the Jonathan Old-bucks of future times.

Roman Camp.

At Battledykes, in this parish, are the remains of a great Roman camp. Maitland accurately surveyed it in his day, and, according to his measurement, the mean length of the camp was about 2970 feet, and its mean breadth 1850, embracing an area of 80 acres. It was nearly three times larger than the famous camp at Ardoch, with which it communicated by the Roman Road which passed from Ardoch northward through Perthshire and Angusshire. It is commonly believed that this camp was occupied by Agricola in A.D. 81. On the farm of Battledykes, and within the limits of the Roman camp, are the King's Palace, the

King's Seat, and the King's Bourne; significent names, and which seem obviously to point to a period when Finavon was a royal demesne and residence.

Tannadice.

The bonnie wee toon on the breist o' the brae.

We have been tempted to linger perhaps somewhat long at Finavon Castle, but the district is interesting and pretty. Returning to "The Red Lion," we now start along a fine road to the really ideal village of Tannadice. Soon after leaving the Inn, we get a "peep" of the fine old mansion of Tannadice, snugly embowered amongst trees, and facing a beautiful stretch of the South Esk. This property was long in the possession of the Ogilvy family, but the present owner is Mr Neish, a London lawyer. Another mile, and we cross over the new line of railway between Brechin and Forfar, which here spans the river on a girder bridge.

As we round the shoulder of the belt of wood which skirts the grounds of Tannadice House, we obtain a pleasant glimpse of the tower of the Parish Church, and the blue reek rising in quiet curling wreaths from the humble yet cosy homes of the villagers nestling secure in the embrace of the braes around the quiet dell, which prevent "a' the airts the wind can blaw" from visiting it unkindly.

The neat church and manse, and beautifully-kept graveyard, where

> Each in his narrow cell forever laid,
> The rude forefathers of the hamlet sleep,

first attract our attention. But a short halt will well repay the visitor, who will enjoy the scene from the

TANNADICE FROM THE SOUTH ESK.

TANNADICE.

river below the churchyard, and a walk through the picturesquely situated little hamlet, with its fragrant garden plots, and rustic cottages, while

> 'Neath the brae the burnie jouks,
> An' ilka thing looks cheerie.

Here we also find the homely Inn, the Schoolhouse, Her Majesty's Post Office, and "the merchant," from whom we can purchase

> Ham and needles, daidles and cheese,
> Loaves and aprons, treacle and teas.

Also the shoemaker and tailor; the blacksmith and joiner—those handicraftsmen that are necessary for the convenience of every rural district. There is nothing, save the church, of an architectural nature in the village. The houses are simple—a few still covered with thatch and stained with lichen and moss—some of them picturesque little structures that would look well on canvas. At every step a new combination of landscape beauties greets the eye, while on every bank and brae, and in every bosky dell there is a profusion of wild flowers, and the cheerful chorus of birds. Indeed, the village, with its pretty walks all around, must, we feel assured, now that the railway is so near it, soon become a popular health-resort.

We are told that the Church of Tannadice is one of the oldest ecclesiastical settlements. Tannadice was a thanedom at the date of the first reference we find made to it. In 1363 David II. gave it to John de Logy, supposed to be the father of his second Queen, Margaret Logy. David's nephew, Robert II., afterwards gave the thanedom to Sir John Lyon, as dower with his wife, Princess Jane, the King's daughter.

On the north side of the South Esk, and near the present Bridge of Shielhill, says Marshall, stood Queich

Castle in days of yore. No vestige of the Castle is now to be seen; but the site of it, on which a plain cottage stands, is "a precipitous rock, looking sheer down through deep and yawning chasms, upon a rush and turbulence of water, and almost isolated and rendered nearly inaccessible, and altogether romantic, by the river." Queich Castle was the property, and one of the residences of a historic family, the Earls of Buchan, the first of whom was a half-brother of James II., and who, about 1466, married Margaret, the only child of Sir Alexander Ramsay of Auchterhouse. By this marriage he succeeded to the estates of the Auchterhouse Ramsays; and these continued in the possession of the Earls of Buchan for very nearly two hundred years, when they passed, by purchase, in 1653, to the Earl of Panmure. But no memorable event, connected with the Buchans' possessions in Tannadice, or with their sojournings in Queich Castle, has come under our notice.

There was another Castle in Tannadice on the side of the Esk, which has also quite disappeared, and of which we know nothing more than that it was near Auchlouchrie, on the eminence still bearing the name of Castlehill, "overhanging a deep gorge of the river, and having round its base a semi-circular fosse, twelve feet deep and thirty wide."

Cortachy Castle.

Here we might so far digress as to suggest that, should the visitor at this point have the time at his disposal, and be able to make an extra day of it, an exceedingly pleasant tour might be made through Glen Clova, taking in Cortachy Castle and district, and resting for the night at the comfortable modern Jubilee Hotel, Dykehead. Cortachy Castle, the residence of the Earl of Airlie, is a magnificent mansion, standing in a beautifully-wooded amphitheatre on the romantic banks of the South Esk, which flows through the policies. Part of it is ancient, having, it is said, been erected by Thomas, third son of John Ogilvy, third baron of Inverquharity, who acquired the lands of Cortachy and Clova in the reign of King James IV. At a still earlier period the district of Cortachy had been the property of the Earls of Athole, of the stock of the royal family of Scotland; for we find that during the episcopate of John, Bishop of Brechin, and Chancellor of the kingdom—who died in 1482—Walter Palatine of Strathearn, Earl of Athole, and Lord of Brechin and Cortachy, granted the Church of Cortachy to the Bishop of Brechin and his successors for ever. Extensive additions have from time to time been made to the Castle, and it is now one of the very foremost of the many lordly mansion-houses of Forfarshire. The natural beauty of the situation has been greatly enhanced by the hand of art, so that scarcely in all broad Scotland can there be found a fairer domain than that which now surrounds Cortachy Castle.

It requires, says A. H. Millar in his admirable volume, "Historical Castles and Mansions of Scotland," no special skill to see that the building has been erected at separate periods and in widely divergent circumstances. . . . A door in a wall of the drawing-room communicates with the room in which Charles II. slept in October, 1650, during one of the crises of his tempestuous life, and, in proof of this there is in the Register House, Edinburgh, a letter from him dated "Cortaquhy, October 4th, 1650. The Castle has twice suffered from fire, and on each occasion has risen from its ashes with renewed splendour. The grounds are laid out with great taste, and their sheltered position has permitted the successful cultivation of many rare flowers and shrubs without artificial protection. The most interesting part is that devoted to the "Garden of Friendship" —an extensive plot which has been cleared and is now planted with trees, placed in their present position by members of the family or by visitors to Cortachy Castle, and each bearing the name of the planter. Conspicuous amongst them is a tree planted by H.R.H. the Duchess of Edinburgh, on the occasion of her visit in August, 1881, and another lofty conifer preserving the name of the late Professor Jowett of Balliol College, Oxford. Within the rustic summer-house that commands a view of these memorials a tablet has been placed, inscribed with the following graceful poem by the late Viscount Sherbrooke (Right Hon. Robert Lowe), expressing the sentiments with which he regarded the scene :—

Is life a good? Then, if a good it be,
Mine be a life like thine, thou steadfast tree,
The self-same earth that gave the sapling place
Receives the mouldering trunk in soft embrace—
The self-same comrades ever at thy side.
Who know not envy, wilfulness, or pride,
The winter's waste repaired by lavish spring,
The rustling breezes that about thee sing,
The inter-twining shadows at thy feet,
Make up thy life, and such a life is sweet.
What though beneath this artificial shade
No fauns have gambolled and no dryads strayed;
Though the coy nurslings of serener skies
Shudder when Caledonia's tempests rise,
Yet sways a cheering influence o'er the grove,
More soft than Nature, more sedate than Love,
And not unhonoured shall the grove ascend,
For every stem was planted by a friend,
And she, at whose command its shades arise,
Is good and gracious, true, and fair, and wise.

CORTACHY CASTLE.

The family of Ogilvy is descended from Gilibrede, or Gilbert, third son of the second Earl of Angus, who fought at the Battle of the Standard in 1138, and obtained the lands from William the Lion. It was in 1369-70 that Cortachy was acquired by the family. Of the sixth generation, Sir Walter de Ogilvy was Sheriff of Angus. His son was the "gracious gude Lord Ogilvy," celebrated in the old ballad of the battle of Harlaw, in which both he and his son George were slain.

> Of the best amang them was
>   The gracious gude Lord Ogilvy,
> The Sheriff-Principal of Angus,
>   Renownit for truth and equity—
> For faith and magnanimity
> He had few fellows in the field,
>   Yet fell by fatal destiny,
> For he nae ways wad grant to yield.

Of the seventh generation, Sir Walter de Ogilvy was High Treasurer of Scotland, and Treasurer of the Household of James I. James, the sixth Lord, was a faithful servant of Queen Mary, for which he suffered a long imprisonment. James, the second Earl of Airlie, was a zealous Royalist. He was taken prisoner at Philiphaugh, tried, and condemned to die; but he escaped from the Castle of St Andrews in his sister's clothes, during the night before the day fixed for his execution. But it is not necessary for us here to enter into farther details of the career of this distinguished family. The present Earl of Airlie, David Stanley William Ogilvy, was born in 1856. He entered the army at an early age, and served in the Scots Guards in 1875-6, changing then to the 10th Hussars, of which regiment he is now Major. He took part with distinction in the campaign in the Soudan, having been twice wounded in action.

Lord Airlie was chosen a Representative Peer in **1885**, and in the following year was married to Lady **Mabel-Frances-Elizabeth Gore**, daughter of the **fifth Earl of Arran**.

The Battle of Saughs.

We would now take the visitor to the Churchyard, a short distance from the Castle. It can be entered by a shaded pathway from "The Garden of Friendship" —referred to on page 40—a place of exquisite beauty situated at the bottom of a vast green basin, formed by a girdle of gentle eminences. The "field of graves" is surrounded by stately and time-honoured trees, and the quiet spot is not only interesting on account of its containing the elegant burial vault of several Earls and Countesses, but here we also find the grave of one who took part in an affray known as "The Battle of Saughs." The tombstone, which is of the old table fashion, is near the south east corner of the church, and bears the following inscription, which is slowly becoming obliterated:—

"I. W. 1732.—This stone was erected by Alexander Winter, tennent in the Doaf (? Doal) in memory of James Winter, his father's brother, who died on Peathaugh, in the parish of Glenisla, the 3d January, 1752, aged 72.

> Here lyes James Vinter, who died in Peathaugh,
> Who fought most valointly at ye Water of Saughs,
> Along wt Ledenhendry, who did command ye day—
> They Vanquis the Enemy and made them runn away."

The date of the "Raid" is somewhat uncertain; but it would be of interest to briefly narrate the tradition now, although it is perhaps more strictly connected with the Fern district, for the parishioners there were the actors, although the "battle-field" is within the confines of the parish of Lethnot.

> Calm was the morn, and close the mist,
> Hung o'er St Arnold's Seat,[*]
> As Ferna's sons gaed out to Saughs
> M'Gregor there to meet.

The accounts of the "transaction" are varied—some asserting it to have been about the middle of the 17th century—others, between 1703 and 1711. Jervise gives it as between 1690 and 1700, when Winter would be in the prime of life. It was the outcome of an unusually bold incursion of the Cateran, headed by the "Hawkit Stirk." The inhabitants were called together, among the tombs of their fathers, by the ringing of the kirk bell. As they were anxious to regain their horses and cattle, the day was spent in discussing the question as to what was the proper course for doing so; but, fearing the superior strength of their antagonists, many of them lost heart, so that the pursuit would have been abandoned, had not young Macintosh of Ledenhendry, enraged at the cowardice of his fellows, stood up on an eminence and called out—"Let those who wish to chase the Cateran follow me." Eighteen young men left the multitude, and rallied round the valiant youth, pursued the reavers, and overtook them by the Water of Saughs, camping around a blazing fire, and cooking a young Fern cow for breakfast. To settle the case between them, single combat was agreed on. A shot from the Cateran, killing one of the Fern men, upset this arrangement, and not the chiefs only, but all under them, forthwith closed in deadly combat. Seeing Macintosh hard pressed by his antagonist, James Winter, stealing behind the bandit chief, hamstrung him; and, though he fought on his stumps, Macintosh soon pierced him to the heart.

---

[*] A prominent object on the top of one of the neighbouring hills.

Lang time they faucht in doubtfu' strife,
　Till Peathaugh, stealthfully,
Hamstrung M'Gregor unawares,
　And drave him on his knee.

Thus on his knees, or on his stumps,
　He hash'd and smash'd around;
But Ledenhendry pierc'd him through,
　And laid him on the ground.*

Seeing their chief fallen, and several of their party biting the dust, the Cateran fled; **but** the tradition is that not one of them escaped.

So ceas'd the strife, and a' was still,
　And silent o'er the glen,
Save glaids and corbies i' the air,
　That hover'd o'er the slain.

Whase mangled bodies i' their gore,
　Lay reekin' o'er the green;
A sight o'er sick'nin' for the saul,
　O'er painfu' for the een.

We will leave the "Raid" by merely stating that the name of the "Hawkit Stirk" was given to the Cateran chief from a supposition that he was the same person as was laid down, when an infant, at the farmhouse door of Muir Pearsie, in the Parish of Kingoldrum, and from the gudewife desiring her husband to rise from bed about midnight to see the cause of the bleating cries which she heard; but having a pet calf that was in the habit of prowling about under night, her husband lay still, insisting that the noise was merely "the croon o' the hawkit stirk." Hearing a continuation of the same piteous moan, the gudewife herself rose and found a male child, of a few weeks old, lying on the sill of the door, carefully rolled in flannel and other warm coverings, and, taking it under her charge, brought it up as one of her own family.

* "Raid of Fearn," by Alex. Laing, schoolmaster, Stracathro.

Nothing of the foundling or his parents was ever positively known; but when about sixteen years of age, he departed clandestinely from Muir Pearsie, and from the resemblance of the leader of this band to him, they are said to have been one and the same individual.

Inverquharity Castle.

The Quharity's a bonnie stream,
 It winds by haugh and shieling,
Where rays of light thro' rowans gleam,
 Their coral beads revealing.

. . . .

Here bending beeches veil thy face,
 Deep mirrored in thy flow,
There, gean trees cast their clouds of lace
 Upon thy stream below.
Linger awhile by ruins gray,
 That fondly gaze on thee—
The dwelling place, for many a day,
 Of many an Ogilvy.
Thy waters, as they speed along,
 Amid thy fleet career,
Re-echo the unchanging song
 Their fathers wont to hear,
Tell of their warlike deeds of old,
 Their loyal ancestry—
How noble names can ne'er be sold
 Like land, and tower, and tree;
Pausing—transmit the ancient lore
 That celebrates their fame,
Then in the Esk for evermore,
 Lose both thyself and name.

This ancient Keep, in the immediate neighbourhood of Cortachy Castle, is well worth a visit. A pleasant hour can be spent in studying its features, and its surroundings afford many ideal "pic-nicing" spots. We give, by kind permission of Mr Lowson, Forfar, from his deeply interesting volume of "Tales and

INVERQUHARITY CASTLE.

Legends," a view of the Castle from the banks of the Quharity, or Carity. The ruins are on an elevation formed by the junction of the Quharity with the South Esk. Surrounded by fine old trees, and although little but the roof is visible from a distance, the old baronial pile forms a very pretty picture.

Built, says Mr Lowson, in the 16th century, in two wings at right angles to one another, with the door and stair in the angular corner, the almost complete disappearance of one wing, coupled with the fact of the other remaining nearly intact, at once attracts attention. Whatever agent acted as the destroyer, the work has been done very effectively, and apparently quietly, as nowhere have we been able to find any mention of it.

Time, which is fast removing all trace of one half of the building, has dealt kindly with the other, only pausing to soften the harshness of lines and angles, and to mellow its colour with the beauty of age. Its walls are of ashlar, the stones being all well hewn and squared. The window openings are narrow and carefully guarded with heavy iron stanchions and cross bars. The glass has been kept near the face of the wall, and the opening boldly displayed to the inside in order that the little light admitted might be as widely diffused as possible. Light was necessary, and might be very desirable, but security from attack was the first consideration, and what avail were walls eight feet in thickness if the windows were wide, and would admit a storm of missiles? This thickness of walls allows of a walk about four feet wide between the roof and projecting parapet, with its embrasure cope. The stones forming the pavement of this walk are very large and heavy, and must have taxed the ingenuity and mechanical appliances of the builders in getting them into position. Immediately over the entrance the corbelling supporting the parapet assumes a bolder proportion in order to admit of machicolations from which the inmates could assail unwelcome visitors with bullets or molten lead. Strange irony of time, that corbelling designed with such sinster intentions should now only serve to beautify the building by the play of its light and shade!

The castle doorway with its pointed arch is protected by a massive iron gate. Similar gates are to be found in various parts of the country, and another may be seen at Invermark Castle in Glenesk. They were erected by special license from the king.

Immediately adjoining the doorway is the stone spiral stair, which gave access to all the floors of both wings, and to the battlement. The first floor is of wood, supported on beams carried by large cortels, but the second and third are of stone, the building being arched from wall to wall. Little wood has been used in the construction, but where it is employed, as in the elaborate rafters, it gives an insight into the carpenter's work of that time, all the joints being formed by mortice, tenon, and pins. The internal arrangements are extremely simple. Huge fire places, to afford room for chains in the ingle-cheeks, stone benches in the window recesses, and a few presses, or stones in the thickness of the wall, all show that utility was studied rather than ease.

Originally a possession of the Earls of Angus, Inverquharity was given by charter, by Margaret, Countess of Angus, to Sir Alexander Lindsay, of Crawford, in 1329. It continued in the possession of the Crawfords till 1405, when it was resigned in favour of Sir Walter Ogilvy, Carcary, Lord High Treasurer of Scotland. In 1420, Sir Walter conveyed the property to his brother Sir John, the founder of the Inverquharity branch of the Ogilvys. It passed by purchase, about 1790, to the family of Lyell of Kinnordy.

The Inverquharity Ogilvys seem to have, unfortunately for themselves, been of a warlike disposition, as we find Sir Alexander, the third baron, was wounded at the Battle of Arbroath in the year 1445. After the battle the Lindsays were let loose on the Ogilvys' lands, which were pillaged, and the south-east wing of the Castle of Inverquharity was razed to the ground. A brother of Inverquharity's took part with the Lindsays, and had a gift from Earl Beardie of Clova, Wateresk and Cortachy. About 1573 the following licence was granted:—

"Rex—Licience be the Kinge to Al. Ogilvy of Inercarity to fortifie his house, and put ane Irne yhet therein—James be the grace of God Kinge of Scottis. To all and sundry oure liegies and subdits to qwhais knowlage thir our Leiz—sall cum gretinge—Wit yhe vs to haue gevin and grauntit full fredome facultey and spele license to oure loud familiare squir Alex. of Ogilvy of Inercarity for to fortifie his house and to strength it with an Irne yhet—Quharfor we straitly bid and commaunds that na man tak on hande to make him impediment Stoppinge na distroublace in the makinge Raisin hyninge and vpsettinge of the said yhet in his said house vnder all payne and charge eftir may follow. Gevin vnder oure signet at Streviline the xxv. day of September, ande of oure regne the seviut yhere."

Baron Ogilvy, of Lintrathen, was created Earl of Airlie in 1639, and in the following year the castles of Forter and Airlie were both burnt by the Marquis of Argyle. It was from the latter that Lady Ogilvy, in the absence of her Lord, was expelled, an incident which suggested the touching old ballad of "The Bonnie House of Airlie." The place had been regarded as an almost impregnable natural stronghold, and had already, under Lord

Ogilvy, who had been left in command by his father, the Earl, resisted a party under Montrose and Kinghorn; but on Argyle's approach with 5000 men the garrison fled. The following is a copy of the original directing the famous "raid" referred to above. It has neither date nor place given, but addressed thus :—

"For Dougal Campbell, Fiar of Innerarie" "Dougal—I mynd, God willing, to lift from this the morrow, and therefore ye shall meett me the morrow at nicht at Stronnar, not in Strathardill, and caus bring alonges wt. you the haill nolt and sheepe that ye have fundine partaining to my Lord Ogilbie. As for the horsi's and maris that ye have gottine pertaining to him, ye shall not fail to direct thame home to the Strone-moor. I desyre not that they be in our way at all, and so send thame the nearest way home. And albeit, ye be the langer in following me, zeit ye shall not faill to stand and demolish my Lord Ogilbie's house and farther, see how ye can cast off the iron yettis and windowis, and tak doun the rooff; and if ye find that it will be langsome, ye shall fyere it weill, that so it may be destroyed.

"Bot you neid not to latt know that ye have directions from me to fyere it, onlie ye may say that ye have warrand to demolish it; and that, to mak the work short, ye will fyere it. Iff yee mak any stay for doing of this, send forward the goodis. So referring this to your cair, I rest your friend,

(Signed)   ARGYLL.

Of the Angus gentry taken prisoners at Philiphaugh, there were Lord Ogilvy, Alex. Ogilvy of Inverquharity, and Andrew Guthrie, the Bishop's son. Lord Ogilvy escaped in his sister's clothes, Guthrie was beheaded, and young Inverquharity, a beautiful lad of eighteen, hanged, upon which occasion Mr D. Dick, a Presbyterian minister, said—" the guid wark gaes bonnilly on."

In 1690 Captain James Ogilvy, son of the baron, fought for James VII. at the battle of the Boyne, and afterwards went abroad. Enlisting in foreign service he fell in an engagement on the Rhine. He was the author of the beautiful song "It was a' for our richtfu' King." As several of the best collections of Scottish song do not contain this ballad, and as it is not so well known as it should, we think no apology is necessary for inserting here this beautiful and pathetic ballad :—

"It was a' for our richtfu' King
  We left fair Scotland's strand ;
It was a' for our richtfu' King
  We e'er saw Irish land, my dear,
  We e'er saw Irish land.

Now a' is done that man can do,
  And a' is done in vain ;
My love, and native land fareweel,
  For I maun cross the main, my dear,
  For I maun cross the main.

I'll turn me right and round about
  Upon the Irish shore,
An' gi'e my bridle-reins a shake,
  With 'Adieu for evermore, my dear.'
  With 'Adieu for evermore.'

The sodger frae the wars returns,
  The sailor frae the main ;
But I must pairt frae my true love,
  Never to meet again, my dear,
  Never to meet again.

When day is gane an' nicht is come,
  An' a' folk bound in sleep,
O think on him that's far awa',
  The lee lang night, an' weep, my dear,
  The lee lang night, an' weep."

Miss Dorothea Ogilvy, Broughty-Ferry, daughter of the Hon. Donald Ogilvy of Clova (whose paternal grandfather was 7th Earl of Airlie), inherits, as did her brother the late Donald Ogilvy, the poetic gifts of the family. Amongst several volumes of poems we might note "Doron," Poems by Dorothea and Donald

Ogilvy, published at Aberdeen in 1865, and "My Thoughts" (Edinburgh, 1873). Miss Ogilvy has sung the loves, the joys, the rural scenes and simple pleasures of the romantic glen Clova, in so sweet and so lovely a strain as to be admired throughout the length and breadth of the land:—

> Lone glens of sunny gleams, of sparkling rushing streams,
>   Where mountains rise in purple, green, and gold;
> In your dusty woods at dawn I have roused the sleeping fawn,
>   Where the fountains glimmered pure, and clear, and cold.
>
> 'Mid the scattered rocks of grey, where the raven seeks his prey,
>   And the wind sweeps evermore around the cairn,
> Thy lakes lie deep and still, in the shadow of the hill,
>   In a wilderness of heather, moss, and fern.
>
> Among the purple bells the heather lintie dwells,
>   And the wailing curlew wanders wild and free;
> In each bosky birchen grove softly croons the cushat-dove,
>   And the blackbird sweetly whistles on his tree.
>
> There many a crumbling keep crowns many a rugged steep,
>   And many a moss-grown wreck of hut and hold,
> Memorial tomb and stone of generations gone,
>   And of bloody fields in war-like days of old.
>
> Thy moorlands spreading wide in all their purple pride,
>   Linns that foaming fall, and rise in silver spray;
> Each burnie's brattling song, thy hazel haughs among,
>   Thy grand old mountains stretching far away.
>
> I see Glen Clova smile, and each dim and deep defile,
>   Mantle rosy in the sunset's crimson glow,
> Each cot and hamlet white, in a blaze of golden light,
>   While the river mourns and murmurs far below.
>
> I've a rapture all my own, in the torrents' distant moan,
>   In the bees' low drowsy hum amid the flowers,
> In the berries ripe and red, in the heather's fragrant bed,
>   In the birch trees lending sweetness to the showers,
>
> Dear land of cakes and cairns, of broth and brosy bairns,
>   Of kebbucks, parritch, sowens, and lang kail—
> Here's a health to every class, Highland lad and Lowland lass,
>   May their bannocks, peats, and whisky never fail.

Before taking the reader to Clova, however, we might merely state that the lands of Downiepark and Kinalty were originally part of the Inverquharity estate. The fine mansion house is a prominent object before crossing the Prosen on the way to Clova. It stands on a terrace amid beautiful surroundings, overlooking the venerable castle of Inverquharity. About 1880 the late Earl of Airlie purchased the house and grounds from the trustees of Colonel Rattray's family.

Clova.

Far from the stir of man
Lies Clova's lonely glen,
Tracked by the gray South Esk meandering towards the seas;
On either hand are seen
Vast walls of living green,
Spotted with crags that mar their verdant harmonies.

Earl of Southesk.

A run through this picturesque glen will prove very enjoyable and interesting. The very spirit of peace seems hovering over, as "Auld Eppie" puts it,

The grand towering mountains, the bright flashing fountains,
The cairns o' the clansmen, sae loyal an' true;
The bright dancing brooklets, the sweet shady neuklets,
The saft fleecy cloudlets that skip o'er the blue.

Its wealth of flora fills with fragrance the soft summer air, and it has for many years been the happy hunting ground of botanists. Several important works have been written on the subject of rare flowers and plants peculiar to this beautiful little glen. We are told that in the year 1327 Bruce gave charters of Clova and other lands to his nephew Donald, 12th Earl of Mar. The lands continued in the hands of the Mar family till Countess Isabella, wife of the Wolf of Badenoch, resigned them in favour of Sir David Lindsay of Glenesk in 1398.

In 1445-46, when Thomas Ogilvy, a younger brother of the Laird of Inverquharity, joined the Lindsays against his own clan at the battle of Arbroath, "Earl Beardie" gave Clova over to him, reserving the superiority to his own family. It continued in this way till at least the years 1513-14; for at that date the seventh Earl of Crawford was infeft in the barony of Clova, as heir to his nephew, the previous Earl, and George, Lord Spynie, succeeded his father in the half of the same lands and barony so late as 1646.

The conduct of young Inverquharity at Arbroath was, as might be expected, the signal for family hostility and revenge. A series of desperate feuds was speedily commenced betwixt the houses of Clova and Inverquharity, and the former, being backed by the Lindsays, was always successful; but, an arrangement being made in the time of the fourth baron of Inverquharity, these hostilities were brought to an end. This agreement was made in the true spirit of feudalism, by written indenture "at the Water-side of Prossyn," on the 26th of March 1524, in presence of various kinsmen and other witnesses, whereby the lairds of Inverquharity and Clova, under heavy pains and penalties, "remit the rancour of their hearts to others (each other), and shall live in concord and perfite charity, and sic-like efter the said sentence be given, as guid Christian men and tender friends should do, under the pain of eternal damnation of their souls, because that is the precept et law of God." In strict fulfilment of the conditions of the "Indenture," the laird of Clova, now weaned over to the sdie of his kinsmen, conspired against the noble-hearted Edzell, on his advancement to the peerage, when the Earldom was cancelled in the person of the "Wicked Master," —joined the Ogilvys in besieging the Castle of Finhaven, harried Crawford's lands, and otherwise tried to prevent his succession—a proceeding which, as already seen, was only prohibited by the peremptory mandate of royalty.

The band had thus the desired effect, and the descendants of Thomas Ogilvy, the family traitor of 1445, continued lords of Clova and Cortachy till towards the close of the sixteenth century, when the former was given to Sir David, third son of the first Earl of Airly, who like his older brother that fell at Inverlochy, bore a prominent part in the great civil commotions of his time. He erected a mansion at the Milton of Clova, several of the hewn stones of which were built into the walls of adjoining cottages, and the initials and date "D · O · 1684 · I · G ," on one of the stones referred to him and his wife Jean Guthrie.

The boundary of the old garden is yet traceable, but the foundations of the house are completely erased. It is not so, however, with those of the previous Castle or Peel, for it is still a prominent object on the west side of Benread (a comparatively smooth or tame mountain, as the name implies), north of the Milton. The Peel commands an extensive and delightful view of the Glen, and consists of a fragment about twenty feet in height, with walls fully four feet thick. It is traditionally attributed to the time of the Lindsays, and the occupant, says the "same authority," having rendered himself obnoxious to his brother barons, a party marched against him under night and set his castle on fire. Amidst the confusion and smoke attendant on the burning, the luckless baron fled to the adjoining mountain and took shelter, first under a large piece of rock, still called the "Laird's Stane," and afterwards in the Hole of Weems, a well-known cave in the face of a hill near Braedownie. Others ascribe the destruction of the Peel to the soldiers of Cromwell and Montrose; but perhaps the real cause and time were in

1591, when, "vnder silence of night," five hundred "brokin men and sornaris houndit oute be the Erll of Ergyll and his freindis," entered Glen Clova in September, "invadit the inhabitants, and murthourit" and slew "three or foure innocent men and women and reft and took away ane grit pray of guidis." It is also worthy of note, that when Charles II. duped his keepers at Perth in 1650, he rode to Clova, in the hope of meeting Lord Ogilvy and some of his other friends; but "finding very few to attend upon him, and very bad entertainment," he returned to his captivity on the following day.

Clova, honoured by Her Majesty and the Prince Consort with a visit in 1861, only a short time before the death of his Royal Highness, was long an independent parochial district, but was united to the parish of Cortachy in 1608, on condition that the minister should receive the teinds of both, and preach on two Sundays at Cortachy, and on the third at Clova. From that period the parochial matters of both districts have been managed conjointly; and the records, which begin in the year 1659, show some glimpses of the curious local customs of the age,—such, for example, as when parties went to Church on the first Sunday after marriage, they were accompanied by the inspiring strains of the Highland bagpipes; and, in 1662, there was no sermon at Cortachy because of the minister being in Clova, at "the executione of Margaret Adamson, who was burnt there for ane witch."

Loch Brandy.

> In days o' auld lang syne I wis,
> Maistlin' frae Adam's time to this
> The kintra o' the Ogilvys.

The view from The Ogilvy Arms Hotel, so romantically situated, and so comfortable within, is extensive and beautiful. Behind and before, the grand old mountains are glittering in the sun as in coats of burnished mail, while the long meandering streamlets are flashing faraway in avalanches of stone and rock in a lengthened maze of loveliest living light. Such a picture—so extensive and so wildly beautiful—would of itself abundantly reward the journey of a long summer day.

Loch Brandy—a loch of surpassingly wild grandeur from which issues a stream, rejoicing in the same exhilarating name—is reached after a somewhat stiff climb to the top of the hill immediately above the hotel. But the sight will well repay the effort, and posts are placed at intervals for the guidance of visitors. As we proceed, the hills seem to increase in altitude, and the glens behind us to deepen into a more sublime profoundity. At length, between

> "Mountains that like giants stand,
> To sentinel enchanted land."

the loch appears to rise suddenly before us. A wild amphitheatre, it is girt with the wildest and most picturesque beauty, as with a girdle. Mountain after mountain rises on either shore, and down their sides streamlets dance from linn to linn, until they subside into sleep in the bosom of the lake. This rampart of cliffs, and peaks, and wildly jagged summits—a strange jumbling of the fantastic and the sublime—has a most impressive and imposing effect—the mists in whirling wreaths are rolling down the steeps. Shadows linger in the corries as if the "skreich o' day" still clung reluctant to depart from their silent and solitary recesses, and, as if to deepen the charm, a sweet Sabbath calm rests over all, which subdues the soul to a perfect peace.

It might be noted that the South Esk rises at the head of Glen Clova, and, after a course of about 40 miles, it falls into the German Ocean at Montrose. Lochs Brandy and Wharrel are feeders of it, and so are the Whitewater, the Prosen, the Carraty, the Lemno, the Noran, and the Pow. A visit to the source of the South Esk, by way of Glen Doll, would be greatly enjoyed. Its scenery is varied, and it is described as a botanical paradise, and is much visited by scientific men.

But we must retrace our steps. May the wild flowers haunt thy loneliness ever as they do now—spring coming to thee with the primrose and the violet, summer with the wildling rose, and may autumn linger to the latest ere she lays her searing finger on the verdant fringe with which thou art girt.

Along the flowery margin of the Esk we wend our devious way—the playful streamlets from the hill sides realising, in the minutest feature, Burns' inimitable description—

> "Whiles ower a linn the burnie plays,
>   As through the Glen it wimples,
> Whiles round a rocky scaur it strays,
>   Whiles in a well it dimples;
> Whiles glitterin' in the noontide rays,
>   Wi' bickering dancing dazzle,
> Whiles cookin' underneath the braes
>   Below the spreading hazel."

Now it is leaping in whiteness over some channel stone, now it sweeps sullenly 'neath some overhanging cliff, lichened and gray, or velveted with the greenest moss; and anon it reflects in its glassy bosom some solitary birch or drooping group of saughs. There are many fertile slopes and green meadows, where an occasional wreath of smoke greets the eye of the wanderer.

But on the mountain sides there are not a few ruined humble cots crumbling in slow decay, and covered with lichen and moss,

> "Like the dew from the mountain,
> The foam from the river,
> Like the bubble from the fountain,
> They're gone, and for ever."

Glen Ogil.

> Whaur gowden blossoms o' the whin
> Fa' i' the deep resounding linn;
> Whaur cowslips kiss the daffodils,
> An' roses redden by the rills;
> Whaur tasselled broom o'erhangs the cairn,
> An' honeysuckle gilds the fern;
> Whaur ivy climbs the granite walls,
> An' willows woo the waterfalls;
> Whaur hoary mists and creeping clouds
> Wrap the blue hills in silver shrouds;
> Whaur doon the rocks the burnies rin,
> An' rise in reek frae linn to linn.

It is said that, probably towards the end of the 15th century, the lands of Ogil, on the braes of Angus, were possessed by the descendents of William, brother of the third and fourth Lords Glamis. Another authority asserts that James Fenton of Ogil, was one of the arbiters in the dispute between the Ogilvys of Inverquharity and Clova, arising out of the desertion of his clan by a son of Inverquharity at the battle of Arbroath, for which service the Earl of Crawford gave him a charter of Clova.

The Fentons of Ogil had acquired the estate of Findowrie in 1558. Four years before David Fenton sold Findowrie, he and several others were charged for "abiding" from the raids of Leith and Lawder that year. David and his brother James were accused of the slaughter of William Currour, and the mutilation of Thomas Currour of his right hand. They were sons of Andrew Currour of Logie Mill.

Whatever the Fentons may have been in early times they appear to have become a wild, turbulent family in later years. In 1571 David Lindsay of Barnyards, in this parish, killed John Fenton. The slaughter of the Currours arose out of an ancient family feud, but the cause of the slaughter of Fenton is not known. Such outrages show the excited state of society in the latter half of the sixteenth century, and the little value the Angus lairds set upon the lives of their neighbours at that period.

In 1585 Fenton of Ogil, Denchar of that Ilk, Dempster of Careston, and David Waterston, portioner of Waterston and other adjoining lands, were charged by the Bishop and Chapter of Brechin with having taken possession of, and built houses upon, and cultivated part of the commonty of the city of Brechin. Lord Gray, then Sheriff of the county, declared the whole muir to be a commonty belonging to the Bishop and Chapter, and to the citizens of Brechin. This common was of great extent, extending from the Gallows Hill of Keithock on the east westward to the Law of Fern, being about eight miles in length by nearly one and a half in breadth. The city of Brechin draws feu duties from those parties who have buildings upon it.

The lands of Ogil are watered by the pellucid Noran; which, rising in the southern ranges of the

Grampians, flows through Glen Ogil into Strathmore, and for some distance separates this parish from Fern. The Lyons appear to have succeeded the Fentons in Easter Ogil. They were proprietors in 1684-5, when Ochterlony wrote his account of the shire, and for some time thereafter. It was acquired by the Grants, who built the old manor house in 1744. It was one of the Lyons of Easter Ogil who in 1745 carried off the famous sword which belonged to Deuchar of that Ilk, in the parish of Fern, and because it was too long for his use, had some inches taken from its length. After the Rebellion the then laird of Deuchar recovered the sword from the Castle of Coul, where it had been left by Lyon. The property was ultimately acquired by James Forrest, banker and merchant, Kirriemuir. At his death he was succeeded by his son, William Forrest, who is the present laird of Easter Ogil. James Forrest erected an excellent house on the site of the one built by the rebel laird. It is in the Elizabethan style of architecture, and is pleasantly situated on the eastern or left bank of the crystal Noran, among fine sylvan scenery.

The old Castle of Cossens, built by the branch of the Lyons from whom this family of Glen Ogil are descended, is now a ruin. The arms of David Lyon of Cossens, impaled, are still to be seen sculptured on the north wall of what remains of the castle. The late George Lyon of Glenogil sold the upper or highland Glenogil to David Haig of Edinburgh, who built a fine residence, which he called Redheugh, on a picturesque site near the Noran, and a short distance to the east of St Arnold's Seat. This beautiful hill is wooded nearly up to the summit, and it is a commanding object in the landscape. There is a large cairn on the top of the hill, but this proprietor

ON THE NORAN.

removed many of the stones to build a wall. The prospect from the cairn is still one of the widest, most varied, and grandest which can be seen from any point on the Braes of Angus, and none should visit the district without ascending the hill to feast their eyes with the glorious views. David Haig died in 1848, and was succeeded by his son, James Richard Haig. From him the property passed to John Leveson Douglas Stewart, from whose representatives the present proprietor, Stephen Williamson, M.P. for the Kilmarnock Burghs, bought the property, which he has in many respects greatly improved.

On the north side of the Esk, near the place where the bridge of Shielhill now stands, the Castle of Queich formerly stood. It was the residence of the Earl of Buchan, who owned some property in the parish. The situation was well adapted for the abode of a feudal chieftain, as it afforded him security from enemies. It was built on a precipitous rock overhanging the river, with a deep chasm on each side of it through which a stream pours down. It was therefore assailable from only one point. No vestiges of the Castle were to be seen when the Old Account was written, a humble cottage then occupying the site of the lordly keep.

The old Castle of Wester Ogil stood near the junction of the burn from the west which falls into the Noran near the lower end of Glenogil, but the ruins of it have disappeared. A mansion has been erected a little to the north of the site of the old Castle. It stands on a rising ground on the right bank of the Noran. It is of two floors, with lofty windows on the lower or ground floor. The building is plain, but very chaste, the bold banks of the beautiful stream, the lawn, gardens, rich shrubbery, and thriving plantations around combining to form a pretty and picturesque scene. The falls on the Noran, at a little distance from Glenogil House, add to the variety and attraction of the scenery.

It may interest some readers to mention that the nervous disease, popularly called "loupin' ague," prevailed much in former times, especially in the Glen of Ogil district. The Rev. John Jamieson, Forfar, who wrote the "Old Statistical Account of Tannadice" in 1795-6, says:—

"The most common distemper in the parish is the low nervous fever, which may indeed be considered as the characteristic distemper of this county. Twenty or thirty years ago what is commonly called the *louping ague* greatly prevailed. This disease, in its symptoms, has a considerable resemblance to *St Vitus's dance*. Those affected with it when in a paroxysm, often leap or spring in a very surprising manner, whence the disease has derived its vulgar name. They frequently leap from the floor to what, in cottages, are called the *baulks*, or those beams by which the rafters are joined together. Sometimes they spring from one to another with the agility of a cat, or whirl round one of them with a motion resembling the fly of a jack. At other times they run with astonishing velocity to some particular place out of doors which they have fixed on in their minds before, and perhaps mentioned to those in company with them, and then drop down quite exhausted. It is said that the clattering of tongs or any similar noise will bring on the fit."

The Castle of Vane, Deuchar, Fern, &c.

*Nor hill nor burn we pass along
But has its legend or its song.*

The ancient Castle of Vane is situated on a precipitous rock on the north bank of and overlooking the Noran, which here flows through a romantic and

beautiful den, adorned with many trees of great age and large size. Three stones removed from the ruins of the Castle, have been built into the walls of the farm offices for preservation. They appear to have been lintels of doors or windows, and they respectively bear the following legends :—

Disce meo exemplo formosis posse carere.
(Learn by my example to be able to want the beautiful.)

—— *vs Placitis abstinuisce bonis.*
Anno Dom, 1678.
(—— to have abstained with a good will.)

Non si male nunc et sic erat.
(If it is with me now, it was not so formerly.)

There is an Earl's coronet, and the monogram, E.R.S., of Robert, Earl of Southesk, upon the first of the stones above mentioned. The Castle was originally of three storeys, with a circular tower containing a staircase in the south-west corner. It is built of red sandstone, and only small portions of the Castle are now of the original height.

Tradition points to **Cardinal Beaton** as the builder of Vane Castle, but this is not the case, and he does not appear ever to have had any connection with it. It also points to a deep pool in a dark cavern in the river, near the Castle, called Tammy's Hole or Cradle, as the spot where one of his sons fell over the precipice and was drowned. A boy of the name may have been drowned in the pool, and the name originated from the event, but he was no son of the Cardinal and his fair friend. In "Ancient Things in Angus," Carrie says:—

"We have not been able to ascertain who were the owners of the lands of Vane previous to their coming into possession of the Abbey of Aberbrothock, but it is certain they belonged to that Abbey at the time of the Reformation. Tradition assigns the erection of the Castle of Vane to Cardinal Beaton as a residence for one of his numerous mistresses. In the description of the parish of Fern, in the New Statistical Account of Scotland, the following paragraph occurs: 'In a deep pool of the Noran water, near the castle of Vane, a son of an ancient proprietor is popularly believed to have been drowned. The place is called Tammie's Cradle, and the name of the estate is ascribed to an exclamation of the father of the child upon the accident being reported to him: he cried, 'It's a' vain.'"

By the side of the stream, a little east of the Castle, is a large sandstone bearing a deep indentation resembling the hoof of a colossal horse. It is locally known as "Kelpie's Footmark," and is an object which excites the wonder of the superstitious people in the neighbourhood. The stone is of the pudding stone or conglomerate sort, and a pebble may have fallen out and left the depression. In the olden time the district was a famous resort of the Brownies and other supernatural beings.

Deuchar, and Auchnacree a short distance to the north, are places of historic interest in this neighbourhood. The pretty estate and mansion of Noranside ought also to be mentioned. The present proprietor is Mr Clazey. The mansion house of Deuchar stands on an eminence well up in the parish of Fern, and commands a prospect of much beauty and extent, embracing a large portion of Strathmore, Finhaven, Turin, and the Sidlaws. Tradition says that Deuchar of Deuchar received the lands from which they took their surname, and the designation "of that Ilk," for services performed at the Battle of Barrie in 1010. Records show that Deuchars held the lands of Deuchar as vassals to Lindsay of Glenesk, lord of Fern, in 1379. But long prior to that period, indeed from earliest record, the property was possessed by a family named after the estate. It is said that Deuchar, who was with Keith at the Battle of Barry, was a man of gigantic stature, and of vast strength, having six fingers on each hand, and as many toes on each foot. While in pursuit of the Danes he fell by a stroke or thrust from some of the Northmen. Mr Thomas Thomson is the present owner of Deuchar, his wife being a daughter of the late Mr Marnie of Deuchar.

The following local rhyme, containing an enumeration of place-names in the district, is somewhat curious :—

> " Deuchar sits on Deuchar hill,
> Lookin' doon on Birnie Mill :
> The Whirrock, an' the Whoggle ;
> The Burnroot, an' Ogle ;
> Quiechstrath, an' Turnafachie ;
> Waterhaughs, an' Drumlieharrie."

We have referred already to the prominent part

played by the men of Fern in the Battle of Saughs. Speaking of Fern we might note that Macintosh, or Ledenhendrie, as he was usually called, from the farm he occupied, ever after "the battle" went armed with sword and pistols, as a protection against the attacks of the caterans or other enemies. In the church he laid his naked swords and pistols on the desk in front of his seat. On being expostulated with by the minister for carrying arms, he replied if he had only spiritual enemies to contend with he would lay them aside, but he had once nearly lost his life by mortal enemies when unarmed, and he would therefore carry them till the day of his death. Ledenhendrie was buried inside the Church of Fern, but notwithstanding what he had done for the parishioners at the Water of Saughs, no monument was put up to mark the spot where they laid him. When the old church was taken down in the beginning of this century, a large unhewn stone with a hole in it was found. It was called Ledenhendrie's stone, and is set up in the graveyard a short distance from the front of the Church, at his supposed grave, but there is no inscription upon it, or any evidence of its connection with the leader of the heroic youths of Fern at the Battle of Saughs. Winter went to reside in Glenisla. It had been arranged between him and Mackintosh that whoever of the two died first the other should attend the funeral and have it conducted with the barbaric pomp of the age—the pibroch playing the coronach, and the mourners armed. Winter died first, and Macintosh kept his promise. A monument—the inscription of which we quoted on page 43—was raised to his memory near the south-east corner of Cortachy Church.

Careston Castle.

The Past, thy storied record bids us cherish,
The Present, views thee with admiring eye.

Careston Castle is the next place of interest, and a visit to it completes our first tour. It stands on a beautiful lawn, amidst luxuriant trees. It was one of the most splendid baronial residences in Angus, but having passed through many families, and on account of neglect, more than from the wearing influence of the "tooth of time," it has suffered much dilapidation both within and without. The present proprietor, Mr W. Shaw Adamson, however, has, with great taste, done much to atone for this neglect. The principal rooms in the original castle have been tastefully repaired, the valuable sculptures replaced in the former positions, and the staircase, walls, cornices, doors, and windows restored as in the olden time.

Ochterlony thus quaintly describes the place as it existed two hundred years ago:—" A great and delicat house, well built, braw lights, and of a most excellent contrivance, without debait the best gentleman's house in the shyre; extraordinare much planting, delicate yardes and gardens with stone walls, ane excellent avenue with ane range of ash trees on every syde, ane excellent arbour, for length and breadth, none in the country like it. The house built by Sir Harry Lindsay of Kinfauns, after (wards) Earl of Crawford." The author of the "New Statistical Account" says that the Castle was erected about 1400, but he gives no authority for the statement.

In the preface to the *Registrum vetus de Aberbrothoc* mention is made of Bricius as "judex" of Angus. In 1219 Adam was judex of the Earl's Court, and some years later his brother Keraldus succeeded to the office. The dwelling of Keraldus received the name of "Keraldistone," then Caraldstoun, and the office of judex becoming hereditary, and taking its Scotch style of "Dempster," gave name to the family, who, for many generations, held the lands of Caraldstoun, and performed the office of Dempster of the Parliaments of Scotland. This, Warden considers, the most probable source from which the name of the estate and of the parish had its origin.

Moniepennie, in his description of Scotland, published in 1612, mentions "the Castles and Towers of Melgund, Flemington, Woodwre, Bannabreich, Old Bar, with the parke, Carrestoun, and Balhall." These had all been existing, probably inhabited and well known, in the early part of the seventeenth century. The proprietors of Careston, prior to its passing to the Lindsays, may have resided on the site of the present Castle, and Sir Harry Lindsay had either made additions to the ancient castle, or taken it down and built a new one, which may be the most ancient portion of the present building. It is evident that its external appearance has been transformed at various dates, and the interior also frequently changed—some of the proprietors having ornamented the principal rooms in a very artistic manner. Warden gives interesting details of the alterations it has undergone.

The Castle, as originally erected, must have been a

CARESTON CASTLE.

TANNADICE.

grand and imposing structure. The front consisted of a centre building of three storeys, flanked by two wings of four floors each, which project about twenty feet from the main building. The space between the projecting wings has been covered in with lead at the height of one storey, and forms a fine entrance hall and lobby. On the roof of this section there is a pleasant and safe promenade. One of the additions made by a former proprietor to the old Castle consists of lofty but heavy-looking battlements and turrets. This portion of the mansion is very massive, has a grand appearance, and is the most castellated part of the edifice. One of the proprietors of Careston had found the Castle too small for his family, friends, and retainers. He was careful to procure increased accommodation, and adopted a novel mode of attaining his object. He incased a considerable part of the exterior walls of the Castle by building a new wall at some distance outwith the ancient walls. The space between the original and the modern walls was divided into floors and rooms, and covered with a roof. In this way the number of apartments in the Castle was increased, but some of the original rooms, instead of having light and air from without, as formerly, had only borrowed lights, which rendered them all but useless. The new outer apartments completely enclose the corbels of the turrets, and prevent them from being seen outside the Castle. The battlemented heads of the turrets rise above, and are seen over the top of this curious addition, but as the turrets are not seen in their entirety, their stunted appearance, and the objectionable outside building, tend to disfigure the external aspect of the grand old baronial Castle. All the principal rooms in the Castle and the old staircase were particularly rich in sculptured and other decorations. They chiefly consisted of armorial bearings, allegorical representations, and curious grotesque ornaments

Above what was at one time the grand entrance to the Castle, on the north side of the low building, are the arms of Carnegy of Balnamoon. The magnificent sculptures, figures, blazons, and other embellishments in the Castle were for ages the glory of the baronial walls of Careston, and the pride of the Lords of the barony.

The dining and drawing-rooms, the grand staircase, and about half a dozen bedrooms are decorated with the sculptures and heraldic bearings to which we have referred, and we will only further give a short account of a few of them. The mantelpiece of the dining-room has the Airlie Arms in the centre, with the motto, *A. Fin.* On each side of these are nude figures with urns, from each of which a serpent is issuing. On the right and left of the fireplace are male and female satyrs. A well-executed sculpture of the Royal Arms of Scotland, around which are banners, shields, and other military trophies, and two nude human figures riding on lamas, adorns the mantelpiece in the drawing-room. Figures of a man and a woman, about life size, with cornucopiæ in their hands, festooned in a tasteful manner, and united by a *Pan's* head, decorate each side of the fireplace.

The grounds in front of the Castle must have presented an extraordinary appearance to the astonished occupants on the morning of the 5th April, 1645. Instead of the sheep and oxen which usually grazed in the spacious park, many hundreds of armed men, firmly bound in the arms of Morpheus, lay thickly strewed in all directions, while about one hundred caparisoned horses fed around them. These wearied men and horses were the heavy armed portion of the troops of the Marquis of Montrose, with their brave and impetuous leader at their head. In the evening of the 3rd April he left Dunkeld, and marched rapidly to Dundee, which he reached early the following forenoon. His troops at once stormed the town, and were proceeding fast with their work of destruction when Montrose was informed that General Baillie with the Covenanting army was close at hand. It was with great difficulty that he got his drunken soldiery to leave so rich a town unsacked, and so much spoil behind. At last he got the troops to leave the town by the east, after setting fire to the Hilltown, as Baillie entered the town from the west. Montrose proceeded towards Arbroath as rapidly as he could get the intoxicated men to move. He then altered his course, turned to the north-west, reached the South Esk, which he crossed at one of the fords near Balnabreich, and onward to Careston Castle, on the lawn in front of which the men at once lay down, and immediatly fell asleep. The men had had no sleep for two nights in succession. They had marched nearly seventy miles, skirmishing frequently on the way from Dundee to Arbroath, and they had stormed Dundee, and indulged in many excesses there. No wonder that after such a masterly retreat and so great fatigue their slumbers were profound, but they were not destined to be of long duration. Montrose had given Baillie the slip, and also Hurry, the other Covenanting General, who was lying in wait for him at Brechin, but this only stimulated their exertions to overtake him. On learning of their near approach Montrose had his men roused again, but so overcome were they with fatigue and sleep that many of the soldiers had to be pricked with swords before they could be awakened. Once on the move they immediately made for Glenesk, and were soon within its bounds, and for the time being,

E

safe. Mr Adamson, father of the present proprietor, in making the alterations upon the Castle, found in the upper or attic floor three *Queen Bess* muskets, which doubtless had been left by some of Montrose's soldiers on the memorable occasion of their visit to Careston. These interesting memorials now add to the adornment of the grand staircase of the Castle.

The people in and bordering upon the Braes of Angus, says Warden, were very superstitious in the olden time. They firmly believed in ghosts, and many people, both young and old, would have made a long detour rather than pass alone in the dark spots supposed to be haunted by a ghost. A *White Lady* was one of the most common appearances which ghosts assumed, and few parishes were without one of these fair but dreaded apparitions. Careston was not behind its neighbours in respect of its supernatural visitors. It had its *White Lady*, who had been wronged while in the body, and who, now that she was a spirit, was wont to traverse the district around the old Castle of Careston where the woods were close, but though harmles, she was feared, and her haunts avoided.

Before leaving Careston, and returning to the city by what is known as the "high," or Barrelwell Road, we might note that the parish formerly known as "Caraldstone," was only erected into a parish in 1641 —it having previously formed part of the parish of Brechin. This was brought about on account of the "ignorance of the tenantry," or on account of "the distance of their abodes from the Parish Church of Brechin." In the Reg. Epis. Bre., Careston is spelled no fewer than eighteen different ways. It is one of the smallest parishes in the Kingdom—indeed it is said that there are only four smaller—and both the church and churchyard are correspondingly small.

Although in our first trip our course has been occasionally of the zig-zag order, and we have on our homeward way necessarily had to go over the same ground which we had already traversed, we now don our "seven-league boots," and find ourselves back to the Ancient City sometime within the bounds of "elders' hours."

Second Tour.

ALDBAR, ARDOVIE, MELGUND, AND FLEMINGTON CASTLES; SCULPTURED STONES OF ABERLEMNO, ANGUS HILL, &c.

Aldbar and its Castle.

"Thus saith the preacher, 'Nought beneath the sun
Is new,' Yet still from change to change we run."

"There's not a heath, however wild,
   But hath some little flower
To lighten up its solitude
   And scent the weary hour."

STARTING on our second tour, we again hold west, diverging, however, to the left shortly after passing the second Brechin Castle Lodge. The first object calling our attention is the range of buildings and gate-way, known as "The Kennels," now silent, but "in the time of the Auld Lordie," a lively and noisy place. In the valley below is the shooting range of the Brechin Volunteers, and while crossing the bridge over the South Esk we cannot fail to feast on its lovely surroundings. Above, we admire the richly wooded policies of Maulesden—to which we have already alluded—the fine mansion nestling almost on the bank of the river, with its delightful sylvan accessories, forming an excellent subject for the landscape painter. Below, we have a pretty "peep" of a portion of the Brechin Castle policies, the south bank of the stream here becoming quite precipitous until a short stretch brings it under the "Image" bridge, of which more anon. Altogether the circle of scenery visible from this "coigne of vantage" is very pleasing and varied.

Little more than a quarter of a mile, keeping to the left where the road diverges, and we reach the neat entrance to the beautiful pleasure-grounds of Aldbar, belonging to Patrick Chalmers, Esq. This gentleman, with commendable kindness—as indeed will be found the case with most of the proprietors whose domains we visit—permits respectable strangers to have access to his picturesque grounds, and it is satisfactory to learn that the favour and his confidence is fully appreciated, and is very seldom abused. About half-a-mile from the gate-way, along a drive profusely fringed with verdure and under the shade of majestic trees, brings us to the castle.

The Castle stands close to the burn, at a singularly romantic spot, near a pretty waterfall. During the time of the "antiquarian laird," and more particularly towards the close of his life, large and important additions were made to the house, which, with a variety of other alterations and improvements, greatly changed the general aspect of the building. It was divested of its feudal character, and instead of being a gloomy fortalice, reared for safety rather than comfort, it became, to a great extent, a modern mansion of noble proportions, at the same time retaining its castellated appearance, and the character of a grand old baronial keep—the richly clothed sides of the ravine and the cascade lending variety and beauty to the surroundings. The principal entrance, formerly on the west, was changed to the east, and the old front ornamented with tastefully laid out flower terraces and balustraded walls. A picturesque grotto, overshadowed by rocks and trees, and a number of rustic and other retreats were also formed, the whole combining to make the grounds of a truly charming nature.

The oldest portion of the Castle of Aldbar was built by Sir Thomas Lyon towards the end of the 16th century, and it is an excellent specimen of the Scottish baronial architecture of the period when it was erected. The tower is ornamented with the armorial bearings of the noble house of Lyon, of which Sir Thomas was a distinguished member, being Lord Treasurer of Scotland. It was he who, in 1582, when James VI. wept because he was detained in Ruthven House, said "It is better that bairns should weep than bearded men."

The period of the death of this bold baron is unknown, but it occurred some time after King James went to England, for, on hearing of Lyon's death, he is said to have remarked to the English nobles around him, "that the boldest and hardiest man in his dominions was dead!" Sir Thomas Lyon left a son who succeeded to Aldbar, but, as he died without issue, the lands reverted to his nephew, the Earl of Kinghorn, who afterwards disposed of them to a cadet of the noble house of Sinclair. In 1670 and 1678, various portions of the estate of Aldbar were bought from Sir James Sinclair by Peter Young of Easter Seaton, grandson of that Sir Peter who was almoner to King James VI. His eldest son and successor, Sir James of Innerechtie, knight, was a gentleman of the King's bed-chamber, and father of

ALDBAR CASTLE.

that **Peter** Young of Easter Seaton, who (with consent of his wife, Isabella Ochterlony [perhaps of Wester Seaton] and his son Robert, as life-renter and fiar, and also with consent of **Robert's** wife, Anna, daughter of Sir William Graham of **Claverhouse**), sold Easter Seaton and bought **Aldbar** as previously noticed.

A romantic story is told of the last Young of Aldbar. According to tradition, arrangements were made for his marriage with the daughter of a neighbouring proprietor. It is said that, in token of respect and in remembrance of her proposed wedding, the lady resolved to present her native parish with the rather odd gift of a *mortcloth*. That and her marriage dress, having been ordered from the same person in Edinburgh, were both sent together, and, by some unexplained accident, found their way to Aldbar, where the package was opened. Mr Young, who was probably of a nervous disposition, took the matter seriously to heart, and sending the mortcloth and wedding dress to his bride, he hurried to Montrose, where, it is said, he committed suicide by drowning. His bride died soon after, and the ill-omened mortcloth was first used at her own funeral. It was soon after this sad occurrence that the lands of Aldbar were purchased by William Chalmers of Hazelhead.

It is said that when King Edward I. subdued Scotland, the lands of Aldbar were in the possession of a cadet of the Cramonds, or Kerramunds, of Midlothian. The Aldbar branch ultimately became chief of the family, and in 1541, soon after that event, James Cramond of Aldbar sold the original family properties of Over Cramond and Clairbar, to William Adamson of Craigcrook, and then the interest of the Cramonds in the Lothians ceased. The estate of Cramond, from which the family name was assumed, was held of the Knights of St John of

Jerusalem, and William of Cramond, of the county of Edinburgh, who was clerk of the king's wardrobe in 1278, is recorded to have sworn fealty to King Edward in 1296, at Berwick-upon-Tweed, much about the same time as Laurence de Cramound, who is designed of the county of Forfar. Besides the lands of Aldbar, the Cramonds were early in possession of those of Melgund and Eddrochat or Kintrockat. They were related by marriage to some of the most influential families in Angus and the Mearns, and held their estates until the latter half of the sixteenth century, when their affairs became embarrassed, and, the lands being heavily mortgaged, John, Lord Glamis, who was Chancellor of Scotland in 1577, became the proprietor.

Since 1296, when Lawrence de Cramond swore fealty to Edward I. of England, the barony of Aldbar has been in the possession of noted families—in that of the Cramonds till 1577, and afterwards in those of the Lyons, the Sinclairs, the Youngs, and the Chalmers's. Thomas Ruddiman, the eminent grammarian, taught for a short time in the Castle after finishing his University course at Aberdeen in 1694. Mr Robert Young of Aldbar, the great-grandson of Sir Peter Young, preceptor of James VI, engaged Ruddiman to be the tutor to his son David. It would appear that his situation in the Laird's establishment was not very enviable; for within a year he accepted the humble office of schoolmaster in the parish of Laurencekirk.

In 1753, Aldbar was purchased by William Chalmers of Hazelhead, representative of the old Aberdeenshire family of Chalmers of Balnacraig, who was at one time Governor of Gibraltar, and who amassed considerable wealth as a merchant in Spain. Indeed, it is said that the family can trace back their pedigree for considerably more than five centuries, if not, says Warden, to the time of King Alexander the First (1106-24).

In 1765 Patrick Chalmers succeeded to the estate of Aldbar, on the death of his father, William. He was Sheriff of Forfarshire from 1769 to 1807. It may be interesting to know that he acted as Sheriff-Substitute for the whole of Forfarshire for the sum of £150 a year. In 1785 he had the painful duty—for he was a man of much kindliness of heart—of pronouncing sentence of death on a young man who was found guilty of house-breaking and theft, adjudging "the pannel to be hanged at the west end of the Hill of Forfar, betwixt the hours of 12 mid-day and 4 in the afternoon." This was the last person in Scotland upon whom such a dread sentence was passed by a Sheriff. "The Shirra" died in 1824 in his 93rd year, and the property then came into possession of his only son, Patrick, who was born at Aldbar in 1777. He was for many years a merchant in London, and founder of the well-known firm of Chalmers, Guthrie & Co., Idol Lane. He married Francis Inglis, daughter of John Inglis, merchant in London, and a Director of the East India Company. He died at Aldbar in 1826, when his eldest son, Patrick (born 1802), Captain in the 3rd Dragoon Guards, succeeded to the estate. On the death of his father he retired from the army, and took up his residence on his estate. From 1835 to 1842 he represented the Angus Burghs in Parliament, and was, altogether, one of our most distinguished Commoners. He rendered invaluable service to the burghs and county by the influential support which he gave to every measure conducive to their interests, and he was a model proprietor, believing and practising the maxim, that if property has its rights, it has also its duties. He did much to enhance the value and the amenity of his Castle and lands, and he did it with a philanthropist's delight in the employment which he thus gave to the artizan and labourer. A warm friend of education, he erected and endowed on his own estate one of the best schools in the shire.

In the republic of letters, and more especially in the department of Scottish history and antiquities, Mr Chalmers occupied a high place, as is testified by his able assistance in the editing of some of the publications of the Bannatyne and Spalding Clubs, and, above all, by his magnificent volume on "The Ancient Sculptured Stones of Angus." This work was the means of directing more attention to the study of these remains of antiquity, which are to some extent peculiar to Scotland, and of which we are finding the districts we are traversing possess so many interesting specimens. The style, so admirable in its antiqueness, in which he raised from its ruins the old chapel in the beautiful and romantic Den of Aldbar, conveying to it from the parish churchyard the remains of his predecessors, and to which his own were added on his death in 1854, will tell posterity of his general culture, and of his accurate knowledge and exquisite taste as an antiquarian.

Among the Bannatyne Books were the "Registers of the Abbey of Arbroath and of the Cathedral of Brechin." Mr Chalmers was employed upon the latter work at the time of his death. This has since appeared under the title "Registrum Episcopatus Brechinensis," and contains a memoir of Mr Chalmers by the late Mr Cosmo Innes, his fellow-labourer in both works. It was presented to the Club by his brother, the late Mr J. I. Chalmers. "It is matter of regret," says Jervise, "that he was not spared to complete the 'Register,' since his vast local knowledge must have contributed greatly to its value and interest." But the two volumes did not appear until two years after his death.

Failing health induced our zealous antiquarian to visit the Continent in the spring of 1854, but he died at Rome on 23rd June of that year. His remains were brought home, and interred in the Old Kirkyard. With an appropriateness which cannot but be admired, his grave is marked by a monument similar in design to those for whose preservation and illustration he contributed so much, and with which his name will continue to be associated.

In the ruins of the chapel Mr Chalmers found a curious and interesting stone, which he transferred to the vestibule of his Castle, and of which Pinkerton thus wrote :—

"It is well known that there exist in various parts of Scotland, but chiefly on the east side from the River Tay, singular erect stones, generally with crosses on one side, and upon the other sculptures, not ill executed for a barbarous age. Three are found at Aberlemno. That at the Chapel of Aldbar is singular, as, instead of horsemen and spears, there are two persons sitting, probably religious, and beneath them, a man seemingly tearing out a lion's tongue—perhaps Samson—and opposite to him a curious figure of an antique harp, and under these a man on horseback, a lamb, and other animals."

The author of the Statistical Account of the parish remarks :—

"It is most probable that this was either an altar piece, or that it was intended in some way to ornament the sacred edifice—whence it was taken. The subject is evidently a Scriptural one, although from the introduction of the harp, it is most probable that it was David, and not Samson, whom the sculptor designed to represent as achieving a victory over some beast of prey."

Aberlemno was not behind its neighbours in its Jacobitism. John Ochterlony, who had been minister of the parish, and was chamberlain on the estate of Melgund, and proprietor of Flemington, signalised himself by his Jacobite zeal. In 1701, he was accused of withdrawing the people from those sent to preach by the Presbytery, overawing them by threatenings, and preaching to them in a meeting-house. He replaced himself in the church in 1703, and was deprived by a Justice Court. He intruded again in 1716; and was prosecuted before the Lords of Justiciary for "intruding into parish churches, lesson-making, and praying for the Pretender:" but the Solicitor-General deserted the diet in respect of His Majesty's Act of Grace. He still kept hold of the poor's box, mortcloths, &c., which the Kirk-Session was obliged to demand of him in 1722. He had a place of worship at Flemington for several years. In 1726 he removed to Dundee; and was that same year constituted Bishop of the non-jurant church of Edinburgh. The district of Brechin was assigned him in 1731, and he died at Dundee in 1742.

The old chapel, as we have said, was long a ruin, but the portions of the walls that were standing were repaired, and the old stones used, as far as possible, in the renewed building. The restoration was made by the father of the present proprietor, in accordance with the intention of his deceased brother, and of a plan approved of by him. The den is here about one hundred and fifty feet in depth, and the steep sides and the umbrageous trees make the chapel and its precincts an impressive and quiet spot, with its old graveyard surrounded by sylvan foliage and undergrowth of suitable evergreen shrubs, while the quiet peacefulness is only broken by the musical "tinkle o' the burnie"—

> There's the tinkle o' the burnies, the fragrance o' the flowers,
> The shaded blinks o' sunshine that bless the leafy bowers.

As Colin Sievwright has it in his "Garland of Love Songs of Brechin and its Neighbourhood," in one of his numerous interesting historical notes—"The Den o' Aldbar, one of those beautiful romantic little ravines common throughout the howe o' Strathmore and the braes o' Angus, is certainly one of the finest specimens of nature, aided by human art, that we have ever had the pleasure of seeing. Surely there is nothing better, and we know not of anything nearly so good, within the sound o' the bell o' Brechin.

> Down the Den the burnie twines,
>   An' violets busk the brae;
> And tufted broom, wi' gowden bloom,
>   Gars Aldbar look sae braw;
> The birdies sing the vesper hymn
>   As shades o' evening fa'.

Trees, shrubs, and wild flowers; rugged rocks, and rustic bridges; shady nooks, and glorious gleams o' sunshine; singing birds, and rippling waters; Castle Ha', and ancient church. Such we believe is the Den o' Aldbar still; only that the little church has been restored, and once more, when the 'disciples meet together on the first day of the week,' the voice of prayer and praise frequently awake the echoes of the Den, and rises, amid the dewy breath of even, to the great white throne of the Eternal Father."

As we have thus seen, the highly gifted laird was succeeded by his brother, John Inglis Chalmers. In 1838 he married Margaret, daughter of John Bellingham Inglis of Verehills, Lanarkshire, who is still alive. He died in 1868. His son, Patrick, the present proprietor, was born in 1841. Mr Chalmers was a lieutenant in the famous 59th Regiment, and is a J.P. and Deputy-Lieutenant of the county. He resides chiefly at Aldbar, where for generations there has been a herd of pure polled Angus doddies, the members of which are well-known for the vigour of their constitutions and purity of descent. Since the present proprietor succeeded to the estate he has devoted great attention to the herd, and by judicious purchases from the best-known strains in Scotland—many of which were secured at long prices—he now possesses a herd the surplus sales of which attract breeders from all parts of the country.

Ardovie.

Before setting out for Melgund Castle a visit to the ancient residence of the Speids of Ardovie—rather less than two miles to the south, leaving Aldbar by the upper or south gate—would well repay the trouble. The house is a neat old-style residence, with a flight of steps up to the doorway, and flanked by Corinthian columns, fronting the west. Over the doorway is a window with a triangular canopy, crowned with three antique vases. The building has two wings, and the approach, by what is known as "the laburnum walk," is very pretty. It is embosomed in a profusion of wood, in belts and clumps, and individual specimens of the most stately proportions. There are old lawns of the most velvety pasture, dotted with trees of great beauty; there are gardens of rich luxuriance, bosky banks where the wild blossoms love to dwell, and the fern holds forth her freshest plumes.

The lands of Cookston or Quygstone were occupied in 1410 by persons called William Johnston, Robert Adyson, John Alexanderson (Saunderson), and Nicholas Speid. The last named was ancestor of George Speid, who had the lands of Ardovie (or Auchdovie) from Sir Robert Carnegie of Kinnaird in exchange for his part of Cookston in 1549. From that date the Speids have continued to possess Ardovie. The old name of

Speid (success) is thought to have been conferred on a remote progenitor for having performed some heroic feat in days of old. "Cuikstone" (Cookston), we might note in passing, is said to have been a pretty extensive hamlet in old times. It had brick or pottery work from at least the middle of the seventeenth century, and a number of cinerary urns found in ancient stone coffins in this quarter seem to be composed of the same sort of clay as that which was got in the neighbourhood of Cockston.

James Speid of Ardovie was styled the ninth recorded generation of this ancient house. He died in 1853, and was succeeded by his brother John. This gentleman died some twenty years ago, and the present proprietor, Henry, has for many years resided in America. Mr J. Shiress Will, M P., is the present tenant of the mansion and shootings.

Over the doorway of the family burial vault in the old churchyard of Brechin, the family crest is sculptured in bold relief, and under it—"Speid of Ardovie, MDXIX." A stone, now inserted over the front door of the farm house of Mains of Ardovie, bears the shield of arms, and initials well sculptured, with the date 1636. The initials, if our memory serves us, stand for Robert Speid and his wife Christina Grierson, who was the daughter of Homer Grierson (or Grigorson) of Balluno (Ballownie) Stracathro, who married Isobel Doig of the Cookston family. This was an offshoot of the ancient family of Grier of Lag, Dumfrieshire, whose remote progenitor was Gilbert, second son of Malcolm, who died 1374, said to be armour-bearer to the Earl of Douglas. On an ancient dove-cot in the Den of Ardovie is a slab with the letters " RS. M.G.-1743." Visitors should test the celebrated echo in this den, and also see the curious three wells, almost adjoining each other, and fed from different sources.

MELGUND CASTLE.

Melgund Castle.

> The turrets are fallen, the vaults are flown,
> And the bat rules the halls they called their own.

Leaving the grounds of Ardovie, and driving along a pretty woodland path—

> Amang the knowes, where heather grows,
> And gently waves the fern;
> Where summer rings the dead man's bell,
> Aboon the hero's cairn,

we regain the high road little over a mile beyond where we left it at Aldbar Public School, and soon find ourselves, on the right, approaching Melgund Castle, the erection of which has been ascribed to Cardinal Beaton.

The surname of Beaton, (or Bethune) is said to be of French origin. The first mention of the family is in the reign of William the Lion, between 1165 and 1190, when Robert of Betun is found as a witness to a charter by De Quincy, a Norman Baron, who flourished in Scotland betwixt these dates. Barons of the same name were at the celebrated inquest in 1286 regarding the division of the pasture belonging to the barony of Panmure. David, Comptroller and Treasurer to King James IV., was father of one of the "Four Maries," who went to France with Queen Mary, and remained in her suite long after her return to Scotland. She became the wife of the first Viscount Stormont, and is thus commemorated in the beautiful ballad regarding the fate of Mary Hamilton, who, according to tradition, was executed at Edinburgh:—

> "Yestreen the Queen had four Maries,
> The nicht she'll hae but three;
> There was Marie Beatune and Marie Seaton,
> And Marie Carmichael, and me."

John Betune, elder brother of the comptroller,

married Elizabeth Monypenny, daugher of the Laird of Kinkell, and had six sons and five daughters. The third son was David, afterwards Cardinal of Scotland, and by far the most remarkable man of that or perhaps of any contemporary family in the kingdom.

The history of this celebrated ecclesiastic need not be here dwelt upon. Although tradition assigns to him the erection of many of the castles in Forfarshire, that of Melgund, in the parish of Aberlemno, is the only one which it can be said, with any degree of certainty, that he built. The castle in its general design bears a strong resemblance to that of Edzell, but had always been much inferior to it in grandeur and extent. Standing on the verge of a steep bank, overhanging a pretty little streamlet (the Melgund) which meanders along the charming dell beneath, the castle consists of a massive square tower, connected with a variety of apartments in the eastern wing by means of a spacious room, which appears to have been the castle-hall. In the north-east angle of the east wing is a ruined tower. At the south-east angle the falling away of the bank has laid bare great part of the foundations of the castle on that side. The ground floor had been vaulted in the same way as most old castles. In its palmy days the castle had been surrounded by extensive gardens and pleasure grounds, of which some traces still remain.

* The stalwart quadrangular tower is lichened and grey, and bears undoubted evidence of antiquity in its narrow windows and loopholes, while architectural remains in various stages of decay are scattered around. Here we can muse in a vault, sympathise over the captive's woes, thread the mazes of a narrow staircase, or pace the lordly hall where now the swallow has

---

* By the kindness of Mr Lowson, Forfar, we are enabled to give a picture of the hoary building from his work, "Forfarshire Tales and Legends."

taken up his abode, and the winds are free to play, while the rank weeds are waving on the floor and trailing over the prostrate stones—

> "The lichened walls look grim and cold,
>   That totter all around;
> The carvéd work of ages old
>   Lies withering on the ground;
> The casement's antique tracery
>   Has wasted in the dew,
> And the cold breeze whistling mournfully
>   Creeps keen and weirdly through."

As in so many districts throughout Scotland, the dreadful storm in November 1893 made sad havoc with the stately "girdle of tall ancestral trees" leading to the ancient fabric. Previously, through the dense umbrageousness of the "green-robed senators" even the vertical radiance of noon sent with difficulty only a few golden beams to fret the mid-day gloaming,

> Tall trees they were
> And old, and had been old a century
> Before my day. None living could say aught
> About their youth. . . .

Altogether the castle is still a fine ruin. Initials and armorial bearings, supposed to be those of the Cardinal and Marion Ogilvy, are to be seen in different parts of the building. From the Beatons the barony passed, in 1580, to Thomas Lyon, second son of the seventh Lord Glamis, who also owned the adjoining estate of Aldbar. On the decease of Mr Lyon's son John without issue, the estate of Melgund was acquired by Henry Maule, cousin of Patrick, first Earl of Panmure. Mr Maule flourished in the reigns of Kings Charles I. and II. He was a colonel in the British army, and an author and antiquary of some repute, and said to be the author of a "History of the Picts." He left an only daughter, who died unmarried about the year 1690, when his line of the Maule family became extinct. But he appears to have disposed of Melgund during his lifetime, for in the year 1678 we find a gentleman of the name of Murray designated of Melgund, and ranked among the minor barons of the county of Forfar at that time.

Tradition has it that about the beginning of last century his son, with his family, most unaccountably disappeared one night at supper time. The repast was set out in the hall, as usual, but none of the family ever entered the room to partake of it, nor was any one of them ever afterwards seen or heard of in Forfarshire. According to popular belief, the supper-table, laden with the dishes and comestibles, remained for a long time untouched in the hall, no person daring to meddle with them. At length, some one, more venturesome than the rest, had the courage to go into the hall and seize upon and appropriate to his own purposes the entire table array. According to Carrie the elucidation of this mysterious circumstance is:— Mr Murray and his family were known to have espoused the cause of the dethroned royal family, and the laird had doubtless committed himself in regard to some of the secret transactions that preceded the abortive attempt of the old Pretender, the Chevalier de Saint George, to recover the throne of his ancestors. They had no doubt been duly apprised of the advance into Forfarshire of the royal army under the Duke of Argyll, in the month of February 1716; and in order to avoid arrest as a rebel the laird considered it prudent to depart, along with his whole family, into voluntary exile. In consequence, the castle became neglected, and fell rapidly into decay. By a female descendant of Maule, through Murray of Philiphaugh, the property came to the Earl of Minto, and from it his eldest son receives the title of Viscount Melgund.

Regarding the lands of Melgund Jervise informs us

that a William de Anaund did homage at Berwick-upon-Tweed, after King Edward returned from the north. It was this baron who figured so conspicuously at the defence of Stirling in 1305, and the lands of Melgund, in the parish of Aberlemno, were those for which he swore fealty. In the year 1354, David of Anand was one of the prisoners whom the English Commissioners engaged to use their influence to liberate without ransom. The same person or his son was forester of the ancient hunting forest of Plater near Finhaven, which he resigned in 1375, and in which he was succeeded by Sir Alexander Lindsay of Glenesk. In the year 1368, Anand appeared in Parliament regarding the falsing of a sentence of the Justiciary; three years afterwards he was present at the coronation of King Robert II., and in 1391, a person bearing the same name and surname paid the sum of £30 to the King's Chamberlain as relief duty for his lands of Melgund. The family held these lands until the year 1542, when the heiress, Janet of Anand, with consent of her second husband, Balfour of Baledmouth, sold them to Cardinal Beaton.

Flemington Castle.

We now steer our course towards the village—which is neither pretty nor picturesque—passing a goodly number of comfortable-looking pendicles, over which the very spirit of peace seems to hover. Wending our way by Mains of Melgund and round the side of a belt of thriving trees, we reach the highway, known as the old Forfar road. Facing us to the right is the summit of Angus Hill, which shall yet claim our attention. For the present we hold to the left, and before referring to the celebrated "standing-stones" near the village would remark that there is a small castellated building situated a short distance to the eastward of the church of Aberlemno. It stands on the left bank of the rivulet called Henwellburn, which flows through the parish, and passes Melgund Castle. In the New Statistical Account of the parish it is said that the Castle of Flemington was a perfect specimen of a defensive mansion, being strong, stately, and dungeon-like. It had been occupied by the proprietor until within a few years of 1842, the date of the report. It is now inhabited by the farm servants.

In the time of King Alexander II. a knight called Bartholomew of Flanders, or the Fleming, settled in Angus. The property he owned is not known with certainty, but probably the lands of Flemington had belonged to him, and received their name from his nationality. Sir William Dishington had a grant of an annual payment from the lands of Flemington, and subsequently a member of that family had a grant of the property from King Robert III. The Rev. John Ochterlony, the last Episcopal clergyman in the parish, was subsequently proprietor of the lands and Castle of Flemington. As we have already seen, he was repeatedly ejected from the parish church on account of his persistency in again and again taking the pulpit and intruding himself upon the Presbyterian parishioners. When finally ejected he went to reside in his Castle of Flemington, and continued to minister to those of his own persuasion until about 1742, when he left to take possession of the See of Brechin. Flemington was afterwards acquired by Mr John Spence of Bearehill, Brechin (now possessed by Mr Robert Duke), who was grandson of Mr Ochterlony of Flemington. The property was acquired from him by Colin Bruce in 1807. In the year 1809 Colin Bruce and his spouse sold the estate of Flemington to John Webster. He died intestate in 1830, and was succeeded in the property by his brother, Robert Webster. On his death, in 1836, his brother James succeeded to Flemington. He died in 1848, and by his trust disposition and deed of settlement left Flemington to his nephew, Patrick Webster of Westfield, and his heirs. Near to this property is another small manor called Tillywhanland, adjoining the village of Aberlemno. Prior to the Reformation the estate belonged to the see of Brechin, and the bishops of that diocese had a summer residence upon it, which has now entirely disappeared.

The Church and Parish of Aberlemno.

A rural church—some scattered cottage roofs,
From whose secluded hearths the thin blue smoke,
Silently wreathing through the breezeless air,
Ascended, mingling with the summer sky,—
And here and there a venerable tree
In foliaged beauty.

Warden, in his "Angus in Parishes," tells us that the Church of Aberlemenach (Aberlemno) belonged to St Andrews, and was dedicated by Bishop David in 1242. It was dependent upon the Priory of Resteneth, and both church and priory were attached to Jedburgh Abbey. David Lindsay of Pitairlie, a cadet of the noble house of Lindsay, Earls of Crawford, held the cure in the middle of the sixteenth century, immediately after the Reformation. He was at same time minister of the churches of Forfar and Resteneth, his stipend for all the three being 200 merks, or £133 6s 8d Scots.

As we have said, Aldbar (Gaelic Alt-barr, a high burn), was originally a distinct parish, but in the seventeenth century the parish was suppressed, and divided between the parishes of Aberlemno and Brechin. At the founding of the College of Methven, in 1433, Walter Stewart, Earl of Athole, granted the church of Aldbar to the College, and the Provost of Methven was thereafter rector of Aldbar. After the Reformation the Presbyterian minister of Methven called himself Provost of Methven and Chaplain of Aldbar, and he drew the tiends until the suppression of the parish. Until the abolition of patronage in the Church of Scotland the patronage of the Church of Aberlemno was alternately exercised by the Crown, and by Smythe of Methven, the latter coming in room of the Provost and Canons of Methven.

The site of an ancient Church is still visible close to where the Lemno debouches into the Esk, and this may have been the ancient church of the parish, as it accords better with its name—the mouth of the Lemno. The present church was erected in 1722, partly on the walls of the ancient Romish church.

The hills of the parish rise to a considerable altitude, Turin, the highest, being about 800 feet above the level of the sea, and 600 feet above the neighbouring lakes of Rescobie and Balgavies. Many stones, the ruins of an ancient stronghold, called Camp Castle, lie on the top of Turin Hill. The view from the summit is extensive, varied, and beautiful. Turin is the diminutive of Tur, a castle, and signifies a little castle. It probably was so called to distinguish it from the royal castle, which stood in the vicinity of the hill, within which Donald Bane was confined by his nephew, King Edgar. The Lindsays are reputed to have taken the castle on the hill by force from the proprietor.

Celebrated Sculptured Stones.

> There is a pleasure on the heath
> Where warriors old have been,
> Where mantles gray have rustled by
> And swept the nettled green.

The Parish of Aberlemno abounds in sepulchral remains. Cairns and stone coffins seem common. On

Pitkennedy, some years ago, a stone coffin was found containing a clay urn, and near it were scattered a number of beads, of jet or cannel coal, of which more than a hundred were gathered, forming, it has been said, "a necklace, probably the most complete hitherto found in Scotland." A little west of the Castle of Melgund are three tumuli, large enough to cover a hetacomb of the slain. On clearing away the foundations of the old Castle of Woodray, in this parish, in 1819, another sculptured stone was discovered, and sent by Lord Minto's factor to Sir Walter Scott, and is now at Abbotsford. It has a cross and various animals on the obverse, and two men on horseback, animals, and the spectacle ornament, on the reverse. These remains are clearly enough the wrecks of war; and, as the Statistical Account of the parish expresses it—"It is evident that the neighbourhood of the church has either been the scene of a succession of sanguinary conflicts, or else some great and protracted struggle has rolled hither and thither its tide of death over the adjoining fields."

The celebrated sculptured stones of Aberlemno, in a field close to the roadside, a little above the village, are considered to be monuments of the same dire visitation. "A few hundred yards to the north of the church"—we quote again from the Statistical Account —"there is a monumental stone, about eight feet in height, ornamented on one side with a cross, richly carved and with two female figures in the garb and attitude of mourning. The other side is sculptured *in relievo*, with men, some on horseback and others on foot, intermingled with dogs. Near to this one are two smaller stones, which also have been ornamented; but the hand of time has greatly defaced them." The larger of the three stones was described by Boece, and also in 1569. According to Mr Chalmers, this fine cross is said, by tradition, to commemorate the fall of a body of Danes on their retreat from the battle of Barry. The figure on the cross is less elaborately formed than the one on the stone in the churchyard, and the horsemen and other figures on the reverse appear to be engaged in the chase rather than in war. In a compartment underneath the hunters is a centaur bearing a branch of a tree. Over them are the crescent, sceptre, and other symbols. The figures on these stones are in relief. The adjoining stone is sculptured only on one side with symbols of the spectacle ornament, comb, and mirror, and others, all incised. If the other stone, which stands near the latter two, ever had any sculptures, they are now obliterated.

"One of the most perfect," says the Statistical Account, "is in the churchyard. On one side there is a cross in bold relievo, and entirely covered with flowered ornaments. On the reverse, towards the upper part of the stone, is another ornament, having no obvious meaning, but intended for ornament only. Beneath it there are some figures of men on horseback, armed *cap-a-pie*, with helmets. Two of these seem to be flying, but a third appears as if he were stopped in his flight by three men on foot, the first of which bears in his hand a weapon of a round form; the second has the same sort of weapon in his left hand, and in his right hand a spear which he is pointing at the man on horseback. The third figure is nearly obliterated. Below these there are two other equestrian figures, one of which holds a baton in his right hand, while the other appears to be in the attitude of encountering him." It thus seems that the figures of armed warriors, &c., on the one side of these stones were symbols of the conflict and the havoc of the war. About the cross on the other side there can be no dubiety. That consecrated symbol not only pointed to the work of Calvary, but told also of the faith which, even in that rude age, those who erected and adorned these stones had in the Saviour. Regarding sculptured stones in general, Warden says:—

The rude uncivilized primeval inhabitants of Caledonia were well satisfied when they had reared a huge amorphous monolith, a cromlech, or other bold and striking memorial over the sepulchre of a revered chief, content that their enduring handiwork should tell its story to those of their kindred who succeeded them. This it may have done for generations after its artificers had themselves been consigned to the tomb, but untold ages have made such memorials dumb to us. As civilization advanced, and the arts improved, and as tools adapted for the purpose were procured, these standing monuments of a people's respect began to be hewn into a more seemly shape, and to be adorned with symbolic figures. This transition was natural and easy. At first these were rude, but with practice, and an improved taste, the desire sprung up for something more artistic, and with it the power and skill to gratify that desire. Many of the old obelisks, and some of the cross slabs have marginal embellishments, with heads and bodies and limbs of animals entwined with foliage, forming designs that would do credit even to modern artists.

Warriors on horseback and on foot, with their weapons; and hunters with their dogs and symbols of the chase frequently appear. By the middle of the twelfth century, blazonry, or the distinction of nobility, of knighthood, and of others entitled to bear arms, or coats armorial, came into general use in Britain, and shortly thereafter such insignia began to be sculptured upon standing stones or obelisks, and on other monuments in Scotland.

What, then, was the war which had desolated Aberlemno, and of which these sepulchral remains and sculptured stones are the memorials? It was the war with the invading Danes in the beginning of the 11th century. The Annals of Ulster make mention of a great battle at Aberlemno in 697, in which "Conquar MacEcha M'Maldwin and Aod, the tall King of

Daleriaid," were slain. But it is not to be doubted that the remains and the stones with which we are now dealing, are chiefly, if not exclusively, the memorials of the battle at Aberlemno between Malcolm II. and the Northmen in 1012. One version of the story is, that it was fought with a detachment of the Danes, who were flying from Barry after their defeat there. Another version is, that the Danish host divided into three; that one division landed in the South Esk at Montrose, another at Lunan Bay, and the third at Barry, and that when the last was overthrown, one of the remaining divisions took to their ships and escaped; but that the other, endeavouring to reach the mountains with the view of passing to Moray, was overtaken and cut off near Brechin, which is understood to have been at Aberlemno. Which of these versions is to be preferred we do not wait to consider. Either sufficiently explains the monuments in question. Both agree in making Aberlemno one of the great battlefields of the shire.

Forfar and District.

"The ruins of a Palace thee decore,
A fruitfull Lake, and fruitfull Land much more,
Thy Precincts (it's confest) much straightened be,
Yet Ancient Scotland did give Power to thee :
Angus and other places of the Land,
Yeeld to thy Jurisdiction and Command,
Noblis unto the People Laws do give,
By Handy-Crafts the Vulgar sort do live.
They pull off Bullocks-hydes and make them meet
When tanned, to cover handsome Virgins' feet."

To the tourist who can spare another day in this interesting district, we might here suggest a run of six miles to the County Town, from which Glamis Castle and other places can be "done." Forfar is a town of considerable antiquity. Authorities tell us that its name is derived from the Gaelic *fuar*, "cold," and *barr*, " a point "—that is the " cold point." In old writings the parish is designated Forfar-Restennet —Restinoth probably being the original parish.

At Restennet there are the ruins of a Priory. It must apparently have been originally wholly surrounded by water and approached by a bridge. The spire of the priory, and part of the walls of the priory and chapel, are still standing, and a spot is pointed out as the burial place of one of Bruce's sons.

Like other towns in the district, Forfar's chief industry is the manufacture of linens, although as far back as the sixteenth century, the staple trade of the town was shoemaking, the shoes made being that peculiar kind called *brogues*. Johnstone, in his poetical panegyric on Forfar, published in 1642, gives prominence to the chief handicraft of the place.

If Johnstone may be believed, Forfar may well boast of the antiquity of its shoe manufacture :—

"The ancient Greeks their Boots from this Town brought,
And also hence their Ladies' slippers sought."

From this manufacture came the designation, the Sutors of Forfar, and it helped to give point to the satire of Drummond of Hawthornden on the town. Visiting it in 1645, it refused to receive him, probably from fear of the plague, which was then prevailing in many parts of the country. He betook himself to Kirriemuir, where he got a hearty welcome, and where he played off a most ludicrous joke on the Magistrates of Forfar. Learning the quarrel then raging between Forfar and Kirriemuir about the Moor Moss, Drummond addressed a letter to the Provost of Forfar. That worthy somehow assumed that the letter was from the Parliament, then sitting at St Andrews, and convened the Council, with the parson, to see the document opened, and to hear it read, when its contents turned out to be as follows:—

> "The Kirriemarians and the Forfarians met at Muir Moss,
> The Kirriemarians beat the Forfarians back to the Cross;
> Sutors ye are, an' Sutors ye'll be—
> Fye upon Forfar, Kirriemuir bears the gree!"

The parish church was erected in 1791, altered in 1836; and had a spire, 150 feet high, built in 1814. It may be of interest to some to know that the Rev. Dr Jamieson, author of several standard works of much value, including the well-known "Scottish Dictionary," "Historical Account of the Culdees," &c., was minister of the Secession congregation in Forfar from 1780 to 1797. The old jail is not now used as a prison, the lower part being utilised for the Free Library, and the upper part for the county meetings. In that hall there are some excellent portraits by Raeburn. The old County Buildings, adjoining, were built in 1820. The County Prison is outside the town, and close to it were erected the Sheriff Court Houses in 1871. A hall for public meetings was built in 1869, by Peter Reid, of "Forfar Rock" celebrity, and presented to the town. In the Public Library is still preserved a "witch's bridle," an instrument formerly used for gagging women burnt at the stake for witchcraft. The "bridle" is described as a skeleton iron helmet having a dart-shaped gag of the same metal, which entered the mouth and effectively "brankit" the tongue. On the circle is punched—"1681 Angus." With this the wretched victim of superstition was led to execution in the Witches Howe, where the public washing-green is now situated. The object aimed at in applying so dreadful a gag to those who were condemned to the stake as guilty of witchcraft was not so much the purposed cruelty attending to it as to prevent the witches from pronouncing the potent formula by which it was believed they could transform themselves at will into other shapes. From 1650 to 1662, in consequence of the passing of the celebrated Statute by James VI. for the punishment of witches, there were no fewer than nine victims of fatuous stupidity who suffered at the Witches Howe of Forfar. According to one document, a Royal Commission was addressed to the heritors and magistrates of Forfar to deal with certain women who confessed themselves guilty of witchcraft. One, for example, confessed—

"That about three years, the last oateseed time, she was at a meeting in the kirkyaird of Forfar, and that yr were first there the devill himselfe in the shape of a black iron hieved man, and a number of other persons; that they all danced together; and that the ground under them was all fyre flaughter;"

and on another occasion—

"That after dancing a whyle, she and the other women went into a house and sat down, the devill being present at the head of the table; that after making themselves mirrie with ale and aqueavitae, the devill made much of them all, and especiallie of Marion Rinde."

The Town Council, with all due solemnity, approved of the care and diligence of an inn-keeper, who brought over "the pricker of the witches in Trennent" to assist in the detection of suspected culprits. They had to secure the services of the Executioner and "scourger of the poore" of Perth to administer the extreme penalty of the law. Before the Rebellion of 1745 it is said there were not above seven tea kettles and watches in Forfar.

The neighbourhood of Forfar is interesting. Forfar Castle, which formerly stood on an elevated site to the north of the town, was a royal palace, and though the exact date of its erection cannot be fixed with certainty, it possessed more than usual historic interest from the fact of its being the supposed place of meeting of the first Scottish Parliament, convened by Malcolm Canmore.

Forfar Loch, a little to the west of the town, is nearly a mile in length by half a mile in breadth. Formerly of greater extent it was partially drained at the end of the eighteenth century. At a public meeting held about the draining of the Loch, the Earl of Strathmore said he believed the cheapest method of draining it would be to throw a few hogsheads of good mountain dew into the water, and set the "drucken writers of Forfar" to drink it up. A number of weapons, &c., were then found, and were regarded as evidence of the truth of the tradition that the murderers of Malcolm II. at Glamis Castle were drowned there while attempting to cross the the ice.

We are told that Forfar basked for centuries in the sunshine of Royalty, beginning to do so as early as the reign of Malcolm Canmore (1057-1093). On the conquest of England by the Normans, Edgar Atheling, the heir of the Saxon line, with his mother Agatha, and his sisters Margaret and Christian, sought and found refuge in the court of Malcolm. This led to Malcolm's marriage to the "beautiful, accomplished, and pious" Margaret; and they resided much in their Royal Palace or Castle at Forfar. Where it stood is not certain; but it seems not improbable that it is the foundation of it that is yet seen on Queen Margaret's Inch—the artificial island near the northern shore of the Loch of Forfar. If that ruin marks the site of the Royal Castle, it is a place of singular interest. In it, it may be presumed, Malcolm, when he had defeated and slain Macbeth, held the assembly of his Maormors, or

Great Barons, in which were passed several of those measures on which some have rested his claims to be reckoned a great legislator. In it, too, were doubtless performed many of those good and holy deeds for which his consort was canonised.

Malcolm Canmore was a monarch of high patriotism, bravery, and energy, and his reign forms an important era in the history of Scotland. Malcolm had no education, but he could worship at Margaret's feet with boundless respect and affection; and he did so, and confided to her the chief care of the kingdom. As her biographer, Turgot says, " Malcolm respected the religion of his spouse, was fearful of offending her, and listened to her admonitions. Although he could not read, he frequently turned over prayer-books, and kissed her favourite volumes. He had them adorned in gold and precious stones, and presented them to her in token of his devotion."

It was in the reign of William the Lion (1165-1214) that the Old Royal Castle at Forfar was superseded by the New one: for, though Boece was long sneered at as a fabler for writing that " Forfar was strengthened with two roiall Castles, as the ruins doo yet declare," charter evidence of the accuracy of this assertion has been discovered. The New Castle stood on the Castlehill, that conical mound to the north-east of the town, now surmounted by a tower. It was that Castle which was the occasional residence of William the Lion, whom we read of as holding a Court and an Assembly at Forfar. His son, Alexander II., resided in it more frequently than his father had done, holding Parliaments at Forfar in 1225 and 1227, and giving charters dated from it till towards the end of his reign in 1249.

In 1291, Gilbert de Umfraville had the command

of the Castle of Forfar; and when King Edward of England demanded the surrender of it, he refused, declaring that he had the castle in charge from the Scottish nation, and that he would not surrender it to Edward without a letter of indemnity signed by him, and by the claimants of the Scottish Crown, and the guardians of the Scottish realm. In 1296, Edward and his suite visited Forfar, and lodged in the Castle from the 3d to the 6th July—two Churchmen and four barons there doing the invader homage. In the following year, while Brian Fitzadam held the Castle for Edward, Wallace either captured it, or it was deserted at his approach. But the English must have soon recovered it: it was in their possession in 1308; and, soon after, King Robert Bruce, assisted by Philip, the forester of Platane or Plater, took it by escalade, put all the English in it to the sword, levelled it and its fortifications to the ground, and it was never rebuilt. When Royalty afterwards visited the neighbourhood, it sojourned either in the Castle of Glamis or in the Priory of Restennet. After he had demolished the Castle, Bruce had a house at Forfar, and we may infer that he was not a stranger in it from the fact that, only two years before his death, he gave his falconer in the shire of Forfar, Geoffrey of Foullertoune, and Agnes, his wife, the lands of Foullertoune in Forfarshire.

The names of many localities in the neighbourhood are to this day memorials of the residence of our Kings at Forfar in those olden times. Such are the King's Moor, the King's Burn, the King's Seat, the Queen's Manor, the Queen's Well, the Palace Dykes, and the Court Road. The tenures by which certain farms in the neighbourhood were held are also memorials of the same thing. Tyrbeg, *alias* Turfbeg, and Balmashanner, were held on the condition of furnishing the Palace with three hundred cartloads of peats from these lands when the Court was at Forfar; and Heatherstack was held on the condition of furnishing heather fit for fuel to the Royal kitchen.

Archibald Douglas, son of James, second Marquis of Douglas, was, by Charles II., created Earl of Forfar in 1661. Archibald, second Earl of Forfar, was presen at the battle of Sheriffmuir, in 1715, and died of his wounds at Stirling. The Earl left no issue, and the title and estates devolved on the Duke of Douglas.

The Revolution having been accomplished in 1688, a detachment of the forces of William and Mary was next year stationed at Forfar. The immediate neighbourhood was Jacobite enough, not to be above the need of them for its peace and security; but the special object of the detachment was to watch the movements of the rebels, who, after the battle of Killiecrankie, swarmed for a time about the base of the Grampians, and were continually passing to and fro between Dunkeld and Brechin, though nowhere was the spirit breathed in the celebrated Jacobite song more rampant—

> He's pu'd the rose o' English loons,
> And broken the harp o' Irish clowns;
> But our thistle taps will jag his thumbs—
> This wee, wee German lairdie.

Forfar is the place which James VI. named as furnishing the model of Scotch hospitality, of which he made his boast to the English. On his way to London to succeed Elizabeth on the throne, he was entertained with great splendour in one of the English towns. The Mayor, in honour of the occasion, kept open house for several days: and some of the courtiers ventured to hint that James must have seen few examples of such munificence among the narrow dignitaries of Scotland. "Fient a bit o' that are they," cried the King ; " the Provost o' my burgh o' Forfar, whilk is by nae means the largest town in Scotland, keeps open house a' the year round, and aye the mae that comes the welcomer." The Provost of Forfar at that time kept an ale house ; so that James's words were literally true.

It was in Forfar that the famous case occurred, which led to the judicial decision that no charge can be made for the stirrup dram. Marshall tells of a brewster's wife having one day "brewed a peck o' maut," and set it to the door to cool, a neighbour's cow passing by drank the browst. The alewife took the case into court, when it was decided that, as by immemorial custom, nothing was ever charged for a standing drink or stirrup cup, the defendant ought to be assoilzied ; the cow having swallowed the browst standing, and at the door.

The Castle of Glamis.

> How rich with legend is our land !
> Its hills and dales and rock-girt strand—
> Each doth its dread, mysterious tale,
> Low ominous whisper in the gale ;
> The scowling loop-holed donjon keep,
> The frowning walls that round it sweep,
> The stately castle, old and grey,
> All chant some weird mysterious lay.

This ancient baronial residence, the chief seat of the Earl of Strathmore, is styled by various authorities as one of the most interesting residences of feudal times in Scotland that has survived decay. It is situated about five miles west of Forfar, and near to the old village of Glamis, which contains many relics of former days. Millar in his valuable and interesting work—" The Historical Castles and Mansions of Scotland," says :—The main gateway is a triple-arched structure, battlemented, and surmounted by carved lions, *rampant opposant*, the heraldic designation of the Lyons, Earls of Strathmore. A Dutch carver, Jan Van Sant Voort, who first appeared in Scotland, where he executed much of the ornamental work of Holyrood, is said to have carved, in 1684, the gladiators and the satyrs and lions which adorn the two principal gates.

Shortly after entering the gateway the arboured foliage ceases, and the avenue is led between wide, grassy parks, terminating in the imposing pile. On each side a grassy plain extends, bordered on the right by the wood crowned hills which form Glen Ogilvie, and on the left by the river Dean and the distant slopes which enclose the Howe of Strathmore. The towering ridges of the Grampian Mountains, with their numerous intervening spurs, make a background of surpassing grandeur.

The immediate surroundings are grandly beautiful and picturesque—the scene and its accessories presenting the very choicest of those harmonious combinations of colour and form which the landscape limner loves to gaze upon and fondly endeavours to transfer to the living canvas. On the lawn, in particular, a group of yew trees arrests the eye. They count their age by centuries, but how many we cannot tell. Their fine trunks and wide-spreading branches twine in serpentine convolutions, and their dark foliage, thrown into relief by the rich green turf, render them striking objects when seen from the grounds, but much more so when viewed from the top of the Castle. The extensive vineries and gardens, on the other side of the Dean, appear from the summit, glittering like a rare gem with a gorgeous setting; the windings of the river, spanned by three bridges brighten the scene; the spacious park, divided and sub-divided by fine carriage-drives, studded with many noble trees, and alive with herds

of pure Angus Doddies; and the thick woods beyond
the Dean complete a foreground of exquisite beauty.
Beyond, to the east and to the west, stretches the
Vale of Strathmore. Every spot in it may not be
equally pretty, but viewed from the summit of the
Castle the scene on either hand is rich and strikingly
beautiful.

Apart altogether from its associations, the castle
is suggestive of profound and solemn grandeur, and of
perfect detail. Embosomed among sombre woods, as
we have said, the vast pile proudly rears its castellated
towers, the level nature of the surrounding grounds,
however, preventing its being seen from a distance.
The surprise experienced is therefore all the greater
when, entering the long and beautiful avenue by which
it is approached from the south, with all its grandeur
it bursts suddenly upon the view. Nor do these feelings lessen in intensity as we gradually approach its
hallowed precincts. There is such a rare combination
of the various styles of the different ages of Scotch
baronial architecture, that our admiration intensifies
and deepens as we approach. The great tower in the
centre, with its round roofed vaults, narrow orifices
and thick walls, is the earliest period of castellated
masonry, while the rich cluster of cone-topped turrets,
and the wings that crouch beneath, are said to be the
work of Inigo Jones.

The view from the central tower is of the most
magnificent and attractive description. Indeed, it is
scarcely possible to conceive a prospect of greater loveliness or more luxuriant beauty. The whole Strath,
in its length and breadth, lies stretched out beneath
and around you, while the Sidlaws on the one hand,
and the Grampians on the other, form most fitting
back-grounds to the picture, adding a mystic, weird-
like sublimity to the scene.

> Here—Catlaw, like a sentinel grim,
> Lone guards the Grampian mountains dim,
> Which stretch across from sea to sea
> In glorious, solemn majesty.
> There—cleaving high ethereal air,
> Loom Cairn-a-Month and dark Mount Blair;
> And in the glack of yonder glen,
> The wild woods wave in Airlie Den;
> While rugged hills of dreamy hue
> Dim mingle with the azure blue,
> And reach in misty gloom afar,
> The confines dark of Lochnagar.

In the surrounding grounds there were to be seen within the last fifty or sixty years a number of statues and sculptured ornaments, most of which were erected by Patrick, third Earl Kinghorn, and first Earl of Strathmore, who did much to encourage the cultivation of a taste for the fine arts. None of these now remain, except a curious and richly-finished sun dial with its many faces to the sun, an object of great attraction to the antiquary, as, indeed, it is of general interest.

The doorway at the base of the tower is flanked by pilasters, with richly-carved floral capitals. Immediately over it the bust of Patrick, first Earl of Kinghorne, one of the reconstructors of the place, may be seen; whilst along the upper walls of the wings the armorial bearings of the principal Earls since 1606 are marshalled with those of their separate wives. Over the door the Royal Arms of Scotland, fully emblazoned, have been carved. The heavy iron knocker on the oaken door bears the date "1689," when the principal work of reconstruction was completed by the first Earl of Strathmore. Within this door a heavily grated iron gate has been erected, which doubtless formed the guard to the entrance of the original Castle.

Within the doorway three staircases appear, that to the right descending by a few steps to the vaulted crypt, and then ascending to the old portion of the

Castle known as "King Malcolm's Room." The dining-room, which occupies a flat of one of the wings, is one of the finest apartments in the Castle. The walls are of oak, pannelled and decorated with the emblazoned arms of the Strathmore family and the noble houses with which it has been connected. Many interesting portraits are hung in the drawing-room, the subjects of each of them being connected in some way with the history of Scotland. The bedrooms include the room in which tradition asserts that King Malcolm II. died in 1033. Dispassionate historians, says Millar, have surmised that he died peaceably at this time, and was buried at Iona, and have even asserted that the stories of his assassination are mere figments of monkish times, and quite unworthy of credence. Nevertheless, the room in which he expired, after being wounded on Hunter's Hill, may still be seen by the visitor to Glamis Castle. It is perhaps more interesting to examine the chamber in which Sir Walter Scott mused over these traditions, and strove to connect the Macbeaths of Shakespeare and of history. The chapel is, perhaps, the most interesting apartment. The panels are exquisitely painted, and contain the Old Testament Angels associated with the Expulsion from Paradise, Jacob's Ladder at Bethel, Raphael and Tobit; and the New Testament Angels of the Annunciation, the Nativity, the Bethlehem Shepherds, the Temptation, Gethsemane, Calvary, and the Resurrection. The walls and roof are divided into oblong panels, upon which numerous Biblical subjects have been painted. These were executed at the time of the building of the chapel (1688) by J. de Witt, the artist who was guilty of the Holyrood Gallery of Kings

In "Ochterlony's Account of the Shire of Forfar," written in 1684, it is stated that "the Castle of Glamis is the Earl of Strathmore's speciall residence in the shyre—a great and excellent house, re-edified, and furnished most stately with everything necessare—with excellent gaites, avenues, courts, garden, bowling-greens, parks, inclosures, hay meadows, and planting, very beautifull and pleasant. Be-east the house, and within the park, is the Yeat Bridge, by which their whole peats are brought, and by which his Lordship is served from his mosses be-north the water in great abundance, and hath ane other little house there called Cossines. In a little distance to the Castle of Glamies is the towne thereof, all belonging to the Earl. It is a burgh of barronie, hath two great faires in it yearly, and a weekly mercat. There is a cunnigare within the park, and dovecoat at the burn."

There is a legend, which points to the top of the Hunter Hill as the spot upon which the first Castle of Glamis was intended to be built. This resolution was frustrated by certain nocturnal "Little Folks" or fairies, who undid at night what the builders had done through the day. On this being frequently repeated a watch was set, but though no destructives were seen, the work of the previous day was undone. At last a voice was heard proclaiming—

"Build not on this enchanted spot,
Where man has neither part nor lot,
But build thee down in yonder bog,
And it will neither sink nor shog."

The earthly builders obeyed the weird speaker, and built the Castle where it now stands. Whether or not the present Castle was built on the site where it stands at the instigation of the "Fairy Queen" or of an earthly king or lord we cannot pretend to say, but there is no doubt the Castle of Glamis, for an unknown period, has stood where it stands to-day. The family of Lyon have occupied the Castle from the period when Sir John Lyon first acquired it until the present time, with the exception of a few years after Lady Glamis was murdered by James the Fifth for the crime of witchcraf, and the young Lord forfeited, in 1537. For full and interesting details of the noble family of Lyon, and of the alterations in the ancient building, we would refer the reader to Mr Millar's "Castles and Mansions." It was in 1372 that Glamis came into the possession of the Lyons. Sir John Lyon married the Princess Jane, the second daughter of Robert II.; and, as her dowry, the King gave her husband a charter of his lands of the thanedom of Glamis, to be held in Free barony. He was the founder of the present noble family of Strathmore, and fell in a duel with Sir James Lindsay of Crawford, at the moss of Balhall, near Brechin—the occasion of the deadly quarrel being, it is supposed, envy at the royal favours which were heaped upon Sir John. On the execution of Lady Jane Douglas, Countess of Strathmore, in 1537, Glamis was, as we have said, forfeited to the Crown; and the Castle again became for a season a royal residence. James V. lived frequently at it.

The story of Lady Jane Douglas is one of the most affecting in our annals. The crime of which she was accused is sometimes called witchcraft, and sometimes conspiring the King's death by poison. But, as Tytler has explained, in those times "poisoning and witchcraft were very commonly associated." The real charge against her was conspiring the King's death by poison and assisting the Earl of Angus and his brother, George Douglas, who were traitors and rebels. She was convicted, and condemned to be burned at the stake on the Castle Hill of Edinburgh. She heard her sentence with unruffled composure, and endured it with immovable firmness and fortitude;

the crowd looking on equally commiserating and admiring her. She was popularly believed to be innocent, being regarded as the victim of implacable hate which the King had conceived against all connected with the house of Douglas.

Three other parties were apprehended as supposed accomplices with her Ladyship. The first was her husband, Campbell, who, the day after her execution, trying to make his escape from the Castle of Edinburgh, was let down over the walls by a cord which, being too short, he fell on the rocks, and was dashed in pieces. The second was the son she had born to Lord Glamis, her first husband, now a boy sixteen years of age, who lay in prison for five years, till the death of King James, when his titles and estates were restored to him as the seventh Lord Glamis. The third was an old priest, whom the King, when told of the tragic end of Campbell on the Castle rocks, set at liberty.

The Strathmore family was ardently attached to the Stuart dynasty. John, the fifth Earl, fell fighting for it at Sheriffmuir, in 1715. The Pretender spent the night of the 4th January, 1715, in the Castle of Glamis, when on his way to Scone, where he expected to be crowned; and it is said that eighty beds were that night made up for his retinue.

The full designation of the title of the Strathmore family is " Earl of Strathmore and Kinghorn, Viscount Lyon, Baron Glamis, Tannadyce, Sidlaw, and Strathdichty." The present representative of the family was born in 1824. Lord Glamis was born in 1855, and in 1881 was married to Nina-Cecilia, daughter of the late Rev. Wm. Cavendish Bentinck, a relative of the Duke of Portland.

Like many other ancient castles, Glamis has long had a reputation for "hauntings" and "apparitions."

Although the whole pile of buildings appears to suffer under the ban, there is one particular chamber which is especially known as "the Haunted Room." Access to this ominous chamber is said to be now cut off by a stone wall, and none are supposed to be acquainted with its locality save Lord Strathmore, his heir, and the factor of the estate. This wall is alleged to have been erected recently, in consequence of certain mysterious sights and sounds which he had both seen and heard.

"There is no doubt," writes a correspondent of Dr Lee, "about the reality of the noises at Glamis Castle. Some years ago, the head of the family, with several companions, was determined to investigate the cause. One night when the disturbance was greater and more violent and alarming than usual—and, it should be premised, strange, weird, and unearthly sounds had often been heard, and by many persons, some quite unacquainted with the ill-repute of the castle—his Lordship went to the Haunted Room, opened the door with a key, and dropped back in a dead swoon into the arms of his companions; nor could he ever be induced to open his lips on the subject afterwards."

The Village of Glamis.

> There's conthie hames a' set sae sweet
> Alang the Strath's green breast—
> The humble cot, the lordly seat,
> Has each peace for its guest.

Outside of the Castle policies, but from the close proximity really forming a part of them, are the Church of Glamis, with its spire seen through the surrounding trees, and the comfortable manse, beyond which, to the north of the Hunter Hill, is the old and picturesquely situated village of Glamis, embowered among trees and gardens. It is in the centre of the Vale of Strathmore, and consists chiefly of two rows of houses, between which the highway from Forfar to Perth passes. The graveyard around the Church, sloping nearly to the level of the den, is a quiet sequestered resting-place for the forefathers of the parish. The hamlet and its surroundings are tidily kept, and form a pretty picture in the landscape.

The village of Glamis, apart from the historical associations of its neighbourhood, is one of the most beautifully situated of our Scottish hamlets. J. Cargill Guthrie, in his " Scenes and Legends," says :—" Built on the banks of a mountain rivulet, and at the base of a lofty pine-clad hill, surrounded by scenery of the most beautiful and attractive description, and nestling amongst ancient and extensive woods, it presents a scene of retired and quiet seclusion from the busy world quite refreshing to the pent-up denizen of the crowded city. Standing on the bridge, beneath which pleasantly flows the burn already noticed, the view on either side, although necessarily somewhat contracted, is very pleasing and beautiful. To the north appear the barley mill, the church, churchyard, and manse, the village stretching away to our left, and a beautifully wooded dell, with the water of the burn flowing fretfully through its midst, opening up its romantic beauties to our right. Southward—the brook, the rocky ravine, the smithy, and a few straggling cottages, amidst their trim gardens and kailyards, are the principal objects which attracts the eye ; while high above the Hunter Hill, in all its luxuriant sylvan beauty, crowns the scene as with a diadem of emerald, the happy birds meanwhile co-mingling their thrilling notes of gladness with the merry voices of the rustic urchins at roystering play on the village green."

We have said that there are a number of interesting memorials of the past in and near the ancient village of Glamis. Nearly all of them are associated with the name of Malcolm II. Knox, in his "Topography of the Basin of the Tay," says—"There is to be seen in the churchyard of Glamis a rude mass, without inscription, which, according to tradition, is King Malcolm's gravestone, and there is every probability that he was buried under it. An ancient cross stands in the lower portion of the Hunter Hill, between the village of Thornton and the Kirkton of Glamis. According to local tradition it is supposed to mark the spot where King Malcolm II. fell. Another of these crosses stands in front of, and only a few feet distant from the manse of Glamis, and is popularly associated with the same tradition regarding the death of Malcolm. On one of the arms is a ravenous quadruped, and on the other a centaur with the legs and body of a horse, and the upper part of the body, arms, and head of a man, with a battle axe raised aloft in each hand. Below the arms are two human figures, with limbs in air, and heads and bodies in a caldron, underneath which are two men with axes in their hands. On the other side are the head and neck of an animal, suspended from which is a circular dish. St Orland's stone stands in a field at Cossins, about a mile northeast from the Castle of Glamis. On one side is a cross rudely flowered and chequered; on the other side four men on horseback appear to be making the utmost despatch. One of the horses is trampling under foot a wild boar; and on the lower part of the stone there is the figure of an animal resembling a dragon. It has been conjectured by some that these symbols represent officers of justice in pursuit of Malcolm's murderers. Such are the monuments, and such is the reading of their symbols in which we are disposed to rest till a more feasible be offered.

The Vale of Strathmore.

Soft flow thy streams, bright bloom thy flowers,
  Thy birdies liltin' as of yore :
The music of thy fragrant bowers,
  The voice of love awakes once more—
Thou bonnie howe o' sweet Strathmore.

Although the most classical and historically interesting portion of the " Howe of Strathmore " is undoubtedly the Castle of Glamis and its surroundings, the whole valley—independent of these associations—is one of the most beautiful and romantic in Scotland. Surrounded on the south by the long rugged ridge of the Sidlaw Hills, and guarded on the north by the Grampian Mountains, the "Howe" luxuriantly nestling between, the great valley is almost unsurpassed in all that constitutes soft, yet rich grandeur. Hamlet, village, and castle combine with hill, wood, and stream to form a picture, which once seen, will not soon be forgotten.

Strathmore (Strath Mohr), or the great Strath or Valley, in its widest extent, stretches from the German Ocean, in the neighbourhood of Lunan Bay in Angus, and Stonehaven in the Mearns, right across the country to the centre of Dumbartonshire. It is only with the portion of this strath within Forfarshire that we have to do, and it is popularly known as the Howe of Angus. This fair district is flanked by the southern outlying spurs of the Grampians, called the Braes of Angus, which form the southern section of the Highland division on the north, and on the south by the Sidlaw Hills, and their outlying fork like spurs or continuations on the east of the continuous chain of these hills. When emerging out of the defile through the Sidlaws, near Haliburton House, the Queen and the Prince Consort, when proceeding to the Highlands of Perthshire in 1844, were so enchanted with its luxuriant loveliness that the Royal cortege was ordered to pause to afford sufficient time to master the details of such a beautiful picture, chased in framework so lofty and sublime.

> Gae wander Scotland's heights an' howes,
> Owre ilka hill an' glen,
> Through whin-clad moor, an' broomy knowe
> By rashy glack an' fen;
> Hand doon the banks o' burn or brook,
> Row loch, row ferry o'er,
> Search everywhere for fairer nook
> Than beautiful Strathmore.
> Owre ilka knowe, doon ilka glade,
> Gae con them o'er and o'er,
> What age or winter e'er could fade
> The beauty o' Strathmore?

On the east the lower portion of the river North Esk is the boundary of this district, and the west border of the parish of Kettins bounds it on the west. The length of the Strathmore division, as so defined, is about thirty-three miles, and its breadth varies from four to six miles. This region is well watered by the Highland rivers which flow through it, by the chain of lakes which lie in the centre of the Howe, and which attest the existence of more extensive waters in remote times; by the outflow of these lakes, and by other streams which meander along the valley in various directions. These rivers, and lochs, and streams, diversify and beautify the scenery, and refresh and fertilize the land in their vicinity. In the northern district of Strathmore, little hills of no great altitude outwith the Highland region, rear their heads above the surrounding ground, and give a picturesque appearance to that section of the strath. Among these may be mentioned the Hill of Baldovie, and others in Kingoldrum, the hill of Kirriemuir, Deuchar in Fern, the White and Brown Caterthun, and Lundie, which adjoins them. Towards the eastern end and near the centre of the strath there are several prominent hills, the northmost of which are those of Finhaven. Farther south are Pitscandly, Turin, Balmashanner hills, and others. Farther east in the parishes of Dun, Logie-Pert, Craig, and others, there are several pretty eminences. Adjoining some of these hills there are mimic ravines, worn out by the tiny burns which trickle down their sides.

> Soft flow thy streams, bright bloom thy flowers,
>   Thy birdies liltin' as of yore;
> The music of thy fragrant bowers
>   The voice of love awakes once more,
> Thou bonnie Howe o' Sweet Strathmore.

Writing on this favoured region Warden, says:—

"Strathmore is not a level plain, like the carses of Gowrie or Stirling. Strathmore is diversified by hills and dales, by gentle eminences and verdant meadows, tiny sparkling rivulets and bubbling brooks, gliding streams and flowing rivers. Its beauties are diversified by numerous mansions, each nestling cosily in its own quiet grounds; others crown gentle eminences, commanding extensive prospects, ornamented with clumps of trees, and emerald lawns, with trickling brooks winding through them. Here and there are splendid castles, the magnificent seats of the great feudal nobles, or of commoners of ancient lineage, rearing their lofty heads, scarred by the storms of centuries, yet scatheless, in the midst of spacious parks, studded with monarchs of the wood perhaps as old as the castles themselves. Throughout the county there also are castles and mansions, the buildings clean and chaste, as if newly out of the hands of the tradesmen, the creation of modern merchant princes, monuments alike of their successful industry and good taste, and surrounded by many emblems of wealth and comfort. Excellent roads run through and intersect the strath in many ways. In the neighbourhood of the pretty church and finely situated village of Glamis, the hedgerows of hawthorn and beech and holly are trimly kept. The superabundance of old and stately trees on the one hand, and finely wooded hills on

GLAMIS CASTLE.

the other, with the splendid ancient baronial Castle of Glamis, and its extensive and charming grounds, combine to form a scene of rare beauty."

Glen of Ogilvy.

There is a charm in footing slow across a silent plain,
Where patriot battle hath been fought, where glory had the gain;
There is a joy in every spot made known in days of old—
New to the feet, although each tale a hundred times be told.

The Glen of Ogilvy, apart from its quiet beauty, is rich in legendary and historical interest. It is said that St Donivald dwelt in it about the beginning of the eighth century. He had nine daughters who for their pious worth were canonised as the Nine Maidens. They lived in the Glen "as in an hermitage, and led a most laborious, but abstemious, mortified life." They cultivated the ground with the labour of their own hands; they ate but once a day, and their meal was barley bread and water. After their father's death Garnard, King of the Picts, assigned them a lodging and oratory, and some land at Abernethy. Their reputation was such that King Eugen VII. of Scotland visited them at the Pictish capital, and made them large presents. They died there, and were buried at the foot of a great oak; and so honoured were St Donivald's nine "virgin dochtors" after their death, as well as in their life, that their shrine at the Abernethy Allon-bacuth was much frequented by devout pilgrims down to the Reformation. Their feast is on the 15th June. Many churches in Scotland were inscribed to them, among which was Strathmartine. "The Nine Maidens' Well" is within the park of Glamis, not far from the dove-cote.

THE NINE MAIDENS.

Barbaric darkness shadowing o'er,
Among the Picts in days of yore,
St Donivald, devoid of lore,
   Lived in the Glen of Ogilvy.

Beside the forest's mantling shade,
His daughters nine a temple made,
To shelter rude his aged head
   Within the Glen of Ogilvy.

Charred wood-burned ashes formed the floor,
The trunks of pines around the door
Supporting walls of branches hoar,
   Turf-roofed in Glen of Ogilvy.

Poor barley bread and water clear,
And that but once a day, I fear,
Was all their fare from year to year,
   Within the Glen of Ogilvy.

A chapel built they rude at Glamis,
From whence, like sound of waving palms,
Arose on high the voice of psalms,
   Near by the Glen of Ogilvy.

The hermit dead, they left the Glen,
E'er shunning dread the haunts of men,
In oratory sacred then,
   Far from the Glen of Ogilvy;

On Abernethy's holy ground,
From whence their fame spread soon around,
Although no more their songs resound
   In their loved Glen of Ogilvy.

Nine maidens fair in life were they,
Nine maidens fair in death's last fray,
Nine maidens fair in fame alway,
   The maids of Glen of Ogilvy.

And to their grave from every land,
Come many a sorrowing pilgrim band,
The oak to kiss whose branches grand
   Wave o'er the maids of Ogilvy.

Three centuries after their day the Glen of Ogilvy again became famous in connection with William the Lion. King William was one day hunting in the Glen, and in pursuing the chase he got separated from his party, and was attacked by a band of banditti. Earl Gilchrist had three sons, who were partakers with their father in the murder of their mother, and against them, as indeed against all the Gilchrists, the King had declared vengeance, and seized their lands. They betook themselves for safety to the forests and mountains, and dens of the land, and hid in them for several years. They happened to be skulking in the Glen of Ogilvy on the memorable day when the freebooters attacked the King. They were close by, and seeing his danger rushed forward and rescued **His Majesty.** On learning who his deliverers were William pardoned them, restored them to their possessions, and added to these the **Glen of Ogilvy,** giving it to Gilbert, **the brother of** Earl Gilchrist ; and in honour of the place where they saved their Sovereign's life, they took the name of Ogilvy, which they have borne ever since.

The Glen of Ogilvy was the retreat of Claverhouse at a very critical juncture in 1689. A convention of the Scottish Estates assembled in Edinburgh on the 14th of March, and was about to resolve that James had forfeited his right to the crown, and to vote the vacant throne to William and Mary, when, to arrest proceedings if possible, Claverhouse suddenly appeared, alleging that the Covenanters had formed a plot to assassinate him, and demanding that all strangers should be removed from the town. This was at once refused, as it would have placed the Convention at the mercy of the Duke of Gordon, who held the Castle for James ; on which Claverhouse left the Assembly with indignation, and rode out of the city at the head of fifty troopers to raise an army to thwart the Revolution.

> Away to the hills, to the woods, to the rocks,
> Ere I own a usurper, I'll couch with the fox :
> And tremble, false Whigs, though triumphant ye be,
> You have not seen the last of my bonnets and me.

After this flight from Edinburgh, Clavers took up his abode in his country seat of Dudhope, professing to live in quiet, and to offer no opposition to the new Government ; but he was in fact busily engaged in a treasonable correspondence with James and the Highland chiefs, and was only biding his time to take the field. The Earl of Leven was therefore despatched with two hundred men to arrest him ; but, receiving timely notice of his danger, he retired from Dudhope to a small remote house in the Glen of Ogilvy; and there he skulked till the approach of a body of dragoons compelled him to abandon his retreat, and take refuge in the Duke of Gordon's country, where he arranged with his Highland supporters for the intended rising.

Kirriemuir and District.

> Wild, traditioned Scotland!
>   Its briery burns and braes,
> Abound with pleasant memories,
>   And tales of other days.
> Its story-haunted waters
>   In music rush along.
> Its mountain glens are tragedies,
>   Its heathy hills are song.

Mr J. M. Barrie, through his immensely popular works on Scottish life and character, has in recent times made Kirriemuir a place of special interest to tourists. So we cannot be in the immediate neighbourhood without seeing the now famous "Window in Thrums." "Thrums" is a quaint little town, with just enough left yet of the primitive "auld warl douceness" to blend pleasantly with the brisk energy of a small manufacturing centre. Its name is said to be derived from the Gaelic, and signifies "Mary's Kirk." It is pleasantly situated on the north bank of the Gairy, fully five miles north-west from Forfar. It skirts the north side of the valley of Strathmore, and its locality is discernible from a considerable distance, the Hill of Kirriemuir rising abruptly to a great height immediately to the north of the town.

Kirriemuir is a burgh or barony, of which the old Earls of Angus were superiors, and consists of several streets, arranged and mutually connected in a manner similar to the arms and shaft of an anchor. It had undoubtedly been, in early times, a scattered hamlet round the church. In the year 1561 it contained 32 inhabited houses, and the population was 124—the present population being nearly 3000. The Parish Church was the first house in the town covered with blue slate. The spire was added to the church by the late Chas. Lyell, the eminent geologist, and is seen through nearly the whole of Strathmore.

Since the middle of last century Kirriemuir has been the seat of an extensive manufacture of brown linen. The years 1816-17 were peculiarly severe on the weavers in Kirriemuir. The manufacturers were not able to allow them more than five shillings, and there were instances where even a less sum than this was given and accepted for the weaving of a web of linen 146 yards in length. About this time an event occurred which forms an era in the history of the town. The discovery was made that persons could sell their own manufactured goods in any market town in the kingdom. A trial was made by a few adventurers, who confined the scene of their operations to the neighbouring towns. In the years 1818-19 and 20, the trade became general, and all who were possessed of capital or credit began to manufacture such fabrics as they expected would suit the home market; and with these they visited most of the towns of England, and the most distant parishes and islands of Scotland.

At the beginning of the present century, low, clay-built houses, with thatched roofs, were general all over the town, and where two-storied houses made their appearance, outside stairs were the medium of ascent. Several of these appendages were to be seen around the High Street; even the front of the Town House was decorated with one of them, from the top of which, on Sundays, the town's drummer recapitulated, for the sake of the country people, the novelties of the preceding week.

The higher part of the town, or Roods Street, commands a magnificent view of nearly the whole of Strathmore. From the hill above the Cemetery, so picturesquely situated and tastefully laid out, a charming scene opens to the gaze. On the north and west are shelving ascents and mysterious vistas, the far stretching surgy sea of elevations, the mist-gathering mountain pinnacles, and the dark and vastly-varied forms of the Angus and the Perthshire Grampians. On the south, as far as the eye can reach, lies spread out the many-tinted valley of Strathmore, with its pleasing array of towns, castles, plantations, &c., flanked by the soft and luxuriant forms of the long range of the Sidlaw Hills. On the east are the undulating heights of Finhaven hill, and, far beyond them, the Grampians of Kincardineshire belted on the horizon with the German Ocean.

Referring to the diversified, extensive, and charming nature of the view from this eminence, Guthrie says: "To the north the scene is inexpressibly wild and sublime, hill rising upon hill, and mountain upon mountain, stretching grandly away with their cloud-covered summits, to the mystic confines of classic Lochnagar, enshrouded with 'its steep frowning glories,' and casting around its gloomy shadow. Far away in the west, backed by the mountains of Perthshire, amidst a field of classic glory, bright and beautiful in the golden sunshine, rise Birnam wood and lofty Dunsinane hill, associated for evermore with the matchless fancy and transcendent genius of the bard of Avon. To the south, beneath our feet and on either hand, lies in all its unparalleled beauty, the lovely valley of Strathmore, bright with its glittering streams and daisied meadows, luxuriantly fruitful in its orchard woods, and waving fields of corn; and supremely rich in all the delicate tints and gorgeous hues of an eastern landscape, blent with the wilder beauties of mountain scenery as a fitting background of Alpine magnificence."

Deeply interesting as a voiceless relic of the past is the "Standing Stone" on the hill of Kirriemuir. Above the surface of the ground the standing part is nine feet in height, while the lying portion is nearly thirteen feet in length. The purpose for which the stone was erected is unknown. Regarding the cause, however, of the stone having been split into two, tradition saith that, after a most daring robbery had been committed by them, the robbers sat down beside the stone to count their gold, when the stone suddenly split into two, the falling part burying the robbers and their booty underneath. It is currently believed that, by lifting the stone, the treasure would be found, but to this day no one has had the courage to test the experiment!

There are two "rocking stones," or "stones of judgment," a short distance to the north-west of the hill. The most interesting feature in connection with these stones is this, that whereas Huddlestone, in his learned and elaborate notes to his edition of Tolland, authoritatively asserts that no two rocking stones are ever found together, these stones are in close proximity to each other.

Several "Weem's Holes," or caves in the earth, have been discovered in the parish; one on the top of the hill of Mearns, and another at Auchlishie. That on the hill is built of stone, and is about sixty or seventy yards in length. The other is a long subterranean recess in which, when it was opened, a currah and some querns were discovered.

The Den, to the east of the town, is a favourite

retreat. The sweet little burn, the Garrie, which takes its rise in the loch of Kinnordy, runs with the happy ripple through its recesses. An excavation, or canal, in the red rock on the north bank of the stream, is called the "King's Chamber," but what tradition is associated with it we cannot tell. Guthrie gets over the difficulty by unravelling the mystery as follows:—
"Taken in connection with the admitted facts, that the lonely den was the chosen resort of the *Spunkies*, and that the neighbouring farm of Glasswell was nightly haunted by ghosts and hobgoblins, I came at last to the sage conclusion, that as the elfins and fairies were presided over and ruled by a queen, the cave in the rock had been, and was the presence-chamber of the King of the Evil Spirits, where he, in royal state, gave audiences to his mythical subjects, and from whence were promulgated those terrible fiats of vengeance and destruction, which made men's hearts to quake with fear, and the material world to upheave in volcanic throes of expiring dissolution!"

Nothing authentic is known respecting the early traditions of the town. Kirriemuir is very seldom referred to in history, although there is ample proof of its antiquity. That the territory had in early times been thickly populated there is not the slightest doubt, from the many Druidic and other remains that are yet found in the locality. Almost every town in Scotland has some record of a battle having been fought in its vicinity. Some parties are of opinion that it was in the neighbourhood of Kirriemuir where the great battle between Galgacus and Agricola was fought, and on page 101 we referred to the conflict between the "sutors of Forfar and the weavers of Kirriemuir."

The Castle of Airlie.

Bonnie sing the birds in the bright English valleys,
Bonnie bloom the flowers in the lime-shelter'd alleys,
Cloudless shines the sun, 'tis there ye'll see it fairly,
Sweet blinkin' through the mist on the bonnie braes o' Airlie.

The romantic beauty and historical interest connected with Airlie Castle is pretty well known, as it is a favourite resort of tourists and pic-nic parties. The Castle is perched on the point of the rocky promontory formed by the confluence of the Isla and the Melgum, the first running north-west and the other north-east from the Castle. The lofty banks of the Isla are in many places rocky and very precipitous, with natural trees or shrubs growing up in every cleft of the rock, extending horizontally or obliquely from its rugged surface, hanging from every crevice, or trailing down its iron face. In others they are clothed with lofty trees, among which is a profuse undergrowth of many varieties of brushwood and Alpine plants. Judiciously formed walks traverse the den in many ways, with seats at salient points, whence fine views are obtained. The banks of the Melgum are planted with cultivated trees of several varieties, growing luxuriantly on the sloping sides of the stream—nature on the Isla and art on the Melgum striving to outdo each other; or rather each ravine by contrast bringing out the beauties of the other the better, and certainly the whole scene is beautiful and romantic.

The Castle of Airlie is a most interesting memorial, the entrance gateway and some other remains of the Ancient Castle being about four hundred and fifty years old, having been erected about 1432. In that year Sir Walter Ogilvy of Lintrathen acquired the lands of Airlie, and obtained a Royal license, as was then requisite, authorising him to erect his tower of Airlie in form of a fortalice. After obtaining the

Royal permission, Sir Walter, who was Lord High Treasurer to King James I., lost no time in proceeding with the erection of the structure. The site he fixed upon was happily chosen, as extensive defensive works were not required, and it is extremely beautiful, picturesque, and romantic. A small promontory projects out from the mainland at the junction of the Isla and the Melgum rivers. The latter winds past the east and north sides, and there falls into the Isla, which runs along its west front. The beds of both streams lie at a depth of quite one hundred feet below the summit of the promontory, and its three sides are all but perpendicular. All that was necessary to make the Castle a safe abode was a defence to the neck of the promontory. Here Sir Walter dug a deep ditch, from 20 to 30 feet in width, inside of which he erected a wall 10 feet thick, and 35 in height, having battlements on the top, a drawbridge across the ditch, and the gateway protected by strong doors, with an iron portcullis to be let down at will. Inside of this ditch and wall the "Bonnie House of Airlie" was built, and here the Ogilvies of Airlie dwelt securely. Only part of the wall across the promontory now remains, with some modern buildings and a fine lawn within. In 1158-9 Sir John Ogilvy, son of Sir Walter, resigned his lands of Airlie into the King's hands, and obtained from James II. a new charter of the Mains and Castle of Airlie, to be held blench for a pair of gilt spurs, or forty pounds Scots as the price thereof. Since then the Ogilvies have been in possession of their Airlie estate, but the attachment of the family to the Stuart cause put it in jeopardy oftener than once. In 1640, while the Earl was in attendance upon King Charles I., the Earl of Argyll attacked Airlie's Castles of Forter and Airlie, took both, and burned them to the ground. It was this burning which is commemorated in the popular old ballad entitled "The Bonnie House of Airlie."

> Argyle has raised a hunder men,
> A hunder men an' mairly,
> An' he's awa doun by the back o' Dunkeld,
> To plunder the bonnie house o' Airlie.

But the incidents related in the song took place at Forter Castle, Glenisla, where Lady Ogilvy was then residing, although tradition clings to Airlie Castle as the scene of Argyle's cruelties, just as it tenaciously does to the Castle of Glamis as the *locale* of the murder of Duncan and the scene of the deadly combat between Macduff and the witches.

Airlie Castle has also several weird "stories" told about it and the family of Airlie. Here is one "narrated by an Englishman":—

"A drummer boy" is said to go about the Castle playing his drum whenever there is a death impending in the family. It is said that on 19th August, 1849, a young English gentleman was on his way to the Tulchan, a shooting-lodge belonging to the Earl of Airlie. He was mounted on a stout pony, having a stalwart Highlander for his guide across the wild Forfarshire moor. For about two hours darkness had fallen, when the welcome lights, issuing from the windows of the Tulchan, met our traveller's anxious gaze. At the same moment a swell of faint music smote suddenly upon his ear. The sound was that of a distant band accompanied by the drum, and appeared to emanate from the low ridge of ground below the hunting-lodge in front of him. As it was wafted in louder accents across the moor, he could not forbear from feeling that it had something of an eerie and unearthly character about it. Astonished at such an unaccountable occurrence in a spot where the Tulchan was the only house within many miles, and where bracken, brown heath, and morass outstretched far and wide upon every side of him, the young man called the attention of his guide to the strange burst of music which he had just heard. Muttering that such sounds were "no canny," and professing that to him they were inaudible, the Highlander urged on his pony to as great a speed as the weary beast could exert after a journey of twenty-five miles, and in a little while the two riders drew reins at the hospitable door of the lodge. Upon descending the Englishman learnt that his friend and host, Lord Ogilvie (afterwards tenth Earl of Airlie) had been summoned to London on account of his father's dangerous illness. On the following day the ninth Earl of Airlie breathed his last in London, thus affording another testimony to the truth of the old tradition, that weird music and the sound of the drum haunt the dwellings of the Ogilvies prior to the death of a member of the family."

The name of the parish of Airlie is said to have been Airdly, from the Gaelic Aird, signifying a ridge, which exactly describes the locality of Airlie Castle.

There are some objects of antiquity in the parish which deserve notice. At the Parish Church is an old aumry or press for holding sacred vessels. A gaunt human figure, in height about three feet, dressed in a loose habit, is built into the west gable of the church. There is nothing known regarding the stone, whence it came, or who the figure is intended to represent. St Madden's knoll and well are close by the church. It is a copious spring of fine water. In a document, dated 1447, "the bell of the Kirk of St Madden of Airlie" is mentioned. On the farm of Barns a weem was discovered, nearly seventy feet long, which proved to be a very entire specimen of these ancient dwellings.

Den of Airlie and "Reekie Linn."

Now mark the varied coloured hue
Of mountain flowers—some softly blue,
And glistening bright with pearly dew;
Some blooming like the purple bell,
Which loves the lonesome mossy dell;
While some, all hung with silver sheen,
Look pure as angels' robes, I ween,
And gently humming sounds distil,
Like distant song of flowing rill.

How delicate their colours bright
Of petals, purple, blue, and white;
What rich embroid'ry gems the form
Of these lone children of the storm!

The picturesque Den, which is about four miles in length—a considerable part of it being a winding ravine—is admired by all visitors. The lofty banks and rocky lichen-covered gray cliffs, the battlemented  crags and bosky dingles, the projecting rocks and rough woodlands, the green groves and dusky dells, choral with the melody of many warblers, form scenes of much grandeur and great impressiveness. The junction of the Melgum with the Isla at the base of the Castle rock, other ravines of considerable beauty, and the famous "Reekie Linn" add variety and interest to the magnificent scenery around "The Bonnie Hoose o' Airlie." The precipitous banks of the ravine are beautifully clothed with a leafy labyrinth. From every crevice and level spot the mountain ash or rowan tree; the graceful birch, its leaves moving with the slightest breath of air, and reflecting the light in the bright sunshine; the alder and other indigenous trees; juniper, bramble, wild rose; ferns in great variety, foxglove, and other luxuriant vegetation, which delight in moisture and shade, assume their brightest garb as they bend their boughs or fronds to kiss the stream from whence they draw their nourishment.

The ivy-covered hoary walls, whose fame, and love, and glory
Auld Scotland guard shall to the end, the bard-emblazoned story,
The Isla o'er its rocky bed rolls grandly through the dell,
The songsters from their leafy bowers try who can best excel.

The brushwood of the Den of Airlie consists largely of oak, and is remarkable as containing the most easterly remains of natural oakwood on the southern face of the Grampians. Its unrivalled scenery and historical association is also classic ground to the botanical student.

Regarding the "Linn," it might be noted that at the entrance of the ravine some ledges of rock extend across the bed of the stream, over which the water rushes, forming small cascades. The stream now contracts in width, and tumbles over the "Reekie Linn," falling into a deep black pool nearly one hundred feet below the brink of the cataract. As if stunned by the fall, the water here appears to rest a little to gain renewed strength before proceeding farther on the troubled passage upon which it has now entered. The fall is partially broken about half way down when the river is low, but when in high flood it bounds over the precipice at one bold leap, and is then one of the grandest waterfalls in the kingdom. At such a time the water shakes the ground in its neighbourhood, deafens the ear by its loud roar, and sends up a constant cloud of spray far above the lofty banks. Then, when the sun shines, many beautiful well-defined rainbows are formed out of the spray; and the water, dashing over the Linn, sparkles like diamonds, and the spectator is fascinated with their lovely tints. From this rising spray, or *reek*, the fall takes its name.

The surroundings of the Reekie Linn are in admirable keeping. A little distance above the fall the rocky banks of the river rise high over the surface of the stream, and from the chasm at the bottom of the cataract to the top of the cliffs they are little short of two hundred feet in height, and nearly perpendicular. Immediately below the cataract, jutting rocks, at various elevations, project from the sides of the cliffs, points of advantage from which fine prospects of portions of the ravine may be safely viewed. As seen from the balcony of a rustic retreat the fall and its accessories form at all times a picture of rare beauty, but when the river is swollen by heavy rains the cataract is a magnificent, awe-inspiring object.

About a mile below the Linn there is another fall called the "Slug of Auchrannie." Here the water, confined in a narrow, rocky channel, rushes with great rapidity down a very steep declivity, and after a fall of about fifty feet settles in a deep pool.

When the river is in flood the water is thrown with much force over the brink of the incline, and its volume so broken that it appears to be quite a cataract of foam, white as snow, and extremely picturesque. Below this fall, as above it, rapids, cascades, streams, and eddying pool succeed each other in quick succession down to the lower end of the Den.

Kingoldrum.

> "'Tis of the brave and good alone
> That good and brave men are the seed,
> Yet training quickens **power unborn,**
> And culture nerves the **soul for fame**;
> But he must live **a life of scorn**
> Who bears a noble **name**
> Yet blurs it with the soil of infamy and shame."

The church of this interesting parish was in the diocese of Brechin. It was given by William the Lion to the monastry of Aberbrothock, 1211-14, although it is considered that there had been a church on the site ages before the erection of the one given to the Abbey by King William. This supposition is strengthened by the discovery of fragments of ancient sculptured stones, with curious devices cut on them of a mixture of heathen and Christian character, and by an old *scellach*, or bell, made of sheet iron and coated with bronze, having been found there in 1843. A coffin slab, about six feet long, embellished with a cross in relief and a sword incised, lies in the burying ground. Flint weapons and other traces of the early inhabitants have been found in various parts of the parish, and there are some peculiar looking entrenchments and stone circles upon the Scurroch Hill, to the west of the manse.

The parish of Kingoldrum is bounded on the north and east by Kirriemuir and Cortachy; by Airlie on the south; and by Lintrathen on the west. Being situated in the Braes of Angus, the northern portion of the parish is mountainous, Catlaw (2264 feet) being the highest summit in it, and the frontier mountains of the Grampians, from which the prospect is most extensive and varied.

The Melgum, after passing the Loch of Lintrathen, presents pictures of rare beauty. The descent of the stream is very rapid, and it suddenly enters a deep, narrow, and tortuous, rocky channel, in passing through which it is precipitated again and again from a considerable height. Cascade thus succeeds cascade in rapid succession, each having beauties all its own.

The Abbots and monks made perambulations of this parish at three different periods, and the names of most of the various farms and hamlets at the earliest of the three perambulations, made more than six hundred years ago, are continued to the present time. The Abbots and monks had the sole right to hunt in the forest of Kingoldrum. No trace of the ancient Royal forest can now be discovered. The huge mountain Catlaw, with its many summits and outlying ridges or shoulders, are largely covered with heath. Between these shoulders there are small glens, each with its little rill. A visit to Catlaw, and a little time spent wandering among the glens around it, is alike pleasing and healthful. High up on the side of Catlaw and the spurs running out from it, bright green spots are here and there to be seen. Each is a clump of moss, and there is a spring, to become, as it trickles down the hillside, a tiny rivulet, a little burn, swelling in volume ss it proceeds onward.

On the subject of the old Castle of Balfour, Ochterlony says, 1684-5—The laird of Balfour, Ogilvy, hath the greatest interest in Kingoldrum—an ancient gentleman, with a great estate. It hath a great house built by Cardinal Beaton, and much planting. Notwithstanding the *great* things enumerated by Ochterlony, Ogilvy of Balfour is not among the barons of Angus enumerated by Edwards in 1678, the laird of Balfour never having got his estate erected into a barony, as he held off the Abbey of Arbrath, and not off the Crown. The Ogilvys were in possession of

Balfour for more than sixty years before they received the charter from Cardinal Beaton.

Walter Ogilvie, the father of James, the first of Balfour by the 1539 charter, was brother of Marion Ogilvy, the mother of the Cardinal's children, who thus had a deep interest in the Ogilvies. Ochterlony's statement that the Castle of Balfour was built by Cardinal Beaton is a popular error, as is the common report that the Castle of Claypots and others were built by Beaton. It is more probable that Balfour Castle was built half a century earlier by Walter Ogilvy, the father of James of Balfour, than by the Cardinal. It was customary for the great mitred Abbots to have castellated messuages on their principal estates, and the Cardinal or a previous Abbot may have assisted the Ogilvys in its erection, in order that he might have a lodging in it when he visited lands there. Half a century ago the Castle was a noble Gothic ruin, but Thomas Farquharson of Baldovie took down two wings of it to build a farmhouse, which destroyed its beauty greatly.

Bidding adieu for the present to the Howe of Strathmore, we crave pardon for lingering so long in our wanderings and explorations, during which we trust our love of Nature has been strengthened. It is high time, however, to resume our journey, and complete our circular tour as previously planned, taking the reader back to where we diverged at Angus Hill, which we referred to on page 100.

Angus Hill.

A short distance eastward from the church of Aberlemno there is a hill designed the *Hill of Angus*. It was probably the place of rendezvous for the men of

Angus when the country was infested with the Danes and other Northmen, and suffered much from their predatory incursions into the interior of the county.

From Angus Hill the South Esk, which we saw in its upper reaches, glistens in the valley below in many a picturesque bend. Indeed, it does not seem to know its own mind for two consecutive minutes, but keeps turning and winding, now hither, now zig-zagging fantastically from right to left, and occasionally even manifesting a decided inclination to retrace its steps. The bosom of the valley is of the most undulating description—now rising into gentle knolls covered with verdure, or plumed with patches and belts of timber, now sinking into water-worn hollows and dells, and anon spreading out into fertile meads and sunny slopes, where cattle in straggling groups are pasturing or lazily chewing their cud. At various points farm houses peer above their girdles of foliage, over which hover curling clouds of blue smoke—altogether a cozy, sunny scene, which is rendered all the more pleasing by the contrast which its quiet beauty offers to the stern and hoary grandeur of the hills rising in the distance.

In our travels how many picturesque burns have we passed, which in by-gone days gave motion to the wheel, but which is now singing its eerie tune to the echoes of an unbroken solitude. A few stately trees, through which the blue smoke from the miller's hearth may have curled long ago, wave drearily over the spot. No gaucy gudewife, with plump bairn in her arms, now graces the door-check of the miller's dwelling, or watches with motherly pride a number of wee toddlin' things, with flaxen hair, who are tumbling before her on the green. But all is lifeless now. The cheerful din of the happer is heard no more, Nature has resumed her peaceful sway. The rank nettle waves on the site of cheery but-an-ben, and the rabbit may burrow undisturbed around the cold hearth stone.

Third Tour.

MENMUIR, *via* PITTENDREICH, WILLIE MILL'S BURN, BRIDGE OF BLACKHALL. THE CRUICK, TIGERTON, KIRKTON, WEST WATER, LETHNOT, CATERTHUN, BALNAMOON, LITTLE BRECHIN, MURLINGDEN.

MANY *Laws* or *Mounds* in the vicinity of Brechin go to prove that the Druids were a powerful body in this quarter. Huddleston, in his edition of "Toland's History of the Druids," informs us that "the three farms close upon Brechin called Pittendreich, are identical with Pit-an-druach, the burial place of the Druids. Amongst the hereditary offices that existed in feudal times, we find that of the office of blacksmith of the lordship of

Brechin. A document, dated 29th April, 1514, is published in the Miscellany of the Spalding Club for 1853, in which it is shown that Richard Lindsay received nine firlots of good meal of every plough of the tenant of Pittendreich, and one fleece of an old sheep yearly.

Some antiquarians are of opinion that the battle between Agricola and Galgacus must have been fought on the sloping ground now facing us, immediately south of the two hills of Caterthun—as a popular rhyme has it

> "Between the Killivar and the Buckler stane
> There lies mony a bluidy bane."

As the "Killivar Stane" is on the farm of Barrelwell, and the "Blawart Lap," and the "Buckler Stane" are on the farm of Longhaugh, and both being under the western hill of Caterthun, our antiquarian friends presume that the principal struggle had taken place at these points, where the Romans, being defeated, had been driven eastward on their camps at Keithock and Slateford—the old name of the village of Edzell—both of which places will, in another tour, receive our attention.

Around this neighbourhood there are a number of small comfortable looking holdings or "tackies," and we pass a number of old-fashioned cosy looking straggling houses, with well cultivated and smiling gardens, known as Willie Mill's Burn.

> There stands the auld biggin' upon the brae-side,
> An' canty bit garden wi' flowers in their pride,
> Weel watered an' tended, baith lily an' pea,
> How lovely they look by the bonnie birk tree.

We cross the Bridge of Blackhall, or Blackha', over the Cruick, a fine trouting stream, which rises in two head streams at the northern boundary of the parish of Fearn, and, after a run of fifteen or sixteen miles, falls into the North Esk near the mansion house of Stracathro, and within 150 yards of the confluence of the West Water with the same stream. The small clachan known by the name of Tigerton, as well as the Kirkton, and the church, being historic scenes, attract our notice. At the hamlet of Tigerton there was at one time an Episcopalian chapel or meeting house, which was "served" by the minister of Brechin. The parish tradesmen — merchant, shoemaker, blacksmith, and joiner — are still to be found here.

It is curious to note that, but for a passing notice relative to the King's (the last Alexander) gardeners at Forfar and Menmuir, the interesting fact of the art of horticulture having been known and cultivated in Scotland in those days would have been little else than matter of conjecture. These gardeners are the only ones mentioned in this part of Scotland at that period, so that it is probable that both places were frequently resorted to by royalty.

Lethnot and its Glen.

We'll hie up yon glen where the clear burnie wimples,
Where wide-spreading willows entwine with the skies;
Where the kid and the lambkin are sporting together,
By Navar's soft streamlet and green gowany braes.

A run through the Glen of Lethnot would here be very enjoyable, but it would take us considerably out of our course, and we may refer to it again when treating of Edzell. Suffice it just now to say that, descending the slope of the hill, we enter the Glen of Lethnot at the Bridge of Peffray. This strath has one natural opening from the south, which is entered a little beyond Edzell, along the course of the West Water, and naturally divides the once separate parishes of Navar and Lethnot, united 1723. We pass the old churchyard of Navar, half-a-mile to the left, in the corner of a field, surrounded by a rude stone dyke and a row of ash trees. The remains of the church are still traceable.

A little to the east we observe the antiquated, semi-circular bridge at Drumcairn, which spans the West Water, and to the left the schoolhouse and school where the "little charge" are fitted for the varied duties of after life.

> Drumcairn stands on the broomy knowe,
>   The burn comes jinkin' doon ;
> The auld kirk jouks i' the hiddlin' howe,
>   The ba'field beiks i' the sun.
>
> An' Clochie wons by the water side,
>   Where the fragrant birken grows ;
> An' t' e braes are clad wi' the heather bells,
>   An' the bloom o' the sweet wild rose.

A little farther on, to the right, are the church and manse, and the lonely burying ground, where

> The rude forefathers of the hamlet sleep.

The stillness is broken only by the water rushing onward in its deep and rugged channel. Here and there are tiny cascades, dark pools, deep clefts of rock; the water now turning itself into foam and fury, and again falling into something like the placid sleep of an infant. Tradition bears that this parish had its Castle, called Dennyferne, which was one of the residences of the Lindsays.

It might be mentioned that the largest tributary of the West Water is the Water of Saughs, and towards the end of the seventeenth century its banks were the scene of the fierce and bloody conflict—the Raid or the Battle of Saughs—to which we referred at pages 43-46.

The Church of Lethnot was dedicated to St Mary, and was formerly a Prebend of Brechin. In 1591 John Lindsay, son of John Lindsay of Barras, was minister, and became "servitour to the auld laird of Edzell, and was one of the eight followers of David Lindsay, younger of Edzell, who, clothed 'in geir,' made an attack, 5th July, 1607, on his cousin David, Master of Crawford, and killed his uncle Alexander, Lord Spynie, while endeavouring to heal the breach between them."

Here, as in Glenesk, Episcopacy was held in great esteem, and the chapel, which stood at the Clochie, was burned in 1746. It was said that the soldiers forced the farmer, who was a Jacobite, to carry peats from his own hearth, and straw from his own barn, and with drawn swords over and around, made him set fire to his own beloved Zion.

Navar was always conjoined with Brechin in one lordship; and many of the Lords thereof ranked among the highest historic personages of their day. The first of them was David, Earl of Huntingdon, brother of William the Lion. Among his successors may be named his grandson, Sir William de Brechin, one of the great barons in the time of Alexander III., and one of the guardians of the kingdom in his minority; his great-grandson, Sir David, who married a sister of the Bruce, and, after the battle of Inverury, espoused his cause, and continued faithful to it; and his great-great-grandson, also Sir David, who suffered for his complicity in the conspiracy of Lord Soulis; Sir David Barclay, who married Margaret de Brechin, Bruce's niece; Walter, the second son of Robert II., by Euphemia Ross, who married the only daughter of Sir David Brechin, and was executed for the share he had in the death of his nephew, James I.; David, Earl of Crawford, and afterwards Duke of Montrose;

James, Duke of Ross, the second son of James III., and afterwards Archbishop of St Andrews; Sir Thomas Erskine, Lord Brechin; the Earl of Mar; and the Earls of Panmure, who acquired Brechin and Navar by purchase, in 1634. Such an illustrious galaxy of nobles should invest Navar with great historic interest.

THE ARCH FIEND AND ONE OF THE LORDS OF BRECHIN.

In the " Lands of the Lindsays" we are told that the arch-fiend held his own with one of these Lords of Brechin. The farmer of Wirren had long nursed his wrath against his neighbour, who had somehow offended him. Learning by which road that neighbour would one night return home at a late hour, he resolved to waylay him, and to have his revenge on him. The farmer's wife, dreading that mischief was in the wind, employed all her art of persuasion and entreaty to induce him to stay at home. At last she asked who was to be her companion in his absence, and was answered by her infuriated husband, "THE DEVIL IF HE LIKES!" And he did like. From the middle of the earthen floor of the room in which the poor woman sat the Devil rose and presented himself before her! With admirable presence of mind she managed to slip her son, a mere boy, out at a back window for the minister. He, with some neighbours, soon neared the house, when feeling the smell of "brimstane smeik," he returned to the manse for his gown and bands, and Bible. Boldly entering with this armour, he attacked the enemy, setting on him with his sword; when, in the midst of a great volume of smoke, and uttering a hideous yell, the fiend shrunk aghast, and passed from view in much the same mysterious way as he had appeared. An indentation of the ground floor of the farmhouse was long pointed out as having been caused by the descent of Satan!

The victorious minister, it has been asserted, was the Episcopal minister of Lethnot, a Stuart devotee, who prayed for " the heads and patriots of the Rebel Army, and that God might cover their heads in the day of battell;" as also, " for his noble patron the Earl of Panmure, that the Lord might preserve him now that he was exposed to danger;" gave thanks for " King James the Eighth's safe landing in these his native bounds;" and entreated " that the army appearing against Mar's army might be defeated," &c. As may readily be supposed, for these and similar good deeds, Satan seems to have had a special pique at him. He even ventured to enter the manse, and to torment him there. If he sat in his study on an evening to read or to write, his book or paper was forthwith covered with darkness, and so faintly did the candle burn that he could hardly see from one end of the room to the other! As he himself used to tell it, " One day when I sat down to my desk, the fiend took his stand just behind me, so that I could not get on with a word of my sermon. At length it occurred to me to write the first promise on a small slip of paper, and, without looking over my shoulder, to throw it to my tormentor, saying, " Tak' that, Satan; it's low water wi' ye noo!" when he instantly departed, and has never troubled me in my study since."

The minister of Lethnot was not so deft a soldier; and, eventually, it fared very woefully with him. On a dark winter night, in the time of a great snowstorm, and during a gust of wind which threatened to overthrow the manse, Beelzebub entered the study by the chimney, in the shape of a large black cat! "How he found his way none could divine, for the minister did'nt see him enter, and saw nothing of him save his long hairy fangs, which suddenly extinguished the candle! Running in pursuit, however, he saw him clear the steep and narrow stair which led to the lower flat of the house, and falling from head to foot of it himself, Mr Thomson (such was the minister's name) was so greatly injured from bruises and fright that he never recovered!"

The accuracy of this item of the old traditional history of the parish has lately been challenged in a convincing manner, and, as we understand the present respected and gifted minister of the parish—the Rev. F. Cruickshank, who has presided over it since 1854—has in preparation a work on the history and antiquities of Lethnot and Navar, he will be able, after much painstaking research and thought, to simplify some of these traditions, and at the same time furnish a book of much historical value. A recent writer says—This is one of the class of stories which, with a slight difference in detail, are found current in almost every district. In this case, however, there is a foundation in fact.

The following account of the circumstances may not be so amusing, but it has at least the merit of being true:—

The minister was not Mr Thomson, who was the last Episcopalian minister of the parish, and was deposed by the Presbytery of Brechin in 1719, for having taken part in the Mar rebellion, and thereby broken the condition on which he had been allowed to retain the living, and who was succeeded, not as the legal minister of the parish, but as the Episcopal clergyman of the district, by the Rev. David Rose, great grandfather of the distinguished Sir Hugh Rose, now known as Lord Strathnairn. The minister to whom the story relates was the Rev. John Row, the last minister of Navar, as a separate parish, and the first of the united parishes of Navar and Lethnot. He died in

1745, and was buried within the kirk of Lethnot, a neat mural tablet marking the spot. He was a strong-minded, but thoughtful and sagacious man, who had a difficult position to fill during the unsettled times betwixt 1715 and 1746, and filled it well. Earnest in promoting education in his parish, he strove to discourage as far as possible the superstitious ideas and practices which were then so prevalent.

At that time, and for long after, the popular feeling, as is well known, forbade the burial of suicides in the kirkyard. In one instance the minister made a strong effort to obtain the rites of ordinary sepulture for the body, and succeeded so far as to have it buried in the kirkyard after the sun was set, "between the sun and the sky," as the old saying is. There was a superstitious belief that whoever stepped over a newly-made grave would meet with some great misfortune within a short time. Mr Row, thinking this a good opportunity of teaching his people a practical lesson as to the absurdity of such a belief, jumped three times over the grave. Returning immediately thereafter to the manse, which then stood close to the present south-west gate of the kirkyard, he went upstairs to his study, or chamber, as it was the custom to call it. It was not yet so dark as to prevent his perceiving that some strange animal was in the room. Going outside the door he called downstairs to his servant girl to bring a lighted candle and a stick. She brought the candle, but, instead of the stick, a long-shafted straw fork. The mysterious animal turned out to be a large black cat, which, on seeing the light, bolted out at the open door. The minister, stepping back a pace or two to get the chance of a stroke at it with his somewhat unwieldy weapon, came against the frail wooden railing, which gave way, and, unable to recover his balance, he fell backward into the lobby beneath and broke his back.

This is the true story of the black cat of the manse of Lethnot. The writer's informant was an old lady who lived till well nigh 90 years of age, and died in Edinburgh in 1880, retaining to the last her wonderful bodily vigour and the full possession of her mental faculties. She was the daughter of a former minister of Lethnot, and in her youth was well acquainted with the woman (by that time of course aged) who as the minister's servant girl held the light for him.

Probably the minister's untimely end, occurring under such circumstances, had the effect of confirming belief in old superstitions. It is certain at all events that years after his death, suicides continued to be refused the rites of Christian burial. Sometime, it is supposed, between 1760 and 1780, the remains of two such poor unfortunate persons, a man and a woman, were taken to the top of Wirren, the highest hill in the parish, and there interred.

The two churches of Lethnot and Navar were within a mile of each other, but separated by the West Water. When the parishes were united, the minister of Navar made it a condition of his becoming minister of the united parishes that a bridge should be erected to connect Navar with Lethnot to enable him to visit his parishioners in both districts. This was done, and the bridge has been of great service to the inhabitants of the whole district. Previous to, and till the union of the parishes, Lethnot and Lochlee were served by one minister, who preached twice at Lethnot for once at Lochlee. Warden tells us that the road the clergyman took in going between his two churches was by the east side of the West Water, past Achourie and Clash of Wirren. It is still known as the Priest's Road. In former times it was the great road from Banffshire and the western part of Aberdeenshire to Brechin and the low country, and was kept in fair order. It was much frequented by smugglers, Highland shearers, and others up to the end of the first decade of this century. By this road Brechin and Ballater are within thirty miles of each other. When the church of Navar was demolished, shortly after the union of the parishes, the bell disappeared, but it was subsequently discovered, and is now in the Museum at Arbroath, with a description by the Rev. Mr Cruickshank. It bears the date 1655.

The church of Lethnot was rebuilt in 1827. The Rev. Mr Cruickshank has no doubt that it occupies a site which has been a place of worship from the earliest appearance of Christianity in the country, if not in old Druidical times. In the early part of the century, during the incumbency of Mr Symers, several pieces of silver coin were found in cleaning out a fountain near the church, which is known as St Mary's Well. These had been votive offerings, cast in by devout worshippers before the Reformation. The baptismal font in use in Romish times was long turned from the holy purpose for which it was formed, and made to do duty as a watering trough. It was lost sight of for thirty years, but was discovered and claimed by the present minister, and now lies in front of the church.

Menmuir.

Manmure Church, or Menmur, as the name of Menmuir was variously spelled in former days, was a vicarage in the Diocese of Dunkeld. It was dedicated to S. Aidan, and a fine spring in the vicinity bears his name. S. Aidan flourished in the seventh century. The present Parish Church was built in 1842 to replace the old church, which was erected in 1767. The Rev. J. L. Thomson has been the much-esteemed minister of the parish since 1875. At Lochtie, in the south-west district of the parish, there is a Free Church, of which the Rev. George Monro has been the highly-appreciated minister since 1854.

The parish is about five miles in length by about two in medium breadth. It is bounded by Stracathro and Lethnot on the north, on the east by Stracathro and Brechin, by Careston and Brechin on the south, and on the west by Fearn.

The earliest known charter of Menmuir is by King Robert Bruce, dated 1st May, 1319. It is a grant of the office of keeper of the forest of Kilgery, &c., to Peter de Spalding, a burgess of Berwick-on-Tweed, who, on the night of the 2nd April, 1318, by stratagem delivered Berwick into the hands of the Bruce. The town and castle had then been for some twenty years in possession of the English. His wife was a Scotswoman, who no doubt encouraged him in his purpose to aid the Scots in taking that important border town. Spalding excambed his tenements in Berwick with the King for the lands of Ballourthy and Pitmachy (Balzeordie and Pitmudie) with the above-mentioned office, and right to half the foggage. Spalding was subsequently slain by the Scots.

LAWLESS RAIDS.

Other portions of the thanedom of Menmuir was granted by David II. to several parties—notably John de Cullas, the first Collace of Balnamoon, a possession we will refer to later on. From 1360 to 1632 this estate was held by his race. He is said to have cost the rebels the loss of the battle of Brechin, for which the Earl of Crawford (Earl Beardie and the Tiger Earl) took terrible vengeance on him, harrying and desolating his lands; resting with his men at the spot where, in honour of the noble savage, the village bears the name of Tigerton. John de Collace led by his encroachments to the inquest for fixing the boundary between his lands and those of the Bishop of Brechin; and was so lawless as to remove the landmarks which the Assize set between them. Robert de Collace so fanned the long standing feud between Balnamoon and Brechin that it broke out in deeds of mutual violence. Along with 52 of his tenants he had to find caution to "underlie the law for collecting a large body of armed men, and under night, going to the Roods of Brechin, destroying cairns, and fighting and slaughtering some of the inhabitants." Reprisals were made by a large body of the citizens, who attacked his servants, and destroyed some of their houses and cattle. This shows the lawless state of things at that period.

TRAGEDIES.

David Lindsay, of Edzell, the ninth Earl of Crawford, purchased Balhall in 1555. It was in Balhall Moss, in 1382, that Sir James Lindsay, then chief of the Lindsays of Crawford, and High Justiciary of Scotland, slew Sir John Lyon, of Glammis. He seems to have envied Sir John for his favour with the King; for he had risen to some of the highest offices of the State, and to be the King's son-in-law. Meeting in the Moss of Balhall, they settled their quarrel with the sword, at the cost of Lyon's life. He was honoured with being buried at Scone in the sepulchres of the Kings. Lindsay fled the country; but, though stained with blood, he retained his office of Justiciary, and, on performing a pilgrimage to the shrine of St Thomas a Becket at Canterbury, he was called home and pardoned.

The Northern border of Balhall was the scene of another tragedy. The Laird of it and a neighbour had differed about the march between their lands. Witnesses were called in to settle the strife. One of them swore against Balhall, deponing "that the land on which he stood" (the disputed ground) was Balhall's neighbour's. Enraged at his falsehood, the Laird drew his dagger, and despatched him. The perjury of the scoundrel was proved, by its being found on examination that he had filled his shoes with earth from the neighbour's land, to which he suited the words of his deposition. His name was Beattie; and a cairn called Beattie's Cairn, and a ridge called the Misworn Rig, are said to be memorials of his guilt and punishment.

We may add here that there was till lately another cairn in Menmuir, the memorial of a much more recent tragedy. Little more than a hundred years ago, Donald M'Arthur, the Tigerton shoemaker, visited Brechin to make purchases for his marriage, and quarrelling with certain parties in the town, was waylaid by them on his return home in the darkness of the night. Concealing themselves in the wood of Findowrie, when Donald reached it they pounced upon him and savagely abused him; and, a well-known highwayman coming up, they hired him with a paltry sum to complete Donald's murder. A cairn was raised to mark the spot where the murdered body was found, and as few passed by without adding a stone to it, Donald's cairn had attained an immense size when the presiding genius of agricultural improvement gave orders for its removal. "The bride died of grief soon after the murder of her lover, and the peasantry were often alarmed by mingled cries of distress from the weird of the unfortunate shoemaker, while the favoured form of his betrothed hovered nightly around the cairn so long as any stones remained."

There was a hermitage in connection with the grant of Kilgery, and the Chapel of the Blessed Virgin Mary of the forest of Kilgery appears to have been part of the gift. It stood in a field near the Chapelton of

Dunlappie. The chapel was demolished, and the stones were used in building the farm steading. A fine spring a short distance south of where the chapel stood is still known as the Lady Well. The office of hermit of the chapel had been acquired by Hugh Cominche. On 28th May, 1445, James II. gave to John Smyth, citizen of Brechin, the office of hermit of the hermitage of the chapel of the Blessed Mary in the forest of Kilgery, with the hermitage, cemetery, and green, and three acres of land. In 1461 John Smyth sold the lands, office of hermit, and other pertinents to William Somyr of Balzeordie for one merk of yearly rent from a tenement in Brechin. The hermitage of Kilgery was on the south of Brown Caterthun, and between it and the White Caterthun. The name is still retained there. Among the Southesk charters at Kinnaird are many relating to the hermitage and the office of hermit.

SEPULCHRAL REMAINS.

The parish of Menmuir is rich in sepulchral remains. Many stone cists, inclosing urns, have been dug up in the Moss of Findowrie. About a mile north of the church is a cluster of burrows. On the line from the Caterthun to Keithock are frequent tumuli and cairns; and there fragments of arms have also been found. As the couplet, somewhat different from that already given, has it—

> 'Tween the Blawart Lap, and the Killievair Stanes,
> There lie mony bluidy banes.

All these things tell of war; of which it can hardly be doubted that the sculptured stones, found in the foundation of the old dyke of the churchyard, are likewise the memorial. According to the common tradition of the district, they tell of battle upon battle between the Picts and the Danes; but it is very likely that they specially point to a great battle fought in 1130 between David I. and Angus, Earl of Moray. Angus claimed the Scottish throne in right of Gruach, the grand-daughter of Kenneth IV., and the mother of Lulach, the grandfather of Angus. The men of Moray supported Angus in his claim; and coming southward at their head, he met the King in this neighbourhood, and was completely overthrown.

WITCHCRAFT AND OTHER SUPERSTITIONS.

Menmuir was as othordox as its neighbours on the subject of witchcraft. The Parochial records of 1496 have this entry:—"No lecture this week, because the minister was attending the Committee appointed by the Provincial Assembly for the trial of witches and charmers in their bounds."

Notwithstanding all this diligence, the witches, instead of diminishing, seemed rather to multiply; and the fairies were no less rife. Even as late as fourscore years ago they were strongly suspected of having performed one of their pranks at Tigerton, viz., stealing a fine healthy infant from fond parents, and substituting for him a sickly, ricketty one! The wise woman of Tigerton knew how the suspicion might be tested: Place the infant over a blaze of whins; if of fairy stock, he will fly away to Fairyland; if a human being, he will abide the fire, and suffer only a *scaum!* The mother going from home for a day, left the infant in charge of a neighbour. The opportunity of bringing his species to the touchstone of experiment was too good to be lost. A select company assembled in the "ben end" of the house. "A bundle of whins was lighted, and, stript to the skin, the poor child was placed upon the tongs, and held over the flame by two of the learned conclave. He screamed and yelled, as elder people would do in like circumstances ; but, as he never attempted to fly out at the chimney, he was declared by the devilish hags, in council assembled, to be merely a human creature after all !"

> Far abune the mystic ring
> Merry laverocks lilt an' sing:
> Down the sunny slopes o' Wirran
> Wimples mony a heelent burn,
> Blythesome as the simmer morn.

The Hill of Wirran, which bounds the northern parts, was used in the ages of credulity and fanaticism as the burial place of suicides. On the very ridge of the hill numerous grave-shaped hillocks point out the resting places of those infatuated beings. At no distant date, when a suicide was found on one of the farms in the neighbourhood, the farmer, rather than allow the body to be conveyed in at the barn door, had a hole struck out of the front wall for that purpose, and although the hole was built up "ower an' ower again, the biggin' wudna bide, but aye fell oot?"

A kettle filled with silver is said to lie in the Craig of Stoneyford, on the west side of the mountain, and, when the sun shines in full lustre, the bow of the kettle, and its precious contents are often seen to glitter. Many attempts have been made to secure this treasure, but without success. If the story is correct, the searchers have little cause to complain, for, alike with the kettle of gold which is said to be secreted in the well on Caterthun, the reward is instant removal from this sublunary sphere—constant labour until the world ends, and perpetual wailing thereafter!

This district is famous as being the locality where the last wolf was seen in Scotland. A servant girl had been at the mill with a *melder* of corn. On her return, she felt so overpowered by fatigue that she lay

down on a bank to rest, and soon fell asleep. She
slept soundly until day-break, when, to her horror she
found a huge shaggy wolf lying beside her asleep.
She quietly fled, and set the neighbourhood in search
of the delinquent, whose depredations amongst the
flocks in all parts of the glen had been severely felt.
He was found nestling on the West Shank of Wirran,
and was shot by the laird of Natbrow.

Caterthun.

> Catherthun, thy matchless ring
> How shall I attempt to sing?
> When 'tis known that learned men
> Are unable to attain
> Perfect knowledge as to how
> That ring was placed around thy brow.

Caterthun is in the parish of Menmuir, and
presents the finest and most interesting example of a
British Hill Fort that is known. There are two of these
forts on the summits of detached conical hills, about
the line where the Grampians begin to swell into
mountains. They are a mile distant from each other,
and are familiarly known as the "Brown" and the
"White" Cater. The last mentioned is peculiarly
interesting, being the better defined of the two. Rings
of white stone encircle the one, and dark turf the
other, and hence their names. The White Caterthun
is at an elevation of about nine hundred feet. Its area
is oval in form, measuring more than five hundred
feet in length, and two hundred in breadth. The wall
enclosing this area is composed of large loose stones,
and is at least twenty feet thick at the top, and about
one hundred feet at the bottom. Outside the wall
was at one time a clearly defined broad deep ditch,
with an earthen breastwork on its outer side; and

beyond **this** there was a double entrenchment of **wall and ditch** running round **the slope** of the hill.

The position, naturally **strong, when thus fortified** must have been impregnable **to the assaults of such artillery as could** then be brought to bear against it. Some think **that the works on the** Brown Caterthun had been thrown up by a besieging army, which was attempting to reduce the large camp on the **White Caterthun.** The elevation of Brown Caterthun is less, its dimensions **smaller, and its walls composed entirely of earth.**

Within **the centre area of the White Cater are the** foundations of **a rectangular building, and a hollow, now** nearly filled with **stones, which appears to have been** the draw-well **of the garrison. The literal translation** of the **word Caterthun is camp-town ; and it may** be added **that it forms one of the various native** strongholds, **which have been conjectured to have been** the camp of Galgacus, **the leader of the Caledonian host, which** attempted **to withstand the Roman invaders** in the famous engagement **of Agricola.**

The labour **of amassing such a prodigious quantity** of stones **as are** here **built, and of carrying them to** such a height, **is inconceivable,** and **would surpass** belief **if we** had **not, in the ruins of the fortress, ocular** demonstration **of what the labour accomplished.**

THE WORK OF THE WITCHES AND FAIRIES.

Local tradition **gets over** the **difficulty by asserting that the fort was erected for the abode of Fairies, and that the architects and masons were the Witches.** A **brawny witch, in the course** of **a single morning, carried in her apron all the stones used from the channel of the West Water to the top of the hill ; and how many more she would have carried, and how much larger the structure would have been, if her apron** strings had not broken, no mortal knows. The string broke with the largest of the stones. It was allowed to lie where it fell, and it is to be seen even now on the north slope of the hill. Mr C. Sievwright, in his "Garland for the Ancient City," says:—

"Some think that it is the remains of an old fortress, built in the days of other years for war-like purposes; while others, with perhaps an equal amount of seeming truth, maintain that it is evidently the remains of a great Druidical temple. I confess myself utterly unable to decide between them. But there is a beautiful old legend still in existence, invented, most likely, by the pious monks of some neighbouring monastery, which contradicts neither the one nor the other, and yet, when properly understood, fully accounts for the building of the wonderful and mysterious 'Ring':—

> "Yes, the story I receive,
> And the country fouks believe,
> Is, that Sin, the Devil's mother,
> Brought these rugged stones together,
> Piled them round and built the Ring;
> Till one day her apron string
> Broke beneath the mighty weight
> Of a stone that even yet
> From the flowery banks so green,
> In the river may be seen."

ANTIQUARIANS DIFFER.

This great work has been the subject of much disputation amongst antiquarians. Huddlestone thinks the camp on the White Caterthun was a Druidical place of worship, and naturally derives the name by which it is known from the Gaelic—*Caither-Dun*, the temple or worship hill. But Miss Maclagan is of a different opinion, and thinks that the derivation of the name is from the ancient British word *Cader*, which signifies a fortress. Indeed there is now, all but universal acquiescence in the opinion that they were forts, hill forts (as *Cader-dun* or *Caither-dun*, signifies) erected by our remote ancestors for retreat and security in times of danger. When they were erected, and who the race was that first manned them, we know not. These, says Burton, " seem questions idle to be asked, since the chances of any answer being ever made to them appear so utterly hopeless."

Huddlestone, who wrote his account in the year 1807, says :—" The chief object of the Druids was to have their temples on an eminence commanding an extensive prospect. Thus although Caterthun could only have been an indifferent fort against modern artillery, it was particularly well adapted for a Druidical cairn, commanding as it does a prospect at once grand and impressive. The extensive view from this hill of the low country to the eastward, and southward upon the vast expanse of the German Ocean, pointed it out as an eligible station for watching the movements of the Romans, Danes, and other hostile invaders. The natives, having plenty of materials ready on the spot, demolished the cairn, levelled the summit of the hill, and built the stone dykes which presently surround it."

> When the Romans endeavoured our country to gain,
> But our ancestors fought, and they fought not in vain.

" Yet," says Carrie, " it is likely that the primitive works were erected long anterior to the first Roman invasion of Britain ; and if the Druidical worship was ever celebrated there it was only as an accessory pertaining to the residential and military encampment then existing upon the hill itself. We think that the camps are vestiges of pre-historic times."

In his instructive pamphlet on " The Brechin District," Mr Jas. A. Campbell of Stracathro, in treating of the Battle of the Grampians, and the claims of the district as being the site of the battle, says :—

On the lands of Keithock, two miles north of Brechin, on the farm of East Mains, there was a Roman Camp— the camp of Wardykes or Blackdykes. All traces of it are now almost entirely removed, but it was described at the end of last century as in the form of an oblong square, with an area to accommodate 12,000 men, and otherwise presenting marked features. The road from Keithock gate towards Newton Mill, on the way to Edzell, passes through a corner of it. The camp extended to the bluff above Keithock Burn, towards the north. Between the camp and the hills there was ample room for the Roman army, and on the Caterthuns for the Caledonians. The strength of the case for this district is Caterthun. There we have a Caledonian camp—an oval area of two acres, surrounded by a wall or dyke of large stones, with lower circumvallations of earth-works on the summit of a hill, 750 feet above the strath, with an adjoining hill (the Brown Cater) with similar earthworks—and commanding an extensive view up and down Strathmore, and across to the coast and the sea. It is situated too so as to command a view of the passes from the hills. No one can look from Caterthun without being satisfied that it was a post of safety and of observation.

The view from the top of Caterthun on a clear day is extensive and magnificent (though in recent years greatly interfered with by an objectionable belt of dense trees). To the south is the city of Brechin, with its mysterious Round Tower, and the venerable grey spire of its Cathedral; the Tower of Johnston on the Hill of Garvock, near Laurencekirk; and, in the farther distance, Arbroath and its ancient Abbey; the Bell Rock, the Firths of Tay and Forth; with the whole Valley of Strathmore from Perth to Aberdeen at our feet. Certainly the prospect contains within its scope material for countless delineations.

Gratified by our visit to this mysterious and interesting relic of the past, a run down hill and we pass the old Mill of Balrownie and the miller's house, with the usual pleasing accompaniments of poultry in capital condition and rosy-cheeked bairns frisking about the corn yard. A little under a mile brings us to the entrance, on the right, to the long winding carriage drive to

Balnamoon.

The Laird maun hae his ain again,
The Laird shall hae his ain again ;
Let us loup an' lilt fu' fain,
The Laird will hae his ain again

The mansion-house of Balnamoon—locally pronounced "Bonnymune"—is a fine old oblong building, believed to have been built about 1632, and enlarged and re-modelled about 1828. A stately edifice, albeit somewhat weather-worn, it is evidently the product of various periods, the more ancient portions, with their peaked gables, projections, and narrow closely-set windows, approximating even to the picturesque. It is surrounded by splendid specimens of great hoary, ancestral trees, and by extensive and well kept pleasure grounds and gardens. Very beautiful are the many winding walks, terminating often in quiet, foliage-shrouded cozy nooks, from which, here and there, rich fields are seen peeping hopefully and cheerfully, and picturesque groups of cattle are lazily chewing their cud. The pleasing quietude is broken only by the trickling of the burn in the wooded dell, and the glad music of the warblers of the balmy grove.

AN INTERESTING FAMILY HISTORY.

Here it may be interesting to briefly trace the lineage of the different branches of the Balnamoon family. We have mentioned that a member of the family of Collace—who held the lands from the year 1347—acquired considerable notoriety for the part he took at the Battle of Brechin in 1452, which resulted in the tide of victory being turned against his superior, the Earl of Crawford. Robert of that name sold Findowrie in 1574, and one of his daughters was married to James Rollo of Duncrub, and became the maternal ancestor of the Rollo family. John Collace—who in 1632 was served heir of his grandfather, John Collace of Balnamoon, in half of the lands and barony of Menmuir, including Balnamoon and others—was the last of the family of Collace who possessed the lands of Balnamoon. On a stone built into the west wall of Balnamoon House are the initials of John Collace, with the date 1584. This is the only visible trace of the family in the district. John Collace could not have long retained the lands of Balnamoon, for we find that Sir Alexander Carnegy, brother-german to the first Earls of Southesk and Northesk, "had a charter of the barony of Menmuir in the same year—1632." Sir Alexander Carnegy's arms are sculptured on the family burying vault at the church of Menmuir. He died in 1657, and was succeeded by his son, Sir John, who married, first, Lady Elizabeth, daughter of James, Earl of Airlie, by whom he had a son, James, who succeeded; secondly, Miss Graham, daughter of Graham of Claverhouse. Sir James died in 1662, while his son died in 1700, and was succeded by his eldest son of the same name, who was fourth of Balnamoon. The latter, dying unmarried in 1704, was succeeded by his brother, Alexander, who, having joined in the rebellion of 1715, forfeited his lands, which he, however, re-acquired in 1728. At his death, in 1750, his son, James, became sixth of Balnamoon, and was known in history as the "Rebel Laird." He married Margaret Arbuthnott, heiress of Findowrie, and died in 1791.

According to M'Gregor Peter's "Baronage of Angus and Mearns," the progenitor of the Findowrie family was Robert Arbuthnott of that Ilk, and his third wife Helen Clephane, who had charters of the lands of Findowrie, in conjunct fee and life-rent, and, David, their eldest son, in fee, from Robert Collaiss of Balnamoon, on the 14th February 1574. In 1616, Robert, son of David Arbuthnott of Findowrie, wedded Margaret, daughter of Sir William Graham of Claverhouse, and widow of George Somyr, younger of Balzeordie. James Carnegy, Esq. of Balnamoon, "the rebel laird" of "'45," great-great-grandson of Sir Alexander, wedded Margaret Arbuthnott, daughter, or at least heiress, of Alexander Arbuthnott, the last of the lairds in the male line of Findowrie, through whom the estate came to Balnamoon. He died 1791.

Many amusing anecdotes are related of the boisterous humour and conviviality of the "Rebel Laird." It was this laird of Bonnymoon, as it is locally pronounced, of whom the laughable story of the wig is told by Dean Ramsay. On returning home from a dinner party, where, by mistake, he had partaken of sherry brandy instead of port wine, his hat and wig fell off in Montreathmont Muir. The driver of his gig went out to pick them up. The laird was pleased with the hat but not the wig, and said—"It's no' my wig, Hairy lad." Hairy replied—"Ye'd better tak' it, sir, for there's nae waile of wigs on Monrimmon Moor." On reaching home, Hairy, sitting in front, told the servant to "tak' out the laird," but no laird was there. He had fallen out on the moor unobserved by Hairy, who at once went back, found the laird, and brought him home. A neighbouring laird having called a few days after, and having referred to the accident, Balnamoon quietly added, " Indeed I maun hae a lume (a vessel) that'll han'd in."

On another occasion, when returning home from a dinner party, accompanied by John, his servant, in passing the river at a ford he fell off into the water. " Whae's that faun?" inquired the laird. "Deed," quoth John, " I witna, an it be no' your Honour." It is said that on one occasion, in his cups, he mounted a stone wall and spurred his fancied steed the livelong night. One Sabbath morning two gentlemen, one a stranger in the district, called at Balnamoon and were invited to dinner. They joined in the forenoon devotional exercises, which the laird conducted himself, and the stranger was much impressed with his piety and religious deportment. After dinner he pressed them to drink until they had to be carried to bed. The stranger said—" Sic a speat o' praying, and sic a speat o' drinking, I never knew in all my life."

In Glenmark, Lochlee, a large natural cavity, with a small opening, is still known as " Bonnymune's Cave." Here the " Rebel Laird" long contrived to evade his pursuers. Many in the neighbourhood not only knew that Balnamoon resided there, but made him their welcome guest on all safe occasions; and, notwithstanding heavy bribes and the vigilance of spies, his hiding-place was never divulged. The parish minister—a sworn enemy of Episcopacy—is said to have heartlessly put the enemy on the scent of this famous fugitive. One cold, wet day, when he had gone to the adjacent farmhouse to warm himself, and while sitting by the wide chimney of the kitchen, a party of soldiers entered the house in search of him. The farmer, urging them to partake of his hospitality, gruffly ordered Balnamoon (who was disguised in the ordinary garb of a hind, and frightened to leave the spot) to go and clean the byres, and give place to the strangers. The hint was enough. Balnamoon at once made himself scarce, and was safe in the retreat of his cave as soon as his feet could carry him to it. He was ultimately arrested, however, but being set at liberty in consequence of some "misnomer," he retired to his family seat; and, as long as he lived, showed his gratitude to the worthy farmer of Glenmark, by making him his familiar guest when he came to the low country.

Jervise, in his "Land of the Lindsays," takes Gillies to task for the *stories* he tells in his "Memoirs of a Literary Veteran" about the "Rebel Laird." "Of all these Carnegies," Jervise says "the most conspicuous was he who married the heiress of Findowrie, and who, with a company of vassals, bore a prominent part at the battles of Preston, Falkirk, and Culloden. He was governor of Forfarshire on behalf of the Prince. Although he was remarkable for humour and conviviality, it is not to be concluded that he was the illiterate Goth who is said to have cut the fine old books of his ancestors to fit the crazy wooden shelves. It has been shown that he not only was married and left a family, but that he also, to a considerable extent, augmented his patrimony by purchase. And although it cannot be said on any authentic grounds that he was the author of the popular old song of "Low down in the broom" (which is generally ascribed to him), the intelligence which was requisite to fulfil the important and trustworthy office, which he held during "the forty-five," ill agrees with the sottish and illiterate character certain writers would give him.

"The Rebel Laird" was succeeded by his eldest son, who died unmarried in 1810, when his nephew, James Carnegy Knox, son of the proprietor of Keithock and Markhouse, came to the property, and assumed the name Carnegy-Arbuthnott. He was married to a daughter of Mr David Hunter of Blackness, and by her he had a family of four sons and five daughters. He died in 1871 at the patriarchal age of 80 years, and was buried at Menmuir. His four sons all predeceased him. His eldest surviving daughter—Anne—succeeded to the estates. She died about two years after that event, and her next sister—Helen—became proprietrix. Through her liberality and public spirit the name of Miss Carnegy-Arbuthnott of Balnamoon became a synonym for all that was considerate and kind, and she was a liberal supporter of all public charities. She died in June 1892, and the estates went to her sister, Mary Ann, wife of Mr Arthur Capel, East India merchant, London, whose eldest surviving son, James Carnegy-Capel, was married in 1894 to Ethel Lydia Hill, eldest daughter of Mr Arthur Gibson Hill, of Walton Brough, East Yorkshire.

Before referring to Little Brechin—where we arrive a few minutes after again reaching the public road, which we left on entering the "drive"—it is worthy of mention that Balhall, a property in the neighbourhood, is associated with families of distinction. We have already referred to the tragedy on "The Moss of Balhall," and also to "Beattie's Cairn" and the "Mis-sworn Rig," on the northern confines of the estate. Previous to 1440 it was possessed by Sir John Glen of Inchmartin—a forebear of the same name being one of the ten barons selected to make the peace of Scotland with Edward I. in 1305. It was afterwards owned by Sir David Lindsay of Edzell, by a descendant of the old Lairds of Aldbar—Hercules Cramond, and the Hon. David Erskine of Dun. It continued in that family until it was sold, along with the patronage of the church of Menmuir to Alexander Erskine, who became heir-male and chief of the Erskines of Dun, and died in 1855. Balhall then became the property of his two daughters, Mrs Ellis and Mrs West, who each received a portion of the estate, which was then termed Easter and Wester Balhall. Captain Scott, a nephew of Mrs Ellis, is now owner of the former, while Miss E. M. West is proprietrix of the latter.

Little Brechin.

> Some o' the hoosies are biggit wi' divots,
> An' covered wi' wattles an' thatch;
> An' O, sic bonnie kail-yairdies—
> A' buskit wi' daisies an' thyme,
> Applerenzie, an' flow'ries wi' tamies
> Dauld Rob in himsel' cou'dna rhyme.

The earliest mention we find of Little Brechin is in the year 1728, in which year the Town Council of Brechin resumed the practice, forborne for some years, of riding their marches. They also then feued off a piece of the Muir of Brechin to John Ogilvie, under the name of "Little Brechin," and this grant was soon followed by other feus. The village is within two miles to the north of the City of Brechin, and is about the centre of that tract of ground denominated "Trinity Muir," of which the Town Council of Brechin are the superiors. The incorporations became alarmed in case all the "common guid" was to be sold off, so that, to quiet them, the Council, in 1729, voted a sum in name of a grant to the poor's box of the six trades, and as a consideration for their trouble in riding the marches.

The village of Little Brechin consists of a number of cottages and small "holdings" and "lairdships" scattered picturesquely about. The only buildings of any pretension are the public school and school house, erected soon after the beginning of the days of School Boards. The houses are in the majority of cases plain, and of one storey, with fertile kail yards attached to them, and lying "east and west of the road," with a strong tendency to avoid anything like orderly arrangement. Here the usual branches of old-world village trades have taken their departure —such as the tailor, the joiner, the blacksmith, &c. —the soutar alone being left. His sign may be "a wee thocht agee," but is he not also the dealer in a heterogenous assemblage of scones, pencils, paraffin, newspapers, and tape. He is a man of "weicht" in many respects, for he is the Provost of the place, and also the postmaster. Indeed on one occasion the Postmaster-General sat on his stool and listened attentively while John expressed his opinion on subjects of vital importance.

Murlingden

Is our next point of interest. The estate has been owned by several well-known families, and in 1889 it was purchased by Geo. M. Inglis, formerly Geo. M. Inglis of the well-known nitrate firm, Jas. Inglis & Company, Iquique, Chili. For the greater part of the year Mr Inglis resides in London, coming, however, during the shooting season, along with Colonel North, "the Nitrate King," and other friends, to " The Retreat," Lochlee, of which he has had a lease for a number of years.

Mr Inglis' brother, Mr David Inglis, who resides at St Ann's (noticed in our first tour), is proprietor of the island of Hoy, Shetland, and of the estate of Kergord, formerly owned by the late Mr D. D. Black, town clerk of Brechin. Both are cousins of the gifted and genial author of " Oor Ain Folk," and other works—the Hon. James Inglis, of Sydney, Minister of Education, New South Wales, regarding whose forebears we will have something to say as we proceed.

"Murlingden House," says M'Gregor Peter in his "Baronage," "is a neat yet massive mansion, having a portico supported by Corinthian columns. Over the portico is a window canopied by the effigy of a man standing on two steps. On each side of the doorway the front juts out semi-circularly—in semi-circle is placed three windows in each storey. It is flanked on west end with a wing of two lower storeys."

A reference to Murlingden would be incomplete were we to overlook its associations with the dreadful "plague" with which Brechin was visited in 1647-48. The session records state " there was no session, neither collection, from the 4th April, 1647, by reason the Lord inflicted the burgh of Brechin with the affecting sickness until the 7th November;" and even on the 7th November, when a collection is made, there is no session, by reason the ministers and elders are afraid to keep company, or, as the records of the *Landward* session bear, "be reason the moderator and remanent sessions feared to convene under one roof." A stone in the old churchyard of Brechin records that, in 1647, no less than six hundred died of the plague in Brechin in the course of four months. Another stone, placed between double columns, supporting a Saxon arch, records the death in that year of Bessie Watt, spouse of *bailzie* David Donaldson, and their daughters, Elspet and Jean, all of whom most probably also died of the plague.

Tradition asserts that the more deeply afflicted of the town's people were sent to the common muir, where huts were prepared for them, and that there they were allowed to die unheeded, and be buried by their surviving fellow-sufferers. The latter part of this story, however much it may savour of inhumanity, is by no means improbable, and the first portion is corroborated by the kirk-session records, where entries occur, in the months of January and October 1648, of payments having been made by the kirk-session to several persons who are described as " lying in *the sickness in the huts*." Record is silent as to the precise place of the exile of these unfortunate creatures, but tradition affirms that the estate of Murlingden, which was feued off the common muir, received its name in consequence, and was known of old as *Mourningden*. A burn runs through that den towards Cruick Water, and the sides of the den seemed at one time as if studded here and there with artificial works about six feet square, surrounded by low walls of mud or turf. Tradition also says that, instead of the weekly markets being held in the town at that time, they stood upon the estate of Kintrockat, about two miles to the westward, and also that a caldron was used for purifying the money which was exchanged on these occasions.

THIRD TOUR. 175

The pestilence seems to have continued in and around Brechin for the greater part of the year 1648, for in January the treasurer of the session takes credit for thirty shillings (Scots of course), " given to William Ross lying in ane hutt ;" while in August it is twice recorded there was " no session be reason the infection was begun again in the toun ;" and finally, in October £3, 12s additional are given " to buy malt and meall to those in the *hutts*." " These huts," says David Black in his " History," " are said to have been erected in the Glen of Murlingden, and before the present garden of that property was made out we remember small mounds at different places which were reported to have been huts or houses pulled down over the inmates who had died there of the plague."

Mr Colin Gillies, one of the former proprietors of Murlingden, war a man of great enterprise. He was not only a flour and corn merchant, but owned several extensive spinning, bleaching, and weaving factories in the counties of Angus and Mearns. He contributed the linen statistics to Sir John Sinclair's great work, and was for several years Provost of Brechin. Indeed throughout the counties he is said to have had more influence than any individual trader —until 1811, when fortune took a turn.

Mr Gillies belonged to a remarkable family. His father, Robert, was a merchant in Brechin, and there was a large family of sons and daughters. John, the eldest, was the well-known historian of Greece, and author of many other works. Before reaching his twentieth year, he attained such proficiency in the Greek language, that he was appointed teacher of the University Class during Professor Moore's last illness, and would have succeeded to that chair on Moore's death had he not preferred a journey to the

Continent, whither he went as guardian to the sons of the Earl of Hopetoun. On the death of Dr Robertson he was appointed Historiographer-Royal for Scotland, and died in 1836, at the advanced age of ninety. Though his pursuits were of a classical and historical character, he had a clear perception of the ludicrous, and entertained his friends with couplets descriptive of the peculiarities of the more singular *characters* of his native town. He epitaphised a maternal relative, who was bred a shoemaker, but preferred the more exhilarating avocation of a *courier*, and other out-of-door exercises, to his immediate calling :—

"Here lies John Smith, shoemaker by trade,
Who wore more shoes than ever he made."

Dr Gillies' youngest brother, Adam, was Sheriff of Kincardineshire, and was raised to the bench in 1811. He was a judge of high authority, of few words, and terse argumentation; and, unlike his learned predecessor, who loved to use the broad Scotch dialect, he affected an ignorance of it, and assumed the English accentuations. While on circuit on one occasion, a case came before him, in which some of the witnesses examined were natives of Brechin. In course of giving evidence, one of them, an old man who had known Gillies from his infancy, happened to give the name of the article *hat* the sharp provincial accentuation of *het*. His Lordship immediately interrogated the deponent—"What do you mean by a *het*, sir?" "I thocht," said the unabashed witness, "that yer honour had been lang eneuch aboot Brechin to ken what a *het* was!"

On leaving the pretty grounds of Murlingden by the some gate as we entered we hold direct for the Ancient City. Crossing the "Cattle Rake," which before the days of railways was the droving road between Aberdeen and Perth, we ascend the hill, and on the right, before entering Brechin, pass the old estate of Cookston, now known as Cookston Farm.

In 1766 the Dove Wells of Cookston were purchased from the proprietor of that estate, and water was introduced into the town by means of lead pipes, the expenses being defrayed by an assessment of 1s per £, laid on for fifteen years. The water was of excellent quality, but increase of population in the course of a very few years led to the introduction of a supply from Burghill. This too was inadequate, and ultimately, in 1874, the Mooran Water Supply was brought in, which has proved plentiful for the wants of the town.

In 1694 Mr John Carnegie, laird of Cookston, and his son are said to have " almost mastered the burgh " through a dispute about the giving off to Mr Carnegie part of the adjoining Loan. A Commission sat on the subject in Edinburgh, and the record narrates that " young Carnegie had, four years previously, struck Alexander Low, a burgess, in his own house, and had broke Bailie Cowie's cart, and therewith forced open his outer gate, and the windows of his dwelling-house, and, finally, fired a gun at the worthy bailie when standing at his own window ; and that Carnegie, being imprisoned for this riot, had broke the jail and come out of it with a cocked pistol and drawn sword ; for all which he is directed to be prosecuted. But the minute holds out the olive wreath, provided the bailies and town-clerk can agree with Cookston regarding the Loan ; and we rather infer that such agreement had been made, for next day " James Carnegie, younger of Cookston," is created an honorary burgess, and we hear no more of the matter.

Passing under the new Forfar and Brechin Railway, we find, on the right, Springfield House (Captain Cargill), and reach the Ancient City at the widely known North Port Distillery, an establishment erected on the site of the old Gallows Hill.

Assured of receiving a kindly and substantial welcome, we enjoy the soothing quiet and pleasant reflection that follow a well-spent day, after having arranged on the following morning to seek out scenes where

> Mossy crag and mountain grey,
> An' rain-brew'd spates a-roarin',
> Yield us delight. Then onward stray—
> They're there for your adorin'.

Fourth Tour.

TRINITY VILLAGE, NEWTON MILL, INCHBARE, EDZELL, THE MOORAN, THE WOODS OF THE BURN, GLENESK, TARFSIDE, LOCHLEE, INVERMARK CASTLE, THE QUEEN'S WELL, &c.

TO-DAY we intend to explore the beauties of Glenesk and district with such feeling of enjoyment of the beautiful and sublime as we are capable of. To enable the visitor to accomplish this all the more successfully we commend him to furnish himself with our "Historical Guide to Edzell and Glenesk Districts," which fully and attractively describes their picturesque scenery, antiquities, and curious traditions. Thus provided, it is only necessary for us in this tour to touch briefly on the more outstanding features of interest.

As there are no hotels in "the Glen," it is necessary to provide "for man and beast" before starting. Excellent provision is made for the journey by all our local hirers, whose 'busses and other traps await the arrival of visitors for Edzell at all the trains. They have also trustworthy and experienced men for the use of private parties; while Mr Knowles' (Crown Hotel) splendidly equipped four-in-hand coach—"Ye Olden Times"—is in waiting, as in the "good old coaching days," from June to September as advertised—though the Brechin and Edzell Railway, now in course of formation, may to some extent soon change these arrangements. However, we have to do with the present, and the sleek and well-groomed horses seem impatient to start; the red-coated driver handles the "ribbons" with that calm expression of face that betokens entire confidence in himself and his team, while the guard, also in scarlet and top boots, assists, in a civil and obliging manner, the passengers to take their seats. The guard blows a blast on the horn, and we are off.

A piece of ground termed "Kirk Dun Keyis," is described in a charter of 1578 as lying between the lands of Unthank and Caldhame, on the east side of the road leading to Unthank, being, as we understand, says Black, "the first field of that property on the east side of the road, going northwards from Brechin."

Trinity.

Again passing under the Forfar and Brechin Railway, we have, on the right, as we ascend "Unthank Brae," Glencadam House (the residence of Ex-Provost Lamb), embowered amongst luxuriant foliage.

TRINITY MUIR ON MARKET DAY. (From a Painting by D. Waterson, Brechin)

FOURTH TOUR.

One mile to the north of Brechin, on the left, we have Trinity Muir, notable as the site of the old-established markets for the sale of sheep, cattle, and horses (at one time ranking next in importance to the Falkirk Trysts, but now fast dying out owing to the popularity of Auction Marts.) There is also the collecting reservoir of the Brechin Water Works.

The Mooran Burn, which is the source of the supply, springs from the top of Craig Soales, one of the spurs of the highest mountain of the Grampian range, in the Glenesk district. About three miles from the source of the stream, and about two miles from the Bridge of Mooran, are the Brechin Water Works, the collecting reservoir being constructed in a naturally formed basin, almost entirely surrounded with hills. The water is conveyed in pipes, by way of Edzell, to the reservoir at Trinity Muir, large enough to hold a six days' supply to the town, at the rate of 300,000 gallons per day. The whole water route is twelve miles in length, and the total cost of the scheme amounted to £15,000. The water was "turned on" at the Trinity Muir reservoir on the 10th October, 1874, by Lord Dalhousie, C.B., (Lord Ramsay, of Glenmark, 1875). His Lordship succeeded to the titles and estates on the death of his cousin, Fox Maule, 11th Earl of Dalhousie, in 1874. He died at Dalhousie Castle in 1880, and the above was his first and only "public function" in Brechin, for although he had spent a long and honourable career in the service of his country, he seldom spoke in his old age at public meetings, though he took a deep interest in public matters.

Trinity—a thriving and prettily situated village, next arrests our attention. Its site was sold by the Brechin Town Council in 1836 to a number of persons who erected neat residences. Recently quite a number of handsome villas have been erected. It is the centre of numerous pleasant walks, and is accordingly a popular resort for summer lodgers. Half a mile further, to the right, is Cairnbank, past which leads to Huntly Hill, the scene of the Battle of Brechin, in 1452, to which we will refer in another tour. Another half-mile along the turnpike, and the road to the left leads to Edzell, Lethnot, and Lochlee, passing the ancient mansion-houses of Keithock, and of Newtonmill. Keithock is now owned by Mr M'Nab, formerly of East Lothian, while Mr Alex. Adams is the proprietor of the latter estate, and has lately greatly improved it by the erection of neat and pleasantly situated cottages. It was formerly owned by Captain Livingstone Ogilvie, the representative of Sir George, sixth and last Baronet of Barras. This family obtained the baronetcy for their services in preserving the ancient Regalia of Scotland during the siege of Dunnottar Castle.

On crossing the Bridge of Cruick, a fine view of the Grampians is obtained, with the celebrated fort of Caterthun, three or four miles to the left. About half a mile to the left is the Kirkyard of Stracathro (or valley of the king's battles), the scene of King John Baliol's penance to Edward I. in 1296. Previously, in 1130, a battle was fought in the same neighbourhood between David I. and Angus, Earl of Moray, which ended in the defeat of the latter.

We now reach the hamlet of Inchbare, with its rural Post Office, its general merchant and tailor's beild. The agricultural implements at, and the horse-shoe on, the door of another biggin' tells, in unmistakable terms, where the smith is located, and we perceive at a glance where the joiner's establishment is by the bright-coloured carts without wheels strewn helplessly

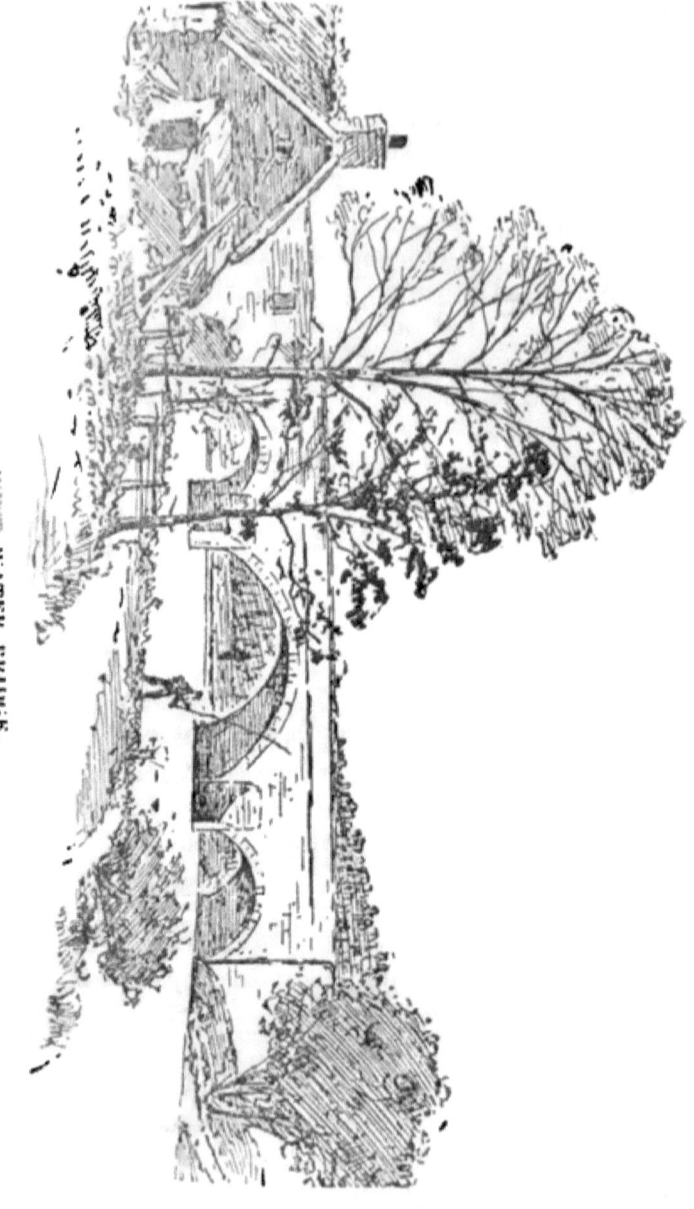

WEST WATER BRIDGE.

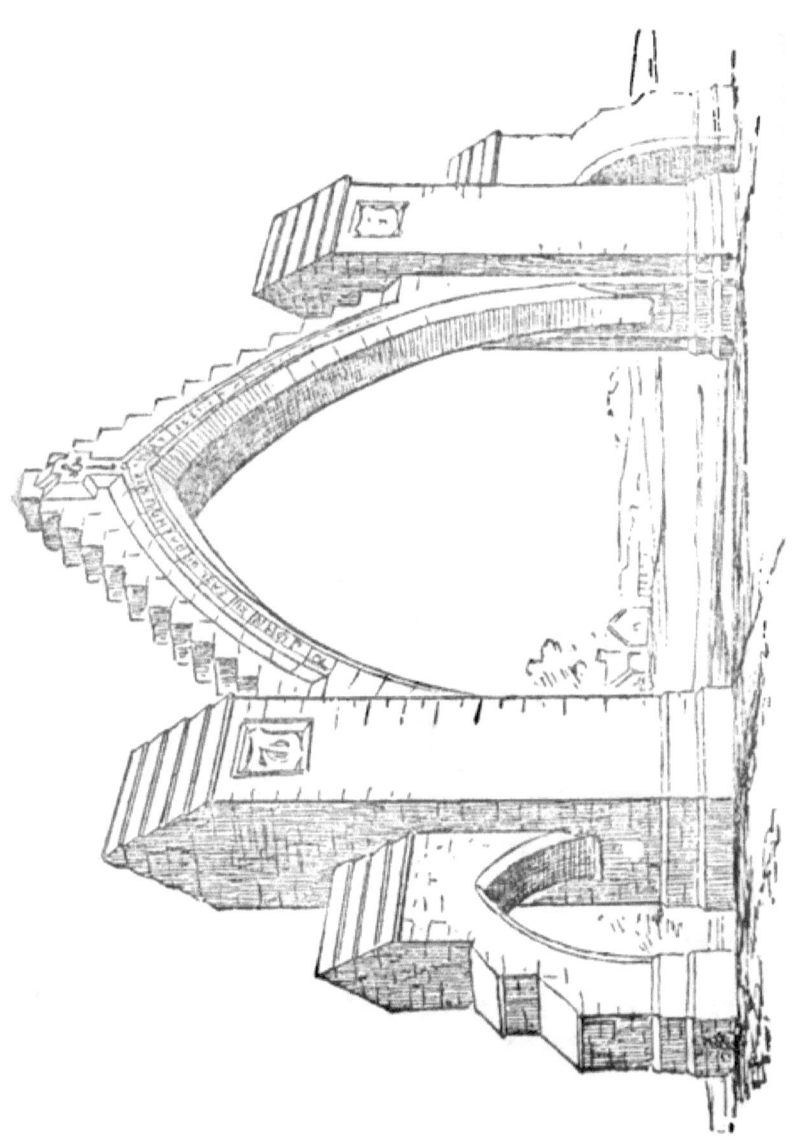

about on the ground, and the wheels without carts lazily lying against the wall. The view up and down the river from the **West Water Bridge** is very pleasing.

> All things are beautiful; if we survey
> The mighty landscape, stretching far away,
> We see the level valley seem to rise
> In beauteous lines, until it meets the skies.
> The sweet perspective of each grove, where trees
> Diminish as they rustle in the breeze.
> The wide-spread river looks a little rill,
> And shadowy azure gathers round each hill.

THE DALHOUSIE MEMORIAL ARCH.

A run of a little over two miles along a splendid level road, and we pass through the Dalhousie Arch, erected in 1889 by the tenants on the Brechin Castle, Edzell, Lochlee, and Lethnot estates, in memory of John William Ramsay, 13th Earl of Dalhousie, aged 40, and his Countess, Ida Louisa Bennet, aged 30, who died—the former on 25th, and the latter on 24th November 1887. The arch, which is 18 feet high, commemorates the memory of a much-loved, tender, and true-hearted nobleman, who devoted during his short life that personal attention to the affairs of his tenantry, which, coupled with the absolute honesty of the man and his sincerity of purpose manifested in all he did, endeared him to the hearts of all classes. In the structure the nature of the surrounding landscape has been kept in view. In the distance is the old, roofless, ivy-clad tower of the "Lichtsome Lindsays." In the crumbling walls and ruined tower of Edzell Castle we have the past vividly imaged in stone and lime—rigid, but with traces of decay. Beyond is many a dark, purple hill, in the bosom of which lie many a bonnie green glen. The design of the arch,

L

too, partakes a good deal of what one might imagine the entrance to a stronghold in lawless times. But although the monument suggests much of the old baronial style, "peep" through the arch, and see the quiet, cheerful-looking village, and its peace-loving inhabitants; think of the industrious and contented tenantry, and we at once realise that the times are changed.

Edzell.

We have now reached the clean and salubrious village of Edzell. This neatly-built village is much resorted to by summer visitors for its dry situation, healthful air, riverside walks, and romantic scenery. Fifty years ago, the houses were mostly of one storey, thatched, and by no means well built. Now, the march of improvement is conspicuous. It has a number of (but still too few for the requirements of the numerous summer visitors), superior houses, instead of its former mud cottages, a Gas Work, Post Office, Bank, Established and Free Churches, Schools, Literary Society and Reading-Room, Horticultural Association, Bowling and Curling Clubs, Golf Course, Annual Games, two excellent inns, and, during summer, a very fashionable society.

The village consists of two parallel streets with connecting thoroughfares. The cottages are neat, with little front plots smiling with many coloured flowers, and back gardens for vegetables. There are several handsome villas, with tastefully laid-out grounds and healthy-looking laburnam, lilac, and mountain ash trees. About the middle of the principal, or High Street, a lane strikes off to the right, by which the river can be reached. The first object which arrests the attention is the airy-looking suspension bridge, already mentioned, over the North Esk for foot

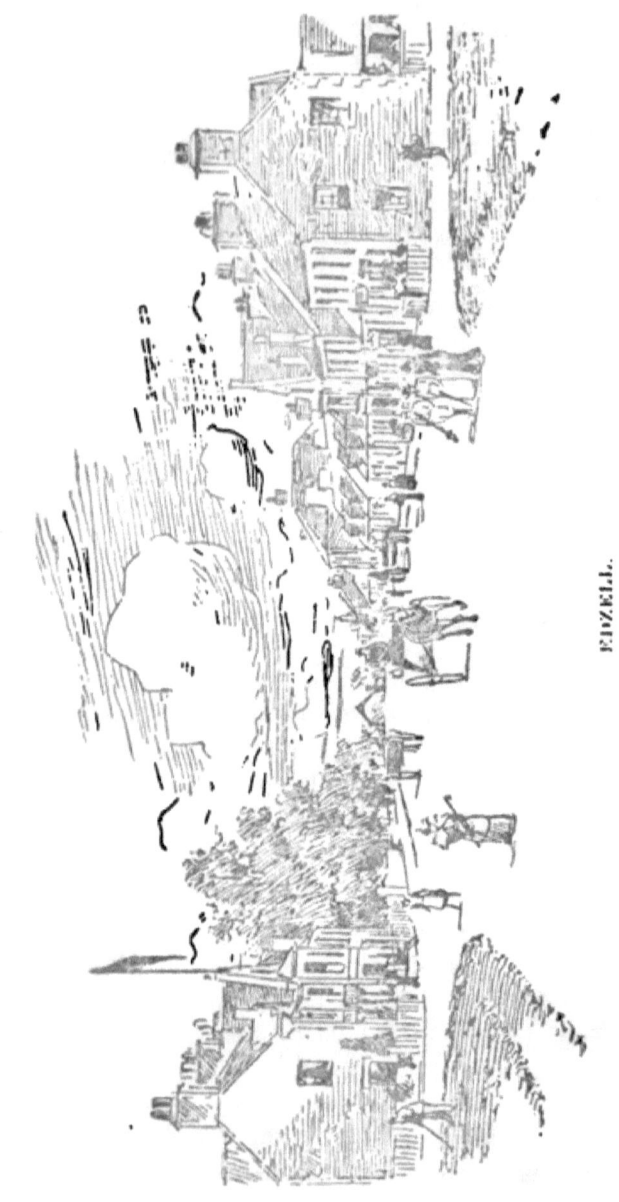

FOZELL.

passengers. It connects not only the two banks, but also the counties of Forfar and Kincardine—the river being the march of the two counties from above this place and downwards to the sea. For the information of those who visit Edzell for the benefit of their health, we may mention that, about a mile below the suspension bridge at Arnha', is a mineral well of rare medicinal value.

Pursuing our course up the right bank, we find the road gradually ascending, and the aspect of the river changing at almost every turn. The woods begin to gather about it, first on the one side and then on both, and the banks get higher. Now the stream is spread over a rough bottom, and goes brawling along, and then it is sweeping on, dark and silent, under the overhanging woods. On the opposite side the bank appears the height of two ordinary trees, and the foliage in all the glorious richness of summer is piled up in every variety of beauty. Far down below the path there are rich coronals of ferns, with tall fronds, while now and again a dripping tributary enters the stream from either side. The blossom of the rowan scents the air all around. By and by the banks get higher and higher; thence different ranges of trees are seen on the opposite bank, and the river bottom becomes rough and bold, with the cropped out strata of hard rocks, which, jutting out at an acute angle toward the north-west, catch the stream as it were right in the teeth. The rocks are worked into little caverns, and the stream is broken up into pools and eddies. A waterfall rushes down the rocky bank, bespangling the leaves of the trees with glittering drops, and filling the dell with sound. Here the path leads on to Gannochy Bridge.

But at present we return to the village, one mile

distant, by the high road, which cuts through the centre of the common ground or muir. On the green is ample space for cricket, golf, and bowling, and also a curling pond, while opposite the Panmure Arms Hotel is a flag-staff and seats for invalids who may not be able to take long strolls.

Here we also find the church, with tower surmounted by an open iron belfry of the most aerial type. In Vol. III. of Scott's "Fasti," we learn that the parish of Edzell was supplied by Mr Thomas Ramsay "reader," from 1567 to 1571. In 1644 David Fullarton was minister; and, living in troublesome times, he had no sermon 30th Nov., 1651, "the English army having come to quarter, and scattered all the people to goe and provyd corn and strae."

In 1714 the minister (Robert Gray) found the doors of the church shut one Sabbath morning, by order of the laird of Edzell, and therefore preached in the churchyard from the Song of Solomon iv. 16. "When his co-presbyter, Mr Johnston of Brechin, went to preach that day four weeks, he also found the doors shut and barricaded, and not only so but both he and the people he had brought with him were inhumanly and barbarously treated, and rabbled by a great many people whom David Lindsay of Edzell hounded out and hired for that purpose. The Lord's day following Mr G. was stopt on his way to church by those that were with the laird, who did violently beat several of those who came with him, with staves to the effusion of their blood, and thrust at the breasts of others, with naked knives and dirks, and violently beat them, and strike them with stones and rungs, and bruised them to that degree that some fainted, others lay dead on the ground for some time, and others they drove into the West-Water, running by the church, and forced them to wade, and pass hither and thither in the said water, until they were almost drowned. David L. of Edzell gave the rabblers money, with ale and brandy, to intoxicate them that morning."

The Reverend George Low, the eminent naturalist, was a native of Edzell, his father filling the humble office of beadle of the parish. He was the author of "Fauna Orcadensis," and accompanied Pennant in his famous Shetland tour.

As a whole day might have been enjoyably spent around Edzell, we, for the benefit of those desiring to do so, will, before proceeding further, refer to some of the places of historical interest and great natural beauty.

Edzell Castle.

> Green ivy cleeds the roofless wa's—
> An' through ilka arch the tempest blaws;
> While here and there, in dusky raws,
>   The feather'd nations
> O' howlets, kaes, and huddy-craws.
>   Haud consultations.

A mile to the left, along the Lethnot Road, are the extensive and imposing ruins of Edzell Castle. It stands in solemn dignity at the base of the lower range of the Grampian mountain-chain. Ancient-looking trees, mounds and grassy hillocks, quiet and impressive gloom, are the appropriate introduction to the silent and deserted ruin. With perhaps the exception of the Stirling tower, or the large square keep on the south side of the castle, the whole had been built by David, ninth Earl of Crawford, and his son, Lord Edzell.

The ruins, taken as a whole, are considered the most magnificent of any in the shires of Angus and Mearns, with perhaps the exception of Dunnottar, which rival them only in point of extent. It seems to have been admirably planned with a view to defence—loopholes being seen everywhere, and every approach and staircase commanded.

The garden wall is ornamented, as we have said, by a number of elaborate carvings in stone, and forms one of the most interesting memorials of the kind in Scotland. These artistic embellishments surround nearly half-an-acre of ground, which formed the flower garden, and greatly interest the visitor. The walls have representations of the celestial deities, sculptured on oval panels.

The castle, built at different periods, consisted of two stately towers connected together by what had been once a range of magnificent apartments. The walls of the keep are from four to six feet thick. The base floor of the tower consists of two damp, gloomy vaults, to which a glimmer of light is admitted through small apertures. These are supposed to have been wards or prisons for holding condemned prisoners.

The modern portion, which stretches from the keep northward, was the work of David of Edzell, and is now the most ruinous part. The foundations of old bathing rooms, at the south-west corner of the garden, were brought to light some years ago, and, together with the old picturesque summer-house, put into a good state of repair. The donjon, or Stirling Tower, to which we have already referred, is even yet an imposing and almost entire structure. The outer walls of the Castle are pretty entire; but the inner have suffered sadly, as have most of the vaults, which had been carried around the whole. Instead of being strewed with rushes, or decorated with tapestry, as in the olden time, the acrid nettle, and other indigenous weeds, until recently, luxuriated on the floors and crumbling walls, and the screech owl and raven nestled in the crevices.

Now, the smooth surface of the enclosed court or garden is beautiful with neatly-trimmed grass, and has a well-kept walk round it. Everything possible is now done to keep the ancient pile in preservation. The grounds have been trimmed with excellent taste, and the bare and solemn surroundings are in keeping with the sombre air of departed grandeur which pervades all ruins, while sympathising Nature sits silent around.

The Castle of Edzell was honoured with the presence of Mary, Queen of Scots, on the 25th of August, 1562, while her Majesty was on her well-known northern expedition to quell the Huntly Rebellion. It was on her return, accompanied by Lords Murray, Maitland, and Lindsay (the last of whom afterwards forced her to resign the crown at Lochleven), that she held a Council, and remained for the night, from which time the room where she slept, though its locality is now unknown, was ever after called the Queen's Chamber.

From the magnificent style in which cookery was

conducted at Edzell Castle, and the liberality of its owners to the poor, it was familiarly known by the title of "The Kitchen of Angus." Oxen were roasted whole, and everything conducted in a correspondingly sumptuous style. Each day, after the family had dined, the poor of the parish congregated in the courtyard, and, taking their seats on the stone benches (which still remain on both sides of the outer entrance passage), received their quota of beef from the hands of the lady or daughters of "the proud house of Edzell."

The quaint old summer-house, in which a book for visitors' names will be found, is fitted up for the reception of visitors, of whom, since the ruins were cleared of rubbish, and otherwise put in order, there have been over 2000 annually. The house contains some fine specimens of oak carving preserved in frames. The room is fitted up with a stone table and seats, while the keeper occupies the upper floor, and courteously and very intelligently attends to the wants of the numerous visitors.

On two occasions since the Castle was deserted by the Lindsays in 1715, has the great kitchen fire been kindled, and a dinner cooked for the proprietor. The first was on the 2nd October, 1856, when Lord Panmure (Fox Maule, afterwards Earl of Dalhousie) was entertained within the flower garden by upwards of 200 of his tenantry. Then, on 1st Nov., 1882, the late Earl, John William, entertained his tenantry to a sumptuous banquet in a large marquee, erected in the ancient flower garden. The scene was one to be remembered. The gaunt skeleton-looking windows, and the niches above the elaborate carvings on the wall surrounding the old flower-garden, were lighted up by Padella lamps, and similar lamps were placed at intervals on the tops of the ruin, and throughout the whole buildings. In the darkness of the night the effect was very striking. The gathering of the tenantry in such a place, and the smoke seen re issuing from the chimney of "The Kitchen of Angus" was worthy of the name of Ramsay, and of one who was not like his "forebear," "the Laird o' Cockpen," merely "ta'en up wi' affairs o' the State,' but who dealt not only in kind words, but made good deeds the rule of his too short life.

> Well at thy feet might hal'owed Ceres bow,
> For countless debts her sons unto thee owe,
> Thy liberal hand supplied the needy day,
> And cheered the poor thro' life's sad chequer'd way,
> And with one voice, the wise of many creeds,
> Confessed thy worth, and hail d thy generous deeds.
> The honoured name was music to the ear—
> The needy's friend—and Scotland's pattern Peer.

THE OLD LAIRDS OF EDZELL, THE OLD CHURCH, CHURCHYARD, AND LINDSAY BURIAL VAULT.

It is worthy of remark that the old kirk was perhaps the earliest *slated* of our landward churches. So early as 1641, we are not only informed that a payment was make to "the sclaitter for poynting the kirk," but have a glimpse at the extras of over payments of the time in the curious item of "mair of drink silver to his boy, 6d." The old bell of St Lawrence was lost sight of for a long lapse of years, and was accidentally recovered by being dragged from the bottom of the old well of Durayhill, in the early part of the present century. It lay in the church down to the period of its demolition, and has since been completely lost sight of.

The old kirk and kirkyard were within the same delta as the original Castle, by the side of the West Water. Few rural burying grounds are more charmingly situated. Of the place of worship, where so many of the proud lords of Edzell and their humble retainers bowed the knee, there is little left. The vault was repaired by the Dowager Countess of Crawford and Balcarres in 1881. The vault underneath, that was built with the aisle in or just before 1549, by David Lindsay of Edzell, the ninth Earl of Crawford, and in which he himself and his Countess were laid, was also cared for. It will be felt that these repairs were a becoming tribute due to the memory of one of the most honoured families in Forfarshire, and entirely agreeable to the great respect in which the name is still held. Down to the year 1818, when the present place of worship was erected at the village, the church stood within the burial ground. A broken octagonal-shaped font, about 20 inches in diameter, of rude workmanship, is preserved within the aisle; and also fragments of a tombstone, bearing the Lindsay arms, much defaced. These fragments are the only visible record of the Lindsays at the church of Edzell.

The first Lindsay of Edzell was Sir Alexander, a lineal descendant of Walter of Lindsay, an Anglo-Norman, who came to Scotland about 1116. Sir Alexander acquired to lordships of Edzell, Lethnot, and Glenesk, by marrying Katherine, a daughter and co-heiress of Sir John of Stirling. Sir Alexander's eldest son succeeded to his mother's patrimony; and in 1397, on the death of his uncle, Sir James Lindsay, of Crawford, he became chief of his family, and heir to the Lindsay estates in Clydesdale, &c. He married Elizabeth, daughter of Robert II., and was created Earl of Crawford, 21st April, 1398. The fifth Earl was created Duke of Montrose, a title which none of his successors appear to have assumed, and when it was claimed by the late Earl of Crawford, the House of Lords gave an adverse decision, owing to some real or supposed restriction in the patent. His Lordship, who died at Dunnecht House, 15th December, 1869, aged 86, was Premier Peer of Scotland. He was succeeded by his eldest son, Lord Lindsay, author of the "Lives of the Lindsays," and other interesting works. His Lordship died at Florence, in Dec., 1880. His remains were brought to the family residence at Dunnecht, Aberdeenshire, and interred in a vault, which had been constructed shortly before, under his Lordship's directions. The sacrilegious rifling of the tomb, and the mysterious disappearance of the body in Dec., 1881, will still be fresh in the memory of the reader.

Sir David Lindsay left a daughter, who became the wife of the chief of the house of Dalhousie, and the mother of Sir Alexander Ramsay, a distinguished warrior. It is a remarkable circumstance that, after a period of more than five hundred years since this first inter-marriage of the families of Lindsay and Ramsay, a scion of the latter now owns the Castle of Edzell. In 1714 David Ramsay sold the Castle and estate of Edzell, and the estate of Glenesk, to James, fourth Earl of Panmure; and so the ancient possessions of the Lindsays in Glenesk became merged in the extensive properties of the House of Panmure. By an inter-marriage of the Houses of Maule and Ramsay a junior branch of the latter succeeded to all the estates belonging to the House of Panmure. The succession in the junior line failed at the decease of Fox Ramsay-Maule, second Baron Panmure in the Peerage of Great Britain, who became Earl of Dalhousie in the peerage of Scotland on the decease of his cousin, the Marquis of Dalhousie, Governor-General of India. In consequence, the Panmure estates all reverted to the elder branch of the house of Ramsay, which house is now represented by the youthful Earl, Arthur

George Maule-Ramsay, born at Brechin Castle, 1878. He was only in his 9th year at the time of the lamented death of his father, John William, 13th Earl of Dalhousie.

Space will not admit telling at any length the story of the avaricious sexton who attempted to secure the jewellery which loaded the body of a lady, buried in the Lindsay vault, while in a trance. Bent on obtaining the treasure at all hazards, he went, under night, and soon succeeded in putting himself in possession of the whole, except the massive rings which girded the swollen fingers. The idea of amputation flashed through his relentless mind, and instantly the fatal blade of his knife made a deep incision. A slight movement of the body followed, and the faint "Alas!" soon staggered his valour. With a heart grateful for the restoration of life, she kindly permitted him to retain his sacrilegious spoil, and the sexton was never more heard of. This and other traditions, as well as particulars of the ancient proprietors of these lands, will be found detailed in our "Guide to Glenesk Districts."

It serves our present purpose, however, and it will interest the visitor, to refer particularly to Sir David. His early life was a striking contrast to that of his later years. When young, he exhibited the hot-headed character of feudal times, and was indifferent to bloodshed. It has been said that later in life the sword, the pen, and the pruning-hook were equally familiar to his hand, as well as the geologist's hammer. He also had a taste for architecture and design, and his proficiency in literature is shown by the King making him one of the Lords of Session; while the extensive additions which he made to the Castle, begun by his father, are still apparent in the ruins of those gigantic and tasteful structures.

He re-built the garden wall in a style of architectural decoration almost unparalleled, representing the Theological and Cardinal Virtues, the Seven Sciences, the Planets, &c., in the allegorical style and manner of the fourteenth century, the sight of which still calls forth the admiration of every intelligent visitor.

DAVID, THE LAST LAIRD OF EDZELL.

The painful nature of the farewell visit of David, the last Laird of Edzell, is pathetically told as follows by Lord Lindsay, in his "Lives of the Lindsays":—

The Laird, like his father, had been a wild and wasteful man, and had been long awa'; deeply engaged with the unsuccessful party of the Stuarts. One afternoon the poor Baron, with a heavy heart, followed by one of a' his company, came to the Castle, almost unnoticed; a few old servants had been the only inhabitants for many months. The broken-hearted ruined man sat all night in the large hall, sadly occupied—destroying papers sometimes, sometimes writing, sometimes sitting mournfully silent—unable to fix his thoughts on the present or to contemplate the future. In the course of the following day he left the Castle in the same manner in which he had come: and, turning round to take a last look of the old towers, he drew a last long sigh, and wept. He was never seen here again.

He had two sisters, Margaret and Janet. Janet, who had been followed in her walks about Edzell by a pet lamb, fell the victim of a vile seducer, and died in England in infamy. Margaret became the wife of Watson of Aitherny, in Fife, and her visit to Edzell Castle Lord Lindsay has also told most touchingly:—

"Year after year passed away, and the Castle fell to ruin—the pleasance became a wilderness, and the name of the old proprietors was seldom mentioned, when a lady arrived one day at Edzell, in her own coach, and drove to the Castle. She was tall and beautiful, and dressed in deep mourning. 'When she came near the ancient burying-place,' says the same faint voice of the past (tradition), 'she alighted and went into the chapel. The poor lady wept sore at the ruin of her house and the fate of her family. After a while she came out, and was driven in a coach up to the Castle; she went through as much of it as she could, for stairs had fallen down and roofs had fallen in. She found her way to what in former days had been her own room, and there, overcome with sorrow, she sat down and wept.' And such was the end of the 'proud house of Edzell.'

The hospitable fire was quenched, the hearth was soon rendered desolate, and the place became the common rendezvous for traffickers in illicit goods. Thus the cherished abode of a long race of the most powerful barons of the Kingdom was reduced to its present condition; and the courtyard of the Castle no longer echoes with the war-cry of the mailed warrior issuing to battle, or rings with the tramp of his charger."

After many a glance at "the ancient tower of Edzell," as Sir Walter Scott calls the old pile, we climb up the rising ground behind, and rapturously gaze on the beautiful scene it commands. At out feet lies the noble Castle, and a little beyond are the picturesque kirkyard and the birch-fringed banks of the river. Here, in the summer evenings, noble maidens of the olden time would doubtless sit enjoying the fine prospect, and probably Mary, Queen of Scots, also sat here on the occasion of her visit in 1562. Time, however, will not permit us to linger. Suffice it to say that if we keep the line of the picturesque and pleasant road along the side of the West Water for three or four miles we reach Lethnot at the point we left it in our last tour.

> Yellow whins and bells of blue
> Mingle with the turf's green hue,
> While the thistle in his pride
> Woos the wild rose by his side.

The Bridge of Mooran.

We have a special feast of good things in store when we start our next tour, so that, as we have a rich treat as we journey onwards to-day, we hope our friends on reaching the Gannochy Bridge will merely stop for a few minutes and view the prospect up the North Esk—the lower part between this and Edzell having already been described—reserving until to-morrow investigating the folk-lore of a scene where unsurpassed

> Beauty and wildness meet together—
> Blend with the rocks, the woods, and heather.

Driving from Edzell to Glenesk, and just as we come in sight of the ivy-clad shooting lodge of Gannochy, to the left, the road to the Bridge of Mooran leaves the main road, and enters Glenesk on the west side of the river. As this is a scene of wild beauty not until recently known by tourists, we would do well to draw attention to it, as no more enjoyable drive or walk for an afternoon from Edzell could, amongst the many in the district, be suggested. It shows the Glen from a different standpoint than the Glenesk Road, and from the elevation attained you obtain wide and sweeping vistas of the beautiful scenery.

After passing above Gannochy the aspect of the country gradually changes from lowland fertility to the "land of brown heath and shaggy wood." The glen opens out between the hills, and glimpses of the silver waters of the Esk are caught between the glades of birch and hazel that fringe its banks. On the right, Mount Battock rears his bare bluff crest above his lesser satellites. On the left the spurs of Wirren creep down into the valley, forming beautiful green holms and sequestered glades.

Past the farm of Dalbog, cultivation ceases, and we now enter a region sacred to muirfowl and black cock —a wilderness solitude, the silence of which is unbroken save by the bleating of sheep on the hills, and the rushing of the mountain stream over its rocky bed.

A more delightful spot for a picnic than the plateau beside the bridge could not be desired. Here the rugged and the picturesque are admirably combined, and form a scene of natural beauty that would well repay the pencil of an artist. At this point the Mooran joins its waters with the North Esk. The Mooran, scarcely more than a Highland burn, cuts its way through a deep narrow glen, the banks of which are clothed with birks and hazel, through which the brawling stream is seen rushing over a boulder-strewn bed. A quaint old bridge of one arch spans the ravine about fifty yards from the meeting of the waters. Here the Esk has worked for itself a passage through a rocky barrier, and its stream, contracted to a few feet, rolls on, black and sullen, between the sandstone ramparts that rise, rugged and precipitous, on either side to a height of fifty or sixty feet. A dense growth of birch, rowan, alder, and pine wave on the summits and upper slopes of the lofty banks, their umbrageous shadows overhanging the stream in many parts.

In various parts of its course jutting crags on either side send the living stream with greater rapidity to the right or left, singing in chorus with the moaning of the wind among the trees on its banks, or hissing and roaring in unison with the wild howling of the breeze when boreas is making himself heard and felt.

On the opposite side (the site of the old Castle of Auchmull, to be referred to as we wend our course in Glenesk), the character of the river, and of the country through which it flows, becomes quite changed. Its upland freedom is curtailed, and its waters confined between steep and lofty rocky walls. The deep gorge into which it now enters commences near the Bridge of Mooran and is continued through the property of The Burn, and, as we have seen, some distance beyond.

The rank vegetation on little level spots under jutting rocks, the lofty cliffs covered with lichens which harmonise with the colour of the rock, the waving trees which here and there spring from the clefts and dells on each side of the stream, and other accessories unite to increase the picturesque grandeur of this wild gorge.

Scarcely anything can surpass the impressiveness of the rocks at this place, which, apart from the surrounding birks of Corneskorn, are shaded by a cluster of other trees of surpassing elegance and beauty. About two miles up the hill road and over a stretch of heather, the visitor will find the simple "intake" of the Brechin water supply referred to on page 181.

M

The Burn.

Resuming our route where we left it—at the Gannochy, and continuing for a short distance, turning to the left, we are soon overshadowed by the Woods of The Burn—the beautiful and romantic residence of Colonel M'Inroy. Many visitors, however, prefer to walk by the river side from the Gannochy, and arrange to meet their conveyances at the top of the woods. We purpose now doing so. With the exception of the private grounds between the mansion house and the bridge over the North Esk, above the house, visitors are allowed to walk by the river side. On both sides of the river there are fine walks, which are connected, a little below the house, by a beautiful suspension iron bridge. In several places the walls are cut out of the solid jasper-veined rocks, and thus

> We walk on stairs both up and down
> On gems might grace th' Imperial Crown.

The Burn is described as a place for which Nature has done much, by cutting out a pass about six miles in length, and surrounding it with heathy hills, and pouring through it the North Esk, a rapid mountain stream, which, from the peculiar nature of the rocks through which it flows, assumes the colour of dark purple wine, and, after rain, becomes " black as blood mingled with ink." Art has done her part in covering the sides of the pass with the richest and most varied woodlands; in spanning the stream with, here and there rustic foot-bridges, overlooking cataracts, up which you can often see the salmon leaping as if on wings of spray. The whole is surmounted with an old tower, standing lonely, at the very head of the pass, on its lofty crag, and looking down in pensive pride on the gorgeous chaos of hills, woods, crags, and waters; while the towering mountains in the background give grandeur to the landscape of an indescribably romantic and picturesque nature.

The late Rev. George Gilfillan said that, if he had the choice of a spot to die at, and were disembodied spirits permitted to choose some particular scene for an eternal sanctuary, his should be found by the side of those clustering woods.

Down to about the year 1780, when Lord Adam Gordon (Commander-in-chief of the forces in Scotland, and brother of Lord " Lewie Gordon," celebrated in Jacobite song), bought the Burn this beautifully-ornamented and wooded place was almost destitute of trees or shrubs, or of any sort of cultivation. No sooner, however, had his Lordship acquired possession than the work of improvement began, and as has been well said, by his disinterested labours, he, within a score of years, "created a desert into an Arcadian grove." Under his skilful treatment the grand natural scenery that had hitherto blushed unseen became a thing of beauty which has been a joy to many a tourist who has since visited the charming spot.

We are now winding ourselves into the bosom of those mountains which, at a distance, appeared as an effectual barrier against all intrusion. The wayside is agreeably fringed with the graceful birch and the rowan, while the modest wayside flower nestles humbly "low doon amang the broom." About a mile and a half above the Woods of the Burn, we arrive at the Bridge of Auchmull. Opposite the Burn of Auchmull, but almost lost to the view of the traveller, on the west side of the river, are, as we have seen, the Bridge and Burn of Mooran, the vicinity of which is perhaps the most romantic part of the North Esk. As we proceed, its windings open up new views, and a continual succession of pictures in every variety of colour, richly painted and drawn by the hand of Nature. These possess much of one character, yet they are diversified by details which the Master painter knows so well how to throw off with matchless skill and indescribable effect. No deformities of expression, no inconsistencies or incongruities mar the picture; sun and shade are profusely mixed together, giving endless changes to the varied scenery.

The hills are not generally abrupt, and being crowded together, they present a rounded outline.

They embrace, however, many a picturesque glen, cheered with its native burn, glowing with wild flowers, and sending up the peaceful smoke from the cottages in the midst of a cultivated patch. Large flocks of sheep speck the sides of the mountains, while the deer may occasionally be seen against the sky line peering from their summits.

Our road now necessarily lies along the river banks, from which the heath-clad hills rise abruptly, leaving but contracted haughs for the labour of the husbandman. Four miles from Gannochy Bridge, on the right, stood the old Castle of Auchmull, where young Lindsay took refuge after the murder of Lord Spynie, in the High Street of Edinburgh in 1607. This Castle was occupied by the farmer down to 1772, about which time he found it so inconvenient that he offered to bear the cost of a new house, provided the proprietor would allow him the wood and iron, and other materials of the Castle, with which to erect it. Unfortunately, this was acceded to, and ere long the famous refuge of the murderer of Lord Spynie was sadly mutilated; and the work of destruction, once begun, had only its limits in the complete annihilation of the stronghold. Only a small portion of the foundation is now traceable.

STONE CIRCLES.

We're round the knowe, whaur Druid folk
Communed aneth their sacred oak,
And shattered rocks o' ponderous size,
A feast for geologic eyes!
Wh ther they've drappit frae the skies,
    It mak's nae odds;
There's here what could Macadamize
    Our country's roads.

About seven miles from the Gannochy, we find ourselves descending into a beautiful valley, formed by an unusual recession of the mountains. Just as we begin the descent we find, on the right, and at a short distance from the road, a farm-steading, and, in its immediate vicinity, the remains of two of those stone circles, that have been called Druidical. These "Stannin' Stanes" of Colmeallie, as they are called in the district, are thought by some to have been temples, or places of heathen worship; by others, again, that they were used as primitive places of burial. The priests are said to have made the people believe that the rocking stones could be moved by the gentlest touch of those whose breasts were pure, but remained fixed and immovable when approached by traitors or other wicked individuals.

The circles of Colmeallie had been of the common concentric kind. The largest boulder lies on the ground, and is nine feet five inches long by seven feet five inches broad. Near a place called "Johnny Kidd's Hole," in Glenmark, and within the recollection of some of the oldest inhabitants, the Rocking Stone of Gilfumman was an entire and interesting object. This stone was long considered an infallible revealer of future events; but some sacrilegious individuals having turned it off its magic pivot, the spell was broken.

We now cross the Turret, which has its source in the springs of Mount Battock, and is the boundary line of the parishes of Lochlee and Edzell. On the east side of this water, between the bridge and the Esk, the shooting lodge of Millden, belonging to Lord Dalhousie, stands on a rising ground, surrounded with trees. The extent of the building, with its cone-roofed turrets, gives it quite a castellated appearance.

Here the "live and let live" Lord Panmure, who built the mansion, delighted to spend the summer during his later years, and hold familiar intercourse with his tenantry. He occasionally wandered *incog.*, and, disguised as a common beggar, would journey through his extensive possessions. In connection with these wanderings we give, in our "Glenesk," several humourous stories.

The bold mountain range, apparently terminating on the opposite side, is Wirran Hill, which stretches away towards the west. We are now getting upon a high level; and, looking around, are struck with the appearance of a conical protuberance on the brow of a hill, at a considerable distance before us towards our left. That is Craig Maskeldie, rising from the western end of Lochlee.

THE MASON'S TOWER.

A number of ancient funeral cairns have been found in various parts of the Glen. But the most conspicuous cairns are two modern erections, the one upon the Rowan Hill, and the other upon the Modlach. The former, which is pyramidical in its form, was erected by Fox Maule, Earl of Dalhousie, in honour of the ancient family of Maule; and the latter, which consists of a tower, with a place for shelter, was built by the Freemasons of Lochlee.

We are now moving along the side of the Hill of Modlach—*i.e.*, the law, or the hill of the court of justice, which may have been so named from the baron's court having assembled there. On the top of the hill stands the Mason's Tower, which has for some time attracted our attention. The brethren of the mystic tie (St Andrew's Lodge, No. 282, Tarfside) are said to occasionally walk to it in procession on the annual feast of their patron saint. This road was wont to be much steeper than it is now, for instead of winding along the side of the Modlach, it went over the hill. Here many unfortunate travellers lost their lives in snowstorms. It was mainly with the laudable view of lessening the number of these calamities that the Lodge of St Andrew's erected this Tower, and had recesses formed at the base of it, where benighted travellers could shelter in comparative safety.

Before coming to the pretty little clachan of Tarfside, we find our way agreeably fringed with the

graceful birch and the rowan, forming a pleasing contrast to the steep rugged barreness we have experienced for the past few miles. These are known as the Birks of Ardoch, among which, on the braeside on our right, is snugly ensconced the cottage appropriately called The Retreat, which was built by the late Admiral Wemyss, and is now occupied as a shooting lodge.

TARFSIDE.

A little further on we reach the well-sheltered and pleasantly-situated Free Church Manse, then the Free Church itself (Rev. J. Paul, minister), with its handsome tower, forming a conspicuous and suggestive feature of the landscape. Two beautiful stained glass windows are on each side of the pulpit—the one erected in memory of Lord Dalhousie by his sister, Lady Christian Maule, the other was presented by the family of the late Rev. Dr Guthrie. On the right hand we come to the neat buildings comprising the parish school and teacher's house. Close by, we find a two-storied house, the upper floor of which is the St Andrew's Mason Lodge. These, with a few other

cottages, form the village of Tarfside, now the only hamlet in the parish. Here we find also the merchant, from whom we can purchase

> . . . . ham and treacle, needles and teas,
> Loaves and razors, coal scuttles and cheese!

Also the shoemaker and the tailor—those handicraftsmen that are necessary for the convenience of every rural district—with the post office, and the haven of the weekly carrier to and from Brechin.

We get a glimpse of the neat Episcopal chapel (Rev. Mr Presslie), parsonage, and school on the right as we cross the Tarf, a little above its junction with the Esk. The new chapel—the church of St Drostan, the patron Saint of the Glen, whose memory is kept green by such names in the district as Droustie's Meadow, Droustie's Well, &c.—was erected in 1880 by Lord Forbes, as a memorial of his distinguished relative, the late Rev. Alexander Penrose Forbes, D.C.L., who for many years presided over the See of Brechin. In the east end of the church are three windows filled with stained glass—the Good Shepherd in the centre, and on the right and left St Andrew and St

Peter. We now cross the Bridge of Tarf, which, according to the quaint entry by the poet Ross in the parish register, was built for the purpose of allowing the poor " to pass and repass in quest of their living,"

and for people "coming and going to and from the church." The Tarf is a fine specimen of a mountain torrent, and the scene at the Bridge at Tarfside, when the river is in high flood, is extremely grand.

Besides the old foot-path, or Priests' Road, from Ponskeenie— a picturesque old bridge of three arches near Dalbrack—to Lethnot, there is a rugged road through Glenturret to Charleston of Aboyne. Another road leads from Lochlee by Glenmark and Mount Keen to Ballater, &c. Though seldom travelled, save by tourists, it was by the last-named route that Her Majesty the Queen and the late Prince Consort and suite came from Balmoral to Fettercairn.

We are now four miles beyond Millden, and within five of Lochlee. As we ascend the rising ground, we can still trace the remains of what had been numerous happy little homesteads, marked by tumbling walls and a solitary tree. We now note the "grey cairns" that are so numerous along the side of the

Rowan Hill on our right. This hill is represented as the scene of conflict between the followers of Bruce and those of Comyn, Earl of Buchan. The artificial looking cairns which we now pass are called the graves of the slain. Indeed, the name of the hill is said to have had its

origin in the adventure of that day, when, as tradition runs, the king rallied his forces by calling out *Row-in!*

Through the ravine on the opposite side of the Esk, flows the romantic Effock. It tumbles down a beautiful glen on the south side of the river, a mile below the head of the North Esk. Another mile brings us to the Branny, which hurries its tributary waters from our right to the Mark, and in the angle formed by the road and the stream, we find the Parish Church of Lochlee, encompassed by its graveyard.

The parish church and manse (Rev. Mr Stewart, minister) were both erected in 1803. Since then, with the exception of old residenters, who still have a natural desire to lie beside their kindred, the modern kirkyard has become the common place of burial. Some of the tablets in this graveyard are of more than ordinary interest, arising from the circumstances of a painful nature which they record. One marks the grave of an Aberdeen youth who perished amongst the snow; another records the death of two brothers who fell over a precipice while collecting their father's sheep.

A little onward, and the Mark, a larger tributary than the Branny—comes rolling from the same side, and in the angle formed by it and the Lee stands the tower of the old castle of Invermark. The meeting of the rushing waters, the bright foliage of the waving trees, the walls of the towering keep, and the noble mountains by which this spot is surrounded, unite in forming a scene of wondrous beauty. The Lee and the Mark, which had been previously joined by the Branny, here unite their waters, and become the North Esk.

> Gang forrit to the steep rock's broo—
> The angry torrent's roarin' fou,
> Splitting the quaking crags, and through
>   This ghastly rent,
> His everlasting, wild halloo
>   Is upward sent.

The Mark is considered the finest specimen of a mountain torrent within the whole boundary of the parish, and traverses a distance of ten or twelve miles through a singularly romantic district, which in many places presents an almost insurpassable wildness, and, in others, flat and undulating swards of the richest grass. In its course there are about a dozen different falls, but only half that number are more than cascades, though all have their own peculiarities, and each in its way is pretty. The Mark is joined by the Ladder Burn, and other burns from Mount Keen, and from the other lofty summits which form the watershed separating Glenesk from the Vale of the Dee. Here, and in other parts of Glenmark, rugged lofty precipices rear their scarred bald heads high in air, frowning defiance, inspiring awe, and casting their dark shadows over the stream and its emerald banks. Seen at a little distance, they appear to bar the way and stop farther progress, but as they are approached, the rugged paths open up, and admit to other kindred wilds. Glenmark is also interesting on account of its historical and traditional associations.

THE OLD CASTLE OF INVERMARK.

The most picturesque parts of Glenesk are in the neighbourhood of Invermark, where is yet to be seen the roofless and ivy-clad old stronghold of the "lichtsome Lindsay," with its curiously-constructed *yett*. The surrounding landscape will amply repay a visit. The Castle buildings occupy the crest of a green mount, and had originally been a place of considerable strength. It commands the opening of several glens, and formerly, when garrisoned by the feudal retainers, was well calculated to afford security to the inhabitants of the country lying around.

The Castle is supposed to have been built in 1526.

It was within this building that the ninth Earl of Crawford died, in 1558, bequeathing his soul "to the Omnipotent God, and the whole Court of Heaven," and his body to be buried "in his own aisle within the church of Edzell." The castle, at a later period, was one of the resorts of the Earl's unfortunate grandson, when skulking from the pursuit of justice for the murder of Lord Spynie. After the forfeiture of the Earl of Panmure, it became the property of the York Buildings Company, and now, instead of the banner of the Lindsays, the mountain rowan waves from the crumbling wall.

> An ancient house, and a noble name,
> An honest heart, and a spotless fame
> By the viper's sting, and the demon of play,
> Shall be blighted, and lost for ever and aye

Down to the beginning of this century, the Castle was in much the same state of preservation as during the palmy days of the Lindsays, being entered, we are told, by a huge drawbridge—one end of which rested on the door sill of the second floor, and the other on the top of a strong isolated erection of freestone, which stood about twelve feet south of the front of the tower. This was ascended on the east and west by a flight of steps, and the bridge being moved by machinery, the house was rendered inaccessible at the will of the occupant. The heavy door, of grated iron, which was erected by Royal permission, is now reached by a flight of worn stones. This door is said to have been manufactured of iron, found in the neighbourhood, and smelted at a place called Bonnie Katie, on the banks of the Tarf, where Lord Edzell had a furnace.

At the time alluded to, it was surrounded by the old offices, which were tenanted by shepherds, while the main building was occupied by two maiden ladies,

but when the present church and manse were erected, the offices were torn down, and the tower completely gutted, to assist in their erection. We may here mention that, in 1593-4, smelting-houses were erected in various parts of this district for "minerals of gold, silver, brass, and tin." Sir David Lindsay and his brother, Lord Menmuir, were so eager to ascertain the extent of these, that miners were brought from Germany and other places.

The only floor now in the Castle is that formed by the roof of the vault. The dark dungeon below, into which only a faint glimmer of light is admitted through those loop-holes common to the baronial remains of the period, is reached by a crazy stair, but presents nothing of note. It is thought probable that the site of Invermark Castle had been that of previous strongholds, from the fact that it commands the important pass of Mount Keen to Deeside. The garrison of Invermark, though tending greatly to diminish the number of invasions by the troublesome Cateran, does not appear to have been altogether effectual, for in one of their inroads they are said to have carried off about half of the cattle and sheep in the Glen. In the language of Ross in his "Helenore;"

> Nae property these honest shepherds pled,
> And all alike, and all in common fed.
> But ah! misfortune! while they fear'd no ill,
> A crowd of Kettrin did their forest fill;
> On ilka side they took it in wi' care;
> And in the ca' nor cow nor ewe did spare.
> The sakeless shepherds stroove wi' might an' main
> To turn the dreary chase, but all in vain;
> They had nae maughts for sic a toilsome task,
> For bare-fac'd robbery had put aff the mask.

Opposite the old Castle is the parish manse, which, in 1803, was erected of material from the castle. The manse is said to occupy the site of the public-house of Drousty, which had been as welcome to the traveller over Mount Keen, as the castle was terrible to the hostile invader.

The bard of "The Minstrel," in his poetical address to his old friend Ross, after complimenting him on the beauty of his "Helenore," takes occasion to speak thus of the inn:

> But ilka Mearns an' Angus bairn,
> Thy tales and sangs by heart shall learn;
> And chiels shall come frae yont the Cairn
> O' Mount, richt vousty,
> If Ross will be so kind as share in
> Their pint at Drousty.

In the neighbourhood of the parish manse we have Lochiemore, where the shop of the general merchant once held out its varied commodities. A saying connected with this place indicates the manners of a former age. When one neighbour asked another, "Weel are ye gae'n to the kirk the morn?" the answer would not unfrequently be, "I dinna think it, man: for there's neither snuff at Lochiemore, nor good ale at Drousty;" as they had taken the opportunity when in the neighbourhood to replenish the *mull*, before going to church, and to prove the quality of the ale at the close of the service. The receptacle of "snuff and tobacco" is now swept away, and the manse has supplanted the ale-house, and the minister kindly gives the use of his stable—a privilege that is frequently very gratefully taken advantage of.

But we now observe on the brae before us the handsome shooting quarters, twice honoured by Her Majesty the Queen, called Invermark Lodge. It is sheltered among the natural birches, and commands an extensive view.

FOURTH TOUR. 217

This is a spot of rare beauty—the rocky mountains of Invermark forming the background. The lodge overlooks the Loch and water of Lee—" the auld kirkyard," the peak of Craig Maskeldie, and a variety of other points of great natural beauty, with a gently sloping lawn to the south making up a complete picture of Highland scenery. Composed of rough native rock, it is built in the fine picturesque style of

old English architecture; and while harmonising with the surrounding cliffs, forms a pleasing contrast to the towering ruins of Invermark Castle. It was built in 1854; and about the same time the whole north-western part of the Glen was thrown into a deer forest, which, united with the extensive preserves of the late Prince Consort and the Earl of Airlie on the north-west, and those of the Marquis of Huntly on the north-east, form one of the finest and most extensive sporting fields in Great Britain.

Leaving Invermark Lodge, we can either turn to the right towards the "Queen's Well," or to the left, and visit the ruins of the old church and the Loch. We prefer taking the former route first. A nicely laid-out walk takes us past the shooting targets, and through the birches to a wooden bridge across the Mark, about half a mile distant from the Lodge, where we get on to the path to

THE QUEEN'S WELL.

Looking up Glenmark, which we have already alluded to, and which stretches away in a north-westerly direction, reminds us that most of the roads that the visitor might take, in proceeding from the upper districts of Deeside into Glenesk, would converge in this beautiful Glen. Perhaps the chief attraction of this locality to the tourist is "The Queen's Well," so-named on account of its sweet waters having refreshed the Royal party on their visit to Lochlee over the hills from Balmoral.

In commemoration of this event, and the death of the Prince shortly afterwards, the noble Earl (Fox Maule)

had the memorial erected. The well has been surrounded with six flying buttresses composed of granite, which, rising to the height of nearly twenty feet, form by their union an imperial crown, surmounted by a cross. The structure is ten feet in width between the buttresses, and the water flows into a basin, bearing, in raised letters, the following:

> Rest, traveller, on this lonely green,
> And drink and pray for SCOTLAND'S QUEEN—

a request loyally complied with by visitors to this enchanting spot. A black marble slab, inserted in one of the buttresses, is thus inscribed:

> Her Majesty, QUEEN VICTORIA,
> and His Royal Highness the PRINCE CONSORT,
> visited this Well and drank of its refreshing waters,
> on the 20th September, 1861,
> the year of Her Majesty's great sorrow.

From the Well the view of the Glen is magnificent. On the right, Mount Keen towers aloft over the neighbouring mountains which surround this part of the Glen, enclosing it like the arena of some mighty amphitheatre. Huge shoulders, projecting from the monarch mountain of the range, and from the lofty crags on the south side of the Glen, seem to lock and interlock into each other. On the south is a terrific precipice (a northern shoulder of Craig Braestock), many hundred feet in height, round the base of which the Mark flows. On the east, high mountains rear their heads, the only egress from the green lawn-like valley being along the edge of the stream as it flows downwards to fraternize with the Lee at Invermark.

THE AULD KIRK AND THE GRAVE OF A NOTED POET.

Retracing our steps towards "The Loch," we are first attracted to the ruins of the old church, situated at the north-east corner of the loch. There had been nothing striking about the style of its architecture, but from its peculiarly romantic situation, it possesses many picturesque attractions, which render it specially interesting.

To the lover of Scottish poetry, the auld kirkyard

of Lochlee must be ever dear, as containing the ashes of Alexander Ross, the parish schoolmaster, and author of the delightful pastoral poem of "Helenore, or the Fortunate Shepherdess," and its vicinity as the place where he spent the greater part of his quiet and uneventful life.

Ross was born in the parish of Kincardine O'Neil, and was nearly 70 years of age before he published his poems. His salary was one hundred merks, or £5 11s 3d sterling, six bolls of meal, and feal and divot in the hill of Invermark, together with six acres of arable land, in lieu of the two crofts and pasture for twenty sheep. As session-clerk and precentor, he is reckoned to have had about £2 more, and a trifle for the school fees of five or six families.

The humble headstone the poet placed in the old churchyard at the grave of his wife, Jean Catanach, is read with much interest by the visitor who enters the hallowed spot. There, too, the body of her eminent husband, who, as we have observed, taught the " noisy mansion" of the parish for upwards of fifty-two years, was laid on the 29th of May, 1784, at the ripe age of eighty-four. A granite tablet was erected by subscription in memory of this remarkable man, who has furnished us with so graphic and faithful delineations of the manners and customs of an age which has passed by comparatively unrecorded. It bears the following inscription:

Erected
To the Memory of
ALEXANDER ROSS, A. M.,
Schoolmaster at Lochlee,
Author of " Lindy and Nory ;" or,
" The Fortunate Shepherdess,"
and other Poems in the Scotch Dialect.
Born, April 1690,
Died, May 1784.

THE POET'S HOME.

Laigh it was, yet sweet, though humble,
Decked wi' honeysuckle round ;
Clear below, Esk's waters rumble,
Deep glens murmuring back the sound.

The humble dwelling of the poet is still represented by the rude walls of his cottage and schoolhouse. They are just a park-breadth north of the kirkyard. The ruins are behind the walls that form a sheep-cot, but cannot be seen from the road. It had been the very minimum of humble dwellings, and consisted of only a ground floor, divided into two small rooms—the largest not ten feet square. One of these was considered sufficient for the school of the parish. There Ross sat during many dreary winters hearing the lessons of his charge. The other apartment was the kitchen, parlour, nursery, study, and bedroom of the humble and contented bard, and here he wrote poems and songs which will live as long as the Scotch dialect is understood.

The romantic description of rural life and manners of the early part of last century, with which "Helenore" abounds, are familiar to all lovers of national poetry. Dr Jamieson, in his "Scottish Dictionary," has paid Ross a high tribute, as one of our Scottish classics, by drawing largely on his works in illustration of our vernacular. His songs, "The Rock an' the Wee Pickle Tow," or "Woo'd an' Married an' a'," and many others, are known and admired wherever the Scottish tongue is spoken.

Chambers in his "Scottish Biography," says—"In Aberdeenshire and in Angus, the Mearns and Moray, there is no work more popular than 'The Fortunate Shepherdess.' It disputes popularity with Burns and the Pilgrim's Progress; is read, in his idle hours, by the shepherd in the glens, and wiles away the weariness of the long winter night at the crofter's fireside." On its appearance, Beattie predicted that—

> Ilka Mearns and Angus bairn,
> Thy tales and sangs by heart shall learn.

The prediction has been amply verified, and a hope which Ross expressed in one of his unpublished poems, has been realized:—

> Hence lang, perhaps, lang hence may quoted be,
> My hamely proverbs lined wi' blythesome glee;
> Some reader then may say, 'Fair fa' ye, Ross,'
> When, aiblins, I'll be lang, lang dead an' gane,
> An' few remember there was sic a ane.

Dr Longmuir, describing in his edition of the poet's works, a visit to the hut, says:—

We do not know how it may affect others, but we confess we should have enjoyed more pleasure in finding the cottage still inhabited—perhaps by some lone widow of the glen, turning a loop before the door of the house in which so much had been written in a cheerful spirit and a Christian strain, whilst some kind neighbour would of an evening have "delved in the yard," and preserved the poet's "bed o' camowyne," than in seeing the walls, bulging to their fall, employed as part of a sheep-fold, and overgrown with nettles.

As the late Lord Dalhousie is understood to have prevented these walls from being entirely removed, would it not be a suitable tribute to genius if his successor were to go a step farther, and preserve them from the inevitable effects of neglect?

LOCHLEE.

Lochlee is in several respect the most interesting of the Forfarshire lochs. As the Lee from the north flows in at the west end and out of the east, the Loch may be said to be a depression and expansion of the river, where it pauses awhile after its turbulent and restless run through the wild moors, glens, and gorges It has traversed in its downward journey from its homes on the mountains. It is somewhat more than a mile in length, and about half a mile in breadth. In some places the Loch is about sixteen fathoms deep, except at the western extremity, where a process of silting has evidently been for ages gradually going on. For a considerable distance from the margin, the "sand-bed," as it is appropriately called, is not covered by above two feet of water, but the next step might suddenly plunge the unwary explorer into a depth of as many fathoms. The greatest depth, however, shows what an immense hole thus forms the bed of the Loch, and forcibly suggests the idea of its having one day been the mouth of a volcano—

> Thae shapless, n'ony-nookit blocks—
> If we can credit learned folks
> Were hirsled frae the impending rocks,
> By lichtnin' rent;
> Or by some warld convulsing shocks
> In times unkent,

Warden in his description of the Loch, says:

The banks of the Loch are boulder strewn, a few stunted indigenous trees lead a precarious life on spots on its borders, heath and briar, fern and bent thrive near its

margin, grouse and other upland game inhabit its mountains, and the adder is well known in the district. Nowhere can the beauties of the morning and the evening sky be better seen than by a spectator low down on the margin of the Loch, or high up on its romantic banks, with the tiny rocky promontories and bays around them. Its rough banks and their varied clothing, and the adjoining mountains from base to summit, are depicted on its smooth and silvery face. The evening sky, seen from an elevated spot, appears to clothe the still lake with a dress of shining gold, changing with the altering tints of the heavens to streaks of rosy hues, to shades of brilliant purple, fading gradually away as darkness draws on. How changed the scene when the fierce storms, so frequent in these Highland glens, sweep over the Loch. With little warning the wind comes through the glens with mighty force, covers the surface of the water with a white surf, dashes the angry waves against the banks, and throws the wild spray far out on the hill sides.

The Loch is surrounded by high hills, which sink down abruptly upon its brink. It lies deep in the

bottom of the valley, at the head of Glenesk. Its waters are hemmed in by Craig Buck on the north, and by Craig Our and other lofty summits on the south, while Craig Maskeldie and its neighbours tower away to the west.

Mount Keen (the highest summit in the parish of Lochlee) is seen to the north-west and north, and Mount Battock to the west—the former rising considerably over 3000 feet, and the latter to a height of about 2555 feet. From Mount Keen is seen much of the central course of the Dee, a large portion of Aberdeenshire beyond, the lofty Cairngorm summits, the sea of mountains to the south and west, and portions of Glenesk; from Mount Battock, the eastern portion of the vale of the Dee and Aberdeenshire, the Kincardineshire mountains and the ocean beyond, and the course of the Tarf, and central parts of Glenesk are seen. The view on a fine day well repays the labour, **but**

> Whae'er the rugged sides would climb,
> Maun hae gude breath and strength o' limb;
> Your water-wagtail Cockney slim—
>   He mount them?—whew!
> Hyde Park, an level roads for him—
>   This winna do!

The Eagle's Craig has bold, abrupt, and lofty faces on the north and east round which the Lee runs, but the southern side of the mountain, called "The Rock of the Eagles," is a terrific precipice, which confronts you in walking up the Glen. It rears its bare crown more than a thousand feet above the Unich and the Lee, which meet in front of it. The circular wall of cleft and furred rocks of Craig Maskeldie, which encircle Carlochie, and stretch away beyond it on both sides, is a giant enclosure of vast magnificence. From the top of the lofty precipice the view down into the cauldron at its bottom is impressive, while the outward prospect is on all sides extensive and varied. Every high mountain for a considerable distance around is seen, and to the south objects beyond the Grampian range are visible on a clear day. Nearer at hand, the course of the burns in the valleys and ravines can be traced, and the beautiful Lochlee, and the ruined church, with the Castle of Invermark, and the fine grounds of Invermark Lodge, form a charming picture.

The Unich and the Lee are the original tributaries of the North Esk—the former rising some seven or eight miles south-west of the Loch, and the latter from four to five miles north-west. They are both united immediately under the northernmost ridge of Craig Maskeldie. These two hurried, sparkling streams are known from thence, for a distance of four miles, by the name of the Lee. The Lee has its fountain head in the Cairn of Lee, and after running two or three miles it comes over the north-east shoulder of the Eagle's Craig, forming many pretty cascades and cataracts in its restless course. The clear sparkling stream has cut its tortuous way through granite rocks, and, tired with the violent exercise, it finally lands in a pretty glen, where it meets the Unich.

This stream has two heads, the one in the Lair of Aldararie and the other in Cairn Derg. Uniting, the burn runs rapidly through a wild and winding rocky Highland district, receiving in its course the Longshank and other burns. It then enters into a deep gloomy gorge, which it has worn out for itself between Craig Damph on the north, and Craig Maskeldie on the south, from which it emerges in front of the terrific precipice of the Eagle's Craig, in the cliffs of which these famous birds of prey still have their eyrie and yearly rear their young. The precipitous, if not perpendicular cliffs, between which the stream forces its way, are very lofty, and approach so closely to each other that it is all but impossible to fathom the depths, or scale the heights of either of them. Leaving the dark ravine by a bold leap of about fifty feet, the water, white as snow, falls into a deep pool at the bottom of the cataract. The high crags by which the cataract is surrounded form an exceedingly sublime scene. The Eagle's Craig securely guards the *White Lady,* as the fall is aptly called, from northern intruders. A high and picturesque shoulder of Craig Maskeldie, which, viewed from near the bottom of the Eagle's Craig, shows a singularly beautiful and curious outline. The stream, when viewed from below the fall, appears to emerge from a cavern in the mountain, and the water tumbling over the cataract is the first announcement of the presence of a river in the rocky wild. At the foot of the cascade the scene changes as if by magic of an enchanter. Above there is a chaos of bare rocks, below there is an open glen with a beautiful green sward, through which the Unich flows peacefully, to be united with the Lee a little way down the glen. As the *Lee*, they flow down the quiet but lovely glen for a couple of miles.

A little below the junction of the Unich and the Lee, on the south, and about four hundred feet above their channel, the immense basin-shaped cavity, scooped from the very heart of Craig Maskeldie, is a natural curiosity of some interest. This is the site of Carlochie, whose beautiful little lake reposes in the bosom of the rugged mountain. The loch is about a mile in circumference. The water is of crystal purity, and the overflow finds an outlet at its eastern shelving bank, whence it descends by leaps and bounds to the Lee. The lofty cliffs are often beautifully mirrored on the surface of the Loch, and, when clear of mist, every projection and crevice of the surrounding rocks is revealed in a halo of beauty.

Here, if the traveller has patience to scramble over huge tablets of rock, he may stumble upon the narrow entrance to a dark recess, called "Gryp's Chamber," where a notorious reiver of that name is said to have dwelt for many years, carrying on a system of lawless plunder. Another noted spot—a hollow near the top of the hill—bears the name of "The Bride's Bed," and is so called, it is said, because of a young and beautiful bride having lost her life there, when crossing the hills from Clova.

At the south-west corner of the Loch is the old farmhouse of Inchgrundle, which, for more than twenty years, formed the autumn home and Highland resting-place of the late Dr Thomas Guthrie. He had a great affection for the Glen, as he invariably called it, and he was often seen musing on the banks, or rowing his lonely boat in the midst of the Loch by sunlight, and moonlight too.

The Loch is noted for its "char," and Dr Guthrie once humorously remarked that he believed the monks introduced it as a delicacy for the sake of fast-days, little thinking that they were providing food and recreation for a Presbyterian minister. The Loch, he said, like the Lake of Galilee, and all such mountain girded waters, rose on a sudden. Like a hot angry man, it was soon up, and soon down, and soon up again. Dr Guthrie occasionally preached in the open air by Invermark, when his audience—peer and peasant, rank, and power, and beauty, within long walking distances, and some few beyond—would hang spell-bound on his words. It must have been thrilling to hear weather-beaten shepherd folks and stately noble men joining together in pealing out the Old Hundred among the solemn grey hills, bringing vividly to imagination the scenes witnessed in still ravines, on heather braes, and bare hillsides, during the covenanting times, when our forefathers conversed with God, with buckled sword and open Bible, ready, in face of fire or death, to hold their conscience true.

We are now for the present at the end of our journey. We have had pure air, and healthful exercise for the limbs and the mind too. We have experienced pleasure in clambering up the steep and craggy mountains. We have traversed long sheep-tracks and foot-paths, skirted with bright golden broom. We have looked on the airy mountain tops, now half-buried in mist, then lit up with a bright sun—the near hills sharp and clear, while the distant masses were enveloped in dark grey vapour, which added to their mystic grandeur, and increased their gloomy vastness. In the words of the old Scottish Gaberlunzie:—"Consider yoursel' daunderin' aboot amang the hills, the fou'-flowing tide o' thought rowing through your bosom;—to lie down on the crisp heather, an' gaze up into glory, watching the varying shapes o' the wee pearly cluds floating through the blue ether, an' the sma' black specks o' music warbling an' winging in mid-air like so many blessèd spirits, blending heaven and earth together; to listen to the heather linties around ye chirming an keeping up the chorus, and hear the low, sweet, and harmonious notes o' the bonny hillside warblers o' auld Scotland echoed frae the choirs aboon;—to gaze upon the mountains towering to the lift, bold, rugged, an' gigantic, yet tapering wi' airy form an' graceful elegance, their sides a' thickly studded wi' bonny green spats o' rich verdure; thack-roofed cots, wooded knowes, dark ravines, an' sparkling waterfa's;—to see a' these grand features alternately in light an' shadow, the rays o' light dancin' an' flickerin', an' playin' at bo-peep amang the heights an' howes, an' the cluds throwin' fantastic shadows across the green slopes an' the dark ridges;—it is amang scenes like these whaur the wanderer feels his ain greatness, **an'** his ain littleness, an' whaur he may weel exclaim in the emphatic language o' Scripture—'It is good for us to be here.'"

Fifth Tour.

THE GANNOCHY, THE BURN, BALBEGNO, FETTERCAIRN, FETTERCAIRN HOUSE, FASQUE, KINCARDINE CASTLE, GLEN OF DRUMTOCHTY, AUCHINBLAE, THORNTON CASTLE, LAURENCEKIRK, INGLISMALDIE, LUTHERMUIR, UPPER NORTH WATER BRIDGE, OLD CHURCH AND CHURCHYARD OF PERT, LOGIE-PERT, STRACATHRO, &c., &c.

The Gannochy.

HAVING again gone over the same road by way of Edzell, we hold direct to the Gannochy. When we diverged in our last tour, and visited the Bridge of Mooran, we merely attempted to give an "inklin'" of the grandeur of the scene from our starting point to-day—The Gannochy Bridge. Here the river is seen struggling and rushing, and leaping through its rugged channel, and with the precipitous and lofty banks, adorned with trees, shrubs and wild flowers, a scene is produced in no small degree picturesque. The bridge, built in 1732, and widened in 1795, unites the rocky banks of the North Esk by a single arch, which spans the foaming stream seventy feet below. The tale of the ghostly visitor, whose humanity urged the erection of the bridge, and whose engineering skill pointed out its proper site, adds the necessary ingredient to render it one of the most interesting spots in the district.

The magnificent view from the bridge has long been an object of admiration. The flowing river, its rocky bed and banks, the luxuriant foliage by which they are clothed, form a scene romantic and picturesque in the extreme, and few can cross the stream without stopping to view and admire the beautiful pictures presented on either hand. Here the geologist, the botanist, and the lover of the picturesque will each be delighted.

The traditional origin of the Gannochy Bridge might be briefly told. A worthy farmer, who had no family, was understood to be very wealthy; and, as his neighbours had often experienced the inconvenience of of round-about roads and the dangerous nature of the fords of the North Esk, and were also aware of his weak side and heavy purse, they adopted the wily scheme which induced him to confer this boon upon the district. During the winter of 1731, when several lives were lost in the river, the spirit of one of those unfortunate individuals is said to have called upon him on three successive nights, and implored him to erect a bridge, and thus save farther loss of life. Unable to find peace of mind, or withstand longer the request of his nocturnal visitor, the farmer set about erecting the bridge at the very spot which the *spirit* had indicated.

Such is the story current in the district, but here are facts: The bridge was erected in the year 1732 at the sole expense of James Black, tenant of the farm of Wood, in the immediate vicinity. He employed a mason to prepare the materials and erect the stonework of the bridge, but he constructed the parapets with his own hands. The expense of the erection amounted to 300 merks, about £200 Scots money. At his death he left fifteen merks, to accumulate at interest, for the maintenance of the bridge. On his tombstone was inscribed the following appropriate couplet:

    No bridge on earth can be a bridge to heaven;
    Yet let to generous deeds due praise be given.

Black's bridge, although ample for the requirements of the time when it was built, was soon found to be too narrow for the traffic that passed along it. It was therefore widened in the year 1795, at the expense of the Hon. William Maule (Lord Panmure) and Lord Adam Gordon.

Balbegno Castle.

Passing the lodge and gateway leading to the mansion house of The Burn (already referred to) on our way to Fettercairn—a village with many interesting associations—we are first attracted to Balbegno Castle, on the left. It is memorable as the residence of Ranulphuss the king's falconer, whose descendants are now represented by the noble family of Kintore. The castle was built by Wood, the hereditary constable of the castles of Kincardine and Fettercairn, and his wife Jean Irvine, 1569, whose initials are below the south window of the tower.

Jervise says: From 1539 (how long before I am not aware), the lands of Balbegno were held by Woods until about 1687, when they were sold to Andrew, second brother of the Earl of Middleton (Doug. Peerage), whose son, Robert, married a sister of John Ogilvy, advocate, son of Ogilvy of Lunan. It is now the property of Sir John Gladstone, whose grandfather bought it from the Hon. Donald Ogilvy of Clova.

The Castle of Balbegno, which is in good preservation, contains an interesting hall with groined freestone roof. Some of the bosses present grotesque ornaments, others floral, and one bears the Irvine arms. The ceiling has two shields, charged respectively with the Scotch lion, and the Wood arms. The vaulted compartments, of which there are sixteen, are occupied by mural paintings of the coats and mantlings, &c., of as many Scotch peers. Upon the bartizan are three medallion heads, one male, with hat, &c., and two female. A male head with beard and helmet is over the garden door. These are all boldly carved in freestone, and in the same style as the famous "Stirling Heads." Several shields, with arms, possibly those of the founder of the Castle and his lady, are upon different parts of the House. The date, 1569, is upon a carved panel on the south side, near the top of the house. About the end of last century, the Ogilvys made an addition to the east side of the Castle, by which the original entrance and front were spoiled.

The Middletons were by far the earliest lay proprietors in the district, of the existence of whom there is authentic evidence from at least the year 1221.

It is said in Law's memorials that one of the Lairds of Balbegno was a companion in arms with Middleton long ere he had acquired much fame; and that before entering the field of battle on one occasion they agreed, in the event of either of them being killed, that the other should return and give the survivor some account of the other world! It is added that Balbegno fell; and one day, while Middleton was a prisoner in the Tower of London, and just as he had finished reading a portion of Scripture, Balbegno's ghost appeared, and taking him by the hand, said—"Oh, Middleton, do you not mind the promise I made to you when at such a place, such a night on the Border?" But, without giving him any account of "the other world," it is added that Balbegno prophesied Middleton's future greatness, and vanished from his view exclaiming:—

"Plumashes above, gramashes below,
It's no wonder to see how the world doth go."

Fettercairn.

We'll etch the vernal landscape as it spreads
At radiant morn, charm'd with these varied views:
The model village, nestling half concealed,
The cultured gardens, glittering in the dew,
The healthy husbandmen, who bends
To dress the grateful soil; the quiet sheep
Which on the adjacent mountain seem to hang
Their fleeces on its sides.

The village of Fettercairn is quite a model, bringing to our recollection the poetic "Auburn" of Goldsmith. Her Majesty and the Prince Consort spent a night here in September, 1861. They were passed off as "a marriage party from Aberdeen." The route pursued by Her Majesty and Prince Albert and their suite extended over sixteen miles, and may be given for the benefit of those who wish to go over the ground. The Royal party having driven from Balmoral to the Bridge of Muick, in the neighbourhood of Ballater, there took ponies and proceeded along a cart road, used for driving peats from the hill of Pullach, through which, extending about a mile, there is scarcely a road at all, and then entered a bridle-road, which conducted them into Glenesk. About six miles and a half from the Bridge of Muick, the road crosses the Tanner, wending its way towards the richly-wooded Glen, to which it gives its name. The road from this point to its highest elevation, on the shoulder of Mount Keen, is very steep; and there the Earl of Dalhousie (Fox Maule) met Her Majesty and party on the boundary of his extensive property. For upwards of a mile the descent is steep and rugged; and hence this portion of it is called The Ladder.

The party then reached Glenmark House, which is now occupied by one of his Lordship's keepers, and there took luncheon. Her Majesty, having taken a sketch of Craig Doon, which lies to the north, resumed her journey. About three hundred yards from the keeper's house, and close by the junction of the Ladder Burn with the Mark, in the centre of a strath of verdant sward, the Queen was arrested by a beautiful mountain spring. She stopped and partook of its cooling waters. In commemoration of this event, and the death of the Prince shortly afterwards, the neat fountain, as we have already seen, was erected. In honour of the visit to Fettercairn, a stone arch, flanked by battlemented towers, has been erected at the end of the bridge. That night the villagers little thought that they had reposed so near "the head that wears a crown," and their consternation next morning cannot be easily conceived, when they found that their Queen had eluded the hearty expression of their loyalty. It soon, however, took a more permanent form than that of loud huzzas—in the fine memorial arch, which commemorates the royal visit. The Queen's room and bed are still shown to visitors at the Ramsay Arms—a hotel which will be found exceedingly comfortable, and is admirably conducted by Mr Kean.

In addition to the common trade of a rural village,

Fettercairn has a widely-known distillery, and several large fashionable looking shops. There are numerous neat cottages, with beautiful garden plots, and the whole place has a fine picturesque look about it. For salubrity of climate, it is said to be almost unrivalled in the county, and the place altogether, with neat and trim houses, and roses and honeysuckle trailing round almost every door and window, the gardens aglow with flowers, together with numerous shady walks makes it a very pleasant summer resort.

One or more intermediate tours might here be suggested, as we will have occasion to note shortly, so that should time permit and our visitors feel inclined, they can *do* several, and spend the night under the kindly care of the "Ramsay Arms" in the apartments honoured by royalty.

A neatly carved and turreted fountain tower stands in the square as a memorial to Sir J. H. Stuart Forbes, Bart. The old Market Cross of Kincardine surmounts an octagonal flight of steps, and has an iron rivet, to which criminals were chained by the *jougs*. The Cross of Fettercairn was possibly erected by the Earl of Middleton at the time he obtained an Act of Parliament to hold a weekly market there. He received this privilege in 1670—the date upon the cross—but long before that, St Mark's fair (named doubtless in honour of the saint to whom the kirk was dedicated), was a market of considerable importance. A. C. Cameron, LL.D., has for many years been the honoured and gifted teacher of the Public School. An antiquarian of repute, he has written much about the district, and is the author of the school "Geography of Kincardine," and other useful works.

Fettercairn was a mensal church of the Archbishop of St Andrews. In 1567, Patrick Bonnele was minister of Fettercairn, and of the three adjoining parishes of Fordoun, Newdosk, and Conveth (Laurencekirk) at a salary of 24 lb., "with the support of the Priour of St Androis." John Thom was reader, or schoolmaster, with 24 merks a year. David Strachan, afterwards Bishop of Brechin, was sometime minister at Fettercairn; also William Chalmers, who presented a congratulatory address to Queen Anne from his brethren in the Episcopal Church. The present place of worship (Rev. W. Anderson), which stands upon a rising ground in the kirkyard, and close to the village, was built in 1803. A handsome spire, or belfry, was added in 1838. In old times, the bell was suspended from a tree, which stood upon the "Bell Hillock."

On a burial stone in the churchyard, surrounding a representation of our first parents at the forbidden tree, is this couplet:

> Adam & Eve by eating the forbidden tree,
> Brought all mankind to sin & misery.

It would appear that Fettercairn is not so rich in "witch lore" as some parishes we have passed through. However, the parish minister of Marykirk, speaking lately at a social gathering, stated that he had been told by old persons of a minute in a parish record which read thus: "Nae sermon here this day—the minister bein' awa at Fettercairn burnin' a witch." As James E. Watt, author of "Poetical Sketches of Scottish Life and Character," puts it—

> "At Marykirk, in days of yore,
>   Ae Sabbath morn the auld kirk door
> A curious inscription bore,
>   Addressed to puir and rich,
> In whilk the minister made mane,
> That there that day he could preach nane,
> As he to Fettercairn had gane
>   To burn a wicked witch—
>
> A hag wha had for mony a year
> The kintra side kept in a steer,
> Till her ill deeds, dune far an' near,
>   Gar't countless fingers itch
> To get her tethered to a post,
> 'Mang lowin' whins an' peats to roast,
> Till she sud yield her sinfu' ghost,
>   As it becam' a witch."

Leaving the village, and within half-a-mile—on the right—Fettercairn House, the seat of the Hon. C. F. R. Trefusis, a grandson of the late Sir John Stuart Forbes, is seen nestling around fine old trees. It was once the property of the Earl of Middleton, whose initials and the date 1666 still mark the oldest portion of the mansion.

THE RESIDENCE OF THE GLADSTONES.

A little over a mile, to the left, we get an excellent view of the magnificent residence of Sir John Gladstone. Fasque House is a fine specimen of castellated architecture, around which cling many associations of the Gladstone family. It was for many years the home of Sir Thomas Gladstone, who died in March, 1889, and lies hid away from the gaze of the ubiquitous tourist. A spacious park, studded with giant rhododendrons and majestic firs and other trees of great dimensions and rare grandeur, surrounds it. To the south-west of the house is an extensive lake, which adds greatly to the attractions of the demesne. The house was built in 1808-9, at a cost of £30,000 by the late Sir Alexander Ramsay, the seventh baronet of Balmain. Fasque estate, which had been held by the Ramsay family, was purchased in 1828 by Mr John Gladstone (Mr W. E. Gladstone's father), who in 1846 was created a baronet by Sir Robert Peel, and who was succeeded in the title and estate by his eldest son, Sir Thomas, on his death in 1851. Between his elder brother and Mr Gladstone, as is well known, there was politically a gulf that kept them wide as the poles asunder; yet there was a personal friendship between the two that united them in the closest bonds of affection and esteem.

The site of the house is a very fine one, standing as it does on the wooded slope of a minor branch of the Grampian range, and commanding to the south a magnificent view of the far-famed Howe o' the Mearns. The house is built of the red-stone found in the locality, and in brilliant sunshine the warm colour of

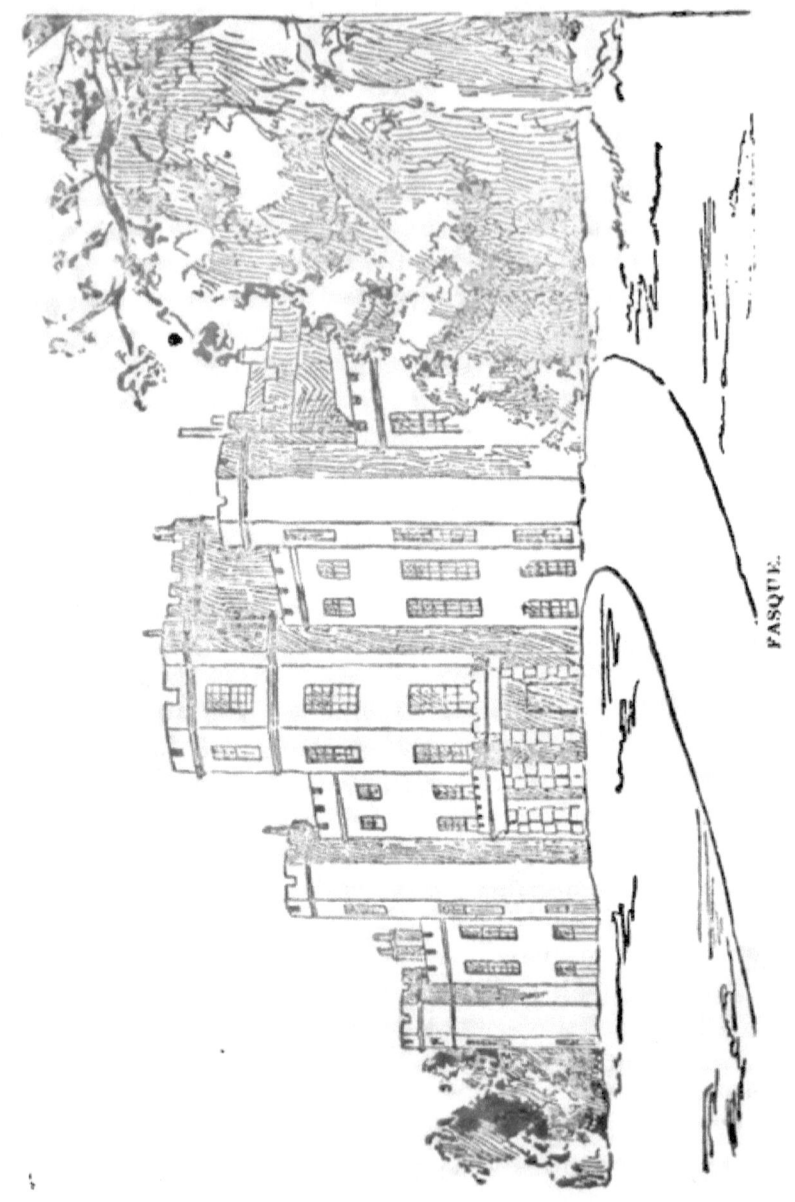

FASQUE.

the stones imparts to it a fine appearance. The property extends from Fettercairn village to Deeside, a distance of fully sixteen miles. The greater portion of the estate lies in the Grampian range, and consists of heath-clad hills intersected by numerous small straths. The estate of Glendye was purchased by Sir Thomas Gladstone in 1865 from the Earl of Southesk.

St Andrew's Episcopal Church, which stands a little to the eastward of the house of Fasque, was built by Sir John Gladstone, and consecrated and opened, 28th August 1847. The original building has been greatly improved by the erection of a new chancel, which was consecrated by Alexander, Bishop of Brechin, 15th April 1869. It is in the early English style of architecture, with deep splayed lancet windows. The east window, which contains representations of St Andrew and the four evangelists, &c., is a fine specimen of art.

Leaving the woods of Fasque, the Burn of Garrol is crossed, and we now enter the historic Parish of Fordoun. On the right hand side, and only a short distance from the road, is the site of the "town" and palace, or castle of Kincardine. The town is said to have extended from the ground at the foot of the castle to the vicinity of Fettercairn House. It was in 1531-2 that the fourth Earl Marischal obtained a charter for making the town of Kincardine "The principal and capital town of the county." But it only maintained that position for about 80 years—the Sheriff and his Deputies petitioning for the removal of the courts to Stonehaven, for want of accommodation at the county town. It had its church, its burial place, its east port, its west port, and its market cross—the last of which was carried off to Fettercairn, and has been already described. The graveyard still remains, but no interments have been made for a considerable time. There is no record when the palace or castle was built, or when it was last occupied. It was a royal palace previous to the death of Kenneth III. in 994, being occupied by that monarch at the time of his murder by Finella.

THE LEGEND OF DEN-FINELLA.

Here is a version of the story of the murder of Kenneth that might be briefly given. It is said that the King had put to death the son of Finella, for treason committed by him in an insurrection in the Mearns. Finella was the wife of the chief of the Mearns, and a daughter of the Maormor or Earl of Angus. In revenge for the death of her son, she hired a band of ruffians to assassinate the King; and they accomplished their purpose at a hunting match at Stracathro, into which they lured him. Justice pursued the murderess. She took refuge in the beautiful and romantic Den-Finella, which has derived its name from her. When overtaken there, according to one class of chroniclers, she was apprehended and executed, while it is said by others that she committed suicide by leaping from the rocks into the deep gully, into which the Burn running through the Den tumbles from a height of 105 feet, at the point where the turnpike road now crosses it.

Dr Cramond, of Cullen, the well-known antiquarian, in his "Stra'finla Top," says:—

Kenneth III. (971-995), like his father and grandfather, also met his end in this locality. Tighernac, in recording his death, merely says he was slain by his own subjects, to which the Ulster Annals add "by treachery." The latter Chronicles state that he was slain at Fotherkern by the treachery of Finvela (Finella), daughter of Cunchar, Earl of Angus, whose only son Kenneth had killed. Later historians represent that Finella caused him to be shot by an arrow from a wonderful piece of mechanism she had erected in her castle.

> As throw the Mernys on a day
> The Kyng was rydand hys hev way
> Off hys awyne curt, al suddanly
> Agayne him ras a cumpany,
> In to the towne off Fethyrkerne.
> To fecht wyth hym thai ware sa yherne
> And he agayne thame laucht sa fast,
> Bot he thare slayne was at the last.
>
> — *Wynton, c, 1420.*

G. L., writing in the *Montrose Standard* on the subject of the legend of Den Finella, relates that Finella, whose family claimed independent rule in the Mearns, "having compassed the death of Kenneth the Third, who had been taking vigorous steps to reduce to submission the Maormors of both Mearns and Angus, fled from Kincardine Castle on being warned of the near approach of the king's troops. While on Garvock Hill information was conveyed to her that the king's men had left Kincardine on her track with sleuth hounds. On hearing this she made swiftly for the upper end of the gorge, since called Den Finella, intending to put the hounds at fault by wading down the water. Various conditions, arising from the particular season of the year, combined to render this idea futile. In this dilemma she swung herself into the treetops, which are said to have been singularly interlaced here, and, passing from one to the other, traversed a considerable portion of the Den before descending. She thus gained time to escape to the sea, as both dogs and men were completely puzzled on reaching the head of the gorge. In after years popular belief has affirmed that the Den, at stated times, is haunted by the spirit of Finella and the baying of bloodhounds at night." Through the courtesy of the proprietor of the *Standard*, we are able to give an excellent picture of the Falls.

> Our grandsire oft the story would maintain
> That, as the gloamin' deepens into night,
> On certain fateful evenings of the year
> When snows are deep on stern old Garvock Hill',
> And trees are bare on wooded Lauriston,
> Weird sights and sounds roll down Dentinell dark,
> And onward pass toward the wintry sea.

Standing on the termination of a small ridge, and surrounded by a morass, the Castle of Kincardine seems to have been a place of considerable strength, and foundations that remain show that it had been of quadrangular shape. That Kincardine Castle was a royal residence is evident from the fact that there are in its vicinity the King's Park, Castlegreen, and Gallow Hill. As showing the originally substantial nature of the building it may be mentioned that the walls are from six to eight feet thick. It is stated by Lord Hailes that it was in this palace that John Baliol resigned his Crown to Edward I. of England, 2d July 1296, although that is open to dispute.

> In him the hills
> 'Circling Kincardine town inspired no thought
> Of independence carried by the sword,
> Or freedom in unpenetrated glens ;
> But Edward's slave was verily no king,
> For Scots are free—a sympathetic pulse,
> Inspired by the freedom of the hills,
> Throbs through the nation's being as one man,
> Defensive of each other's equal rights
> Against the power of shameless perfidy.

About a mile further, on the West flank of Finella Hill, overloooking the Fourdon rivulet, we pass the site of Green Castle (or Green Cairn, supposed

to have been the abode of the notorious Finella), and what has been regarded as a Caledonian or Pictish fort, but more probably it had been a camp where soldiers had been stationed to guard the Cairn o' Mount Road, as it commands an extensive view of it both ways, while it was used as a military road to the Highlands. The view here for about a mile and a half is magnificent, the hills rising on either side till we arrive at

"THE CLATTERIN' BRIG,"

which, as has been truly said by a writer describing **Mr Knowles'** (Brechin) Four-in-Hand drive through Drumtochty Glen, has long been the trysting place for many a pic-nic and excursion party, a broad meadow by the side of the stream being well adapted for this purpose.

> Athwart the lower glens by Birnie's Slack,
> And flippant on the hills danced fairy bands:
> Each moonlight saw them glide from mountain gorge,
> And speed in flight where "Clattering Brig" now stands.
> They murmured with the murmur of the stream,
> They breathed a night-song with the lonely bird;
> Returning in their elfin triumph home
> When every life awaked from restless sleep.

But for the sake of those who would like to *do* Cairn o' Mount, we would here crave the company of our readers, and ask them to dismount, and walk to the summit, a distance of nearly three miles. The road is fairly good, however, and the extensive and charming view from the top will repay the toil.

> The earth was made so various, that the mind
> Of desultory man, studious of change,
> And pleased with novelty, might be indulged.
> Prospects, however lively, may be seen
> Till half their beauties fade: the weary sight,
> Too well acquainted with their smiles, slides off
> Fastidious, seeking less familiar scenes.

Here you can see Montrose, the Bell Rock, and most of the fertile Howe o' the Mearns, while, to the north, the famous Cloch-na-Ben bounds the horizon. From the summit of the Cairn to the Brig o' Dye is about eight miles—almost entirely downhill, and at times exceedingly steep. The scenery through which the Dye flows is very pleasing, and the panorama of river, hill, forest, and heath is something to be remembered. Four miles or so further is the inn of Feughside on an elevated plateau. Here a magnificent view is spread around by a narrow circle of hills, in which Cloch-na-Ben now lying direct south, is in the centre.

A writer in the *Weekly News*—J. W.—in a sketch entitled "Through Kincardineshire," says this excellently appointed inn, comfortable, tidy, and reasonable, is situated exactly on the confines of the parishes of Strachan and Birse, 9½ miles from Aboyne, 6 from Kincardine O'Neil, and 6 from Banchory. Far up the river looms the famous forest of Birse, from which till its junction with the Dee the Feuch "turns and twines," to use the vigorous and poetical language of the gifted Gilfillan, "as if in agony of reluctance to leave a scene so fair." We voted it an ideal place for lounging about at and consuming unlimited tobacco under pretence of fishing. One of us fished with indefatigable zeal, another somewhat intermittently, and between the two as many trouts were captured as made a grand show beside the fowls next morning at breakfast. We then took the road on foot, which runs alongside of the river till its rocky rush into the Dee at Banchory, having traversed from the Gannochy Bridge to the Bridge of Feuch—both alike for scenery—the whole length of the county of Kincardine. From here we hired to Stonehaven, the capital of the county, a distance of sixteen miles, which we reached

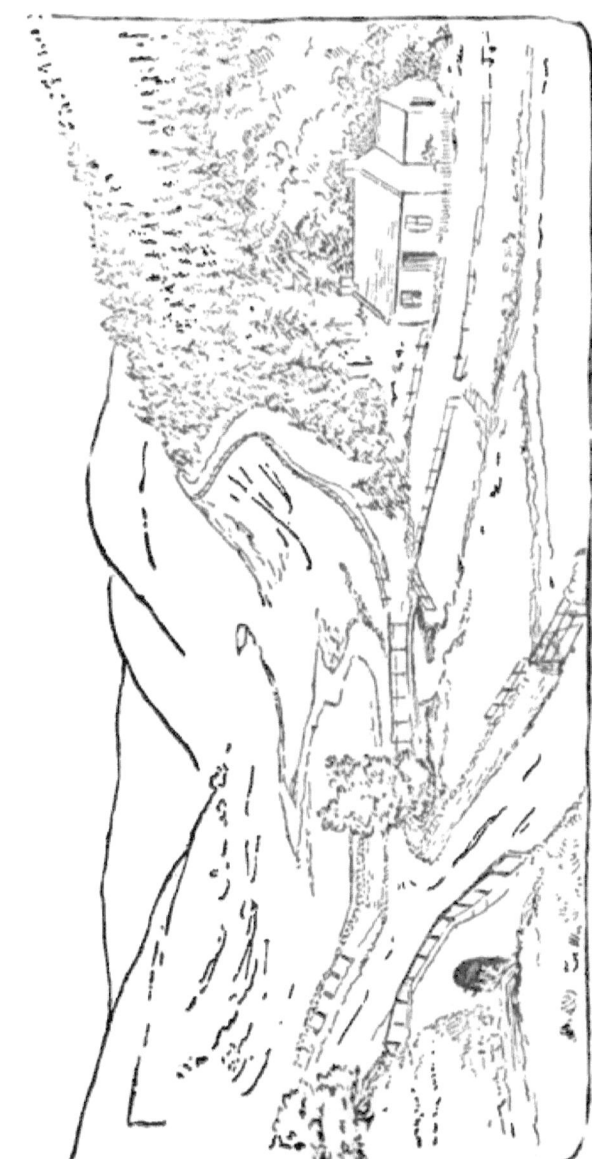

by a beautifully diversified route called the "Slug Road," from one part of which we could see the sugarloaf-like top of Bennachie towering above his *confreres* in the distance.

We resume our journey at the "Clatterin' Brig," after having explored the limekilns and the well, at which we are asked to believe Dominie Young and his jolly company were wont, after a cockfight, to carouse, pouring ten or a dozen bottles of whisky into the well to regale themselves to their heart's content. On fording the Burn of Slack, the route, as will be seen on the right hand side of our illustration, leads up a sharp incline, where the hill scene that meets our eye is very picturesque, and affords a view of the entrance to the Slough of Birnie, on whose shores it is said the parsely fern grows abundantly. At Glenesk Lodge (Miss Donald, proprietrix), the scene changes from rugged hills, and we get a brief "peep" of beautiful and interesting landscape, over the Howe of the Mearns and on towards Brechin. It is only a glimpse, however, and a sudden turn of the road brings to view the Loch of Glensaugh, with swans and wild ducks skimming its surface. The Loch is stocked with trout *imported* from Loch Leven. The route now skirts the loch, and on the left is Bright's Well, which is said to possess wonderful virtues, and where amidst a profusion of ferns and the wild rose many an enjoyable picnic has been held.

We now enter the Glen proper, and for about four miles we are assured that the lover of nature will feel enchanted. At every step new combinations of landscape greet the eye, while on every bank and brae, and in every bosky dell there is a profusion of wild flowers. Wooded slopes and grassy meadows tend, along with the natural formation of the narrow Glen,

P

to form pleasing and ever changing scenes. For botanists this is a favourite resort. About sixteen different varieties of ferns are said to be found within the circle of one mile.

An object of interest, on the right, is the entrance to Friar's Glen, where are still to be seen the remains of a house said to have been connected with the Black Friars of Aberdeen. Here also tradition has it that John o' Fordoun wrote one of the oldest histories of Scotland. The Priest's Well can also be distinctly traced, the water of which joins with the course of the Luther, forming a small burn, which looks, as has been happily said by a writer in the *Dundee Advertiser* describing this route, as though a blessing still existed in it, the meadows through which it passes having a freshness and greenness not to be found around.

A little further on there comes into view the splendid modern mansion, in the castellated Gothic style, of Drumtochty Castle, erected at a cost of over £30,000, after designs by Gillespie Graham. It is the residence of the Rev. James S. Gammell of Drumtochty and Countesswells. The grounds are beautifully laid out, and the natural beauties have been considerably enhanced by the extensive improvements judiciously carried out by the present proprietor. One cannot fail to be struck with the parks of Drumtochty, so tastefully laid out and fringed with belts of beautiful trees.

About a mile to the north-east of the present Castle of Drumtochty stood the Castle of Glenfarquhar, the home of the Falconers. The road is also in sight leading to the moor to which Paldy Fair has been relegated—6th July is St Palladius Day in the calendar—but railways and other causes have shorn the fair of much of its pristine greatness. It was held, as appears in record, in 1506, in the open space, now considerably circumscribed by the churchyard, in front of Fordoun Parish Church. Thereafter, there is some reason to believe, it was held on Gilbert's Hill, overlooking the village of Auchinblae. As cultivated land increased in value the stance was transferred to the barren moor on the top of the Harescha, and a single day is now sufficient to transact the business that aforetime engaged for three days a large part of the population of the neighbouring parishes.

Continuing, we pass the lodge, adjoining which is the church of St Palladius and burying ground. The church, with the large statue of the patron saint, presents an imposing appearance.

After about four and a half miles of a very pleasant drive, we now leave the romantic Glen of Drumtochty, and are again in the open country. Herscha, or Harescha Hill, meets the eye. On the point first seen is a stone circle, and a little to the west is a stone cairn, while, further to the left is the valley and range of hills of Glenfarquhar.

Auchinblae.

> In thee, sweet Auchinblae, whose ample street,
> By houses lined in fascinating rows,
> Ascends in graceful slope—a village placed
> To bask in noon-day sun.

Another mile and we enter Auchinblae, and a halt is made at the Kintore Arms—a comfortable hotel, long kept by a relative of the famous athlete, Donald Dinnie, and now under the very efficient charge of Mrs Dinnie.

Auchinblae appears first in record about 1506. The village is pleasantly situated among the hills at a height of 400 feet above sea-level, has an air of ideal ruralism, and has for many years been a popular health resort. Indeed, it has been styled "a very paradise for retirement." It is famed for its beautiful surrounding walks, and it is said that for over ten days a different direction may be selected every day without any of the same ground being walked over. Thus on all hands you have beautiful landscapes to please the eye and brighten the hours, and many lovely country roads on which to ramble. Auchinblae has an abundant supply of water and excellent sanitary arrangements; also a neat public hall, spacious recreation park, lawn tennis courts, golf course, &c. Part of the village being built on a somewhat steep slope, with the gardens rising in terraces, imparts to it much of a continental appearance.

PLACES OF INTEREST AS VIEWED FROM STRA'FINLA.

As our route has hitherto been round a considerable portion of the base of Finella Hill, or Stra'finla, and we cannot linger over the many places of interest in the district, the next best thing for us to do, so as to get an idea of the attractions of this centre, is to ascend the hill, and have a look from the summit.

This can be done by an easy ascent, and will only take little more than half an hour. The view is magnificent. Across the "Howe o' the Mearns" lies Laurencekirk, with Garvock Hill and Johnstone Tower; towards the east the valley of Arbuthnott, with Bervie raised defiant on the coast. The sea view from this is remarkably fine, whilst the line of the Forfarshire and Fifeshire coasts can be clearly followed with the friths of Forth and Tay, and Montrose and its lofty steeple; while beyond, the hills of Glenesk and Sidlaw nobly rear their heads.

The leading features in this lovely panorama are so graphically and attractively unfolded by Dr Cramond in his "Stra'finla Top," already alluded to, that we cannot do better than give some selections from these sketches.

Directly north of us, on the south side of the Bervie stream, is Gaerlie Hill, where the Rev. Mr Menzies of Fordoun, recently discovered the remains of primitive dwellings. Towards the south side we see the road ascending to the Goyle, on the top of which the parishes of Fordoun and Strachan meet. For several miles the boundary between the parishes of Fordoun and Strachan is the watershed between the Water of Dye, which flows into the Water of Feugh, and thereafter into the Dee; and on the Fordoun side the Luther and its tributaries, and farther north the Bervie. Near the northern boundary of the parish of Fordoun rises the Cowie, which falls into the sea near Stonehaven. The Luther, after flowing through the Howe past Pitarrow, to the west of the village of Laurencekirk, joins the North Esk in the parish of Marykirk. Our view to the north is bounded by the regularly shaped hill Kerloak, from which a view may be obtained of a great part of Aberdeenshire, and, it is asserted, even of the distant Lammermuirs. A little to the south of Kerloak, rises the Bervie, a favourite stream with anglers. It forms the boundary between Fordoun and Glenbervie on the north-east, and for a short distance between Fordoun and Arbuthnott. It then enters the parish of Fordoun, and when near Fordoun Station diverges to the sea, past the seat of the Viscount Arbuthnott, the Castle of Allardyce, and other localities of note. In the latter part of its course it separates the parish of Arbuthnott from Garvock and Bervie, and falls into the sea at Bervie. Bervie is the only Royal burgh in the county. Here in 1342 landed David II. with his Queen Johanna from France. In the same direction may be seen the village of Drumlithie; and were it not for the intervening heights a view might be obtained of the old Church and Churchyard of Fetteresso, remarked by travellers between South and North as so charmingly situated among overshadowing trees. That, too, is the direction of Stonehaven, or Stanehyve, as it is familiarly termed, and the ancient Castle of Dunottar, ever to be associated with the sufferings of the Covenanters, and the preservation of the national regalia.

Dr Cramond recalls, before descending from his stand-point on the top of the hill, some of the notable persons whose progress might have been discerned as they marched from south to north along the Howe. He says :—

About 210 A.D. might probably have been seen the dense mass of the Roman army, under Severus, on its way from the camp at Wardykes, near Keithock, towards Raedykes, near Stonehaven. Edward I., with a large army, was at the Castle of Kincardine on 11th July, 1296, and on his return journey the following month, and he was again there on 17th August, 1303. Robert II. visited in passing the same Castle in 1375 and in 1383, and James V. was probably there in 1526. Mary Queen of Scots marched north with an army in 1562, and the Queen Dowager a few years before. In 1644 Montrose made his presence felt as he marched through the Mearns with his whole army, and the following year, as he advanced from Drumlithie to Fettercairn, plundering and burning all the way. A century later and we see the army of the Duke of Cumberland burning the Episcopal Churches and crushing the rebels. Much of the land within our view formerly belonged to the Church. The Carmelites or

White Friars of Aberdeen, as we have seen, held the superiority of the property of the Friars' Glen, gifted to them in 1402 by Fraser of Frendraught.

Most of the parishes in this county lay in the Diocese of St Andrews, but Glenbervie was in that of Brechin. Fordoun (St Palladius) and Fettercairn (St Mark) were mensal churches belonging to the Archbishop of St Andrews. Arbuthnott (St Ternan) was a prelate of the Collegiate Church of Kirkheugh, St Andrews. Laurencekirk and Marykirk were dedicated respectively to St Lawrence and the Blessed Virgin Mary. The hill on which we have our stand is specially studied by the inhabitants of the district as a prognosticator of the weather.

> When Stra'finla puts on its hat,
> What does Wirren say to that?

From Knock Hill, east of the Harescha, a charming view is obtained. Scattered over the hill, says Dr Cramond in his instructive and well-reasoned sketch, may be seen large boulders well-suited for burial circle purposes, and a single boulder, "The Court Stone," evidently the remains of such a circle, still stands in one of the fields. An attempt has been made to associate this stone with the death of Duncan II., and if this could be proved it would be exceptionally interesting, for it would be the sole contemporary memorial in Scotland erected to a Scottish Sovereign. This much at least is certain that he met his death at Mondynes. Other parishes in Scotland may boast themselves the birth-place of greater men than can Fordoun, but no district in Scotland has seen the death of so many Sovereigns. Donald, King of Alban (889-900), was killed in a battle between the Danes and the Scots.

> Over Fotherdun upon the brink of the waves he lies,
> In the east, in his broad, gory bed,

says St Berchan. Dr Skene identifies this with the

parish of Fordoun, although referring to Dun Fother or Dunnottar as the locality.

Following the line of the Luther, we pass Drumsleed Woods, where traces apparently of an old encampment are visible. So early as the 13th century part of the rents of Drumsleed were gifted for the support of the bridge at Brechin. Still following the same river line, we recognise the farm of Pittarrow by a tall chimney stalk and the old trees around. The old mansion-house of Pittarrow was demolished in 1802, and interesting objects destroyed; but, in spite of all, a feeling of bygone times still pervades the place.

No more honoured name is associated with the parish of Fordoun than that of George Wishart, the martyr, and there can be no reasonable doubt that he was the son of James Wishart, the Laird of Pittarrow, Clerk of Justiciary, the King's Advocate in the reign of James IV. The family of Carnegie, afterwards Earl of Southesk, succeeded the Wisharts in Pittarrow.

The buildings immediately south of Pittarrow, are the Mill of Conveth, a name that appears in charters from the earliest times. Conveth was the name of the parish of Laurencekirk till last century. The word "Conveth" means a due collected by a lord from his vassals, perhaps on journeys. The adjoining parish of Marykirk also changed its name about the same time from Aberluthnot, and the next adjoining parish of Ecclesgreig, or Greg's Church, became St Cyrus, so-named after St Ciricus, the Martyr.

Laurencekirk, of which more afterwards, lies well exposed to our view. It was the creation of Lord Gardenston, who in 1789 erected it into a burgh of barony, as Earl Fife a few years later erected Macduff. It was widely famed for the manufacture of snuff boxes, the special varnish and the secret hinge being the peculiarities. The firm, named Stephen, was appointed "Boxmakers to Her Majesty."

Not far off is Haulkerton—that is, the hawker's town, referring to the King's Hawker or Falconer. The family of Falconer has been associated with that estate for centuries. Garvock Hill, running from north to south, forms the eastern boundary of the Howe.

Further south, but hid from view, is Brownie's Kettle, or Sheriff's Pot, the reputed scene of one of the most improbable stories anywhere to be met with. Briefly, the story is:—"In 1438, while James II. was residing at Redcastle, Inverkeilor, on a hunting excursion, he was waited upon by five Mearns' barons, with great complaints against Sheriff Melville of Glenbervie, for the too rigorous exercise of his authority. The irascible Monarch being often annoyed by such complaints, passionately exclaimed:—"Sorra, giff he were sodden and supped in broo!" They quickly withdrew muttering—as your Majesty pleases! They soon laid a plot to carry out the King's words as if they were a command: they planned a hunting party to meet at a place in the Forest of Garvock, (long since transferred to the shades of oblivion), at a place now known by the names of "Brownie's Kettle," or "Shirra's Pot," a little to the east of Easter Tullochs farm, on the roadside over the hill to Bervie. These rude barons had ordered a caldron to be filled with water, and boiled early on the morning, the Sheriff being unsuspicious was unattended, and when the hunters came to the kettle each and all pretended great surprise, and looking in all around, these five barons tumbled the Sheriff into the boiling caldron, and each being provided with a horn spoon, took a sup of the *filthy broo*; thereby pretending to obey the King's command.

THE CHURCH OF FORDOUN.

> The Parish Church !—Behold its ancient spire
> Peeping from forth the tall ancestral elms,
> Beneath whose shade thousands are sleeping well,
> In undistinguish'd and forgotten graves:
> While here and there are old grey stones inscribed
> With quaint memorials—images of DEATH—
> TIME with his sandless hour-glass and his scythe
> And legends of high hopes for ever crushed—
> Of young loves blighted, and of elder ties
> Dissolved, not broken—Scripture texts,
> Old epitaphs, and rudely chisse'led rhymes.

The parish church (Rev. Mr Menzies), is a handsome Gothic building, erected in 1829. Around it centres much that is of interest to the antiquary. In the churchyard is the old chapel of the patron saint, Palladius, regarding whom, it is said that, in the year 432, he was sent by the Pope Celestine "to the Scots believers in Christ." "St Palladius' Well" is pointed out in the manse policies. As the old ballad puts it:—

> "Twas here he proclaim'd the glad tidings of Life,
>   And first gave us Bishops, they say;
> But after a long and a holy career,
>   He sank to his cold bed of clay.
>
> And within yonder chapel, just over our heads,
>   We are told that his relics do lie;
> And that the poor pilgrims with long staves and gowns,
>   Came here from all airts of the sky;
>
> There knelt they and worshipp'd for days upon end,
>   And fared but from barely stored scrips;
> Nor had they a measure of wine—but alone
>   This water to moisten their lips.
>
> And this crystal stream—thou may'st smile, but it's true,
>   Was long thought so wondrous pure,
> That the deadliest wounds of body or soul,
>   From its virtues received a cure!"

On a tablet fixed over the entrance to the old chapel it is recorded that it was built A.D. 452.

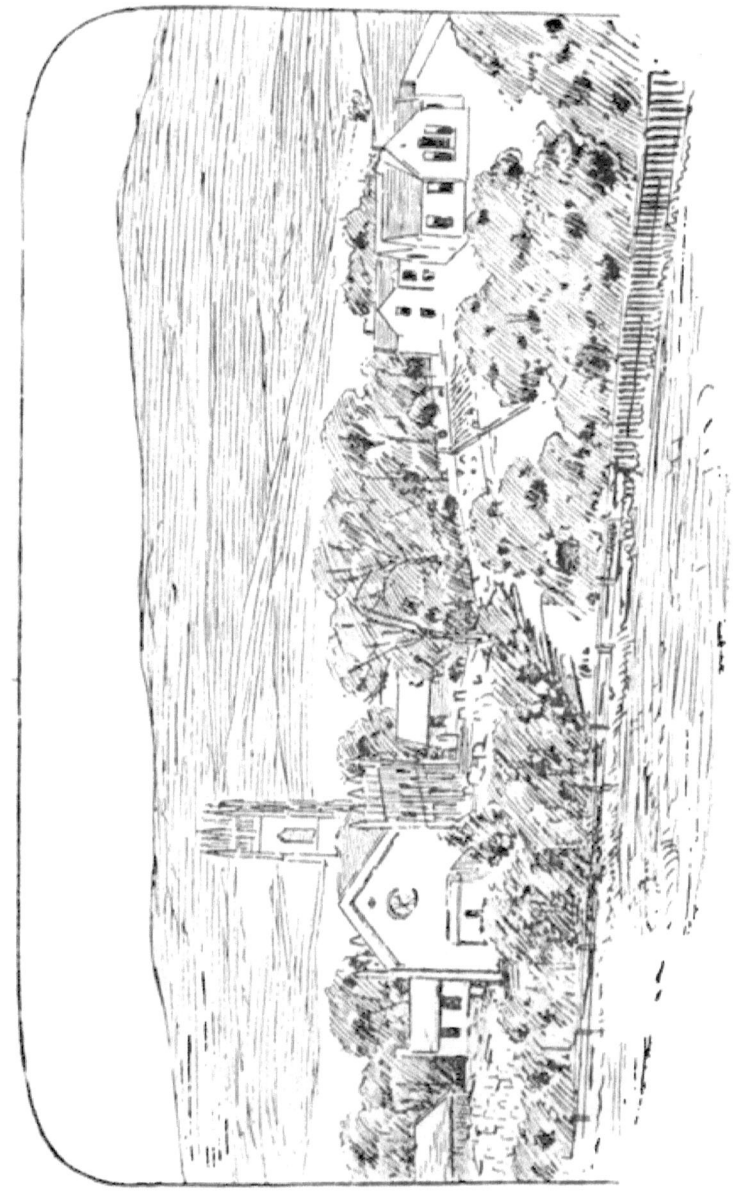

We will not stop to dispute this subject, which has engaged the attention of the learned in such matters, but would merely add that it was dedicated by Bishop de Bernham in 1244. In 1630 we read of "the church of Sanct Palladius, vulgarly called Pade Kirk," and Dr Cramond mentions the oldest district reference to the chapel that he has met with as in a charter dated 1603, whereby the King confirmed to John Wishart of Pittarrow "Sanct Pallades chapell . . . to remain in all future time as the proper burial place of the said John Wishart and his heirs." Inside the chapel now stands one of the famous sculptured stones bearing the spectacle ornament, riders on horseback, and other symbolic figures; also part of an inscription which the Earl of Southesk considers to be "Oeidernoin." There are other old stones within the chapel, also the parish bier, few specimens of which are now to be seen in Scotland. On the outside of the north wall, as the Rev. Mr Menzies was the first to point out, is a cup-marked stone, very rarely to be found on a building of any kind.

An old building that served as a school and schoolhouse stands in a corner of the churchyard. The building is said to have cost about £28, (£340 Scots). By the original plan it was to have a thatched roof, but when the walls were erected the heritors altered the plan so as to have a slated roof, and Sir James Carnegie of Pittarrow proposed a tax on gravestones, which, he understood, was then not unusual, so as to cover the additional expense. One wonders what these heritors would think were they to see the present school buildings and equipments, the cost of which, erected in 1891, was £2717. Beattie, the author of "The Minstrel," was schoolmaster of Fordoun from 1753 to 1758. In his "Ode to Retirement" he thus describes the neighbourhood of the Parish Church :—

> Thy shades, thy silence now be mine,
>   Thy charms my only theme,
> My haunt the hollow cliff whose pine
>   Waves o'er the gloomy stream—
> Whence the scared owl on pinions grey
>   Breaks from the rustling boughs,
> And down the lone vale sails away
>   To more profound repose.

Nestling in a delightful position on the further side of the burn is the Free Church manse. The minister (the Rev. John Philip) received, in 1894, a public testimonial on the occasion of his jubilee as Free Church minister of Fordoun.

A very enjoyable day might be spent in making a circular tour of the Kincardineshire villages and places of interest, starting from Fordoun on to Stonehaven, and along the coast to St Cyrus, from which, over the Hill of Garvock, we arrive at Laurencekirk, the next halting place in our present tour.

Between Auchinblae and Fordoun Station is the estate of Redhall, with its fine old mansion house cozily embedded amongst luxuriant beeches. The genial owner is Captain Carnegie, factor to the Earl of Southesk.

LORD MONBODDO AND BURNS.

The estate of Monboddo is beautifully wooded, and has a fine mansion house, about a mile and a half east of Auchinblae, where Dr Johnston visited Lord Monboddo, a meeting, as described by Boswell, which represents all parties in a pleasant light. The romantic old mansion was erected by Colonel Irvine, the founder of the family of Monboddo, in 1635, and considerable additions were made to it by Lord

Monboddo. Mr Irvine-Burnett's maternal aunt, Elizabeth Burnett, who died of consumption, on the 17th June, 1790, at the early age of twenty-three years, has been immortalised by Burns. Her monody begins :—

> " Life ne'er exulted in so rich a prize
> As Burnett, lovely from her native skies ;
> Nor envious death so triumph'd in a blow,
> As that which laid the accomplished Burnett low."

Lord Monboddo and his daughter were the first to give Burns a hearty welcome to Edinburgh, and he never forgot the kindness thus shown to him. The poet had a warm invitation to Monboddo House while he was in this, the district of his ancestors. When a mere boy, it is said Burns had been over at Stonehaven on a visit to his relatives there, and had been amusing

himself fishing in the Carron, when one of the proprietors ordered him off. He is said to have stood for a few seconds "like one bewitched," and then muttered the following couplet—

> Your water's wee, your fish are sma,
> There's my rod, an' Rob's awa.

—pitching his rudely constructed rod into the stream. The proprietor is said to have made enquiries about the lad, and "took an interest in him ever afterwards."

It is to the woods and walks of Monboddo and to the generous disposition of the proprietor thereof that Auchinblae owes so much of its attractiveness.

GLENBERVIE AND BURNS' ANCESTORS.

The Churchyard of Glenbervie, which is romantically situated about a mile west of the village of Drumlithie, is of considerable interest owing to its containing the remains of several of the ancestors of our national poet. In the neighbourhood—Bogjorgan farm—William Burness was farmer, father of the author of "Thrummy Cap," one of the most popular of chap books. He was a relation to Robert Burns. The Parish Church was built in 1826, having formerly occupied a position nearer the water of Bervie, where still stands the churchyard, and not far off is Glenbervie House, the fine old seat of Mr J. Badenoch-Nicolson. Glenbervie Castle is of unknown antiquity, and occupied the site of the present neat mansion house. In the twelfth century, it belonged to the Melvilles, and more recently to the Douglases, Earls of Angus. The Douglas burial aisle in the graveyard contains a curious monument with a Latin inscription, renewed in 1680, recording the brave deeds and alliances of the lairds and ladies of Glenbervie, as well as their descent from Hassa, a German, (730 A.D.). It was to Glenbervie that Edward I. marched from the Castle of Kincardine in his journey North. This parish was the fatherland of Burns, and four tombstones in the graveyard mark the burial-place and record the names of his ancestors. His grandfather, Robert Burness, was farmer, first in Kinmonth, and then at Clachnahill, Dunnottar.

EMINENT MEN OF THE MEARNS.

Here it may not be inappropriate to remark that much might be said of the men the Mearns has produced. Their ability has, in fact, become proverbial—" I can dae fat I dou. The men o' the Mearns can dae nae mae." The native of the district has no more genuine pleasure than pointing out to the stranger the different localities, humble enough in some cases they may be, all over the district, where men now risen to eminence were born or brought up. It has added many to the learned professions, especially clergymen, bishops, and judges. The Judges that have been connected with the district include Sir David Falconer of Newton, Lord President of the Court of Session (1682), Lord Monboddo, Sir James Falconer, Lord Phesdo, and Lord Gardenston. As we have seen, John de Fordun, author of the celebrated " Scotichronicon," and the most trustworthy of our historians, is supposed to have been born at, and to have assumed his name from, " the ancient town of Fordoun, about 1350." The ancient house of Falconer (keepers of the royal falcons of Kincardine palace), gave three senators to the College of Justice. Cadets of the Burnetts of Leys, and of the Douglases of Tilquhilly, were Bishops of the See of Salisbury, and were considered the greatest men of the age in which they lived. Dr John Arbuthnott, the intimate friend of Pope, was born at Kinghorn. Dr Beattie, author of " The Minstrel," was born of humble parents in Laurencekirk; and David Herd, whom Sir Walter Scott calls the editor of the first classical collection of Scottish song, was born on the farm of Balmakelly, Marykirk. His chief work was a valuable collection of " Ancient and Modern Scottish Songs, Heroic Ballads," &c., which he industriously gathered, and edited with much judgment and care. The collection was published at Edinburgh, first in one volume in 1769, and next in two volumes in 1772. Sir Walter Scott, in his Introduction to the "Minstrelsy of the Scottish Border," acknowledges his obligations to him for the use of MSS., containing nearly a hundred songs and ballads, published and unpublished; and to these he often refers in his Notes to the Minstrelsy. Regarding Lord Monboddo, author of "The Origin and Progress of Languages," &c., it is sufficient to remark at present that, though somewhat eccentric, he was one of the greatest scholars of the age, and his table was open to all votaries of literature and art. To him and his daughter, "the fair Burnett," Burns owed a deep debt of gratitude.

A SMALL COUNTY RICH IN HISTORICAL LORE.

At a recent re-union of natives of Kincardineshire in Glasgow, a Stonehaven gentleman, in the course of a most interesting and comprehensive speech, said:—

There are 33 counties in all Scotland, and in the order of population, Kincardineshire comes in as 23rd. As a matter of fact the whole population of our county is only little over 35,000, and I have no doubt the whole of these could be transferred from Kincardineshire to Glasgow, without causing you serious inconvenience. But in spite of these disadvantages and drawbacks it cannot be said of Kincardineshire that it is an insignificant or uninteresting county. On the contrary, it is a county full of historical associations, and possesses many and great natural beauties and attractions. We have Dunnottar Castle, one of the most interesting of the historical remains of Scotland. With this fine old ruin tradition has associated the name of Sir William Wallace; here were enacted some of the most stirring scenes in the Covenanting struggle: the soldiers of Cromwell besieged it in 1651; and here was concealed for a short time the Regalia of Scotland, afterwards removed to the Parish Church of

Kinneff in a way that was highly creditable to female ingenuity. We have the old churchyard of Dunnottar, also associated with the covenanting struggle, and the scene of the labours of Robert Patterson, who had been immortalised by Sir Walter Scott in "Old Mortality." These, taken from one small corner of Kincardineshire, are sufficient to show you how rich and varied are the historical associations of our county. On the other hand in these days the natural beauties and attractions of Kincardineshire have become more and more appreciated, with the result that several places are now fashionable and favourite summer resorts, and this I think is particularly so with the county town. . . . I may be permitted to say, without giving offence, that the hillsides and braesides and seasides—if I may use such a word—of Kincardineshire are a far greater change to the jaded citizens of Glasgow, and that our climate is more bracing and more invigorating than the somewhat relaxing climate of the west.

Drumlithie.

Drumlithie is an old and irregularly built village and burgh of barony. Its Episcopal Chapel was burnt by the Duke of Cumberland in 1746, and the clergyman imprisoned with others in the county jail. A Mrs Effy Turnbull gave the congregation a house for a chapel in 1792, when they removed from the low thatched building which had been sufficient for their worship when the penal laws were severely pressed. According to Nisbet, the Turnbulls were first settled in Teviotdale, and had a charter from Robert I. of the lands of Bedrule, in that district. Hector Boece, who attributes the origin of the name to a period long after the first assumption of it, says that a person called *Rule* turned a wild bull and wrung off its head, when it was about to attack King Robert the Bruce, who was hunting in the forrest of Callander, for which he received certain estates, and thereupon assumed the name of Turn-bull! In 1689, there were Turnbulls designed of Stracathro and of Smiddyhill, in Angus, one of them, Andrew, collecting the rental of the bishopric of Brechin for the years 1689-91; and in 1698 John Turnbull succeeded his father, also John, in the property of Stracathro.

Stonehaven.

To the seeker after health, rest, or pleasure, few summer resorts can compare with Stonehaven. We are told that it possesses manifold attractions for "all sorts and conditions of men"—a splendid bay, numerous walks along the coast, beautiful shaded paths and woods in several directions, drives through some of the prettiest scenery one could desire to see, places of rare historical interest; all this, along with fishing in the clear-running streams—the Cowie and the Carron—boating, fine roads for cycling, recreation grounds, tennis and bowling, combined with the refreshing breezes from the German Ocean, all go to make a sojourn here pleasant and healthful.

The water supply is plentiful and of most excellent quality. The town is in every way suited to the wants of those who desire to enjoy the luxury of a country retreat, and at the same time to participate in the comforts of a modern town. Indeed, there are few places that can offer such advantages of scenery as the county town of Kincardineshire, and the large number of visitors and the frequency of their return afford the best possible proof that Stonehaven posseses attractions of which few watering-places can boast.

The Old Town (which is situated in the parish of Dunnottar, of which the Rev. Mr Barron is minister), says a writer on "Stonehaven as a summer resort," with its busy fleet of fishing boats, will well repay a visit, especially should the herring fishing be at its height. Several of the houses are at least two or three hundred years old, and have witnessed many stirring scenes. They may have been the abode of those who were butchered by Montrose, or they may have witnessed the triumphal march of Charles II. to Dunnottar.

In the High Street are the market cross; the tolbooth or court house and prison down to 1767; the house of Provost John Clark, which alone escaped Montrose's burning in 1645, and lodged the Duke of Cumberland in 1746; St James' Episcopal Church, which served the Duke for a stable, and the elegant county court-house, rebuilt in 1867.

The new town, founded by Robert Barclay of Urie, stands between Carron and Cowie on the "Links of Arduthie" in Fetteresso parish (of which the Rev. J. Robertson is the minister), and is joined to the old town by a bridge on the Carron. The town contains a spacious square, with wide and regular streets, several of them named after members of the Barclay family.

The old pier was built in 1700 by George, 9th Earl Marischal; and the new one in 1825. By Acts of the Scottish Parliament in 1600 and 1607, the seat of the sheriffdom and county courts, previously, as we have already remarked, at Kincardine, were transferred to Stonehaven.

PLACES OF INTEREST.

The view from the beach is very fine—the bay, from the two outstretching headlands, Downie Point on the south and the Carron on the north, extending nearly a mile. The bathing ground is considered a very safe one, and visitors may take an easy walk to St. Kieran's Well, there to drink the mineral waters. On the south side of the bay the rocks rise to a height of nearly 300 feet for about ten miles along the coast, while the many caverns to be met with will interest the explorer. The antiquarian cannot fail to find many objects worthy of his observation while in this neighbourhood. A walk of a mile or so will bring him to the old Kirk o' Cowie, with its picturesque burying-ground. A short distance south of this, on a well-marked promontory, will be seen a few stones supposed to be the site of the Thane of Cowie's Castle, which was believed to have been erected by Malcolm Canmore.

The old Churchyard where Sir Walter Scott's "Old Mortality" did so much to preserve the memory of others, will be found worthy of a visit; while Malcolm's Mount, a thickly-planted knoll, where Malcolm I. is believed to have been slain and buried in the year 953, and Rae Dykes, the site of a Roman Camp, carry the mind to bygone ages.

Ury Castle, a fine old mansion on the banks of the Ury, with magnificently wooded grounds, is about a mile north of Stonehaven. The Barclays of Ury flourished as far back as 1110. David de Berkeley (1438) of Mearns and Mathers was engaged in the "affair" of murdering Robert Melville of Glenbervie, Sheriff Principal of Mearns, upon which occasion he built the castle of Kaim of Mathers, "where the family lived awhile, for their better security." Captain Barclay Allardice of Ury succeeded his father, Robert, M.P. for Kincardineshire, in 1797. He was noted as a pedestrian and driver; his ordinary walking pace was six miles an hour: but his great feat was his celebrated walk of 1000 miles in 1000 consecutive hours. He could lift half a ton from the ground, and set an eighteen stone man on the table with one hand.

The estate was sold in 1854 (on the death of the Captain) to Mr Alex. Baird, who is now Lord Lieutenant of the county, and whose son and heir, Mr John L. Baird, came of age in 1895—the occasion being observed by hearty congratulations.

CASTLE OF URIE.

DUNNOTTAR.

Fetteresso Castle, about two miles from Stonehaven, is a very elegant and delightfully situated mansion, with a portico, on the canopy of which the family crest is richly sculptured in bold relief. It is one of the residences of Lady Duff, whose husband, Sir Robert Duff, Governor General of New South Wales, died in Sydney in 1895.

Dunnottar Castle.

There hung the huge portcullis, there the bar,
Drawn on the gate, defy'd the war.

. . . . .

Oh great Dunnottar, once of strength the seat,
Once deem'd impregnable, thou yield'st to fate;
Nor rocks, nor seas, nor arms, thy gate defend—
Thy pride is fallen, thy ancient glories end.

When lance and spear, claymore and dirk were the favourite weapons of war, few castles could lay claim to greater strength than Dunnottar, fully a mile south-west of Stonehaven. The peninsula upon which it stands rises to a considerable height above the sea, and the stormy waves of the German Ocean break into foam upon three sides of its base.

The ruins consist of the great tower, 40 ft. high, other broken towers and turrets, the palace, the chapel, the court-yard well, long ranges of roofless buildings and broken arches, dismal halls, damp vaults, and gruesome chambers. Tradition reports that the Picts had a fort on this rock. It was held by the English in 1297, when 4000 of their forces were driven in by Wallace, who, according to Blind Harry, forced his way by a window still shown, and

"Burnt up the kirk and all that was therein,
Attour the rock the lave ran with great din;
Some hung on crags, right dolefully to dee,
Some lap, some fell, some floyter'd in the sea."

Edward Baliol garrisoned the rock with English

soldiers, but it was retaken, in 1336, by Sir Andrew Murray the Regent, and Sir Robert Keith, grandson of "the gallant Keith," of Bannockburn. Sir William Keith, grandson of the above Sir Robert, built the tower and the older parts. When William became 4th Earl in 1530, the family lands were extensive, not only in the Mearns, but throughout all Scotland. George, the 5th Earl, was the founder of Marischal College in 1593. In 1645, William, 7th Earl, Andrew Cant, and fifteen others of the Covenanting clergy, took refuge in the castle at the approach of Montrose and his troops. In 1650, Charles II. visited Dunnottar, and the Scottish regalia were brought to it for safety. In 1651, the Earl, on leaving for the wars, made Ogilvy of Barras governor, and he, with two officers and forty men, held the castle, the last in Scotland, against Cromwell's forces till May 1652, when famine compelled them to surrender. Being unable to deliver up the regalia, secretly removed by Mrs Granger of Kinneff, he was imprisoned, and his lady threatened with torture. From May to August, 1685, Dunnottar was used as a state prison for one hundred and sixty-seven Covenanters, of whom forty-five were females, from the west of Scotland. They were thrust into a damp dungeon, now called the "Whig's Vault." Of twenty-five who tried to escape, fifteen were retaken and tortured—some to death—by the boot, rack, and thumbkin. The rings are yet shown to which prisoners were chained, and the "Martyrs' Monument" in the ancient churchyard serves to preserve the tradition. The monument owes its preservation chiefly to David Paterson, the hero of Sir Walter Scott's celebrated novel of "Old Mortality." It was here, in the summer of 1788, while Scott was spending a few days with Mr Walker, then minister of the parish, that he met with Paterson busily employed in restoring the inscription on this tomb, and it was his singular taste and veneration for the Covenanters that suggested, long afterwards, the idea of one of the best of Scott's works. It was also during Scott's stay at the manse of Dunnottar that he saw Kate Moncur, a Crawton fishwife. It was affirmed by those who knew her that she was the original of Meg Mucklebackit, "The Antiquary." Two "perished comeing donne the rock," as recorded on the stone erected by the survivors, who had returned from banishment in 1688. In 1689 the fortress was occupied by government troops. After the rebellion of 1715, and the forfeiture of George the 10th Earl, this stronghold was dismantled.

THE CHURCH OF KINNEFF AND THE REGALIA OF SCOTLAND.

> They tell how Scotia keeps with awe
> Her old Regalia bright,
> Signs of her independent law
> And proud imperial right.

It is said that one of the Kenneths had a royal residence in the parish of Kinneff, and that the name was assumed from that circumstance. It will interest the visitor to the quaint old church, however, to refer to the preservers of our regalia—Rev. James Granger and his wife. Granger was appointed minister in 1639, and Jervise tells the story in his "Memorials" as follows:—"The old church of Kinneff was, it is well known, the place where the regalia were concealed for a time during the civil wars. It is said that these were carried from the Castle of Dunnottar, at the very height of the siege, by being hid about the person of Mrs Granger, who was aided in her enterprise by the lady of Governor Ogilvy. When they were safely conveyed to Kinneff, they were buried below the pulpit of the church, and carefully watched there by the minister and his wife. They were restored to the

Government at the Restoration; and, as a proof of their sense of Mrs Granger's service, the Estates of Parliament ordered payment to her of 2000 merks Scots 'out of the readiest of his Majestie's rents.' Mr Granger was interred within the church, and a monument, with Latin inscription, now much mutilated, records the share he had in preserving the ancient honours of the kingdom. Besides the Granger's monuments, there are several others, of which the most generally interesting one is to the memory of Sir George Ogilvy of Barras, Governor of Dunnottar Castle at the time of the siege above referred to, and his lady, Elizabeth Douglas. Like that of Mr Granger, this tablet bears an inscription, recording the part which the Ogilvys bore in the defence of the castle and in the preservation of the regalia."

Before touching on Bervie, Allardyce House, Arbuthnott, and Parkside might be mentioned as being places of some historical note. A family of the name of Allardyce flourished from 1300 to 1800, when the estate fell by marriage to the Barclays of Ury. Arbuthnott House is a building of the 16th century. The belfry of the church (Rev R. M. Spence, minister) is still an object of great interest for the student of ancient church architecture. The church, dedicated to St Ternan, has a burial aisle built by Alexander Arbuthnott (1538-83), principal of King's College, Aberdeen, and in it a statue of Hugh le Blund, the founder, in the 13th century, of the Arbuthnotts. Fable says that he received large additions to his estates in consequence of having killed some wild animal that frequented the district, and, says Jervise, a *cannon ball*, preserved in the awmrie of the aisle, is shown as the *stone* with which Sir Hugh killed the animal. About 1482 a James Sibbald was chaplain of St Ternan, and wrote the Psalter, and other beautifully illustrated and illuminated church service books, still to be seen in Arbuthnott house. John Arbuthnott, M.D. (1667-1735), physician to Queen Anne, the friend of Pope, Swift, and others, and the greatest wit of them all, who, according to Swift, "knew his art but not his trade," is said to have had his birth and early education here.

Bervie.

It has been said of the little hamlet of Bervie that it lies upon a kind of shelf in the hillside as peacefully and as contentedly as a babe in its mother's lap. It possesses also a distinct advantage in being a railway terminus, and, as has been said in an admirably written and comprehensive sketch by its historian, D. Brown Anderson, "the tired traveller, or the wearied man-of-the-town finds himself in a quiet haven—no jostling in Bervie—the abode of that restful peace which only the wearied know how to enjoy—possibly as fine a place as any in Scotland for sick nerves."

It has, however, seen stirring times. King David II. landed at Bervie with his Queen Johanna on 4th May, 1342, and founded a chapel here. The site of the house in which the royal pair slept is still pointed out in Market Square. The King gave the town its first charter which, having been lost, was renewed by King James VI. in 1595. In the interval, however, in or about 1567, the Regent Murray conferred upon Bervie the honour of burning it to the ground because it remained true to Catholicism and Queen Mary. The Duke of Cumberland slept a night in the Manse when on his way to Culloden. A long peace then settled upon Bervie.

The first linen yarn mill in Scotland was erected here in 1790. Hallgreen Castle, a stronghold of the sixteenth century, with thick walls, and a modern addition, stands on an eminence within the burgh, and belonged at one time to the Raits, whose coat of arms, and the date of 1683, remain on an inside ceiling. The Carmelites had a seat at Friars' Dubbs (now the site of the public school) till 1567, when it and the town were burnt by the Regent Moray.

Mr Anderson, in the article from which we have quoted, anticipates us in our trip from this point round the coast to St Cyrus. He says:—"There is nothing finer than the walk by Craig David to Kinneff. By the winding path we look down to the right on a fine expanse of ocean, the white sails of the boats wooing the morning's breeze, a large steamer far at sea, while hugging the shore are fishermen's boats returning home. Onwards the path leads by caves and rocks, and then rounds the point from which the small sea hamlet below the church and manse of Kinneff is seen basking in the sun. The transition is so swift as to come with the force of a surprise. Bervie commands the entire section lying between Stonehaven and Arbroath and westwards across Strathmore to Auchinblae and Glenbervie. Running down the coast by rail I am reminded, too, that the district is also rich in song and story. St Cyrus takes us to Beattie's grave. It is impossible to forget the glint of his grave got from the car window through a rent in the cliffs near St Cyrus. At Montrose appears his "Ketty Pert," at Ferryden his "Jamie West," and on the main line between Montrose and Craigo the words of the witch's invocation in "John o' Arnha" runs irresistibly through the mind, so incongruous is the association of unholy rites with the lovely retreat of Martin's Den :—

"Will-o-wisps! wirrycows!
Warlocks wi' your lyart pows,
At three-quarters after ten
Hover round auld Martin's Den."

Benholm Tower is a turreted castle of the 15th century, with walls and battlements five feet thick. It was owned by the Earls Marischal. The estate of Benholm was sold about 40 years ago to Mr Matheson, and given in exchange to Lord Cranstoun for his entailed estates in Ross-shire. An equivalent acreage of Benholm being in this account entailed, it passed in 1869, on the death of Charles, eleventh Baron Cranstoun, to the Baroness de Virte, as heir of entail. The entail was afterwards thrown off, and the property was sold to William Smith, Esq., Stone of Morphie. It is supposed that the Tower of Benholm was built by Lord Airlie; and if so, it is three centuries old. It is an imposing square pile, about eighty feet high; its walls are about five and a half feet thick; and it has massive battlements and turrets at each corner, overtopped by a pent-house. It stands on what was originally a peninsula. Its east and south sides were defended by one of the small streams which run through the parish, and its west by a deep trench or moat; till a passage was latterly formed over the moat, in opening a new approach to the mansion. Rev. John Nicoll is minister of the parish.

Brotherton Castle, within a mile of Johnshaven is the beautiful residence of Hercules Scott, Esq. "Scott's Garden" at Brotherton is stated to have been the hiding-place of the Chevalier St George when on his way to Montrose in 1716, to embark there for France. The Scotts are a very ancient family. James Scott of Logie, Logie-Pert, a cadit of the house of Balweery, Fife, amongst others, purchased the estate of Brotherton, 1570, and gave it to his third son, Hercules, born 1621. According to Sir Robert Douglas, the first of this family who assumed the name was Richard Scot, son of "Uchtredus filius Scoti," who is so designed in the foundation charter of the Abbey of Holyrood house. The castle is a magnificent edifice, in the Scottish baronial style, and is delightfully situated on rising ground overlooking the sea. The policies are well-kept, and present a charming appearance. A deep and richly wooded romantic ravine, through which a streamlet ripples, divides the parish of Benholm from the parish of Bervie, and debouches into the sea at the foot of the gardens. The older portion of the building, on the east side, has a circular turret, and the walls in some places are about six feet in thickness.

Johnshaven is an irregularly built fishing village, and a coastguard station. Some fifty years ago it was more a manufacturing than a fishing village. In almost every house at that period the "click" of the shuttle might have been heard. With the advent of steam, however, the hand-loom had to give place to the power-loom, and the old-fashioned weavers, Hamlet-like, finding their occupation gone, had either to leave for larger centres of population, or become fishermen. The present villagers are a hardy, well-behaved race, and it is said that from few, if any, villages on the whole coast have so many first-class sailors gone forth. It is said that the natives suffered, along with many others, for their loyalty to the Stuarts during the '45, and there is a tradition that the Duke of Cumberland's soldiers plundered the village, and burnt the fishermen's boats for having sent out provisions to the Pretender's ships.

Lauriston Castle (Mr D. S. Porteous, proprietor), is nearly two miles north of the sea; and there is a story

JOHNSHAVEN.

of an unexplored cave on the shore, with much the same fable as that accorded to the Forbidden Cave, near Arbroath. It is said that a blind piper lost his way, and, entering the cave, wandered until he came below the kitchen-hearth of Lauriston, when, according to one version of the story, he was heard to sound his pibroch for some days, but the music becoming gradually weaker, it ceased at last altogether, and at that time the minstrel died: according to another version, he is still occasionally heard!

The estate of Lauriston belonged about 1243 to Sir John Strivelyn, who granted the chapel, together with a pound of wax yearly to the prior and cannon of St Andrews. Tradition asserts that the Straitons (who appear pretty regularly in the Scotch Parliament) possessed Lauriston from a very remote period. In the year 1411, it is recorded that, along with 500 knights and burgesses of the counties of Forfar, Kincardine, and Aberdeen, "Alexander Straton de Laurenston" fell at Harlaw, while fighting on the side of the Duke of Albany. The fall of Straiton is thus noticed in the well-known ballad:—

> "And thare the Knicht of Lawrie toun
> Was slain into his armour scheen."

The romantic valley or ravine of Den Finella forms part of the property of Lauriston, and, as we have already said, tradition affirms that it was so called because Lady Finella, the reputed assassin of King Kenneth III., was overtaken here by her pursuers, when, rather than fall into their hands, she committed self-destruction by throwing herself from the rocks into a deep gorge, where the water leaps from a height of about seventy feet. The stream is crossed at this point by a stone bridge on the turnpike road between Montrose and Bervie, and by another for the Montrose and Bervie section of the

North British Railway. The banks of the den, where the hart's-tongue fern grows luxuriantly, are tastefully adorned with wood, and laid out in walks; and at all times, but more particularly when the stream is in flood, few places in the neighbourhood are better worth a visit from lovers of botany or romantic scenery.

Towards the close of last century, a singular fate overtook the village of Miltonhaven, or Milton of Mathers. It stood on a low, shingly beach, and was protected against the ocean by a projecting ledge of limestone rock. This was quarried for lime to such an extent, that the sea broke through, and, in 1795, carried away the whole village in one night, and penetrated 150 yards inland, where it has maintained its ground ever since, the new village (of Milton of Mathers, provincially called Tangleha') having been built farther inland, on the new shore.

The Kaim or Camp of Mathers is another historic scene in this neighbourhood. It stood on a rocky peninsula overlooking the sea, where its ruins may yet be traced. Till lately, by reason of the encroachment which the sea is here making on the land, they indicated an old fortress, strongly built, and strongly defended, and occupying a most inaccessible position. The tradition is, that the Kaim belonged to the ancestors of the Barclays of Ury; and that it was the refuge of that member of the family, who, as we have seen, was deeply implicated in the horrible murder of Melville, Sheriff of the Mearns, and was outlawed therefor. . We may, without mortal sin, accept the tradition; though the author of the "Agricultural Survey of the Mearns" obviously had no great faith in it. He remarks (but his making Finella *Queen* rather sinks his authority), "the origin of the Kaim of

Mathers is generally cited in testimony of the truth of the extraordinary manner of Melville's death, just in the same way as Queen Finella's journey from Fettercairn to Den Finella on the tops of the trees is alleged, as proof positive, that the country was then thickly covered with wood.

> Now woe betyde the cruel deed !
> And woe betyde the pain !
> And grant good Godde that never more
> The lyeke may come again !

Ecclesgreig, the magnificent residence of Captain F. G. Forsyth-Grant, occupies, it should have been noted, a fine site on the summit of the Hill of Criggie.

St. Cyrus.

The oldest part of this picturesque and popular watering place stands on high ground some distance from the east side of the road, but the more modern portion is almost connected. With its well kept garden plots in front of the grouping of neat cottages, embosomed in rich flowers and covered with gay creepers, the line that skirts the west side of the road has a very inviting appearance. The Parish Church (Rev. R. Davidson) is on a prominent site, and its spire is seen at a great distance. In connection with this parish there are several ancient funds. The Straton Fund, being of a curious nature, is worthy of mention. The interest of £750 is divided annually into four equal parts, and given to the oldest, the youngest, the tallest, and the shortest brides married in the St. Cyrus Established Church, who have acquired a settlement in the parish—six weeks constituting a settlement, the sum being about £7 to each of the four candidates.

There were, according to Davidson's excellent

R

and entertaining "Guide to Montrose and District." two chapels within the parish used as preaching stations, one at Chapelfield, and the other at Mathers, the path to which passes along the top of the braes, and crosses the burn of Mathers by an old bridge, which is still called the " Priest's Bridge," The priory itself probably stood a little south from the Kirkyard, in the direction of the river, which about a century ago rolled its floods along the foot of the braes, and entered the sea at their eastern base. It must have swept away part of the site on which the priory stood, and at one time endangered the Kirkyard itself.

Perhaps in few places is there such a happy combination of all the circumstances that make the sea beautiful as at St Cyrus. From where the sun rises in the east all round to where he stands at noon is the great expanse of the ocean. Even the fields in the distant East Lothian can be seen with the aid of a telescope. Turning the eye inland, Montrose is seen beautifully situated, with the glancing basin of the South Esk behind. A prospect of the sea northward is ever cold and bleak, but here the view is towards the smiling south. Then the sunny braes of St Cyrus are from 200 to 300 feet in height, lowering gradually towards the North Esk. At the northeast they recede, and leave between them and the sea a pleasing expanse of bents and sands.

THE GRAVE OF A POET.

At the foot of these braes, says the biographer of George Beattie, poet and humorist, and author of "John o' Arnha'," is the Auld Kirkyard. There is something, we know not what, in our unconscious nature, which lures us to spend an hour in an old churchyard.

There are few old churchyards so interesting from situation, or from old associations, as the Auld Kirkyard of St Cyrus. The spot can lay claim to

great antiquity. At a very early date this was a Culdee settlement. Strange that this place, now so lonely, should once have been a busy centre of human life. Here, in the Middle Ages, the monks of the priory were busy studying the fathers, copying MSS., engaged in the duties of the cloisters, and waiting for preferment in the church. The youthful and aspiring students once walked here by the river side, or crossed to make an expedition to Montrose, an ancient town, and then more than now a port for foreign ships. Here the barons and their retainers gathered weekly to hear the chanting and the solemn services of the church. But all are gone now. No more the bell tolls for matins and vespers, the intrigues of churchmen are over, and though the sea still breaks on the yellow sands, and the river flows on with a never ending stream, the former haunts of learning have long been deserted. Not a stone of the buildings is left, and even the traditions respecting those times have perished. But of the generations who lived then in this spot, of their manner of life, and the things in which they took an interest, of their sowing and their reaping, and of all their labours under the sun, not a trace is to be found. They have gone to that world of which the Culdees told them, and nothing now remains but—the Auld Kirkyard.

Doubtless the monument of the deepest interest in the sequestered old burying place is that over the grave of George Beattie, near the south-east corner, erected about a year after his death by "the friends who loved him in life and lamented him in death." A marble tablet on the north-east face bears an inscription which shows the estimate formed of him by those who knew him well. The pathos of its simple wording accords but too well with his touching story. A wild honey-suckle, which has grown up in the enclosure, entwines its branches within the railings, and hangs its clusters of fragrant blossoms over the grave.

George Beattie was born in 1785. He studied law and began the practice of it in Montrose in 1807. His talents and his rare social qualities soon gained him a large share of public respect and affection. His society was courted by all classes of the community; and he was the life and soul of every company in which he mingled, and of every circle in which he moved. A disappointment in love upset his mind, and brought his bright life to a premature and tragic close on the spot where his remains now rest, 29th September, 1823, in the thirty-eighth year of his age. Much the lengthiest and the chief of Beattie's poems is " John o' Aruha' ; a Tale." The hero was John Findlay, one of the town officers of Montrose. As the poem introduces several places and scenes of interest in this district, we give a bright summary of the principal points :—

John, the hero, has been at Montrose fair, and on setting out late at night for his native Aruha', falls in with a witch, with whom he has some parleying. He loses his way in the darkness, and finds himself beside the North Esk, where he falls foul of the Water kelpie. Before they engage in mortal combat, John rehearses his exploits, that the Kelpie might know what sort of enemy he had to deal with. Then they grapple, and the unearthly monster, finding himself overpowered, loudly calls for help. At this call, the witches and warlocks appear, to hold their orgies, and work their horrid spells in St Martin's Den—and legions of goblins, demons, and spectres, hasten to the scene, accompanied by the shades of those whom John had slain in his numerous encounters. But, before they make an end of Aruha', Satan bids them lead evidence. The infernal court begins its sitting with music, and then evidence being led, the whole crew assaulted John, but ere they could make an end of him, the grey cock sounded his clarion, the morn appeared, and their hour was past. At the Ponage Pool John lost his way in the gloom, and, plunging through bogs and ditches, found himself in the presence of the Kelpie, beside the pool. The Ponage or Pontage Pool is named from having been the place of a ferry, and is the abode of the Kelpie. The Pool is recognised at once from the red brae on the north side, at the foot of which it lies. Martin's Den, where the witches held their incantations, is a wooded ravine, which enters the broad valley from the south side, further up the river.

Its edges are picturesquely hung with the tangled roots of trees and bushes. On the left hand side, looking downwards, and just beside the torrent bed, the cool, perennial spring, called St Martin's well, bubbles up among the stones. Proceeding down the den, the traveller suddenly finds himself out of the leafy darkness from the thick trees, in the bright sunshine of the open vale of the Esk. Logic Kirk is a little to the west of this, and lies at the foot of the brae on the same side of the valley. The ancient kirkyard is enclosed by a line of overhanging trees, and contains a number of old tombstones. The Auld Kirk has been repaired in the former antique style, and is used as a place of sepulture.

The creations of Beattie's genius are certainly of the wildest and most singular character, in which the grotesque and the ludicrous are strangely mingled with the grand and the horrible. What can exceed in energy his description of the dance of the ghosts and skeletons?—

> The very ghaists play'd antic pranks,
> They screicht an' shook their spindle-shanks,
> Clappit their wither'd hands and leugh
> Till 'mid the din of dance and battle,
> Their banes were heard for miles to rattle.
> And aye's they fell to crockinition.
> Their wizzent timbers stoured like snee hin,
> An' flew like cluds athwart the lift,
> As choakin' thick as yowden drift.
>
> . . . . .
>
> The thunder roar'd—the sweeping blast
> Their reekit, riven rags, blew past,
> An' show'd their parchment thro' the glim,
> Reistit, squalid, swarth, and grim;
> The skin hung down in shrivell'd flaps,
> Like spleuchans o'er their teethless chaps;
> Thro' skinny lips their blasted breath
> Mix'd wi' the wind, and smelt of death.

During the tenth and the early part of the eleventh centuries, the Danes committed much havoc on the east coast, burning Montrose in 980, and Brechin in 1012, but were checked at Luncarty, Aberlemno, and Barry, where the founder of the Keiths is said to have slain Camus their leader. Tradition bears that they were finally defeated at Commieston; and there, in the "Sick Man's Shade," at the "Stone of Morphy" and "Dannie's Den," a number of stone coffins and bones have been found.

The lands of Morphie and Canterland, it may be briefly remarked, were owned for a short time by the Lindsays, having been previously, about 1329, held by Fraser of Cowie, the trusty follower and relative of Bruce, and hence anciently called Morphyfraser. They were sold to Sir Robert Graham in 1629, and subsequently destined by will to the Barclays of Balmakewan, the present proprietor being Mr Barron Graham.

The adjoining property of Canterland was long owned by a family surnamed Ramsay, who held it under the superiority of the Cathedral of Brechin. From the Keiths it passed to the Lindsays—the last of that name who held it being John, nephew of the murderer of Lord Spynie; and the laird of Edzell and Glenesk having died without issue in 1648, he was succeeded by John of Canterland. He was Sheriff of Forfarshire, a person of great worth and a friend of the Covenant, for which, says Jervise, he suffered great losses. He died in 1671, and from his grandson the family possessions of Edzell and Glenesk fell to the Earl of Panmure in 1714—"and the once powerful race of the Lindsays of Glenesk is now represented as proprietors in their native shire by the family of Kinblethmont, who are sprung from a sister of the last Lord Spynie."

But here we have now, on our way to Laurencekirk, to cross the Hill of Garvock. The first mention of the Hill is made in 1282, when Hugh Blond, lord of Arbuthnott, gave the patronage of the church to the Monastry of Arbroath, "in pure and perpetual alms." The present church (Rev. William Stephen) was erected towards the close of last century. Some years ago an old *censer* was found under the floor, and is now preserved in the manse. Bishop David Mitchell of Aberdeen, who superintended Archbishop Spottiswood's "Church History" through the press, was the son of a small farmer in this parish, and Bishop John Strachan of Brechin was born at Redford, Garvock. A hollow to the northeast of the church is said to have been the place where the old barons, already referred to, boiled "an' suppit" their Sheriff, and an oblong spot, near the old site of St James' Fair is known as the "Packman's Howe," where two packmen "fell out," killed each other, and were buried where they fell—their packs being still "seen in the gloamings dancing about the fatal hollow."

Laurencekirk.

In recent years Laurencekirk has grown in popularity as a summer resort. It enjoys a fine climate, and, like Auchinblae, it has its charms and facilities, and very pleasant surroundings. Its authorities are enterprising, and ever willing to add to the attractions of the town. Nature has done much all around. The view from the Hill of Garvock is grandly impressive A fine picture is spread out, backed by the Grampian peaks, robed in pines, and capped with red-tinged heather. Below stretch out the fields for miles and miles on either side, varied in colour as one of our own native tartans. The whole country presents a pleasing aspect—"one glory of cultivation," as Pennant, in 1772, in his memorable "Tour in Scotland," prophesied the district would become.

The credit of having founded the village of Laurencekirk, as well as of having erected the burgh, has usually been given to Lord Gardenstone; but, though his Lordship's merits were great in the way of enlargement and improvement, it is certain that the village was in existence more than a century before he had acquired an interest in the parish. The parish church (Rev. Thomas Scott) was renovated and tastefully modernised during 1895. It was erected in 1804 on the site of an earlier church, built in 1626; but a sacred building, dedicated to Christian worship in 1244 stood on a site known as the Chapel Knap, near the Mill of Conveth. It had doubtless belonged to the Culdee Church, which had existed for centuries before the Church of Rome dominated the country.

The name of Laurencekirk (formerly Conveth) must have been in common use during Ruddiman's (the eminent biographer and grammarian) official connection with the parish, 1695-1700—the first edition of his Rudiments bearing on the title page that he had been "sometime schoolmaster at Laurencekirk." It was then a village with an inn, under the roof of which the celebrated Dr Pitcairnie sheltered himself.

The first occurrence of the name of "Laurencekirk" in the Presbytery records is under date 10th September 1701, after which, with one or two exceptions, the name of Conveth is dropped. The first start to growth and prosperity was given to the village by the advent of Lord Gardenstone as proprietor of Johnston. So early as 1772, David Beattie, his factor, appeared at a meeting of kirk-session "to purchase the loft belonging to the poor, in consequence of the increasing size of the village." When his Lordship purchased the estate of Johnston, Laurencekirk was a mere clay-built hamlet of 54 inhabitants. He built an elegant inn, with a library and museum, a town hall, an

Episcopal chapel, a spinning mill with a bleachfield on the Luther, and established the linen manufacture. Portraits of the original feuars are to be seen in the Gardenstone Hotel. In 1779 he wrote to them his famous letter of admonition, and obtained a Crown Charter, erecting the village into a burgh of barony, and empowering the feuars every third year to elect a bailie and 4 councillors, to hold markets and collect customs. His Lordship's energies, says the Rev. W. R. Fraser, formerly of Maryton, in his admirable "History of Laurencekirk," were first moved in this direction by a feeling which, in a Preface to his "Letter to the People of Laurencekirk," he has described in these characteristic terms :—

"In ancient and heroic days, persons of the highest ambition aspired at a character of being the founders of societies and cities. I have produced an elegant proof of this in a quotation from Virgil; and it is finely illustrated in a story related by Plutarch (I think) of Themistocles. A man of quality in ancient Greece, who seems to have possessed a modern taste of distinction and pleasure, asked Themistocles if he could play on the lute? No, said he, but I can raise a small village to be a flourishing city."

Encouragement was given to strangers settling in the village who were likely to promote its industry; and it soon became a centre of attraction to handicraftsmen and others from all parts of the country. According to tradition, only one branch of industry was at a discount in those early days of the village. A hatter had come from a distance to judge for himself what encouragement was likely to be given to a person in his peculiar line. The few days of his stay included Sunday, when he went to church, and observed that the only hats in the congregation were the minister's and his own. Disappointed, if not disgusted, he left the village early on Monday morning, resolved to prosecute the sale of hats elsewhere.

It was the rapid increase of the population from so many different sources that the Aberdeen Professor had in view when he penned the famous rhyme,

> " Frae sma' beginnings Rome of auld
>   Becam' a great imperial city.
> 'Twas peopled first, as we are tauld,
>   By bankrupts, vagabonds, banditti.
> Quoth Tammas, then the time may come
> When Laurencekirk will equal Rome."

LORD GARDENSTONE'S ECCENTRICITIES.

Lord Gardenstone was the author of several books of travel and "Miscellanies in Prose and Verse." He was Rector of Marischal College, Aberdeen, 1788-89. His lordship's attire was usually of the plainest description; and there is a story related of him which arose from this habit. On a journey from London he was outside passenger on a coach in the inside of which there were some "young bucks." At the end of a certain stage they took breakfast, the outside traveller being shown into an inferior room. The young gentlemen in the best apartment, being seated for breakfast, received a civil request through the waiter that they would allow their fellow-passenger to join them. A haughty reply was given that they were not in the habit of keeping company with outside passengers. His lordship then ordered a *magnum bonum* of claret, which he shared with the landlord, giving instructions for a postchaise-and-four to be put in readiness for him in the meantime. The landlord at the end of the next stage, who knew Lord Gardenstone, received him with all due respect to his rank; he had timed his journey so that the gentle youths were eye-witnesses of his reception. As might have been expected, when the tables were thus turned, the pretentious "bucks" developed into fawning suppliants. A polite note was addressed to his lordship, craving forgiveness, and requesting the honour of his company at dinner. But to the note the only reply was a verbal message, that "he kept no company with people whose pride would not permit them to use their fellow-travellers with civility."

His lordship's eccentricity assumed the still stranger

form of a strong affection for pigs. To one he was so much attached that he allowed it to share his bed; and, when good feeding and rapid growth made it too cumbersome a bedfellow, it was still lodged in comfortable quarters in the apartment. During the daytime it followed him about like a dog. David Cowie, Mains of Haulkerton, had occasion to see his lordship one morning, and was shown into his bedroom. He stumbled in the dark upon some object, from which a loud grunt proceeded, followed by another voice from the direction of the bed, "It is just a bit sow, poor beast, and I laid my breeches on it to keep it warm all night."

THE LAURENCEKIRK SNUFF BOXES.

We have already referred to the celebrated nature of the Laurencekirk snuff-boxes. Mr Fraser gives several examples of their fame, and tells that many years ago an Aberdonian in India met an Englishman, who asked him if Aberdeen was in Scotland. Being informed that it was, he rejoined, "Oh, you come from Scotland; do you know a Mr Laurence Kirk who makes snuff-boxes?" The maker was Charles Stiven, a name-son of the Pretender. His father was spoken of as a "gryte Jacobite," and the principles implied in that distinction seem to have been engrafted in the family. When the Duke of Cumberland had destroyed the Episcopal Chapel at Stonehaven, the members of the persuasion were in the practice of meeting for divine service in the house of Jean Stiven. It was unlawful for more than five persons over and above the household so to meet; and an evasion of the law was attempted by the permitted number assembling in a room, with a clergyman officiating, while the rest of the congregation occupied another within reach of his voice.

Stiven was brought under the notice of Lord Gardenstone, who induced him to remove to Laurencekirk—a likely place, when it is said nearly everybody, male and female, indulged in snuff. Lord Gardenstone consumed it in large quantities. He carried it usually in a leather pocket, made for the purpose, in his waistcoat. His lordship's use of the article was so liberal, that the folds of his waistcoat became a repository of snuff to the villagers, who, when conversing with him, helped themselves. It was customary for a lady in the position of a farmer's wife to receive a box filled with pure taddy as one of the first presents on the occasion of her marriage. For many years a thriving trade was carried on, and at one time there were three establishments devoted to the manufacture.

The present mansion-house of Johnston was erected in 1805 for a summer residence by Mr James Farquhar, a London merchant, who purchased the estate on the death of Lord Gardenstone. Alexander Gibbon, advocate, Aberdeen, succeeded to the possession of Johnston on the death of his uncle, Mr Farquhar. Mr Gibbon's only child became the wife of D. A. Pearson of Northcliffe, Writer to the Signet in Edinburgh. Mrs Pearson, through her maternal grandmother, is a direct representative of the line of Barclay of Mathers. Her succession to the estate gave to the number of landed proprietors in the parish a lineal descendant of John, brother of Humphrey de Berkeley, the earliest one on record, whose possessions in the twelfth century included a portion of the lands which are now attached to Johnston.

It may be interesting to add that Mrs Pearson belongs to the twenty-second generation of the race of Barclays, reckoning from John de Berkeley. Mrs Johnston of Kair and Redmyre is also in the twenty-second generation, though nearly three hundred years have elapsed since the separation of the lines to which the respective families belong.

Before leaving Laurencekirk mention might be made of Thornton, two miles to the west.

THORNTON CASTLE AND THE THORNTONS.

This ancient residence, with magnificent grounds studded with grand old trees and surroundings of great natural beauty, has been added to at various times. What is known as the Round Tower is supposed to be the oldest portion. On the Square Tower there is a slab inserted bearing the following inscription:—"The above now perishing date of this tower is 1531. Alexander Crombie, 1834." Over the entrance door is the date 1662. The back wing facing the garden was erected about 1847. We give views of the castle from the north, and from the south-west.

The first mention of Thornton in the history of the country was about 1204, when the name of Laurence of Thornton is mentioned in a deed by Henry, Abbot of Arbroath. In 1296 it is recorded that John De Thorontone did homage to Edward I. at Berwick-upon-Tweed. We further find that Valentine of Thornton received a charter from King Robert the Bruce of the lands of Thornton. This is the last mention of the Thorntons of Thornton until 1893, when Sir Thomas Thornton became possessor of the estate. Sir Thomas, who was knighted in 1894, and is an LL.D. of St Andrews University, is Town Clerk of Dundee, and holds numerous important public offices in that city, and received the honour of knighthood in recognition of his valuable and numerous services to the Liberal party.

The estate was carried by a daughter—Agatha—to Sir James Strachan of Monboddo, by whom she had two sons. The younger received Thornton, and was subsequently knighted by Robert II. The estate re-

mained in the hands of the Strachans for a long period, and through their valour the Strachans of Thornton rendered their name famous in history. In 1572 the then laird's name appears as having a seat in Parliament; and in 1574 he was appointed Commissioner for Kincardine-

hire to superintend the "making of waping shawings,"

which was then ordered to take place throughout Scotland twice a year. In 1606 the property fell into the hands of Alexander Strachan, who was a Commissioner of Exchequer in 1630. The term by which the Mearns men are so well known took its rise during an engagement under Robert the Bruce, in which one of the Strachans of Thornton took a very prominent part. At a very critical time he most successfully led the Mearns men to the charge, and so well pleased was the King that he exclaimed—"Well done, men o' the Mearns."

From the Strachans the estate passed to the Forbes family, and subsequently to the Fullertons, one of whom sold it to Lord Gardenstone. In 1804 his Lordship's successor, Francis Gordon, sold it to Alex. Crombie of Phesdo, who was followed by the Rev. Dr Crombie, London—a man of some literary fame. On the death of his son, Alexander, who enlarged the castle, the estate went to Alexander Crombie, W.S., Edinburgh, who greatly en'arged the ancient castle and adorned the grounds, rendering Thornton one of the most attractive places in the district.

The burial place of the Thornton families was the aisle built on the south-west wall of the parish kirk of Marykirk in 1615. This house of the dead is now dilapidated, but it was originally a very ornate structure, and had a beautiful monument to Dame Elizabeth Forbes, Lady of Thornton, and her husband Sir James Strachan, Bart. The old statistical account says :—" The pillars, images, and other designs were finely cut, elegantly ornamented, and highly finished." Near the centre of this monument is a Latin inscription, but it is so defaced with age, and by a burning occasioned by the Covenanters at the time of the Revolution, that it is no longer legible. On the ceiling of the aisle, which is of oak, there is a long list of the names of honourable families, with their coats of arms beautifully inscribed, with which the family of Sir James Strachan was connected. In the east end of the aisle there is a font, and on the north-east wall of the church there are two porches near to each other, in which were preserved the sacred utensils. At this entry lie the stocks, almost consumed by age, and on the outside of the church, formerly attached to the wall, are the jougs.

THE BEREANS.

Sauchieburn is the next point of historic interest. Here a Chapel was erected in 1774 for the Rev. John Barclay of Fettercairn, the founder of the Bereans. The name was assumed from the ancient Bereans, whose example they professed to follow in building their faith upon Scripture alone. Mr Barclay was succeeded by Mr Macrae, grandfather of Rev. David Macrae, Dundee. Another of his grandsons was the founder of the Congregationalist body in Laurencekirk. Here are homely incidents connected with three of the pastors of the Sauchieburn Bereans:—David Low, a shoemaker at Laurencekirk, succeeded the first pastor. When asked by a curious neighbour what stipend the congregation allowed him, he replied, "I get nae steepin; they dinna even come to me for their shoon!" John Todd, farmer at Butterybraes, was the next pastor. His discourses were alike practical and seasonable. About the time of Yule he never failed to warn his audience: "My frien's, beware o' cairds an' dice, an' that bewitchin' thing the totum." William Taylor, carrier at Fettercairn, was at first associated with John, and afterwards sole pastor. His services were of a homely description, making up in fervour for any lack of polish. While his colleague survived, the duties of the day were occasionally divided. When William had performed his share, he usually ended with a remark such as, "Noo, John, ye'll come up an' lat's see daylicht through the Romans." The weekly service was continued until about 1840. Soon afterwards the kirk and site were disposed of for the sum of £14 sterling. The congregation was speedily reduced to two aged females. When one of them had gone to her long home, the other remarked with feeling, "Ah, sir! when I gang too, the Bereans'll be clean licket aff!"

LUTHERMUIR.

Luthermuir is a scattered village, built since 1800, on a muir or common, and inhabited chiefly by crofters and handloom weavers, now greatly reduced in numbers, though a faint echo of the buzzing and rattling of the primitive loom of former days can still be heard. The place has a peaceful air about it, and we can see the smoke from the small pendicles lazily lingering for a little, and then getting lost in the blue of the hills beyond.

BALMAKEWAN.

The lands of Balmakewan were owned by Allan Fawsyde from about 1329 to 1371. They were subsequently in the Arbuthnott family till their acquisition by Lord Menmuir, the first Lindsay of Balcarres, who was proprietor in 1580. The mansion, which is pleasantly situated amid fine old trees and policies, near the junction of the Luther and North Esk, has been tastefully renewed and enlarged by the present proprietor, Mr James F. Lowe.

The original mansion was built by Dr Thomas Gillies (a member of a celebrated Brechin family) who amassed a large fortune abroad, and on returning home purchased the estate. At page 176 of this work we referred to this gentleman, who, though of eccentric habits, was a man of great benevolence.

MARYKIRK,

This quiet and cosy-looking little village lies very pleasantly on the side of the North Esk, and contains

the parish church and manse (Rev. J C. M'Clure),

a number of well-built modern houses, the remains of an ancient market cross, and a homely, hearty, old-style roadside inn. Comfortable little holdings seem to rise almost out of the bed of the river, as in a broad stretch it quietly ripples along, glistening like burnished silver, under the long and graceful railway viaduct; and all the gardens are so gay and trim as to suggest to the visitor that the love of flowers must be universal in this country-side. The gate-way to Kirktonhill House is in the village. It is the seat of George Taylor, Esq., is a quaint old edifice, and occupies a commanding situation.

A correspondent informs us that not many years ago old people then alive talked of the church only as "Mary." How a village arose here can be easily understood. The famous well near the Church, like that of St John at Balmanno House, is one of the purest and most refreshing water, and was of old believed to have excellent healing properties for the injured or diseased, whilst the sheltering hill above it, combined with rural lovliness all around, formed a scene where nature evidently intended a village to arise. The people seeking abode naturally came to a spot possessing so many advantages, and ere long houses, humble although they were, arose, and in greater number than now exist. The land was cultivated into crofts, and cottages and ale-houses, as old records attest, stood on what is now the finely sloping lawn of Kirktonhill, and along the quickly flowing burn which bounds it.

Marykirk village is said to have been the first place to see a valuable esculent—the potato—introduced in the district, an Irishman, whose name is forgotten, having in 1727 come from Kilsyth, where it had been for some time cultivated, and reared it in his little garden, without being able, however, for a time to get the villagers to share in his liking for it.

CRAIGO.

The lands of Craigo adjoin Marykirk. The Fullartons owned part of the property in the 16th century, and it was in possession of various proprietors previous to the purchase of the estate by the present owners. The policies of Craigo are extensive, and plantations spread out to a considerable distance in all directions around the mansion, leaving an open park in front. Some of the trees are remarkable for size.

Craigo House is a large building three floors in height, with a long frontage. The entrance is in the centre, the door being surrounded by a small portico, the front of which is supported by four Ionic pillars. Right and left of the doorway there are four windows on each floor, all of comparatively small size. There is a wing extending back from the centre of the house, behind which are ranges of offices. David Carnegie, Dean of Brechin, who died in 1594, was great-grandson of Sir Robert Carnegie of Kinnaird. He purchased Craigo, and was ancestor of this branch of the Carnegies. David Carnegie, third of Craigo, received a Crown charter of half the lands of Craigo, 1705; and another of the lands and Barony of Logie-Montrose, 1713; and another of the lands of Meikle and Little Dysarts, 1739. He married Margaret Dempster, heiress of Logie and Dysart, in Angus, and of Ballindean, in Perthshire, by whom he had eight sons and eleven daughters. Thomas Carnegie in 1785 disponed Craigo, Logie, &c., to his son David and his other sons, whom failing, to Elizabeth, Anne, Clementina, and Helen Carnegie, his sisters, equally among them. David Carnegie succeeded his father in Craigo, in 1793. He married Isabella Agnes, daughter of George Macpherson of Invereshie, and by her had three sons and seven daughters.

In 1881 these properties, and Logie Mills and Bleachfields, in terms of the settlement of their late brother, Thomas, in 1851, came into the possession of Misses Ann Grace Carnegy, Agnes M. Carnegy, Rev. Thomas Bain, Coupar-Angus, in right of his wife, Mrs Agnes Carnegy or Bain, and Miss Elizabeth Carnegy, the latter of whom is now the sole survivor of the family, the owner of the lands of Craigo, Dysart, Balwyllo, Pitforthie, &c. She resides for the most part in Edinburgh, although she spends the summer months at Craigo. Miss Carnegy is a lady held in high esteem by her tenantry, is of a very kindly and charitable disposition, and ever takes a warm and substantial interest in all that tends to the welfare of the district.

Mr Fraser writes thus of the highly esteemed ladies of the Craigo branch, who were remarkable for their longevity :—

Mrs Margaret Carnegie of Craigo, aged eighty-seven years complete; born in Montrose; never had a fever; her eyesight entire to the last. Her sister, Miss Carnegie, was also born in Montrose, and lived for the most part in it, till her death, aged eighty-one years complete. Very healthful all along, and did not lie in bed one day till her death, memory and judgment entire to the last. Their grandfather, David Gardyne Esq. of Gairden, had twenty daughters and four sons, all by one lady Elspet Arbuthnot of Arbuthnot. They lived sixty years in the married state: died at eighty-six years. Both had their memory and judgment vigorous to the last. They had six daughters married to gentlemen of fortune, in the counties of Angus and Mearns, and lived to between eighty-six and ninety years. They were brought up in a cold house, the Castle of Gairden, and had no fires in their rooms till married. Miss Carnegie's aunt, Lady Nicolson, lived till ninety-two years complete, vigorous as to body and mind till her death; and on her deathbed signed a deed of entail sixty times with her own hand. Her sister, Lady Arbeikie, lived eighty-eight years complete, and was cheerful with her friends the night before her death, knowing herself dying. Both the sisters, and the whole of the family were remarkable for temperance.

Logie-Pert.

There were two different churches in this district called Logie—Logie-Montrose, and Logie-Dundee. The first stood, as we have seen, near St Martin's Well, in a hollow on the west bank of the North Esk. Some years ago it was converted into a burial vault by Carnegy of Craigo. In 1565, William Gray, a relative of the father of the celebrated James Melville, was minister of the parish, as well as of the parishes of Pert, Menmuir, and Fern, down to about 1574, with a stipend of £188 15s 6d, out of which he paid the reader at Logie the sum of £20 a year.

The present church of Logie-Pert is situated near the middle of the united parishes. It is a neat, rectangular building, with four large round-headed windows in the south wall. It contains a very fine organ, purchased through the energetic endeavours of the present popular and gifted minister of the Parish —the Rev. James Landreth—from All-Saint's (Episcopal) Church, Edinburgh, to which it was gifted by Dean Ramsay of the "Reminiscences." The spacious manse is situated on the brink of a pretty den, through which the Gallery Burn ripples, and stately old trees shelter the building and lend beauty to the scene.

The old kirk of Pert, which is on the highway, near the Upper North Water Bridge, is a very picturesque ruin, bearing a marked resemblance to "Alloway's auld haunted kirk," and, adds Jervise in his "Memorials," as in the vicinity of that place a poet of world-wide fame was born in a clay-built cottage, so here, in a similar tenement, on 6th April 1778, James Mill, the historian of British India, was born. His father was a humble crofter, and the house in which Mill first saw the light stood for many years near the south end of the North Water Bridge. It is said that Mr Mill owed his early success to the kindness of Sir John Stuart of Fettercairn; and Mr Mill's son, the distinguished writer on political economy, bore the name of his father's patron.

Dr Bain, in his "James Mill: a Biography," says:—The spot of his birth is not far from being a central point in that part of Strathmore, extending into the two counties of Forfar or Angus and Kincardine or the Mearns, called "Howe of Angus," and "Howe of the Mearns." The strath or plain is from four to six miles wide, and lies between the Grampians, here rising to an average of nearly two thousand feet, and a line of coast hills of much lower elevation.

Of the various bridges on the River North Esk the oldest and most important is the one that gives the name to Mill's birthplace; a three arch stone bridge built about three centuries before his time, on the great central line of communication from the north of Scotland to the south; the bridge near the sea for the coast road being built only in the end of last century. The river is for a great part of its course the boundary of the two counties of Forfar and Kincardine. The parish of Logie-Pert, a union of two older parishes, ratified by Act of Parliament in 1661, Logie and Pert, lies along the right bank of the North Esk, and is the last of the Forfar parishes northward. Across the river is Marykirk, lower down St Cyrus—the coast hills and coast parish.

The oldest historic scenes in Logie-Pert are marked by a number of tumuli. Three of these are on the Laws of Logie, about a mile to the west of the House of Craigo; and there is a fourth on Leighton Law, on the border of the parish of Montrose.

A HISTORIC BRIDGE.

The North Water Bridge is a scene to which a melancholy interest attaches. Built at his own expense by the famous Reformer, Erskine of Dun, little did he think of the use that was to be made of it in the next age, in the persecution of his ecclesiastical followers. Argyle's invasion in 1685 ended in his capture and execution; but to a Government whose tyranny, civil and religious, was fast becoming intolerable, it created great alarm, during which the Privy Council ordered all the Covenanters who were in confinement to be sent to Dunnottar Castle for their safe custody. Like a flock of sheep for the slaughter, they were driven to their prison on foot, their hands tied behind their backs, and all manner of indignity and cruelty heaped upon them. At night they were crammed together in unwholesome apartments in jails, where they happened to be within the reach of these. One night they passed between the parapets of the North Water Bridge, which was guarded at both ends to prevent their escape. Regarding this structure popular tradition says:—

John Erskine dreamed that unless he should build a bridge, where three waters ran in one, he would be miserable after death. Going out in a pensive mood one day and walking along the banks of the North Esk, he met an old woman near the spot where the bridge stands, and asking the name of the place, she told him it was called Stormy Grain, where three waters ran in one. Recognising this to be the spot to which his dream alluded, he immediately set about building a bridge there. After the bridge was founded and partly constructed, a spate in the river carried it away. He commenced to the bridge again, and again it was carried away. This so discouraged him that he kept his bed. While there he one day saw a spider commence to weave a web, but it fell down. A second attempt also failed, but it succeeded in the third attempt. Encouraged by this he commenced a third time to build the bridge, and succeeded in erecting the handsome structure which has stood every flood to the present time.

In old times a great market was held at the North Water Bridge upon Sabbath as well as week days. The Brechin Presbytery Records, of date 12th October, 1643, state that the Sabbath was profaned by the market held there, and the minister of Pert was ordained to take notice of those who frequented the fair, and inform their ministers that they might be punished as Sabbath breakers.

GALLERY.

Gallery House is a massive-looking old mansion, weather-beaten by the storms of centuries to a rich variety of tints. It was erected by the late Mr Foulerton of Gallery and Thornton, from whom the late David Lyall, Esq., purchased the estate of Gallery. It is snugly situated on the southern bank of the North Esk, about a mile west from Marykirk village. The building is of three storeys, consisting of a central portion, in the middle of which is the entrance, surmounted by the family arms. There are wings on each end, which project forward some distance beyond the main front. From the side of the westmost of these a range of buildings is carried some distance farther to the west, and half hidden by trees, which are not surpassed in size by many in Angus, and throw an air of dignity over the scene.

INGLISMALDIE.

Towers and battlements it sees
Bosom'd high in tufted trees

Inglismaldie Castle is a noble old mansion, beautifully embowered amongst gigantic firs, picturesque policies, and ancient gardens. Few buildings can boast of a setting more impressive than that of the historic home of the Falconers, for here the elements of the antique and the beautiful blend together till they grow into one harmonious whole. The castle was built in the 17th century by Carnegie of Northesk, but has been much added to at various periods, especially by the present Earl. It was for centuries the seat of the Lords Falconer of Haulkerton, and is now the seat of their representative, the Right Hon. the Earl of Kintore, late Governor-General of South Australia, who is the 13th Lord Falconer and the 10th Earl of Kintore. He was born in 1852, and married Lady Sydney Montagu, daughter of the Duke of Manchester. Her ladyship's artistic tastes are widely known, many fine specimens of intricate embellishment in hammered brass and iron work being seen in the castle. Many of these have been thought out by the Countess, and measured with a handicraftsman's accuracy, and executed from her designs by the local blacksmith. A magnificent oak carved screen was erected by a local man near Inglismaldie, from Lady Kintore's own designs and measurements. The beautiful carved gates were procured in Brittany, the pillars modelled by the carpenter, and the carved figures picked up by degrees.

The surname of Falconer originated from the office of keeper of the king's hawks or falcons, and Hawkerstown had its name from being the place of their residence. These lands are about a mile north of Laurencekirk, near the site of the old Castle of Kincardine, where William the Lion and other Scottish kings sometimes resided; and William Auceps is believed to have been keeper of the hawks to King William, and to have received the lands of Haulkerton for his services. Willelmus Auceps, or William the Hawker, is the first recorded of the noble family of Falconer. He appears in an undated charter, supposed to belong to about the close of the 12th century, and by this he gives certain lands, situated on the banks of the Luther, to the church of Maringtun (now Marykirk). This grant was confirmed, as was the custom of the times, by laying a turf, cut from the land, upon the altar of the church.

Shortly after 1693 the Earls of Kintore acquired the lands of Dunlappie, and held them until about 1860, when the Earl of Kintore divided the lands into six portions, and sold them to as many proprietors, all of whom had previously been tenant farmers. It is said that four of these portions were possessed by parties named Martin, on whom the following triplet was composed—

> "Crawhill, an' Ba'hill,
> Rochie, an' the Greens.
> A' thae three are frien's."

Of these, Dunlappie is now held by the representative of the late William Carnegie; Cairndrum, by John Soutar; and Reidhall, by David Reid. The lands of Lundie, belonging to John Shepherd, are in front of Brown Caterthun. By practical skill and much labour, he has been able to bring a great part of them under high cultivation. Near Lundie House is a romantic den, in which bracken grows luxuriously to a height of from four to five feet. From the top of Lundie Hill the prospect is extensive in nearly all directions, and both pleasing and grand. It is said that Lundie was at one time an oak forest, and that the timber grew there of which the rafters of the Church of Brechin were made. When the rafters were removed and sold, some of the wood was made into snuff-boxes and household ornaments. In allusion to this tradition, the following lines by the author of "Wayside Flowers" were written and put on some of the ornaments, &c. :—

>This box was made from an oaken log,
>That was brought from the forest of Lundie Bog,
>At the foot of the famous Caterthun,
>Full seven hundred years bygone,
>And since that time, till lately, stood
>On Brechin church a rafter good,
>As, by this relic, you well may see
>It was sound at heart, as sound could be,
>Which is more, perhaps, than may be said
>Of you who have this inscription read.

The property of Auchinreoch — formerly called Muirton — was retained by the Turnbulls when they sold Stracathro. The present fine old mansion was built by the last laird of that name, who became embarrassed, and had to sell the property to Archibald Gibson, who changed the name of the property from Muirton to Auchinreoch. His brother Alexander added the property of Chapelton to the estate. Archibald Gibson had been a merchant in Calcutta. Alexander was in the medical service, and Conservator of Forests in India; and another brother, William, was a medical practitioner in Montrose. Archibald died in 1859, and Alexander in 1867. Neither of the brothers was married, and the two properties were left to Patrick, the grandson of their brother, Dr William Gibson, whose father, Patrick, a merchant in Peru, had died at an early age. The estate now belongs to the family of the late Mrs Catherine Gibson or Cumming, and the lands of Chapelton to the trustees of Alexander Gibson. The Rev. F. Cruickshank, in his "Footmarks in Stracathro," says :—

"Auchinreoch" is a recent name which has taken the place of the former one of "Muirton." The late Dr

Gibson, when he bought the property, being interested as a man of cultivated mind in the fact that it had formed part of the battlefield of Stracathro, desired to perpetuate the memory of the great historical event by the name "Auchinreoch, the field of the king." What king he meant does not matter much. He showed much better taste in making the change than some other persons who do away with ancient and significant names, because perhaps they are not very euphonious, substituting those which have either no meaning at all or a misleading one.

The farm of Newton, one of the properties acquired by Mr Campbell of Stracathro, owned at one time by the Livingstons, and from which Lord Newton assumed his judicial title, lies to the westward of the church of Stracathro. It belonged to his Lordship, who was raised to the Bench in 1806, and was esteemed one of the best lawyers of his time. He possessed a great fund of humour and anecdote, became excessively corpulent, and died at Powrie House.

The old suppressed parish of Dunlappie, an estate now owned by William Carnegie, is stated to have had an older proprietary history than any other in the county, having probably been gifted by King Malcolm III. to his valorous adherent Macduff, Earl of Fife, who is traditionally credited with having slain King Macbeth, and thereby restored the throne to Malcolm. The Abernethys were the superiors of Dunlappie (then Dunlopyn) in the 12th and 13th centuries, at which time they probably had a fortalice upon it, for tradition has it that when they returned from the Crusades they "found that the Lords of Edzell had taken forcible possession of their Castle."

Stracathro.

> It stands embosomed in a happy valley,
>   Crowned with high woodlands where the Druid oak
> Stood, like Caractacus, in act to rally
>   His host, with broad arms 'gainst the thunder stroke.

There are not a few important passages in the

history of this parish and district. An interesting and comprehensive treatment of some of these is given by James A. Campbell, Esq. of Stracathro, in his "Brechin District: Some Passages of its Early History;" by Rev. F. Cruickshank, of Lethnot; and by Surgeon-General Don.

On page 182 we have already mentioned that the churchyard of Stracathro is of historic interest, being the scene of King John Baliol's penance to Edward I. in 1296. Previously, in 1130, a battle was fought in the same neighbourhood between David I. and Angus, Earl of Moray, which ended in the defeat of the latter. According to Tytler and others, the Danes who survived the battle of Aberlemno in 1012 are said to have passed through Stracathro in their flight northward; and tradition likewise speaks of a battle fought here at a very distant period between three kings—Pictish, Scottish, and British or Danish —in which all three fell. These bloody conflicts may account for the numerous sepulchral remains found throughout the parish of Stracathro.

THE BATTLE OF STRACATHRO.

Mr Campbell thus refers, in his "Brechin District," to this great battle, the importance of which is shown by its being mentioned in the Anglo-Saxon Chronicle and the Annals of Ulster:—

David I. had become King of Scotland in 1124, on the death of his brother Alexander. His Queen was the Saxon Princess Margaret, sister of Edgar Atheling. It was during his reign that the Norman Conquest of England took place, and partly owing to the position of his kingdom, and partly to his connection with the Saxons through his Queen, his territory was largely frequented by those to whom the Norman rule in England was not acceptable. On entering upon the government of the lowland portion of Scotland, he had been followed into that territory by many of his Norman friends and companions, and had introduced Norman customs. When he received the further promotion of becoming King of the whole of Scotland, he was ready to give an extension to the feudal customs and policy with which he had thus become familiar. But his policy was not favourably received by the Celtic portion of his people, and in the north the opposition was headed by two grandsons of Lulach the successor of Macbeth—Angus and Malcolm. The former was known as Angus the Maormor or Earl; and his brother Malcolm tried to pass himself off as a natural son of the late King Alexander. These rallied the Celtic hosts and passed south over the Mounth with an army of 5000 men. King David was in England when news of the insurrection reached him. The battle was fought within a mile of the Roman camp of Keithock—on the lands of Newton and Auchinreoch. The result was that 1000 of the King's men, and 4000 of the rebels, were slain. The rebels were completely discomfited, and their leader Angus was killed. As to the part taken by King David, there are different accounts. One account would imply that he was present and in command of his army, but another account, probably a more correct one, says that his army was led by his cousin, Edward the Constable. After the battle, the King's army pursued the remainder of the rebels over the Mounth, and invaded and subdued the district of Moray. In the words of the chronicler, "thus David's dominions were augmented, and his power was greater than that of any of his predecessors."

The Church of Stracathro (or Stracatherach)—signifying "the strath or valley where the King fought"—was a parsonage of the Cathedral of Brechin, and the residence of the Chanter. The present church (of which the Rev. R. Grant, clerk to the Presbytery of Brechin, has been the much esteemed minister since 1851) was built in 1791, and was recently considerably modernised. It is a neat and comfortable place of worship, having two double pointed windows in front, and a belfry on the west gable.

The Session Records of 1715 show that the Jacobites carried matters with a high hand in Stracathro—the *factor*, however, spoken of in the following extract, being at one time a licentiate of the Prelatic Church:—

November 2d, Mr John Davie, factor to the Earl of Southesque, intruded on the minister's charge by taking the keys of the church, ordering the Kirk officer to ring the bells at the ordinary time of day, the people being warned the day before to wait on, and join in, the worship of a pretended fast or humiliation day for success to the Pretender's arms, and that under the pain of taking each man, master and servant, to the camp at Perth; which warning so prevailed that it brought the whole parish together at the time appointed to the church, when and where Mr Davie himself came at the head of near eighty men under arms, with beating drums and flying colours, and preached a little in the church, and after that kind of worship was over, he mustered up his men again at the kirk gate, and on their front went to Kinnaird.

Alexander Laing, who was originally a flaxdresser, educated himself, and became schoolmaster of Stracathro. He perished near his own house during a snowstorm in 1854. Laing wrote the well-known balled, "The Raid o' Fern, or the Battle of Saughs," and other poems. In 1840 he addressed the following lines to his namesake, the gifted author of "Wayside Flowers," in allusion to the occupations of their respective grandfathers, the date of their own birth, places of baptism, and their names, trades, and tastes.

> Our grandfathers rang our parish bell,
> . Inviting all to worship God;
> They toll'd their neighbours' funeral knell,
> Now both rest low beneath one sod.
> In eighty-six to life we came,
> And both were sprinkl'd at one font;

> Our names and surnames are the same ;
>   And both have view'd, not climbed the mount.
> To one profession both were bred—
>   Both still are in the land of grace ;
> Grant when we make the grave our bed,
>   That we may see our Father's face.

Surgeon-General Don, in the course of a series of very instructive and interesting articles—" Archæological and other Notes on Stracathro and its Neighbourhood" (suggested by the Rev. F. Cruickshank's exhaustive and painstaking "Historic Footmarks in Stracathro,")—contributed to the *Brechin Advertiser*, says:—

"The Northumbrian Anglo Saxons, who ultimately supplanted both Picts and Scots in the lowlands, were a most masculine race ; for thirty years in the seventh century they actually had the latter nations south of the Grampians under tribute ; and it was the keeping them in subjection which led to Eigfrid's invasion, and his destruction at Dun Nechtanin 685. This battle, of which many of our countrymen perhaps never even heard the name, was really (next to Bannockburn) the chiefest turning point in our history ; but for the destruction of the Saxons, they would probably have overran the entire lowlands in the seventh century ; in which case only our mountains, rivers, and chief natural features would have retained Celtic names ; and we should not even have had the name Scotland, much less the familiar *pits* and *buls* ; all our homesteads, hamlets, and towns, with rare exceptions, would, as in England, have borne Saxon names ; and instead of wonderful variety there would have been only dead uniformity. It would be interesting but unprofitable to speculate which might have been, philologically and historically, had the Saxons triumphed in 685 ; suffice for us to note that their time had not then come, but was delayed until the eleventh century. It then did come in the form of the Norman Conquest, an event usually associated with momentous consequences to England only, but which in reality equally affected Scotland. It was through it that Malcolm Cenmore came to marry the

Saxon princess Margaret, and through her that many of the best Saxons of England found their way to Scotland; and by her son, David I., that their supremacy was finally asserted at the Battle of Stracathro in 1130. David's policy may be summed up in the twin endeavour to plant Roman monasticism, and diocesan episcopacy in the religions, with Saxon colonisation and Norman feudalism in the secular system of our country. He succeded in both."

"In the interpretation of certain Celtic place names in and about Stracathro, I have been fortunate in securing the opinion of an accomplished Gaelic scholar—Dr Cameron of Fettercairn. He interprets the oldest spelling of the parish itself 'Stracatherach,' as the 'valley of the warriors,' which, as he remarks, is quite in keeping with its historical surroundings; at the same time it is also 'very good old Gaelic for the mossy valley of bogs and marshes,' which would express the early condition of the country along the course of the Cruick. . . . The high banks overlooking the Kingford bore the Celtic name 'Portsoy,' which means the 'sitting or resting places of those about to cross the 'port' or 'ford,' it was, in fact, the place where travellers took off their nether garments preparatory to a wade. The next name is Saxon; the bridge over the Cruick near the Manse, is called the 'Chanter's brig,' being the spot where the singers from Brechin Cathedral passed with a chanting sing-song to the affiliated church of Stracathro."

The lands of Stracathro belonged to the Cathedral of Brechin, and appear to have been in the hands of the Chapter until the Reformation, when they were given off to Captain Robert Lawder. After being owned by several families it remained in the hands of the Turnbulls from 1656 until 1764, and was again in the possession of two or three different owners, including a Dr Mackenzie of Jamaica, and of Patrick Cruickshank, who had also acquired a fortune in Jamaica. His heir, Alexander Cruickshank, built the present mansion house, and, according to Warden, made a deer park, and laid out the fine existing gardens. Mr Cruickshank's trustees sold the property in 1848 to Sir James Campbell, long the head of the well-known firm of J. & W. Campbell, merchants, Glasgow, who received the honour of knighthood in 1842 on the occasion of the birth of the Prince of Wales, at which time he was Lord Provost of Glasgow. Lady Campbell died in 1873, and her husband in 1876, and a handsome granite monument stands to their memory in the quiet churchyard. The present widely esteemed proprietor, James Alexander Campbell, LL.D., is the Member for the Universities of Glasgow and Aberdeen—a model landlord in every sense of the word, and one of the ablest and most consistent upholders of the Church of Scotland. As a recent writer (A. T. L.) on "Men of Mark" well says :—

Mr Campbell is one who has never swerved from his devotion and loyalty to the maintenance of the Empire, and one who, alike with voice and with pen, has unobtrusively, yet effectively promoted his country's cause. A good cause finds in him a ready champion ; and when once his sympathies are enlisted and his judgment is convinced, his energy goes forth in prompt and enlightened activities. His contributions to Parliamentary debates have ever been marked by sagacity and insight, and have displayed a faculty not only of acute thinking, but also of vigorous and incisive expression. The cause of education has no more sympathetic and enlightened friend. His speeches on educational matters have been characterised by thorough grasp, by rare practical wisdom, and by a freshness and suggestiveness that were stimulating and helpful. Himself a man of high culture, a remarkable linguist, and an enthusiastic student of literature, he is fully alive to the inestimable benefits of knowledge, and he has a clear comprehension of the true methods for its acquisition.

STRACATHRO HOUSE.

The mansion-house of Stracathro is beautifully situated on the right bank of the North Esk, near the

confluence of that river with the West Water and the
Cruick. Over the entrance, which is in the centre of
the facade, there is a massive portico, supported in
front on two fine Corinthian columns at each side, and
four pilasters, of the same order of architecture, at the
back of the portico. The floor of the portico, which is
slightly raised, is reached by steps in front and on each
side. The centre of the building is recessed, the
two wings surmounted by balustrades, projecting a little
way beyond. Neat buildings of one storey, with

handsome doorway in the centre of each, the front of
which is on a line with the back wall of the house,
project on each end of it, and have a pleasing effect,
as they help to lighten the massive appearance of the
structure. Beyond the one storey building forming
the west wing, and a continuation of the line, is a
handsome conservatory, stocked with a wealth of
floral beauties. Extending from the building, apparently on the level of the main floor, is a stone
terrace, some ten feet in width, running the length of

the house, and surrounded on the exposed side and ends by a stone balustrade. Behind the mansion the contour of the grounds admits of variety in the ornamentation, and this, with great taste, has been turned to good account.

All around is a profusion of gorgeous flower beds, not to speak of the wealth of glass-houses which are evidently attended with such care and skill that one feels on seeing the specimens of floriculture and of the fruit world that they hold the season at their service. Then there are stretches of lawn of the most enchanting kind, studded with great chestnuts and other umbrageous trees, some of them sylvan giants and woodland beauties, which seem to be at home in the rich soil. The eye rests on a highly cultivated country, dotted with homesteads of the most complete and modern design, proofs, if such were needed, of "the laird's" well-known solicitation for the comfort of his contented tenantry. The far-extending green crests and distant hills appear to sleep on the horizon like a cloud, with the blue sky above, which seems enhanced by the velvety verdure at one's feet, all going to form a truly delectable and alluring sight.

But it is time to leave this beautiful domain, for the evening mist will soon begin to rise over the lawns. We therefore retire by the finely sweeping avenue, and are soon again on the highway, within an hour reaching the Ancient City.

Sixth Tour.

Trinity, Cairnbank, Huntly Hill, Dun Church, Dun House, Broomley, Montrose, Ferryden, Craig House, Rossie Castle, Lunan Bay, Redcastle, Auchmithie, Arbroath, Friockheim, Montreathmont Muir, Maryton, Bonnyton, Farnell Castle, Kinnaird Castle, and Brechin Castle.

THROUGHOUT our present tour the elements of the beautiful in nature will again be attractively blended with what is rich in antiquarian and historic interest. Leaving Brechin by way of Trinity, within half a mile along the turnpike, we diverge to the right, and enter a shady road. We first reach Cairnbank House, which is a fine modern mansion, in the Elizabethian style, erected in 1839 by Mr George Smart.

THE BATTLE OF BRECHIN.

When grappling close, the thick ranks for to break,
What dreadful havock broad-swords there do make;
Such various deaths are terrible to tell,
Heads clipt in two on different shoulders fell;
The gushing blood from every wound does spout.
Where death can enter in, or life come out.
Long in suspense the doubtful battle stood,
Till Brechin's green was deeply dyed with blood
Which ran in purple sluices to the flood.

The late Mr D. D. Black considers that the old name of Cairnbank was the Templehill of Keithock, which, in 1444, was conveyed to Bishop Carnoth of Brechin, by David Conan, to be held of the master of the hospital of St John in summer. Speaking of Bishop

Carnoth, we may in passing refer to a dispute during his reign which appears to afford some evidence of the period when either the steeple or the round tower of Brechin was erected. Mr David Ogilvy, rector of the parish church of Lethnot, having failed to pay a sum, said to have been due from the income of the church of Lethnot to the bishop and chapter of Brechin, was repeatedly cited to appear before the consistorial court. He treated the summonses very lightly, and neglected to appear; but a court was held by Robert Wyschart, rector of Cuykstoun, as substitute of the bishop, at Brechin, on the 9th of February 1425, when it is recorded as having been proved that Lethnot was liable in 28 merks annually to the church of Brechin; and that in part payment of this debt, Henry de Lechton, vicar of Lethnot, had delivered to Patrick, Bishop of Brechin (1344-84), 'a large white horse, and had also given a cart to lead stones for the building of the belfry of the church of Brechin' in the time of Bishop Patrick, and which cart was made by Elisha Wright, then residing at Finhaven.

It will be recollected that the Earl of Douglas was murdered by James II in Stirling Castle, in February 1452, because he refused to break a league which he had formed with the Earls of Crawford and Ross. In consequence these noblemen joined the Douglases in open rebellion to the royal authority. Alexander Gordon, Earl of Huntly, was advancing with a body of troops consisting of his own vassals, and of the clans Forbes, Ogilvy, Leslie, Grant, and Irving, with the intention of joining the royal standard, when he was encountered, on 18th May 1452, at the Hair Cairn, near Cairnbank, by the Earl of Crawford, surnamed "The Tiger," from his fierce temper, and "Earl Beardie," from his immense hirsute appendage. Crawford was in command of the "bodies of Angus," and of the adherents of the rebels in the neighbouring counties, headed by foreign officers.

A full account of the battle is given by Lindsay of Pitscottie, and Mr Campbell in his "Brechin District" thus refers to the encounter:—

Huntly's men fought to gain the crest of the hill; Crawford's to resist them and drive them back to the strath. For some time there was a stubborn and cruel fight, with no certain advantage to either side. A reserve of fresh men was then brought forward by Crawford. These having the advantage of fighting on higher ground, rushed fiercely down upon the royalists and beat back their vanguard. This gave spirit to the rest of Crawford's troops, who charged the more impetuously on that part of the line which seemed to be yielding. Victory appeared now to be certain to the Tiger Earl, when an unexpected event turned the fortunes of the day. Among Crawford's troops was a body of men under John Collace or Colless—Pitscottie calls him Colliet—of Balnamoon. They were the best armed of the Angus troops—having battle-axes, long spears, and broadswords; they were the men "in whom the whole hope of victory stood." But their leader had a grudge against Crawford. He had been disappointed the day before of a favour he had expected from him, and now he took his revenge by deserting him in the very moment when victory to Crawford's arms seemed certain. Collace passed over to the side of the royalists, taking his troop of axe men with him. Others of Crawford's men followed, and the battle was thus lost to the Douglas party. The Tiger Earl, deserted by those "on whom he lippened most, was compelled to flee for the safety of his life." The Earl of Huntly gained the battle for the King, but "got not the same without great slaughter of his folk."

After the battle the Earl of Crawford retired to his castle at Finhaven, about six miles west of Brechin, and is reported to have declared, in the frenzy of disgrace, that he would willingly pass seven years in hell to obtain the glory which fell that day to his antagonist, or as tradition has it, "that he wad be content to hang seven years in hell by the breers o' the ee"—the eyelashes. After his defeat Crawford turned his vengeance from the royalists towards those who had deserted him, wasting their lands and burning their castles, and he was left at liberty to do so, as Huntly was obliged, immediately after the battle, to return home to protect his own lands from the ravages of the Earl of Murray.

The Battle of Brechin entirely broke up the Douglas and Crawford confederation; and about a year after the battle the Tiger Earl made his submission to the King.

It is worthy of note that the Earl of Huntly, who gained such a victory for the King at the Battle of Brechin, was afterwards the innocent occasion of his sovereign's death. It was to celebrate the arrival of Huntly, at the siege of Roxburgh, A.D. 1460, that the King ordered all the guns to be fired. One of them burst, and the King was killed by the accident.

In the old Statistical Account of Scotland, under the parish of Menmuir, the Rev. John Waugh writes:—

When the Earl of Crawford fought in this engagement to revenge Lord Douglas' murder by James II., there was in his army one Collace of Balnamoon. This man being affronted at not receiving a promise of the lands of Fern from Crawford, in their eventful victory, left him while the combat was yet doubtful, and brought over to Huntly and the royalists the best part of his commander's forces, consisting of battle-axe, long spear, and broadside men. This turned the fortunes of the day, and forms a very important fact in the history of that time, as several writers acknowledge it was a most critical event to James, and established his crown, which, till that decisive engagement, had only tottered on his head.

Mr Campbell in his "Brechin District" says:—

The place at which the battle was fought was named

Huntly Hill—after the victorious commander. The site was a most favourable one for Crawford's party. It commanded a full view of the country along which Huntly's army approached; it was an easy position to defend, and a difficult one to assail. As you stand at the Hair Cairn, and look in the direction of Brechin, you see a gently sloping tableland, giving ample room for the easy development of troops all screened from the view of those approaching from the north. Looking on the other side, you see a steep declivity extending along the ridge of the hill for a considerable distance, up some part of which the attacking force, from the strath on the north, must come. You see the application of the words of Lindsay of Pitscottie, with reference to Crawford's troops, that they took "thair advantage of the brae syd."

The view from the summit of the ridge which rises between the valley of the South Esk and the valley of the North Esk would require the pen of a Ruskin to depict. The fine mansion of Stracathro and the beautifully wooded grounds by which it is surrounded lie at your feet, with the long level valley, dotted with picturesque cottages and substantial farm houses, extending to the north and west and lending ever-changing light and shade to the charming picture. The course of the North Esk, with its sylvan fringes, until lost in the rich foliage of the Woods of the Burn, like a long and gentle arm, stretches lovingly over the shoulder of many a verdant knoll; the pretty village of Edzell, with the remains of its castle, hoary with age; to the left the Caterthuns, and towering over all are several ranges of the Grampians.

But we cannot longer tarry, for although the prospect is very pleasing, and tempts one to linger, we have many a pretty scene before us on which to feast our eyes. Descending the hill, and passing between the dense woods of Dun, we reach the Church of Dun and Dun House.

Dun House.

How sweitlie shonne the morning sunne
Upon the bonnie Ha-house o' Dun :
Siccan a bien and lovelie abode
Micht wyle the pilgrime aff his roade.

The Church of Dun belonged to the Cathedral of Brechin, and became attached to the foundation of the Nunnery of Elcho, established by Sir David Lindsay of Glenesk. In 1583 the vicarage of Dun (a chapel erected for pilgrimage) and the parsonage of Eglisjohn —traces of which still remain near the house of Langley Park—were united into one parish. The present church (Rev. Alexander Anderson) was erected a short distance to the westward of the old church, within the grounds of the House of Dun, which is finely situated on a plateau, having in front a spacious park gradually sloping down to the highway, between Brechin and Montrose. Erected in 1758, from designs by the elder Adams, it is an elegant structure, the entrance being under a portico adorned with Ionic pilasters. The windows open out on a pretty terrace and a charming flower garden. The noble trees in and around the park are worthy of special attention. They are of great size and variety, including Wellingtonias, Auracarias, and other modern sorts, but perhaps the chief ornaments of the beautiful domain are the magnificent oaks, elms, beeches, chestnuts, and limes to be seen in all directions, raising their heads sixty or seventy feet above the ground. Warden says that from the large size of some of them they appear to have been well grown when the house was built. The present mansion superseded an older one, and it is probable that the larger trees may have been planted in the infancy of the previous house, which in its turn took the place of the ancient Castle of Dun, which stood within the present garden, near the kirkyard, where an old arched gateway, constructed of stone, and with thick walls, prettily covered with ivy, still marks the site of the old baronial residence. As we have it in the old ballad entitled "The Ghost o' Dun":—

>   Once on a time, near yon seaport,
>   An ancient castle stood,
>   Hard by a little winding stream
>   That gurgled through a wood.
>
>   Projected towers erect on high
>   Stood by the little stream,
>   Where minstrels oft were heard to blow
>   And honours to proclaim.
>
>   Those splendid walls, so vast on high,
>   Stood far above the trees,
>   With waving colours on the towers
>   That turn'd still with the breeze.
>
>   Now minstrels and towers are gone,
>   Their form is seen no more,
>   Nor waving colours on their tops
>   Seen from the eastern shore.

The old house of Dun was sacked by the Marquis of Montrose in the time of the Civil War. Erskine was obnoxious to the Marquis in proportion to his influence and zeal as a leader of the Covenanters. Having been pillaged by the Royalists under Irvine of Drum, the people of Montrose, fearing another visit, had the most portable and valuable of their goods removed to Dun House for security. Hearing of the store deposited there, Montrose could not resist the temptation of attacking it while passing from Athole through Angus, gutting the house, and plundering it completely.

The Den of Dun is a pretty ravine to the west of the house, extending to about a mile in length, through which a rivulet, having its rise in Dun's Dish, flows. The walks through the Den afford a cool and pleasant retreat, even in the middle of a bright summer day. The greenhouses, vineries, &c., on the right bank of the Den, are reached by a footbridge thrown across the ravine. Immediately to the south of it is the picturesque graveyard, in which are the ruins of the old ivy-covered Church, and many old tombstones. At the entrance a solemn-looking tree of gigantic proportions threatens the destruction of several tasteful stones around it—the decayed trunk leaning over considerably. We can imagine this to be the tree under which the ghost had a conversation with the miller, and revealed the secret of its distress:—

> I by my brother's hand did fall;
>   He shot me with his gun;
> And from this stately tree I fell,
>   And there my glass was run.
>
> When great Dunnottar fought with me,
>   And showed his mighty pride;
> And said he'd take his daughter back,
>   Who should have been my bride.
>
> And at this tree she died with me,
>   And there our vows were paid;
> And in a tomb not distant far
>   Our bodies two were laid.
>
> But thrice this mighty tree shall fall,
>   And twice be raised again,
> Before that I come back to Dun,
>   Or cross the eastern main.

To the north of the common graveyard is a square plot of ground, enclosed by a lofty iron railing, inside of which are deposited the remains of members of the Erskine family, including Archibald, Marquis of Ailsa, and Margaret Erskine of Dun, Marchioness-Dowager of Ailsa.

Dun's Dish we passed on the summit of the ridge to the north of the mansion. It is a small lake, extending to about 40 acres, with clear water in the centre, surrounded by a considerable extent of marshy ground. It might be made a pretty lake at little cost.

John Erskine of Dun, the future Superintendent, appears to have been in some way connected with the murder of a young priest in the bell tower at Montrose. Strange to say the tragedy tended to accelerate the fall of Popery in Scotland. For the murder of a priest a heavy assythment had to be paid by those concerned to the parents of the priest, besides a severe penance. He had been a good son of the Church before the murder, now he had a pilgrimage to make to some distant shrine before he could obtain absolution. While in the performance of the pilgrimage he made the acquaintance of some of the leading Reformers on the continent. Approving of their religious views he joined the Reformers and returned to Scotland to aid in the dissemination of the Protestant doctrines among his countrymen. Great events sometimes flow from trivial causes. The imposition of a pilgrimage upon Erskine brought to Knox and the other Reformers his powerful aid, and the Reformation.

It is believed that John Knox preached at Dun when on a visit to his friend, John Erskine, the Superintendent of Angus and Mearns, and the pulpit in use is popularly supposed to be the one which he then occupied. It has the date 1615 upon a shield, which bears the Erskine and Wishart arms. Above is the injunction—"Preach the Word." The old house, or Castle of Dun, in which it is said that Knox visited Superintendent Erskine, stood, as we have said, within the present garden of Dun, near the graveyard.

In the year 1555, the great Reformer, at the invitation of John Erskine of Dun, spent a month at his-residence, and is said to have preached every day. The inhabitants, high and low, of Angus and Mearns flocked to hear him. The result was that the Protestant faith made great progress, and the fervent appeals of Knox made so powerful an impression on the minds of the leading families that they bound themselves by a solemn pledge to renounce the Popish communion, and maintain with all their influence the right of Protestants to have the pure doctrine of the Gospel taught. He not only preached, but administered the Lord's Supper in the simplicity of the Reformed mode; while in the mansion house Erskine, Knox, Melville, Durham of Grange, and others often met to take counsel and to unite in supplicating heavenly guidance and blessing in the great enterprise in which they were embarked.

The lands of Dun were Crown property in the time of King William the Lion, who granted them to John of Hastinkes or Hastings He was owner of lands in the Mearns, and was Sheriff, and also Forester of that county from 1163 to 1178. The barony of Dun was then granted to Alexander Bruce, the King's nephew, but it afterwards passed to David of Strathbogie, who sold the lands to Sir Robert Erskine, who is much extolled for his loyality and fidelity to King Robert II. Wynton, in the following lines, states that he was the main instrument in bringing the Stewarts to the Scottish Throne :—

> "Robert Stewart was made King
> Specially throw the helping
> Of gude Sohir Robert Ersking."

Four of the Erskines of Dun fell on the fatal field of Flodden. Although the family, like many other baronial houses in Scotland, was much weakened by that disastrous battle, the Erskines, in the immediately succeeding generation, had a wonderful vitality. In the year 1588 four generations of the family were all living and in manhood. At the same time as these four lairds were living upon the estate there were five ladies, the wives or the widows of lairds, who also derived their living from the estate. John Erskine of Dun was born in 1509, and died in 1589. He thus lived in the time of five Sovereigns, and of seven Regents of Scotland. Members of the family of Dun have twice occupied seats in the Supreme Court under the title of Lord Dun. David Erskine, Lord Dun, was one of the Commissioners of Justiciary who tried certain of the Magistrates and Town Council of Dundee for petit treason during the Rebellion in 1715. Sir Thomas Erskine, a cadet of the family of Dun, was for many years, prior to March, 1543, secretary to King James V. Shortly before the end of the 16th century David Erskine of Dun married Jean, eldest daughter of Sir Patrick Maule of Panmure, and sister of Patrick, first Earl of Panmure. He died at an early age, leaving by her two sons. Their uncle Robert, who lived at Logie, and his three sisters, determined in 1610, to poison the two boys, that he might succeed to the succession. They administered a draught to each of their two nephews. One of the boys died, but the youngest survived. One writer, in the course of lengthy details of the tragedy, says :—

With the view of removing these obstacles, Robert and his three sisters, who lived together at Logie, determined to poison the "two zoung boyis." For this purpose two of the sisters crossed the Cairn o' Mounth and met with "ane notorious witche and abuser of the people," called Janet Irwing, from whom they received a quantity of herbs, with injunctions how to use them. They "steipit thame amangis aill ane lang space," and after much deliberation as to whether the dose should be administered, they resolved in the affirmative; and "about mydsomer" in 1610 the murderers "past al togidder furth of Logy," along with the eldest of their two victims, to the house of his mother in Montrose, where she and the other son were living for a time, and there the "poysoneable drink wes ministrat," and given to their "brother sones."

The uncle was tried and convicted, and executed at Edinburgh. The three aunts of the murdered boy were sentenced to have their heads struck from their bodies at the Market Cross of Edinburgh. Two of them, Isabella and Anna, suffered the penalty, but Helen was banished for life.

John Erskine, the last male descendant of the Erskines of Dun, died in 1812. He was succeeded in the estate by his daughter, Margaret, who was married to Archibald, 12th Earl of Cassilis. John Kennedy, their second son, on inheriting the estate, assumed the additional surname of Erskine. He married Lady Augusta Fitzclarence, daughter of King William IV., and died at Pisa in 1831, leaving a son, William Henry Kennedy-Erskine, whose only son, John William Henry, is the present Lord of the Barony of Dun. He is not a resident landlord, and the mansion house for a number of years has been occupied by Morton Peto Campbell, Esq., younger of Stracathro.

Here an extension of tour might be suggested. On arriving at the highway between Brechin and Montrose, and steering our course over the South Esk a short distance below, and completing our tour after endeavouring to do justice to Kinnaird, the magnificent residence of the Earl of Southesk, we will now direct our course towards Montrose, and continuing our journey, as indicated at the head of this chapter, through a very interesting district rich in national beauty and historic lore. A run of four miles will bring us to the beautifully situated and clean and salubrious town of Montrose. Before starting, however, we cannot help referring

to the graceful and romantic old bridge, of three arches, over the South Esk near the railway station, which was erected by the grandfather of the Marchioness of Ailsa, and was only completed a few months before his death. It bears this inscription:—
"This bridge was founded on the 7th June 1785, and finished on the 27th January 1787 by Alexander Stevens."

The lands now called Langley Park, with those of Broomley, anciently included in the barony of Dun, were given to the See of Brechin by Sir John Erskine of Dun in 1409. At that time they were known as Eaglesjohn. Broomley has again become the property of the Erskines of Dun, but Langley Park has become a distinct estate. Towards the end of the century the estate was acquired by the family of Cruickshank, members of which also purchased Stracathro, Keithock, Glenskenno, &c. The family continue to possess Langley Park. The mansion house of the estate of Langley Park stands on an eminence on the north side of the highway between Brechin and Montrose. Over the entrance is a balcony supported by fluted Doric pillars. In the vicinity of the house there are several large and beautiful birches. Two large old yews are to the north of the front door, and many magnificent beeches adorn the approach from the highway to the mansion. The crowning glory of the place is a Spanish chestnut tree of extraordinay size and beauty. The ground on which it stood appears to have been lowered, and the soil removed, leaving a sloping mound around the trunk. Immediately above this mound the tree is about 26 feet in circumference. Huge arms branch off in all directions, extending to a great distance, and some of them are turned down, and rest on the ground.

Before reaching Montrose we find ourselves in the neighbourhood of the pretty little village of Hillside, a rising "suburb," which perhaps ere long will be connected by a tramway. It nestles snugly amid fine trees, neatly trimmed hedges, and sheltering shrubberies. The cottages and villas, built from tasteful designs, are picturesquely situated on the sunny southern slope of the rising ground to our left. Each building has its garden—from the quaint thatch-roofed cot of the humble resident, with its carefully tended little plot, to the extensive gardens and grounds of the retired men of business, and a visit would prove very pleasing, for in few places are to be seen flowers growing in such gay profusion and perfection.

> Soft Pity turns her eye from these,
> To scenes that humble human pride;
> Where prostrate reason—dire disease!
> Has found a home at Sunnyside.

Almost adjoining Hillside, to the east, is a palatial building around which many sad memories cluster—Sunnyside Asylum, erected 1757 at a cost of about £30,000. As the number of patients yearly increase, (the average number being from 500 to 600) additions have from time to time been made. The grounds are spacious and cheerful, and many forms of light work, amusements, entertainments, and holiday excursions are freely provided with the object of bringing rays of sunshine into clouded minds.

Montrose.

> O, a bonnie wee toon is the toon o' Montrose,
> A canty wee toon is the toon o' Montrose;
> Enriched by the sea, an' adorned by the rose,
> There are unco few toons like the toon o' Montrose.

> It has routh o' auld hooses wi' quaint gable ends,
> An' its braw modern steeple far skywards ascends;
> Its wide-spreading Links are baith fragrant an' free,
> While its borders are washed by the surf o' the sea.
> A broad sheet o' water, where Naiads micht dwell,
> Lies its basin—the mune keekin' in't at hersel',
> A largess o' lustre richt lovingly throws
> On the hamely hoos-taps o' the toon o' Montrose.

It is said that, as early as 980, Montrose was attacked by the Danes, who destroyed both the town and the Castle, and massacred the inhabitants. The Castle occupied a strong position about a mile above the point where the South Esk falls into the sea. The invaders, says Buchanan, "set sail for the mouth of the River Esk, where they landed their forces, seized and plundered the nearest town on the coast, and murdered the citizens without distinction of age or sex."

William the Lion made the Castle of Montrose an occasional residence, dated charters from it, for the space of twenty years, from 1178 to 1198. On the 7th July, 1296, Edward I. of England came to Montrose by Arbroath and Farnell, and continued in it till the 12th of the month; receiving the homage of many barons and clergy from all parts of the country, including several from the neighbourhood. Next year Wallace rescued the town out of the hands of the English, and demolished the Castle, which it would seem was never rebuilt. In 1303, Wallace, then near the end of his career, landed at Montrose, having been solicited to return from France to oppose Edward. Montrose had its Convent, built and dedicated in 1230 to the Virgin Mary. David II. was twice at Montrose in 1369, first in October and next in December; where he confirmed the charters which David I. had granted to it, and conferred on it several new privileges.

It was from the port of Montrose that Sir James

Douglas, with a numerous retinue of knights and squires, set sail for Palestine in the spring of 1330, to fulfil the last charge laid on him by his deceased master, King Robert Bruce. That charge was to carry the King's heart to Jerusalem, and to deposit it in the Holy Sepulchre, which he had vowed that he would be a crusader to recover from the Saracens.

> We bore the good Lord James away,
> And the priceless heart he bore,
> And heavily we steered our ship
> Towards the Scottish shore.

Montrose has always held a comparatively high educational position. Its schools were famous even as early as the days of The Bruce; and he granted twenty shillings out of the public revenue for their support. Since the revival of learning in Scotland, its Grammar School has turned out many first-class scholars; four of whom were Fellows of the Royal Society of London. This supposes first-class masters: among whom was David Lindsay, son of the Laird of Edzell, afterwards Bishop Lindsay. It was he who mounted the pulpit and tried to restore order, when Janet Geddes hurled her stool at the Dean's head, as he began to read the services in St Giles's Cathedral, exclaiming, "Villain! dost thou say mass at my lug?"

The inhabitants of Montrose were among the first in the country to embrace the Reformation; which may be traced to the influence exerted on them from Dun, and to the copies of the Holy Scriptures, which their merchants, who had much intercourse with the Continent, brought home with them in spite of legal prohibitions.

In 1548, in the war in which England courted Scotland for the heart and hand of Mary to Edward, the English attempted to land their fleet in the mouth of

SIXTH TOUR.

the South Esk at Montrose. As they were endeavouring to land, Erskine of Dun, with the dart-men and other light troops which he himself led, attacked them with great spirit and vigour, and drove them to where his other two bands were concealed. In the civil war of the seventeenth century, Montrose was the scene of some sharp passages between the combatants.

The plague visited Montrose in 1648, and, from May that year to February, 1649, filled it with lamentation and woe. Crowds fled from the infected town into the country; and a large proportion of those who remained in it died. A tumulus, still pointed out on the Links, immediately north-east of the town, is said to be the place where its numerous victims were interred.

Montrose figures somewhat prominently in the Rebellions of the next century. At the Cross of Montrose, in 1715, the Earl of Southesk proclaimed the Chevalier St George, under the title of James VIII. of Scotland. The night of the 3rd February James spent in a house at the south end of the High Street of Montrose. There he wrote to the Duke of Argyle the letter intimating that he had consigned to certain magistrates a sum of money, to repair so far the loss which his unfortunate adventure had caused the country. In 1745, Prince Charles Edward repeated the attempt of his father to recover the kingdom. Montrose sympathised with him, as did also the county, which was then strongly Jacobite and Prelatic. There was keen contention between the loyalists and the rebels, as to which of them should have Montrose for their head-quarters. The loyalists had it first; but it would seem that the rebels drove them from it. It was the Duke of Cumberland who crushed out the rebellion in Montrose, as elsewhere. When he visited the town in 1746, he found the spirit of Jacobitism virulent and ascendant in it. The boys made bonfires on the 10th of June, the Pretender's birthday; and "Jacobite gentlewomen got on white gowns and white roses, and made a procession through the streets." As it was ladies that offered the affront, the military officers in the town had gallantly overlooked it; but Cumberland was a man of another mould. The commanding officer he ordered to be broken on account of his leniency; and he threatened "because the inhabitants are nourishing up their children to rebellion, to cause them to be whipped at the Cross, to frighten them from their bonfires."

So much for the antiquity of Montrose and the historic interest attached to the town. But it has many stronger attractions to tourists and summer visitors, and although, as was lately said by the Chairman at an annual reunion of natives resident in Glasgow, "it is unco wee for its age," it has made considerable progress in other respects. "The Jews believed that the name of a child would have a great influence in shaping its career," and so he was inclined to think that the name of the good old town—or its mottoes at least, "must have had a considerable influence on it." The motto, which means "The sea enriches, and the rose adorns," has been amply verified in the case of Montrose—in the harvests of the sea and its fishing wealth, and in the beautiful adornment of its public gardens and links. The speaker also mentioned, as we have hinted, that Montrose was not only amongst the first towns in Scotland to embrace the Reformation and to propagate its principles, but it was also the first that could boast of ever having female burgesses, for, in 1751, the Ladies Jean, Mary, and Margaret, daughters of Lord Falconer of Haulkerston, were raised to that dignity. Another speaker at one of these annual gatherings—Ex-Provost Lackie, one of Montrose's most esteemed citizens, said—

Let us hope they appreciated the honour, and held the corporation in greater esteem than did Miss Carnegie, when a deputation of the Town Council waited upon her, and solicited a subscription for the purpose of raising a small battery at the water mouth for the defence of the town. One of the representatives having addressed her she said, "Are ye ane o' the Toon Council?" He replied, "I have that honour, mam," to which she rejoined, "Ye may hae that *profit*, but honour ye hae nane." There seems to have been no doubt left in this lady's mind regarding the profits of members of the Town Council, for it is said that she was very much opposed to paying taxes, and one day receiving a notice of such payment, signed by the Provost, she broke out and said, "I dinna understand thae taxes; but I just think that when the Provost's wife wants a new gown her man sends me a tax paper."

The very name of Montrose has given rise to many conjectures — the French Minstrois, three hills; the Gaelic "Monross," but the most likely one is that of "Montis Rosarum." It had another name, "Celurca." Wind-mills must have been deemed of some importance, for in the eighteenth century a man of the name of James Young was sent to Holland by the magistrates, to learn the best method of constructing and working windmills. When it received its charter is not positively known, perhaps in the reign of David I. At any rate burgesses of Montrose are mentioned in 1261-62. Twelve of their number went to Berwick and took the oath of allegiance on behalf of themselves and the Burgh. The town was visited in 1773 by Dr Johnston, who cared for nothing Scotch, but on whom the town and its surroundings seemed to have left a good impression. It was also visited by our national poet in 1787, he having relatives in the town. I must confess that we have not shown the same energy or the same enterprise as has been manifested by other towns in the country; still, I do not think there is any appearance of the fulfillment of the old rhyme:—

> Bonny Munross will be a moss,
> Dundee will be ding doon,
> Forfar will be Forfar still,
> And Brechin a braw Burgh toon.

The town of Montrose has been the birthplace of some eminent men, such as Joseph Hume, the great reformer; Alexander Burgess, the great scholar; James Burgess, who distinguished himself in India; James Duke, Lord Mayor of London. It is well spoken of in the 17th century as a goodly town, clean, and regularly built. Well, I think no one will deny that it still sustains the same reputation.

As particulars are given of the objects of interest in and around Montrose in the admirable "Tourists' Guides" published by Mr M. Welsh and Mr D. P. Davidson, booksellers—to both of whom we are greatly indebted for several local illustrations, as well as to the enterprising publisher of the *Montrose Standard* newspaper—we do not require to go at any length into such details.

As a holiday resort, and as a retreat for those in search of health and sea-bathing, few places are so favourably situated, or offer more varied facilities.

Nature has been admirably seconded by Art, for the site of Montrose and its surroundings are most picturesque. It is seen to most advantage from the south—from the high ground above Ferryden, or from Rossie Braes. The view we give from the last mentioned point is from a painting by Mr Madoland, a local artist of more than local fame. The scene is well described by a writer in "Fullerton's Gazetteer" —"To a person approaching from the south, and coming in view of the town from the high ground traversed by the public road in the parish of Craig, the fine sweep of the broad river fringed with shipping, docks, and variform edifices stretching out to the sea on the right; the large circular Basin, set round with richly cultivated fields and forming the foreground to a far-spreading expanse of luxuriant landscape on the left—the town, lifting up several imposing structures, and retiring in a large broad field of architecture in front—the receding prospect behind it exhibiting a fine variety of swell, hill, and plain, and of mansions, fields, and woods, till the eye ceases to discern distinctive features—and the dark, vast amphitheatre of the Grampians, piled shelvingly against the sky, and forming a stupendous mountain-bulwark, at about twenty miles distant—altogether present one of the most diversified and magnificent views in the kingdom."

A gallant captain, writing in 1567, writes of the town in high-flown language when he calls it "a beauty that lies concealed in the bosom of Scotland, most delicately dressed up, and adorned with excellent buildings, whose foundations are laid with polished stones, and her ports all washed with silver streams, that trickle down from the famous Esk." Although this is perhaps somewhat fanciful, without doubt Montrose is entitled to be classed as one of the most

clean and salubrious towns in Scotland, the spacious High Street being admired by all visitors.

The Town House, which as we enter the street seems to terminate a very pleasing and imposing vista, is a large four storey building, with arcade below, and balustrade around the top, decorated on the west front with the armorial bearings of the burgh. It contains council room, court room, and commodious halls, with the public library and reading rooms.

The old bell tower of the burgh was of great antiquity; supposed to have been built by the Picts at a very early date. Inside the tower were bells and a clock, and on three sides of the parapet was a wooden dial plate, about 5 feet square, with hands to indicate the time. It was removed in 1830-31 to give place to the new and magnificent edifice which was built in 1832-4, from a design by Gillespie Grahame of Edinburgh. The present steeple is of elegant design and graceful proportions. It rises to a height of about 210 feet; with four pinnacles at the corners, 32 feet high each, connected with the spire by flying buttresses. The Parish Church, which is a collegiate charge (Revs. J. Niblock Stuart and Hugh Cameron) is one of the largest in Scotland. We are told that towards the end of the eighteenth century negotiations were in progress by the kirk session and heritors for the erection of a new church for the wants of the burgh. The consideration of this matter appears not to have been premature, for the enlargement and renovation of 1643 seem to have been of a temporary nature. In 1690 a meeting of the kirk session and magistrates was convened, in " order to consider the ruinous state of the quier, as also to fall upon such methods as it may be repaired." The only work that was done on this occasion was the supporting of the roof and galleries and the propping up of the walls " with trees brought from Edzell." With this improvement, the building continued to exist until December, 1790, when it was pulled down to make room for the present church, which covers the same site. Its interior, with two tiers of galleries, is somewhat antiquated, although there is a handsome organ. Doubtless the interior of the old fabric will soon be altered to meet modern requirements. Much information concerning the Parish Church and antiquarian matters connected with the town and district are given by the local historian, Mr James G. Low, in his "Memorials," and other works affording evidence of painstaking research; and in the admirable portfolio of etchings by Mr J. M. Smith, teacher of drawing, many ancient buildings and places and objects of interest are beautifully portrayed. Mr Smith has also issued a similar high-class portfolio of views in and around Brechin from his own sketches.

Besides its famous artists, Montrose has also its poets, some of whom have warbled very sweetly. We have already quoted from Mr J. E. Watt, under the heading "Montrose." His volume of verse "Sketches of Scottish Life and Character" has deservedly gained for him wide admiration. We have also referred to Alexander Smart's "Rambling Rhymes," and other works, but there are also James Bowick's "Montrose Characters," Miss Potter, a thoughtful writer, J. Marshall, and others.

The "Guid Tolbuith," spoken of by Guynd, which stood in the middle of the High Street, is now removed, and the site occupied by a colossal statue of Sir Robert Peel. Near by is a statue of the late Joseph Hume, M.P., who was of humble origin—his mother being left a widow with a large family. To help to maintain and educate them she took up a crockery business. Joseph, after receiving a fair education, was apprenticed at the age of 13, to a surgeon and druggist, and afterwards went to Edinburgh as a medical student. Having finished his

curriculum, he was, in 1797, appointed Marine Assistant Surgeon in the service of the East India Company. He continued to advance himself in his studies, and having acquired the native languages, he was appointed, during the Mahratta War, to the office of Persian interpreter in the army.

Speaking of the spacious beauty of the High Street, we might summarise the following particulars from materials supplied in a very exhaustive paper by ex-Provost Japp, who has so long and so favourably been identified with all that has in view the welfare of the burgh. He says:—

Our High Street owes its beauty to the fact that High Street on the west side, and Murray Street on the east, were thrown into one by the removal in 1748 of a row of thatched cottages which ran up the centre of the present street. In a quaint poem on this subject by James Bowick, he says—

> The roofs were made o' auld stob thack,
> The wa's o' plaistered fir;
> So down they came wi' mony a whack
> That ruddied wi' the virr.

What like was Montrose (or Munross) in not very distant times? At first a straggling village, mostly of fishermen, sailors, and the officials of the Castle, it spread along the banks of the South Esk, under the protection of the fort or castle, which in remote times stood on Castle or Constable Hill, where now stands the old Baths and Infirmary at Bridgend. It gradually spread up the slopes, and as far north in time as the North Port at the narrow of High Street and Trades' Hall.

In the fine view of the town by Miss Ochterlony, published in London, 1810, you have the old timber bridge, with drawbridge at its southern end. No bridge existed till this was built in 1794. The ferry at Ferryden was up till that time the only means of reaching the south. The wooden bridge stood till 1827, and the present Suspension Bridge was founded 10th September, 1828, and finished next year. The upper chain on the East side gave way at a boat race on 19th March, 1830, when some lives were lost. In Miss Ochterlony's view we also see the Horologe Hill, which occupied the south end of Hill Street.

On its top stood a massive pillar, with sun dial, and it formed a favourite outlook for the seamen. Also eastward stood the Windmill Hill, on which stood the windmill belonging to the town—once a source of revenue in grinding corn and malt.

The **Old Steeple** was at first without a spire—the weathercock and vane are in the Museum, and bear date 1694, and also the rude iron works of the old clock, the church adjoining it being built in 1791, replacing an old Gothic structure dedicated to St John.

The Academy, as we have said, has been the nursery of many famous men, including Sir William Burnett, M.D., James, and the late Sir Alexander Burnes—the latter relatives of the National bard; John Leech, an old Latin poet; Dr George Keith, author of the "Farmers Ha'"; David Buchanan, an eminent Classical scholar; Alexander Smart, author of "Rambling Rhymes," &c.; G. P. Chalmers, A.R.A., a young artist of great merit, who met a sad end in Edinburgh. It is also noted as the cradle of the Greek language in Scotland, which was taught by M. Marsilliers, who was appointed and maintained by Erskine of Dun at his own expense, and was succeeded by his own pupil, George Wishart, another eminent Montrosian.

The Museum, facing the Mid Links, is a handsome building, in the Grecian style. It was erected in 1845, mainly by the liberality of Lord Panmure, and is well worth a visit. It contains many rare objects of great interest. Connected with the Institution is a vigorous Natural and Antiquarian Society.

Dorward's House of Refuge was founded and endowed by a wealthy merchant of that name, for the education of orphan children, and the protection of aged men and women belonging to the town and parish of Montrose. The building is in the Elizabethan style, and was erected in 1839.

For a golf course, Montrose stands almost unrivalled. Indeed, as far back as 200 years ago, it was placed next to St Andrews in excellence, while recently a high authority declared it to be one of the three best in Scotland. The great stretch of beautiful links also supplies excellent facilities for cricket and other games. For sea-bathing the authorities have provided the most modern comforts—the magnificent sandy beach extending four miles in one continuous stretch along the margin of the German Ocean. This also affords delightful and invigorating walks, while all around is very pleasing and diversified. Amongst the places of interest—outwith our route, and which can only be mentioned here, are Kinnaber (with its waterworks), Charleton, Newmanswalls, Broomfield, Rosemount, Hedderwick, &c.

Passing down Bridge Street (another spacious street) we leave the town by crossing the Suspension Bridge already referred to, which truly beautiful and airy-looking structure was designed by Captain S. Brown, R.N. On the erection of this bridge, the middle of the arch of the old stone bridge across the southern, or narrow channel of the South Esk was also removed and supplanted by a revolving draw bridge, by which means vessels passed up and down the Basin to a small port at Old Montrose, where, at one time, goods were frequently shipped and delivered, but since the formation of the railway that harbour has gone entirely out of use.

In the matter of railway accommodation Montrose is well served. The Caledonian route skirts the town on the east, and a more modern line, wrought in conjunction with the North British system, on the west. This line begins at the south end near the Caledonian Company's Station at Arbroath, thence almost due north through the parish of St Vigeans, and, as we shall see as we proceed, past Inverkeillor to Lunan Bay, where it first emerges on the coast. From this point the sea is kept in sight nearly all the way to Ferryden. Though much beautiful scenery is passed on the route, the most magnificent is undoubtedly that when the train crosses the bridges over the Esk—when the Montrose Basin lies exposed in all its splendour on the west, and Montrose on the east.

The view looking up the river over the tidal Basin, with the long stretch of hills in the background, through the greater part of which we have already traversed, is very pretty, especially by moonlight, and when the tide is well up, the silver streaks rippling on the bosom of the great sheet of water have a fine effect, while occasionally it seems, when the sun is in its full splendour, to be converted into a huge expanse of molten gold.

> The Basin in its sparkling pride,
> Stretching its bright bosom far and wide,
> A lake of gold;
> Where verdant hills, on either side
> Their charms unfold.

The Basin, a nearly elliptical area of about 7 miles in circumference, is described in Davidson's "Guide" as one of the grandest sights a tourist can witness—the small riplets on the water dancing and glittering in the sunshine, while the water being skirted all round with richly cultivated fields, and the receding prospect behind exhibiting a fine variety of hill and plain, alternated with mansion houses and green woods, backed by the shelving Grampians, render the scene perhaps one of the best and most varied that can be met with in Scotland. Passing along the second of the two bridges which span the South Esk, a good view is got of the Suspension Bridge. The prospect below, towards the ocean, will also command admiration. The quaint, old-world looking fishing village of Ferryden is seen opposite the docks, perched, terrace after terrace, in fantastic lines, on the face of the dark grey rocks.

According to the late Andrew Douglas, its historian, Ferryden "owes its existence to the ancient and important commercial and manufacturing town of Montrose, on the opposite bank of the South Esk."

The oldest house in the village, which consisted of mud walls, thatched with rushes and straw, belonged

only to the early part of last century. The forebears of James West, *alias* Bull West, were the next colonists of Ferryden, after, David Pert and family, and they came from the same quarter,—the shores of the Moray Firth—hence, probably the great redundance of the names of Pert and West.

Let us now direct attention, merely in a summary way, to several places around the coast, bringing us in sight of Lunan, which, with Redcastle, &c., we will reach by an inland route.

A short distance down the river, two lighthouses are passed on the north bank—the two, when taken in a line from the sea, marking the entrance to the port. At the entrance to the river itself, stands a magnificent round tower—the Scurdyness Lighthouse —erected by the Board of Trade in 1870, at a cost of about £2700. Scurdyness forms one of the points for the measurement of the breadth of Scotland, the distance from it to Ardnamurchan Point, on the west coast, being 140 miles.

Usan House, the seat of George Keith, Esq., is

delightfully situated on an eminence south east from the village of Ferryden. The harbour is a narrow gorge in the rocks and only capable of admitting one boat at a time, the boats being anchored bow and stern in a single row. As in most fishing villages, traces of superstition still linger here. Recently a woman had to appear before the Sheriff in a case of defamation of character, having blamed a neighbour for purloining an article of dress. On being pretty openly questioned and sharply rebuked by the Sheriff, the woman's face began to betray some concealed emotion that agitated her mind, the cause of which she seemed unwilling to reveal. At last she fixed her eyes on the Sheriff, and spoke as follows, with as much earnestness as if they had been the last words she was to utter, "A' that I ken aboot it, my Lord, is just this—when Mary's name was mentioned the key ran three times round aboot the Bible; that's a' I ken aboot it." The Sheriff answered, "I believe you are perfectly honest my good woman; you should not be so very particular about your character, that is you should not give any heed to the idle talk of your neighbours, who have brought forward nothing to injure your character in the slightest degree." "That's a' very gude, me Lord," replied her ladyship, "but in oor toon, a puir body has maething, me Lord, but their character to depend on." "It is the same everywhere," replied the Sheriff, "but go away home, I believe you to be a perfectly honest and respectable woman."

Apart from superstition, Usan enjoys the reputation of having been the origin of that world-wide saying, so dear to the Scot at home and abroad, "We're a' John Tamson's bairns." The origin of this familiar saying is reported to have taken place in one of the numerous public houses, so common in the parish previous to the passing of the Forbes Mackenzie Act. This house was kept by a certain John Thomson. John was one day, along with several others, helping to prolong the time and finish another bottle, when his wife, wondering what was making him stay so long in the other end of the house, eventually ushered herself into the room where our heroes were busy with the "Nut Brown Ale." After having delivered herself of a harangue of righteous indignation, she was compelled to withdraw, having failed to inveigle John from his potation. After she had retired the company sat for a short time unable to say a word, when all of a sudden the dreadful silence was broken by the following exclamation from the redoubtable John :—" Drink awa' lads! an' never mind—my wife's nae man ava, for we're a' John Tamson's bairns."

At the fishing port of Usan began the "Cadger's Road," which reached westward to the market cross of Forfar. It was the road by which the King's purveyor travelled daily with a supply of fish for the royal table when the court abode at Forfar. The King always reserved a right of road for the royal cadger in the grants of land made by them in that district, from the seashore at Usan onwards to Forfar, "in breadth the length of a mill wand." According to Huddlestone, "before roads and wheeled carriages were brought to their present state of perfection, the conveyance of a mill stone was attended with great labour and difficulty. A long rounded piece of wood, called the millwand, was thrust through the centre of the stone; then a number of men took hold of each end of the wand, and rolled the millstone along on its hem, from the quarry to the mill." The width indicated must always have been sufficient for the passage of a single cart. From an account of the proceedings of an ancient Baron-Court in Perthshire, we learn that the millar had to provide dinner for the tenants when they brought home the runner, or upper-stone, and the laird the dinner when they brought home the bed, or under stone. The cottars had to make the road fit as often as need required.

The "Cadger Path" passed through Montreathmont Moor—a large tract of country, partly situated in the parishes of Aberlemno, Farnell, and Kinnell. About the year 1780, the Moor was parcelled out amongst the conterminous proprietors, who claimed certain rights of common upon it, each receiving a share proportionate to the size of the estate.

The parish of Craig comprehends two titularities— Inchbrayock ("the church island," as the church formerly stood upon the island, on the side still used as the parish burying ground) or Craig, and St Skeoch or Dunninald. In 1618 they were united, and took the name of Craig. Saint Skeoch, or the Church of Doninad (Dunninald) belonged to the Priory of Resteneth. The church stood upon a cliff between Usan fishing village, near Ferryden and Lunan Bay, and there is still a small graveyard on the picturesque rock

> St Skeoch grey rock stands frowning o'er
>   The troubled deep;
> A structure formed by nature's hand,
> A bridge with wave-worn arches planned,
> Whose echoing depths the surges spanned,
>   Where wind and wave
> Their voices raise in concert grand,
>   When tempests rave.

The saint of this name is supposed to have been one of the twelve disciples of St Columba. The present church of the parish (Rev. Robert Scott) was built in 1799. It stands on a commanding position, and the lofty square tower is a prominent object for many miles around, while from its summit the view of sea and river, hill and plain, is truly grand. Over the entrance are the words, "Enter His Gates with Praise."

Dunninald Castle is delightfully situated amid noble trees, near by the frowning rock of St Skeoch. It is the seat of the daughter and heiress of the late Sheriff Arkley, wife of Captain Stansfeld, late of the Scots Greys. The Den of Dunninald is a romantic sylvan breach opening toward the sea, formed by a small streamlet, and thickly wooded. The coast line between this and Lunan Bay is of bold precipitous cliffs, of old red sandstone.

Black Jack's Castle occupied the top of a perpendicular rock rising nearly 300 feet above the ocean, near Boddin Point. The foundations are still visible upon the rock, which is reached by a narrow neck of land. Mr A. H. Millar, in his interesting and able work, "Castles and Mansions of Scotland," says:—

The Keep of Dunninald, which then crowned the cliffs of Boddin Point, was in the possession of James Gray of Invergowrie, a son of Patrick, Lord Gray, and one of the rude nobles of the time, fearless alike of God and King. In 1579 this reckless freebooter had gathered together in his fortress of Dunninald—usually styled "Black Jack" —a band of ruffians worse than himself, and ready for any exploit which the unsettled state of the kingdom would permit. The ancient fortress of Redcastle had often awakened his envy, and, at the time of which we speak, he was aware that the old lord was dead, and the new heir far away from his patrimony, so he deemed this a fitting period to make an attack upon the fort. The inmates of Redcastle were the Dowager Lady Innermeith, her second son, John Stewart, and her daughter Marjorie, the wedded wife of Lindsay of Vayne Castle, and as the Lord of the Manor was not then present, it is likely that the retainers were few in number. Terrified at the fate which seemed to await them, the inmates of the Castle sought refuge in the tower, and though its construction enabled them to defy the attempts of these bandits to execute vengeance upon them, they were compelled to witness, even from their safe retreat, the destruction of the lower portion of the Castle by fire. The forethought of the first Lord Innermeith who had possessed the Castle, had prompted him to build the tower which he erected separate entirely from the rest of the building, else the Lady and her children would have been consumed in the flames which rose all around her.

> But when the ladye saw the fire,
> Come flaming owre her heid,
> She wept and kissed her children twain,
> Said 'Bairns, we been but deid.'

The ruthless marauder, who had thus warred upon innocent women, finding he could not carry the tower of the castle by assault, withdrew at length to his keep, carrying with him such spoil as he could easily obtain.

Taking up our route where we left it to refer to Ferryden, &c., we keep to the right, and drive along a lovely road, skirting the Basin. As we ascend the brae, a prettily situated little bit of public recreation ground, tastefully laid out with shrubs and with secluded winding paths, shaded by fine old trees, arrests attention. This is Rossie Public Gardens, liberally provided by a former proprietor, for the enjoyment of the inhabitants of Montrose and Ferryden. As we proceed, we are charmed with the quiet beauty and the charming situation of a number of cozy-looking quaint cottages that nestle romantically on the ledge of the Basin. They are embowered in rich greenery, shaded by grand old trees, and are aglow with roses, and brightly-coloured creepers form fantastic arches around every porch and door-way, while the great expanse of water, valleys, and hills beyond presents a view that must command admiration.

A small portion of the old Castle of Craig is still preserved within the grounds of Rossie, and Craig House is an old, heavy-looking, ivy-clad mansion surrounded by high walls—the quaint portcullised entrance being flanked by towers. It was the seat of Baron David Wood, progenitor of the Woods of Bonnyton Castle.

Rossie Castle, the residence of the proprietor of the estate, Edward Millar, Esq., is a splendid castellated mansion, erected by the late Hercules Ross, Esq. of Rossie. With battlemented towers, and large square towers at each corner of the main building, with bartizans around the top, the building presents an imposing appearance. It is very pleasantly situated amid noble trees, trim lawns, and extensive and rich gardens. The estate was an ancient feudal barony, and many of the usual appendages of a barony court are to be found in the locality. A field near the castle is still called the Law-field, which shows it to have been the seat of the Justice Court of the regality. Balgove, the name of an adjoining farm, is, we are told, the Anglicized form of the Gaelic Balgobh, literally the withy house or prison. Govan Hill, situated rather more than a mile to the westward, was the withy hill, or place of execution. In ancient times the gallows was always a growing tree, from one of the branches of which the culprits were suspended. The condemned persons were led to the place of execution, having their hands tied together with green withs. Old people generally call a bad, worthless fellow, a "cheat the widdy," because he has so far escaped his merited punishment.

Towards the west end of the estate there is a lofty wooded hill called Kinnoul Hill, which appears to have been the chief beacon-station in the district. There is a tradition concerning the hill, to the effect that an ancient baron of Rossie and his son waylaid the King's cadger, for which offence they were tried and executed on the lofty summit of Kinnoul Hill. It would appear that they exhibited a natural reluctance to mount the scaffold under the fatal tree. The King himself superintended the execution, and seeing their dilatoriness, he called out to them, "Mount, boys!" to which circumstance is ascribed the derivation of the name of Mountboy, which lies on the south side of the hill.

At the south-western base of the Hill of Kinnoul, snugly embowered amongst the woods, is situated Rossie Reformatory, a place for the detention and education of refractory boys. From this admirably conducted institution many a well equipped lad has been sent out into the world who would have otherwise sunk into a career of crime.

Many years ago a lady of the Ross family, then of Rossie Castle, enamoured with the beauty of the situation, built a white-walled cottage of two storeys on the steep southern slope, to which she occasionally resorted to enjoy the scenery in summer. The cottage — like a shooting lodge — is now the residence of the Governor, and for a time, at the commencement, was the only building available for the inmates and officials, until the present buildings were erected.

The Institution was opened in May, 1857—the founder, under the advice of the Earl of Southesk and others, being Lieutenant-Colonel Macdonald Macdonald of St Martins and Rossie, who alone gave £1165 towards buildings, furniture, &c. Since then over 500 have passed through the Institution, every one of whom, in some way or other, had broken the law.

Many a notorious character commenced real life in Rossie, and it is doubtless a great recompense to those philanthrophic gentlemen who commenced the

REDCASTLE.

work to know that they have been instrumental in making good men of not a few. Many of the old lads are now holding responsible places. Several are large employers of labour, two are ministers of the gospel, one a doctor of divinity and Principal of a College in one of our Colonies, and, strange as it may seem, one some years ago held the post of Governor in a Reformatory.

Lunan Bay and Redcastle.

> Redcastle proudly aye doth keep
> Its vigil o'er the mighty deep,
> And in the track of Sol's bright ray
> Serenely shines sweet Lunan Bay.

The roadside as we approach Lunan is beautified with carefully tended flowers and ferns, and as far as the property extends rows of Norway maples and black Italian poplars, and Corsican pines beautify the surroundings. There are few places on the east coast that present greater attractions as a bathing resort than the Bay of Lunan. These advantages have earned for it the title of the Scarborough of Scotland; but hitherto the great hindrance to its development has been the want of adequate house accommodation. The wide extent of beach, flanked on either side with beautiful and romantic rocks, the picturesquely situated hamlet of Torshaven, the commanding ruins of Redcastle, and the bold fantastic cliffs of Dysart are features of natural beauty which strike every visitor to the Bay. There is also plenty of scope for the followers of Isaac Walton in the immediate neighbourhood.

The whole district lying between Montrose and Arbroath abounds in objects of much interest to the antiquary, while the scenery in several parts is grandly impressive. The author of "Traditions and Stories of Scottish Castles," writing on the subject of Redcastle, says:—About seven miles north of Arbroath the east coast-line of Scotland suddenly deviates westward and forms the vast semi-circular sweep known as Lunan Bay. Beyond Auchmithie, the fishing village rendered famous by Scott in the "Antiquary," the cliffs of old red sandstone and trap which form the sea-limits terminate in the Redhead, whose summit reaches an altitude of about 270 feet. North from Redhead the promontory of Boddin Point forms the extreme limit of Lunan Bay, which circles around betwixt these two capes in one long stretch of sand. Were a line carried from the one point to the other it would be found that the shore at the centre of the bay runs nearly three-and-a-half miles inland, whilst it extends fully three miles north and south.

At the bottom of the hill, and before we reach the bay, nestling amid fine old trees, is the mansion-house of Lunan, the residence of Colonel William Blair-Imrie. The old mansion-house—which had several mural coats-of-arms of the Ogilvys of Inverquharity and Guthries of Guthrie, and the date 1664—was pulled down, and a new one built in 1825. It was considerably enlarged during the minority of the present laird, when the garden and beautiful lawn, extending to upwards of five acres, were laid out. These grounds, planned with taste, adorned with great ancestral trees, and kept up at considerable expense, have for many years been thrown open to the public. The only restriction is that a stop has been put to pic-nic parties being held there on Sunday—not visitors, who can find, as the genial and respected laird lately said, " while wandering about a well kept garden on a Sunday afternoon, that flowers are quite as much stamped with the impress of divinity as Calvinistic sermons— they can, in addition, practice the virtue of self-denial by more frequently acting on the principle of 'touch not, taste not, handle not,' than they have hitherto done." As the crow flies, the distance between Lunan Bay Station and the sea-beach is only about 400 yards; but as it is a mile by the road, the proprietor has formed a broad footpath through Buckie Den to the beach. Though somewhat steep, this walk is a singularly attractive one, as it passes several cascades of water, and is surmounted by a thicket of black thorns. Nearly a mile to the north of the house, and standing on high ground, is an obelisk, 45 feet in height, erected in 1850 to the memory of the late Brigadier James Blair, father of Colonel Blair-Imrie.

Upon the summit of a grass-covered hill near the central point of the bay stand the remains of Redcastle. Around the base of the mount, and stretching far into the interior, the water of Lunan flows on in its course to the sea, and dividing at the foot of the hill, it separates its current into innumerable little rills which make their way through the sand until lost in the ocean. The beach for a great distance is formed of fine sand, unbroken by rock or precipice.

From the peak of Redcastle a magnificent panorama of the eastern portion of Forfarshire may be seen. Although it does not stand very high, compared with Redhead or Boddin, its position at the north of the river enables the spectator to obtain a view of the valley of the Lunan, and to overlook, thereby, some of the most fertile portions of the shire. Westward the spurs of the Grampian Hills forming Glen Isla, Glen Prosen, and Glenesk, may be detected upon a clear day enclosing the scene, whilst Mount Blair in solitary grandeur limits the south-western view. Within the range of vision lie the fertile lands of Angus, extending in gentle undulations as far as the eye can reach, and varied with field and woodland in a manner scarcely to be equalled elsewhere in Scotland. With the fertility of the Lothians is combined some of the grandeur of the Ochil district, and the grain-bearing lands and pastures are relieved in artistic effect by the remains of the ancient forests of Angus. Seaward the view is unlimited. The wave which

breaks upon the beach at Lunan Bay has sped through the waste of waters from the distant shores of Norway or Denmark, and the North Sea laves without obstruction the rock-bound coasts of each of these widely separated lands.

> Yonder bright the bay,
> The bonnie, bonnie bay,
> Yonder bright the bay,
> The bonnie bay of Lunan!
> Sparkling white with silver waves,
> Girt with high wild rocky caves,
> Mermaids sing o'er seamen's graves,
> In the bonnie bay of Lunan.
> Yonder bright the bay, etc.

It is remarkable that very little information concerning Redcastle can be gathered from the pages of history, although Mr A. H. Millar, through the recent researches of the Royal Commission upon Historical Manuscripts, has been enabled to tell us, in his "Castles and Mansions," its tragical story more completely than any previous historian.

Tradition points to William I. as the builder of the castle for a hunting seat. Ochterlony says it was the residence of William I. when he built the Abbey of Arbroath. It is certainly one of the oldest castles in Forfarshire. There is the traditional deep dungeon, of which the oldest inhabitants in the neighbourhood have often heard but never seen. The Witches' Pool to the north, and the Gallows Hill to the west, constitute the most striking feudal appendages of the barony. The Gallows Hill, placed in the appropriate neighbourhood of the Witches' Pool and Ironshill, is a large conical mound covered with trees, and is perhaps the most perfect specimen of the kind which this or any country contains.

The first subject found in possession of Redcastle is Henry de Baliol, chamberlain to King William I., and grand-uncle to King John Baliol. He married Lora, daughter of Philip de Valonis de Panmure, with whom he got in dower the lands of Panlathy and Balbinnie, in the barony of Panmure and parish of Arbirlot. There were two witchpools attached to the castle; an artificial one, now filled up, a short distance south of the Gallowshill; and another, a little to the westward of the castle. The latter was a naturally formed pool in the river-bed, which by shifting its course left the pool dry, but the place still retains the name of Witchpool. The purposes for which these pools were used was the ordeal of water-trial, and the punishment of female delinquents.

Redcastle was in a tolerable state of repair so late as the year 1748, at which time the slates and joists belonging to it were removed to Panmure. Afterwards the castle buildings became a common quarry to all the tenants in the neighbourhood.

> Sad are the ruthless ravages of time;
> The bulwark'd turret frowning once sublime
> Now totters to its basis, and displays
> A venerable wreck of other days.

According to Fraser's "History of the Carnegies of Southesk," the last inhabitant of Redcastle was the Rev. Mr Rait, of the family of Rait of Hallgreen, in the Mearns, who, at the Revolution in 1688, was Episcopal minister of Inverkeillor. When deprived of his living he took up his residence in the square tower of Redcastle, and he continued to perform religious services for the parishes of Inverkeillor and Lunan.

It was at Redcastle, during the beginning of the last century, that the curious incident occurred which is recorded in Jervise's "Epitaphs."

Under the apprehension that it was intended to bring him up as an agriculturist, the first William Imrie of Lunan quitted, while quite a youth, his father's house in

Aberdeenshire, without communicating his design to any one, and started for London, walking along the coast road until he reached Redcastle. Having mounted the hillock on which that old ruin stands, he lay down, fell asleep, and dreamt that he was laird of Lunan. He went to England, sailed several times to India, married a woman with money, and became the owner of a hotel in Fountain Court, Strand, London. This hotel was at that time the favourite resort of the Forfarshire lairds when they went to London. The incident at Redcastle left a deep impression on William Imrie's mind, and having become rich in London he returned to Scotland, where in 1759 he realised the dream of his youth by purchasing the estate of Lunan.

After settling at Lunan Mr Imrie was instrumental in bringing thither Robert Huddleston, who, in 1789, was appointed to the office of parochial schoolmaster. Mr Huddleston relieved the drudgery of tuition by the love of letters, which, during his intervals of leisure, he wooed to some purpose, having carved his name in the literary annals of his country. In 1814 he published a new edition of Toland's "History of the Druids," which bears internal evidence of deep study. He edited also Holinshead's "Scottish Chronicles," and was a constant contributor to the magazines and periodical press. A small tombstone, with a modest inscription, marks his resting-place in the Lunan Churchyard.

Since 1189 Colonel Blair-Imrie is the twenty-eighth proprietor of these lands, which were formerly called "The Barony of Inverlunan," and had been constituted into a "free barony" by Robert II. on the 4th January, 1377. In the parish church of Lunan there is attached to the reredos a brazen support for a baptismal font, and likewise a sand-glass stand of the same material. Each of these articles bears an inscription in these words;—"Given to the Church of Lunan by Alexander Gavin, merchant there, and Elizabeth Jamieson, his spouse, 1773." A bell which used to be rung at funerals is also in the possession of the minister (the Rev. Alex. Fridge) and bears a similar inscription. The history of the donor of these gifts and his family is very remarkable. This Alexander Gavin was for many years beadle of the parish of Lunan. Among the duties that devolved upon him in that capacity, were the keeping and preparing the baptismal font for service, the turning the sand-glass during sermon, and the ringing the hand-bell as he walked before the company of mourners who bore their departed friends to their last resting place.

The father of Alexander Gavin was named James Gavin, and he also held the office of beadle. It happened, while James held the appointment, that a Dutch vessel was wrecked in the Bay of Lunan, and the beadle, taking pity on the destitute condition of the castaway skipper, invited him to share the hospitality of his humble abode. This kindly offer was readily accepted, and the acquaintance, so strangely formed, resulted in the marriage of the Dutch skipper with the beadle's daughter, Catherine Gavin. Soon thereafter the skipper with his wife left for Holland, where he renounced his seafaring life, and betook himself to the less dangerous and more lucrative pursuits of commerce. After Catherine's departure, Alexander succeeded his father in the office of beadle, and seems to have made a livelihood from the profits of a small shop. He married Elizabeth Jamieson, and had a son named David. Thus David Gavin, while quite young, was invited to Holland by his uncle and aunt; he became in course of time a partner in the business carried on by his uncle, and married his cousin, the skipper's daughter, who, however, soon thereafter died. Having by industry and intelligence amassed a considerable fortune, David Gavin returned to Scotland, made his father comfortable for the remainder of his days, and purchased, along with other property, the estate of Langton in Berwickshire. In 1770 he married Lady Elizabeth, daughter of the Earl of Lauderdale, and by her had three daughters. One of these, Mary Turner, married John, fourth Earl of Breadalbane, and was the late dowager Marchioness, and mother of John, fifth Earl (second and last Marquis) of Breadalbane, and of Lady Mary who was married to Richard Plantagenet, second Duke of Buckingham. Alexander Gavin, the kirk-beadle of Lunan, was thus the father-in-law of an Earl's daughter, the grandfather of a Marchioness, and the great-grandfather of a Marquis, and of a Duchess. The family of the last are, the Duke of Buckingham, the lineal descendants of a daughter of Henry II., and thus remote heirs to the British throne.

The Rev. Walter Mill, parish priest of Lunan immediately before the Reformation, was the last martyr who suffered in Scotland for his religious opinions. Having renounced Popery and embraced the principles of the Reformation, he was, in 1568, apprehended at Dysart by two priests in the service of Archbishop Hamilton, brought to St Andrews and imprisoned in the Castle. All means to shake his constancy having been tried, he ended by saying, "You shall know that I will not recant the truth, for I am corn, and not chaff. I will not be blown away with the wind, nor burst with the flail, but will abide both." So great was the sympathy with him, that Provost Patrick Learmonth refused to do the part of temporal judge; and not a rope would any individual supply to bind the victim to the stake. His last words were, "I shall be the last that shall suffer death in this land for this cause," and these proved prophetic. A monument to his memory was erected inside the old church of Lunan in the year 1818. When the present church was built in 1845, the monument was destroyed, but another one was placed in the new church in 1848.

The Church of Inverkeillor (formerly Ethie) was built towards the end of the seventeenth century. At a later period part of the back wall was removed, and the Anniston Aisle added. In this addition and in the two ends there are galleries, each of which has a stair for itself inside the Church. The one in the east end is the Northesk gallery, the front of which is very dark oak, with some quaint but beautiful old carvings upon it, and the Northesk arms in the centre. In the west end is the Kinblethmont gallery. The Church (Rev. Andrew Halden) is surrounded by a graveyard, embosomed among old trees. The burial vault of the Northesk family is attached to the east end of the Church. Inverkeillor, which is a clean, well-built and airy-looking village, was known in the old coaching days as Chance Inn.

The mansion-house of Anniston is an elegant structure, consisting of a centre building, flanked with extensive wings. It occupies a beautiful situation on a fine piece of table land in the parish of Inverkeillor, about a mile south-east of the village, close by the road which leaves the Arbroath and Montrose turnpike road at Chance Inn, and leads to Ethie Castle. It is the residence of Colonel Rait, C.B., of Anniston.

Ethie Castle.

Ethie has recently been greatly enlarged, and restored, under the skill and fine antiquarian taste of Dr R. Anderson, the eminent architect. The fine seat of the Earl of Northesk, it is supposed to be the Knockwinnock of "The Antiquary." It was not built by Cardinal Beaton, but was one of his favourite residences; and, notwithstanding several additions made since his day, it is yet in much the same state in which it was when he occupied it. A mansion of such antiquity as that of Ethie could not fail to gather round it singular traditions. So attached to Ethie Castle was the Cardinal, that he did not leave it on his murder. His ghost lingered about it, and, indeed, it still does so. "It is still reported," as an indisputable fact, that "at a certain hour of the night a sound is heard

resembling the tramp of a foot, which is believed to be the Cardinal's." The haunted room, which is in one of the attics, has long been unoccupied. It is always kept locked, and few have been privileged to enter it. The learned author of the "History of the Carnegies" once explored the mysterious room, and found a veritable trace of the Cardinal in the form of a large oak cabinet, the only article of furniture in the apartment.

The estate is finely wooded; and although placed within easy distance of the grandest marine scenery on the east coast of Scotland, it is yet completely sheltered from the rough sea breezes, thus combining much variety of feature in landscape with almost perfect seclusion. In the vicinity of the house is a large tumulus or hillock, known as the *Corbie's Knowe*, which is supposed to have derived its name from the Danish ensign, a black raven (the well-known cognizance of the Scandinavian rovers) having been planted upon it during some incident connected with one of the numerous expeditions of those bold adventurers in this part of Scotland.

During the reign of David II., on 17th June 1329, Walter Maule of Panmure disposed of the lands of Carnegie, in the barony of Panmure to John de Bohnard, who whereupon adopted Carnegie as his family surname, instead of, as previously, Bonhard. This gentleman—who acquired considerable property in Angus—was the ancestor of the Earls both of Southesk and Northesk. David Carnegie, designated of Panbride, sixth in descent from the said John de Carnegie, was the father of David, first Earl of Southesk, and of John, first Earl of Northesk, betwixt whom he divided his properties. John Carnegie was created Lord Lour in 1639. But, disliking this title, he prevailed upon King Charles II. to alter it in 1662 to that of Earl of Northesk. His youngest daughter, Lady Jean Carnegie, married William Grahame of Claverhouse, by whom she was the mother of the famous John Grahame of Claverhouse. William, seventh Earl, was third in command at the memorable battle of Trafalgar, fighting under the leadership of Lord Nelson.

The present peer, David Carnegie, 10th Earl of Northesk, was born in 1865. He succeeded his father in 1891, and married, 1894, Elizabeth Boyle, daughter of Major-General George-Skene Hallowes.

Kinblethmont.

The mansion-house of **Kinblethmont**, which a number of years ago took the place of an ancient structure, is pleasantly situated. The estate of Boysack is of considerable extent. It forms the extreme north-western portion of the parish of Inverkeillor, culminating at the farm of Knowes, where three lairds' lands and three parishes meet, viz., the lands of Boysack, Middleton, and Cononsyth, and the parishes of Inverkeillor, Kirkden, and Carmyllie.

The first owner of Kinblethmont of whom there is certain mention was Richard de Melville about the year 1188. After the estate had passed out of the possession of the Lindsays it belonged for a short time to the Earl of Kinnoul, who sold it to David Carnegie, second Earl of Northesk, for behoof of his second son John, for whom he also purchased the estate of Kinblethmont, and with whose descendants these properties still remain. Mr H. A. Fullarton Lindsay-Carnegie is the present laird of Kinblethmont. His wife, Mrs Lindsay-Carnegie, is a highly-gifted lady, and takes a warm and substantial interest in all that pertains to the welfare of the people in the district.

Auchmithie.

The visitor to this quaint old fishing village, in the words of "Marie" in *Dundee Weekly News* (to the proprietors of which we are indebted for view of "Musselcraig"), will be ready to echo the words of the artist who cried as his eyes fell on Auchmithie— "Commonplace! Why, it's glorious, every step you take shows something quaint and beautiful!" Through a fair landscape you pass onwards towards Lunan Bay, one of the most beautiful bits of coast to be found in Scotland. It has the beauty of Oban, but, alas! it cannot offer the advantages of Oban, for, save for a few cottages, the place is quite desolate. Only the spirit of enterprise is needed to make Lunan as fine a summer resort as Oban and as prosperous. Either by rail or for driving, the country round about presents great attractions.

Just between sea and sky seems to swing the village of Auchmithie as you round the cliffs that so gloriously break the coast line beyond Arbroath. Up

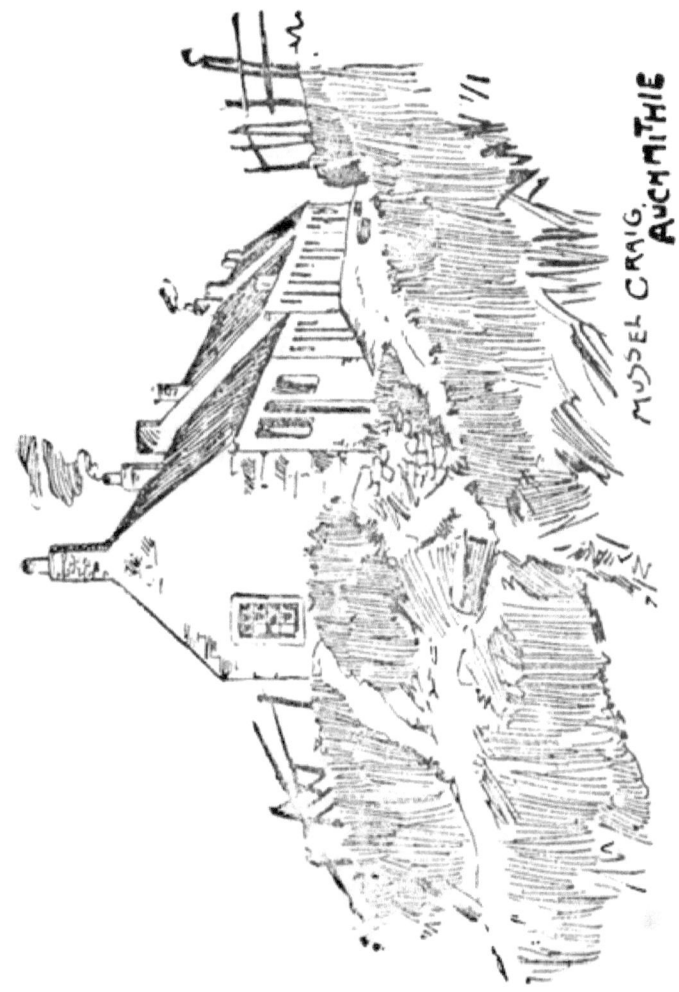

there in the quaint village you find a people whom the mighty whirling of the hoary world has left undisturbed in their primitive and simple ways. As

Mr J. M. M'Bain says in his "Arbroath: Past and Present"—a work of much general interest, and rich in story and anecdote, while faithfully recording the social progress of the burgh—they are the lineal descendants of the immortal "Mucklebackets," whose simple manners and curious habits are worthy of careful study.

> Swans, Swankies, Watts, Cargills, who since the Flood,
> Have burrowed in Auchmithie.

The wondering eyes of bairns will peer at you from beneath masses of tangled gold, and of brightest red are cheeks above tattered blue. The white-crested waves dash themselves against the rocks, ever hollowing out deeper caves and breaking more and more the line of mighty cliffs. Round the cliff head the road sweeps, and ere you have followed its windings you are apt to think it breaks off short just over the rocks that stand up sheer from the ocean.

However dark the winter morning, however deep the snow wreaths, the boats are launched, and the men put forth to sea. Theirs to fight the white riders on the waves for the sake of the women and weans at home! It is not so many years since the women launched the boats and carried the men aboard, wading often over the waist in the surging foam. It was done that the men might set out dry on their perilous and arduous toil. For a day's outing no more beautiful ground can be dreamt of than the round from Arbroath to Lunan Bay by Auchmithie.

The lands of Auchmithie were owned by John Beaton of Balquhargie in the 16th century; but these and many of the neighbouring lands have long been the property of the Earls of Northesk. The village was burned by some fishermen in the end of the seventeenth century. Near the end of last century thirty-three coins were found in an earthen pitcher in the floor of one of the houses in the village. The find comprised some of Henry IV. of France, others of German princes, and others of Charles II. and William III. A few of the coins were of square form.

Referring to the fact of this romantic looking village being rendered almost classical by Scott, on account of its being generally identified with Mussel-Craig of "The Antiquary," we are told that Sir Walter lived several weeks in the village inn, then kept by Mrs Walker, who for half a century occupied the house, and who was as well known in the district as Scott's typical landlady of the olden time, Margaret Dods. Luckie Walker has been gathered to her fathers, but the house is now considerably enlarged and improved, and lovers of the grand and picturesque, after satisfying their tastes amidst the wild scenery along the coast, can, as of yore, have their more prosaic cravings satiated with an excellent fish dinner by the present host, Mr Scott. The bed-room said to have been occupied by Sir Walter is shown to the admirers of the immortal "Wizard." Greatly through the exertions and influence of Mrs Gilruth, Seaton of Auchmithie, a fine harbour was made some years ago.

Seaton House, the residence of the Hon. F. K. Bruce, is a massive structure, within two miles of Arbroath. In former times the chapel and burying-ground of St Ninian, Bishop and Confessor, stood at the Den of Seaton. The site of the chapel is marked by a spring, called St Ninian's, or St Ringan's Well.

Arbroath and its Abbey.

> The wreck of centuries is buried here;
> The very monuments are hoar with age;
> The empty tower that sentinels them all
> Wails when the gusts wild wander o'er the earth,
> And creaks the rusty gate with careless Time.

Until recent times the usual appellation of this town was *Aberbrothock*, from its situation on the mouth of a small turgid stream called the Brothock, which is here poured into the sea. The present name is a commodious abbreviation of the word. It is the seat of a Presbytery of eleven parishes. Little is distinctly known of the origin of the burghal privileges of the little seaport town which arose in the immediate vicinity of the Abbey, on account of the loss of charters in the troubles during the minority of James VI. It is generally understood that the town was constituted a royal burgh by the same monarch who founded the Abbey.

Arbroath has a population of about 23,000, its principal industries being linen, bleaching, and boot and shoe manufacture. From being a place of small importance it, like some other towns in Forfarshire, gradually rose into consequence from its manufactures and exports. From being a quiet little country town, it has become, in recent times, a bustling place of business. The Town House, situated in the widest part of the old-fashioned looking, and somewhat tortuous High Street, has a handsome Grecian front. In this building both the Trades, and the Guildry have commodious public halls, and it also contains public reading rooms and library. The town also has a too little known museum, with a more rare and valuable collection than most local institutions of this sort possess. The Parish Church (Rev. James Thomson) was destroyed by fire in 1892, but a handsome edifice is rapidly taking its place. There is also The Abbey Church (Rev. Andrew Douglas) and several other *quoad sacra* churches.

The history of this ancient town and district, with the interesting historical associations connected with the grand old Abbey, has been most exhaustively treated by Mr George Hay, Mr J. M. M·Bain, the Rev. J. Moffat Scott, and others, not forgetting Mr Buncle's (of the *Guide* newspaper) richly artistic large album of splendid etchings, entitled, "The Round O." The writings of these gentlemen are so well known, and so very highly valued that we do not require to devote so much space to Arbroath and its Abbey as we might otherwise have done, but would express our indebtedness to their researches.

Although nothing very definite is known of the history of Arbroath previous to the reign of "William the Lion," there is reason to believe that it was an inhabited place prior to that. Its Church (St Vigeans) is known to have existed before William's accession, and there is every probability that it was the site of a hamlet before the foundation of the Abbey in 1178. One of the earliest endowments of the monastery was the village of "Aberbrothock, with all the shire thereof and the church of the village, namely, Aberbrothock, with its tiends and pertinents."

There is much in and around Arbroath of interest to visitors. Sir Walter Scott thought so when he selected the town and its neighbourhood as the scene of one of his most interesting novels, Arbroath being the "Fairport" of the "Antiquary." With his magic wand, says Mr M·Bain, he has thrown an air of enchantment over our cliffs and caves which has enticed many of his admirers to visit the spot which he has thus made classical.

With many picturesque and quaint nooks, and intimately associated in Scottish literature with the curious "Antiquary" of our greatest romancer, Arbroath is perhaps best known as the seat of a noble monastery that sheltered kings and nobles, monks and pilgrims, in other days, and witnessed many stirring scenes and notable events in our country's history. The abbey stands at the head of the High Street, and commands a magnificent view of sea and land.

This great religious house was founded by William the Lion in 1178 and finished in 1213. It was intended for the redemption of the king's soul; but it was dedicated formally to St Thomas à Becket, Archbishop of Canterbury, who was murdered by four knights in 1170, at a pillar in his own cathedral. Before the erection of the Abbey of Aberbrothock, there was no hospice or asylum along the rugged coast of Angus and Mearns; and King William's noble house supplied a deeply-felt want. While it was a sanctuary for the sacred service of God and the cultivation of piety and the arts of peace, it was also an hospitable asylum for homeless pilgrims and strangers.

Constructed chiefly in the early English style of Gothic architecture, the Abbey of Aberbrothock was unsurpassed by any in Scotland. The church of the monastery was spacious, forming a Latin cross. Originally it possessed a lofty central square tower and spire, and two western towers, one of which still stands 100 feet high, sentinelling the town, and locally known as *Saint Thomas*. Over the fine circular gateway, once rich in ornament and pillar, there was a choir gallery, and above it "a beautiful rose-window." There were twelve altars, with their chapels, and the sacristy contained many precious vessels, vestments of gold and silver, a pastoral staff, and a fine mitre. Outside the church were two refectories, a dormitory, a chapter-house, a library containing over two hundred books, an ample and well-furnished hospice, an infirmary, and "many gardens wide and fair."

Now the abbey is a great ruin; but the western tower, the high altar, the southern wall, and the gable with the celebrated Saint Catherine wheel window, known as "the Round O," the gateway, the pend, and the weather-worn Regality Tower, "grinning," as Mr Moffat Scott says, "like some monstrous dragon over the busy street," remain to proclaim the greatness and glory of the ancient pile. "The monastery of Aberbrothock," says Dr Samuel Johnson, "is of great renown. Its ruins afford ample testimony of its ancient magnificence. I should scarcely have regretted my journey had it afforded nothing more than a sight of Aberbrothock."

The Abbey of Arbroath was exceedingly rich in goods and lands. William the Lion and Alexander II. conferred on it splendid gifts, and many of the nobles of Angus followed their good example. The property included salmon-fishing on the Tay, the North Esk, and the Dee; the ferry-boat at Montrose; a salt work at Stirling; license to cut timber in the royal forests; and the livings of not fewer than forty-six churches! The income of the abbey, in money and victuals, could not be less than nine thousand pounds—an enormous sum in these days.

Not only did the abbots treat their visitors at home with a profuse liberality, but they maintained *hostilages* at Dunnichen, Dundee, Aberdeen, Edinburgh, and Peebles, for the accommodation and entertainment of their friends and servants. At Stirling there were spacious lodgings and stabling for thirty horses.

Upon the dangerous insulated reef, at the distance of twelve miles from the coast, called the Inch Cape Rock, and in modern times the Bell Rock, one of the abbots attached a bell, which, at high water, when almost hidden by the breakers, was rung by the lashing of the waves, and warned, by its tolling, the seamen who were sailing near its dangerous vicinity.

> When the rock was hid by the surge's swell,
> The mariners heard the warning bell;
> And then they knew the perilous rock,
> And blest the Abbot of Aberbrothock.

The ingenuity and science of modern times have rendered the Bell Rock one of the most serviceable light-house stations on the east coast of Scotland. But, at the period to which we refer, the abbot's bell was all that indicated the dangerous existence of the rock.

The historical associations of the abbey are interesting. Before the high altar William the Lion was buried amid a nation's tears in 1214. Within the monastery Edward I. of England, bent on subjugating Scotland, rested in 1296, when Abbot Henry paid him a most reluctant homage. Here Robert Bruce, the hero-king and patriot, prayed before he fought the battle of Bannockburn, and here he sojourned during the autumn of 1317. The first Scottish Parliament that proudly asserted the national independence and defied Pope John XXII. when he insolently threatened to excommunicate the king and people if they refused to acknowledge the English sovereignty, met in the great church in 1320; and Bruce presided over it, and signed the letter that staggered the Pope. Here, too, were educated two great men—John Barbour, the father of Scottish poetry, and Alexander Myln, Dean of Angus, and the first president of the Court of Session. Within the walls was carefully preserved for centuries the *speckled banner* of Saint Columba of Iona, the famous Culdee symbol carried to battle on great occasions.

Foremost amongst its Abbots were Ralph de Lamley and Bernard de Linton. The former was a good man in a bad time, and when he became Bishop of Aberdeen was wont to travel afoot throughout his diocese preaching the Cross; the latter was a statesman, scholar, and soldier, and fought by the side of Bruce at Bannockburn.

In 1815 the Barons of Exchequer took measures to arrest the dilapidation of the venerable pile, which had been going on during two centuries and a half of neglect, and in the chancel, immediately before the high altar, the clearing away of the rubbish laid bare an effigy covering a stone coffin, in which were the bones of a person of goodly stature; and there does seem good reason for regarding these as the effigy, the coffin, and the bones of William the Lion.

The Battle of Arbroath dates in the fifteenth century. It was fought in 1446, between the

Lindsays and the Ogilvys. The occasion of it was the Abbey Chapter's choosing Ogilvy of Inverquharity as chief Justiciar in their regality, in place of the Master of Crawford, afterwards known as the Tiger Earl, and Earl Beardie. As the combatants approached each other, the Earl of Crawford, being anxious to avert the intended combat, suddenly appeared on the field, and, galloping up between the two lines, was mortally wounded by a soldier, who was enraged at his interference, and ignorant of his rank. The Crawfords, infuriated at the loss of their chief, attacked the Ogilvys with a desperation which soon broke their ranks. They were almost entirely cut to pieces, and five hundred men, including many noble barons in Forfar and Angus, were left dead on the field. Edward I. of England thrice visited Arbroath, and rested in its Abbey, and in 1528 James V., when only sixteen years of age, and attended by a large retinue, was entertained in the Abbey of Arbroath.

Away to the north is a stretch of rocky coast, where Scott has laid the scene of the adventure of Sir Arthur and Miss Wardour. The lofty cliffs present many scenes of beauty and grandeur, and, with the exception of two or three tiny bays, extend onward to the Redhead. They vary in height from 100 to 150 feet, and the Redhead is about 260 feet high. A footpath leads along the top of the cliffs to Auchmithie, affording many picturesque views of the precipitous rocky coast, the outlying shelving rocks, over and upon which the restless waves are ever breaking, and the boundless ocean beyond, while a beautiful, richly cultivated country lies behind you, over which towers, and chimneys, and the lofty ruins of the Abbey of Arbroath stand boldly out. The rocky bulwark is perforated by several caves, some of which extend more than two hundred feet into the cliff. Some of these caves are accessible at all times of the tide, others at low water, others can only be reached from a boat, and the entrance of one or two is some distance up the face of the rock. Wild legends are told of some of these caves. At one period a large smuggling trade was carried on along the east coast, and the caves were often occupied by the smugglers, and made the receptacle of contraband goods. In one or two places, outside the cliffs, isolated pillars stand out bold and gaunt, the softer rock which had surrounded them having been washed away. The most curious of all the wild scenes on this rocky coast is the Geary or Gaylot Pot, in a field not far from Auchmithie. It is a huge pit, about fifty yards in diameter. At high water in easterly storms the water is impelled into the pit with extreme violence and loud noise, and the water boils, and surges, and froths in an extraordinary manner. The bottom of the pit can be reached at low water, as the soil slopes down from the north-west side, but in other parts the rocks are all but perpendicular.

Mr Hay in his admirable history of Arbroath gives a graphic description of the caverns and cliffs between Arbroath and Auchmithie. A long narrow inlet, with a huge rock in the entrance, is known as Dickmont Den. In it there are several caverns, one of which is large, and has two entrances from the Den, and one from the sea. Looking down from the top of the cliffs when the tide is in and the sun shining, there is seen at this cave the appearance as of two large eyes, which have been locally named the "Devil's E'en." There is a very distinct echo in the Den. Among the many objects of interest here, there is also the Stalactite Cave, famous for its beautiful natural pendants; the Needle E'e, the Mason's Cove, a spacious grotto to which the "brethren of the mystic tie" from time immemorial made, and to which they still continue to make, pilgrimages, and in the recesses of which they perform some of their mysterious ceremonies. A visit to these and other points of interest with which that part of the coast abounds will amply repay any effort that may be undergone in its accomplishment. Mr Bain, describing the scene, says:—

Apart from the romantic spell thrown around this part of the coast, one cannot resist a feeling of sublimity arising in his mind as he walks along those cliffs or descends to and explores those wonderful caves. The beautiful panorama which lies stretched before him is perfectly enchanting. The German Ocean here and there studded with fishing boats, while near at hand and in the distance may be seen the white sails of many a merchantman. To the right he sees the Firth of Tay and the sands of Barry, where, in the early days of our Scottish history, Camus, the Danish commander, landed his soldiers in the vain attempt to conquer our country. The coast of Fife, with its hill and dale, add variety to the scene. From any point may also be seen that wonderful beacon, the Bell Rock Lighthouse, as, like a faithful sentinel, it keeps watch and ward over the lives of our hardy mariners. To the naturalist our beautiful cliffs have a special charm. Professor Balfour and other distinguished botanists have scrambled along their grassy and rocky slopes to pluck the carline thistle, the sweet milk vetch, the seaside gromwell and the lovely maiden pink, and to admire their rich and varied maritime flora. To the geologist they have proved no less attractive. Hugh Miller investigated their grandly-piled masses of old red sandstone and conglomerate. They fired Sir Charles Lyell with so much enthusiasm that when tottering on the verge of the grave he insisted on getting into a boat at Auchmithie and gazing on them with a last fond look.

The Town Council, with most commendable spirit, have recently made the access to the cliffs very easy, and at the same time enhanced the beautiful surroundings, by the formation of footpaths and graceful bridges over ravines that formerly made the visit somewhat fatiguing and of a switchback nature.

The bridging and extension of the paths along this, perhaps one of the most romantic seaside walks in Scotland, will, as we have already hinted, no doubt be prized by all visitors to "Fairport." In this connection, it is satisfactory to note that the Town Council is moving, though somewhat tardily, in the direction of making the town, which has so many attractions, better known to tourists and summer residents, now in these days of cheap and speedy travelling, a numerous class of people. Besides its "lions," already referred to, it has a fairly good golf course, a stretch of sands to the west sufficient to give Arbroath a good reputation as a watering place; the Common is an extensive and excellent health-giving recreation ground; while the geologist and the botanist find themselves in a veritable Garden of Eden. As was recently said by the editor of the *Herald*, now that Hospitalfield, Sir Walter's "Monkbarns," has been thrown open to the public, (tickets of admission to be had at the *Guide* office) Arbroath and neighbourhood should be more and more attractive to readers and students of Scott.

But we must now crave pardon for lingering over these cliffs and caves, sandy and rocky shore, ruined castles and far-stretching ocean. We are sure, however, that they will form a grand gallery of pictures, wich will long remain treasures in memory's storehouse.

Hospitalfield—"Monkbarns."

Monastic buildings were not complete without their hospital. The hospital attached to the Abbey of

Aberbrothock was situated about a mile from the Monastery. It was endowed with lands in its vicinity, which are now part of the present estate of Hospitalfield. It appears to have been sold about the time of the Reformation, when the monastic houses were abolished, as Marian Ogilvy was proprietrix of Hospitalfield about 1565.

The mansion of Hospitalfield, which was erected on the site of the Hospital, is about one and half miles from Arbroath. The old mansion house remained without much alteration from its first erection until about the middle of the present century, from which time the late proprietor, Patrick Allan Fraser, did much to improve it. Mr Fraser, through his wife, acquired considerable property, and, out of respect to her, he, with her consent, resolved to erect a fitting memorial in commemoration of her. Shortly after Mrs Fraser's death he acquired ground in the centre of the Western Cemetery, and erected the memorial in the form of a mortuary chapel; the entire building is the conception of Mr Fraser. It is a noble and unique structure, rich in ornament, and likely to tell its story for many centuries.

Mr Fraser resided for some time in Rome, and became a member of the British Academy of Arts there. He was elected President of the Academy, and discharged the duties of the office while there. He was an artist of repute, and the mansion is adorned with some beautiful paintings by himself, and others by most of the leading painters. There are also fine examples of the old masters. Many choice objects of virtue and exquisite statuary, finely arranged, certify to the refined taste of the proprietor, who died in 1890.

Speaking of the mansion, a writer in the *Queen* says:—" Those familiar with the identity of Hospitalfield mansion, with the "Monkbarns" of Sir Walter Scott's novel, "The Antiquary," will find a new interest in the purpose to which 'the residence of Mr Jonathan Oldbuck' is now devoted. By the will of 'the last laird of Monkbarns,' it is provided that an art school shall be erected at Hospitalfield, and that the mansion-house, with its wooded surroundings, will form a retreat for students. Meanwhile permission to view the grounds and galleries has been accorded to the public, on the Fridays of July, August, and September, in the hope that thereby artistic taste will be stimulated as a prelude to the scheme of art education to be ultimately adopted. The main building, with its lofty barbican, standing

in trimly kept grounds, is a model of Scoto-Franco architecture, and there is no more interesting house in the county. Replete with quaint structural devices, rich ornamentations, arcaded galleries and balconies, floral wood carvings, corbel brackets, and heraldic designs, Hospitalfield will form a unique home of art, enhanced as it is by an almost classic environment. Patrick Allan-Fraser, 'the last laird of Monkbarns,' was a man who rose from obscurity to distinction by his brush. He was a pupil of Robert Scott Lauder, and Sir William Fettes Douglas and the late Calder Marshall were amongst his artistic colleagues. Should Hospitalfield, which is a permanent mark of his beneficence to art, be well cared for by posterity, it cannot fail to become a resort of the curious and intelligent traveller."

St Vigeans.

The church of St Vigeans (Rev. William Duke, D.D., F. S. A. Scot.) is very picturesquely situated on a knoll, about a mile from Arbroath. The existence of numerous sculptured stones of the Celtic period render it probable that a church and burying-ground have existed here from the first introduction of Christianity into the country. It seems to have been dedicated to St Fechin, an Irish bishop, who died A.D. 664. Its local name of Aberbrothock, as the parish church of the shire, or whole surrounding district, was retained in common use down to the suppression of the neighbouring monastery, and the erection of the town of Arbroath into a separate parish—but now under the Parish Council regulations designated Arbroath and St Vigeans—after the Restoration.

The numerous fragments of sculptured stones of the Celtic period that stand in the porch, or have been built for preservation into the walls, give a singular interest to this venerable church, while the learning and researches of the esteemed minister have enabled him, in his writings on the subject, to throw much light on these relics. The Droston stone combines the symbols of pagan times with a finely chiselled cross. It is unique in further bearing an incised inscription in the early Celtic language of the country. The inscription on it, Dr Duke says, is " the only specimen of a Pictish inscription that has come down to us. It speaks of a stone as erected to Droston, son of Voret, of the race of Fergus, and a Pictish King Droston was killed at the Battle of Blathmig or Blethmont, a mile or two off, in the year 729; the inscription is on the edge of the stone." Here rests the dust of Peter Young, tutor of King James VI. under George Buchanan. James made him a Privy Councillor and King's Almoner, conferred on him the estates of Seaton and Dickmontlaw, and knighted him Sir Peter Young of Seaton. He died in 1628, and was buried in a vault at the back of the church of St Vigeans, the new aisle of which has a tablet to his memory. Sir Peter's father was John Young, a burgess of Dundee, and his mother Margaret Scrimgeour, of a branch of the Dudhope family, and from him sprung the Youngs of Seaton, Ochterlony, and Aldbar.

In the days when the transport of weighty materials was difficult, the erection of buildings in elevated situations must always have appeared an arduous task. Hence the general consensus of opinion which ascribed all gigantic labours to supernatural agency. Satan is often associated in old legends with the erection of churches and abbeys. The recollection of the assistance he gave in building the old Church of St Vigeans is still perpetuated by the well-known couplet :—

>Sair back and sair banes
>Carryin' the kirk o' St Vigeans stanes.

St Vigeans seems to have possessed sculptured stones of almost every variety of character that is found elsewhere in the north-east of Scotland. Besides the Droston Cross, there are two fragments that contain examples of the spectacle ornament, one of them quite primitive in its simplicity, the other highly ornamental. The representations of the cross are numerous, and of very diverse design. The earlier discovered stones are described and illustrated in the late Dr Stewart's book, " Sculptured Stones of Scotland," Vol. II. An account of those that were found during the restoration of the Chvrch in 1871, was prepared by the minister of the parish for the Society of Antiquaries of Scotland, and is printed with relative plates in the ninth volume of their " Proceedings."

A short distance east from the mount on which the church of St Vigeans stands there is another eminence of about the same height on which stands the farm buildings of Bridgeton. On the top, according to the Old Account of the parish, there was a very remarkable echo proceeding from the east end of the church. It is said the echo repeated very distinctly six syllables, and in a calm evening eight syllables, or a line of the Psalms in metre, and did not begin to reverberate till the voice of the speaker had ceased. When the speaker moved a few yards from his first station two echoes were repeated, and proceeding a little further three echoes were repeated. The growth of trees about the church, however, and other alterations appear to have destroyed the echo.

Letham Grange.

The extensive estate of Letham Grange includes the united properties of Letham, New Grange, and Peebles. Mr James Fletcher purchased the property in 1877, and shortly after he acquired the estate of Fern, referred to in our first tour. He has since built a splendid mansion at Letham Grange, in which he has incorporated the earlier house, built in 1830 by Mr Hay, the previous owner, close to the site of the old mansion house of New Grange. It is charmingly situated, is surrounded by grand old trees, and a park diversified by many a shady neuk, verdant knowe, and clumps of spreading monarchs of the wood. From the railway between Arbroath and Guthrie an excellent view of the house and grounds is obtained.

Mr Fitzroy C. Fletcher, who succeeded his father in the estates, is a very popular landlord, and has fitted up a riding school, and made many other improvements on the property, which add greatly to its amenity and beauty.

Colliston Castle.

The lands of Colliston were part of the possessions of the Abbey of Arbroath, and appear to have been alienated from the covenant in the early part of the sixteenth century, as Gilbert Reid of Colliston is mentioned in 1539.

Henry Guthrie is designed of Colliston 1568-9. Bishop Guthrie, who acquired Guthrie from the old family, was of the Colliston Guthries, and so are the Guthries of Guthrie of the present time, but the estate has been for a considerable time in possession of the family of Chaplin, the present owner being Mr Peebles Chaplin, who succeeded to the estate in 1883. Mr Warden says that the Castle of Colliston was erected in 1583, two years later than the neighbouring castle of Braikie, and it still shows, through subsequent additions, all the interior arrangements of a gentleman's "fortified" house of the period.

Mr Chaplin, who takes a great interest in antiquarian researches, holds according to an ancient

Latin charter, signed by the monks of the Abbey, that "the principal mansion-house of Colyston," was in existence in 1545. Extensive additions of a very tasteful nature, have just been completed at a cost of nearly £5000. The elements of the antique have been skillfully preserved, while the modern portions so blend with them as to produce a harmonious whole. Several ancient stones are built into the walls, these having recently been discovered by Mr Chaplin during building operations. It is conjectured that the stones had at one time been taken from an ancient religious temple which is known to have existed in the vicinity of Colliston.

Colliston Parish Church (Rev. Alexander Mills) was built in 1870 by the minister and kirk-session of St Vigeans, to supply the religious requirements of a large and populous district of the parish. It is situated at the junction of the road from Colliston Station with the Arbroath and Forfar road, about three miles from Arbroath. The site of the church, manse, and adjoining public school was given at a nominal feu-duty by the proprietor of the estate of Colliston. The village, with the usual inn, merchants' places of business, tailor, shoemaker, &c., with flower-embosomed garden plots, is neat and attractive.

Friockheim.

Friockheim is a pleasantly situated quiet-going place, recently, like "Thrums," made more extensively known than ever it was before by the inimitable and widely popular delineations of Scottish life and character, entitled "Cruisie Sketches," and other works, by "Fergus Mackenzie." It also possesses all the attractions of a health-resort, and is likely, as such, to grow in favour. In the neighbourhood are a number of interesting historic old mansions we will refer to before taking up our route where we left it at Maryton to *do* the coast scenery and other adjoining points of importance between Lunan and Arbroath. Should the visitor wish it, however, he can now, as will be seen on consulting our map, cross to Farnell and Kinnaird by way of Montreathmont. Some four or five hundred acres of the Moor of Montreathmont, one of the great Royal forests of Scotland, lay in the barony of Kinnell. It was therefore, frequently honoured with the visits of Royalty, in pursuit of the pleasures of the chase. In 1617 James VI. paid it one of those visits, residing at Kinnaird Castle, the seat of his favourite, Lord Carnegie ; and it would seem that he enjoyed himself for eight days in hunting in his Royal forest in that district.

The ground upon which the village of Friockheim is built was part of the barony of Gardyne, but it was parted with to the Rollocks in 1604. The lands came into the possession of Miss Elizabeth Ogilvy, who sold them in 1792 to David Gardyne for his brother Charles. The land was feued in the early part of this century. The village was at first named Friockfeus, but by public advertisement, dated 22d May, 1824, it was changed from "feus" to "heim," with the consent of T. Gardyne, the superior.

Jervise informs us that, apart from William Gardyne, who did homage to King Edward, until 1408 the name of Gardyne or Gairn is not met with in Angus, but of that date it is recorded that Alexander Gardyne acquired the lands of Borrowfield, near Montrose, on the resignation of William, and his descendants held that estate until 1615. In 1409 the laird of Borrowfield is also a witness to a charter of half the lands and brewhouse of Kinnaird, which Duthac de Carnegie received in dowry with his wife,

Mariota, one of the three co-heiresses of Richard de Kinnaird. The chief of the Borrowfield branch fell at the battle of Arbroath in 1445-6, fighting in support of the Ogilvys.

During the following century, branches of the family were designed of the different properties of Lawton, Leys, Legatston, and Tulloes, in Forfarshire—all in the neighbourhood of the parent house. After this, notices of them become more plentiful, chiefly, however, in the annals of our criminal trials. and in regard to "deidlie feuds" which took place between them and their neighbour, Guthrie of that ilk. This course of lawless revenge and bloodshed, so characteristic in our feudal times, continued over several generations with great loss of life and property to both families, and became so serious that the king was called upon to interpose between them. In 1682, Gardyne was acquired by James Lyell, ancestor of the present proprietor, who is the representative of Lyell of Dysart. Gardyne, Middleton, Cotton of Gardyne, Friock, and Legatston belonged to the Lyells till near the middle of last century. when James Gardyne of Lawton bought Middleton, Friock, Legatston, and Cotton of Gardyne.

Gardyne Castle is situated about four miles east from the parish church of Kirkden. It is a large and elegant building, partly old and partly modern. The old portion is a good example of the castellated architecture of the sixteenth century. It is romantically situated upon the west side of Denton Burn, a tributary of the Vinny; and the Moot or Gallows-hill, still forms a prominent object in the landscape.

In ancient times the parish of Kirkden was called Idvies. The estate of Idvies embraces the greater portion of the western end of the parish, and the estates of Pitmuies and Gardyne, with some other properties, the principal one of which is Middleton, constitute the eastern portion of the parish. The old church of Kirkden was taken down, and a new church erected in 1825 (Rev. James Anderson.) When the new church was built the parish was more populous than it now is, even in the portion that still remains to it; and besides this diminution, in the year 1825, the district church of Friockheim—since 1870 a *quoad sacra* parish church—was formed out of the original parish of Kirkden.

The Castle of Braikie is situated in the parish of Kinnell, at an elevated point about equidistant from Arbroath and Brechin, by the line of the old road connecting the two towns. Soon after the battle of Bannockburn, the barony of Kinnell (which was the name it bore in ancient times) was granted by King Robert the Bruce to Fraser, chief of the clan Fraser. The estates appear to have gone out of the family of Fraser about 1650. In 1688, Charles Carnegie, fourth Earl of Southesk, was infeft in the office of baron of the barony of Kinnell, and also of the barony of Bolshan. Soon after the year 1695 the barony of Kinnell was sold by the Southesk family to James, fourth Earl of Panmure.

By the year 1760 the castle had ceased to be occupied by the family to whom it belonged. The housekeeper in charge, about fifty years ago, was an old woman nick-named Castle Jean, who had her own version of the history of the castle, and everything pertaining to it. She was always impatient of contradiction, and altogether independent of authorities. When questioned as to when and how the castle was built, she generally replied:

Be it cheap, or be it dear,
This house was biggit in ae year;

which version she is said to have sometimes altered to—

> Be the meal cheap, or be it dear,
> Braikie frizel was biggit in ae year.

The word "frizel" appears to be a corruption of fortalice.

The Castle and Barony of Guthrie, in the parish of Guthrie, about equi-distant from Arbroath and Forfar, are now, and for many years have been, the residence and property of the family of Guthrie of that ilk; amongst the oldest in the country, and one of the most respected families of landed gentry in Scotland. The original castle, which was of great strength, consisted of a square tower, about sixty feet in height, with walls ten feet thick. The old part of what now forms the pile of castle buildings stood a few yards eastward of the ancient tower-fortress. About 1818 the intermediate space was filled up by the erection of a Gothic building, the whole then forming a commodious and elegant modern mansion. The grounds around the castle are tastefully laid out, and finely ornamented, the Lunan water winding its onward course directly in front of the castle; while behind it the wood-crowned hill of Guthrie rises to an elevation of 500 feet. The erection of the castle is ascribed to Sir Alexander Guthrie, who together with his son fell in the fatal battle of Flodden field, along with King James IV. and the flower of his nobility.

The Church of Kinnell (Rev. D. Macarthur) is situated in a district a large part of which was the Royal Forest, referred to on page 390. It contains an interesting relic of the battle of Arbroath (page 379) at which the leader of the Ogilvys, the Laird of Inverquharity, was slain. He was buried in the old church of Kinnell, in what was called the 'Ogilvy Aisle,' on which there was this inscription:—

> While girse grows green and water rins clear,
> Let nane but Ogilvys lie here.

The ground on which the Ogilvy aisle stood was opened about thirty years ago, when the remains of a man of gigantic size, according with the description given of Inverquharity, were found. Ogilvy's boots and spur long hung in the church aisle. The boots, much decayed, are said to have been there until about the beginning of the present century. The spur has been preserved, and it is fixed in the vestibule of the present church.

Maryton.

The Rev. W. R. Fraser, in his "Maryton Parish Church : a Centenary Address," says:—The church of the parish, from the time of the Reformation, had as its first minister Richard Melville, eldest brother of the distinguished Reformer, Andrew Melville; and if the same building had continued until 1642, when a new church is said to have been built, it had as its two last ministers the nephew and grand-nephew of the Reformer, who were also successive lairds of Baldovie. That is the church to which two references are made in the quaint words of the autobiography of James Melville, who was the son of Richard. We find him on one occasion saying:—

I remember a certean day my father send me to the smeddy for dressing of hewkes and some yron instruments, the way lying hard by Mariekirk, wherein my father pretched. I begond to weirie soar of my lyff; and as my custome haid been fra my bernheid to pray in my hart, and mein my esteitt to God, coming fornent the kirk, and luiking to it, the Lord steirit upe an extraordinar motion in my hart, and which made me atteans, being alean, to fall on gruiff to the ground and pour out a schort and earnest petition to God that it wald please His guidnes to offer occasion to continue me at the scholles, and inclyne my father's hart till use the saming, with promise and vow that whatever missour of knawledge and letters He wald bestow upon me, I sould, by His grace, imploy the saming for His glorie in the calling of the ministrie ; and rysing from the ground with joy and grait contentment in heart, again fell down and worshipped, and sa past on, and did the errand, returning and praising my God, singing sum Psalms. . . . Going a day to Bonitone, I past by the kirk of Maritone and place where I haid prayed and vowed to God, the same cam in my memorie, with a grait motion of mind and determination to pay my vow, giff God wald giff the grace and mayen.

The present neat ivy-clad church, which was opened by James Wilson, minister of the parish, in 1792, underwent considerable alterations in 1818, when one of the two galleries it then contained was taken out. Mr Wilson removed to Farnell in 1794.

The church, like churches generally in olden times, had been unprovided at first with pews—the practice being for everybody that wished to sit down to bring his seat along with him. The seats were sometimes an occasion of bickering, as the following minute of 1727 will testify :—" It was reported by some that their seats were misplaced without any of their order, therefore the session ordered their Beddle *in presentia* to sett the Stools belonging to the women in such places of the church as they judged most proper, and to prevent trouble or disturbance, afterwards they discharge any person whatsomever to alter any of the same without an order from the session, or some member of the same." It is not said whether the " beddle " had any difficulty in carrying out his instructions. If the spirit of Jenny Geddes had developed itself among the women, to whom the stools belonged, the poor man would have been sorely bested.

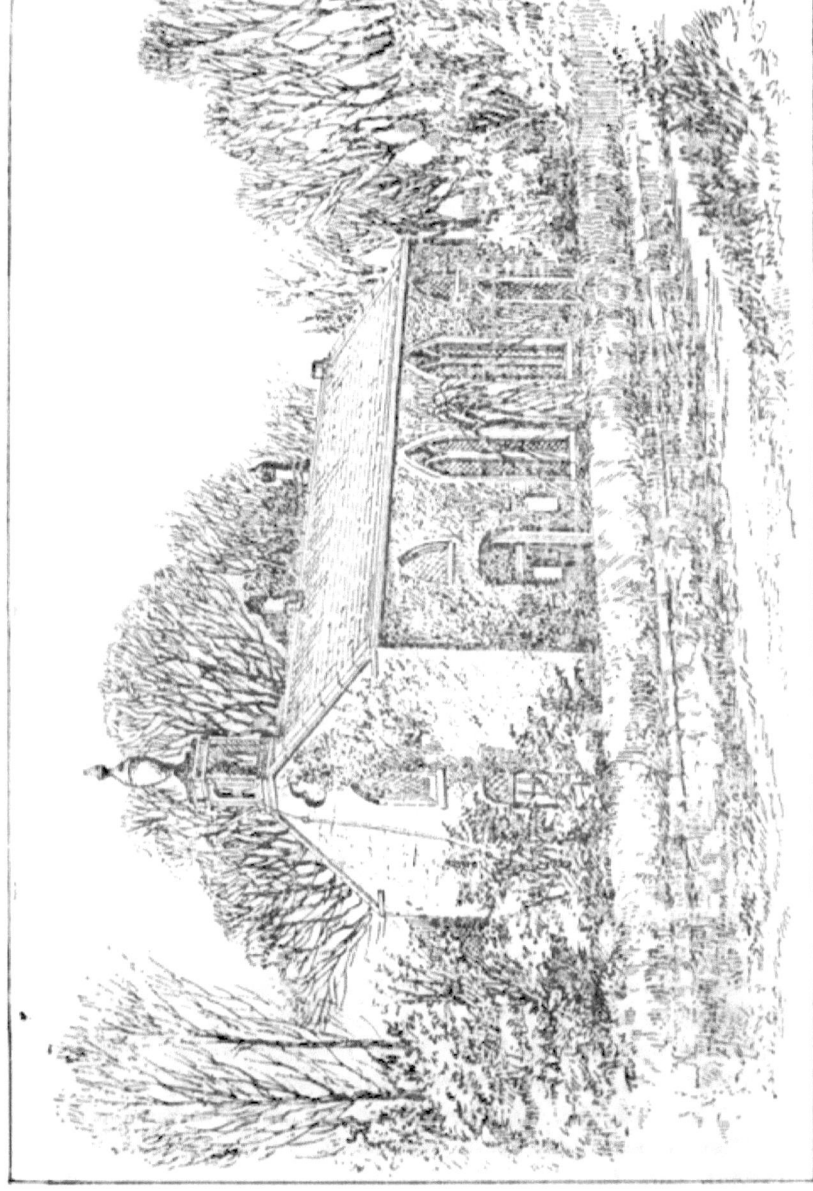

The Rev. Mr Fraser, who, by his writings, has done much to make known in a popular style the ancient history of the parish, as well as of the counties of Forfar and Kincardine, retired from the active duties of the ministry at Maryton some years ago, his assistant and successor being the Rev. R. Henderson.

Mr Fraser, in his interesting "Maryton Records of the Past," tells us that the lands of Maryton were originally constituted what was called an abthen, that is, property of or connected with an abbot or abbacy. The church was called St Mary's of Old Montrose, and was dedicated to the Virgin. It is said to have been a vicarage of the Cathedral of Brechin; but, with all its belongings, it was given at a very early date to the Abbey of Arbroath. The earliest charter known is one between the years 1178-98. These gifts were made and confirmed by kings (notably King William the Lion), popes, and bishops of Brechin—one of the latter bearing the name of Hugh—and the presentation embraced the **church of Auld** Munross, with its chapels, lands, **tithes, oblations, and** all their just pertinents, as well **as a grant to the** monks of the said Monastery of **Arbroath of the** right to **convert to their own use, and for their sustentation, all the** rents and profits of that church, **and** to appoint in the **same** church such chaplains **as they** pleased.

Church collections **during last century were** made for many very different purposes, such as "For helping John Jamieson, a poor man, to buy a cow;" "For William Teveotdale, a lame chapman from Craig, who had been robbed, &c." The Session of Maryton were sorely exercised sometimes with the small bits of coin that formed a part of the contributions. Here is one extract in 1727 —"The rest of this collection, viz., 12s 8d, being all Doitts, was putt into the Box." The same year Margaret Birnie, a poor woman, complains that so much of her money, at last distribution, was "doitts," and so of little, or almost no use to her. The schoolmaster one year *referred* payment of his salary till another time, "in regard the money we had by us was in Brass." Another time we find "the Minr. and Sess advising there should be a comitee, viz., two or three of the elders, for taking out some Doitts, or halfpennies, for the payment of the Presbytery Bursar, and his discharge to be got up when he receives it."

Old Montrose.

Old Montrose is a place of considerable interest. It was from the town of Montrose that Lindsay, the original Duke of Montrose, took his title; but it was from their old seat of Old Montrose, Maryton, that the Grahams took their several titles of Lord, Earl, Marquis, and Duke. They were an old family, the first of them who settled in Angus being David of Graham, who was the grandfather of the patriot, Sir John Graham, who fell at the battle of Falkirk, fighting with Wallace for the independence of his country. The Great Marquis of the seventeenth century was born at Old Montrose in 1612; and the part which he acted in the Civil War of his day is well known. After swearing the Covenant, and being for a time a zealous supporter of the Presbyterians, he deserted them, and went over to the side of Charles. At Philiphaugh he was captured, and conveyed a prisoner to Edinburgh, where he suffered a cruel and ignominious death. Who can read, without feelings of admiration, those lines which he wrote with the point of a diamond on his prison window the evening before his execution?

"Let them bestow on every airth a limb,
 Then open all my veins—that I may swim
 To Thee, my Maker, in that crimson lake—
 Then place my parboil'd head upon a stake;

Scatter my ashes—strew them in the air—
Lord ! since Thou knowest where all those atoms are,
And confident thou'lt raise me with the just."

The ancient house of Old Montrose, in which the great Marquis of Montrose is supposed to have been born, was a plain, white-washed building. Becoming ruinous, it was mostly pulled down by the father of the Earl of Southesk when the present farmhouse was built, about fifty years ago. A portion of the old house exists as part of the offices attached to the stables, which stand close by the public road, near the north entry to the house. Two old gate posts are at this entrance.

Speaking of "Powis" Mr Fraser says there is no evidence of its ever having formed a separate possession—and the Powis of Old Montrose, a name by which it is generally known, would suggest that it formed a part of the original barony of Auld Munross. The name of Powis is evidently from Pow, the old word for stream or burn. The Pow-bridge has an interesting history of its own. It was built first in 1617, while King James was visiting at the Castle of Kinnaird, and enjoying the hunt in the royal forest. And the purpose for which it was erected, according to the Session Records of Brechin, was for "leading his Majesty's provision" while he was the guest of his favourite, the Earl of Southesk.

A handsome Free Church, with manse and other buildings, was erected on a prominent position in the vicinity of Old Montrose. This church is adorned with a neat spire, which is seen from a considerable distance. The surrounding scenery is beautiful, and the church and spire form a pleasing feature in the landscape.

Maryton Law, which commands such a magnificent view of the surrounding district, is supposed to have been vitrified. It is one of those eminences which are popularly believed to have been used as sites for the administration of justice. Last century it was a separate holding; and, judging from the Session Records, it would seem that even in one of its proper centres the law was not always observed.

The Right Honourable the Earl of Southesk, K.T., whose unwearied and learned researches in connection with the antiquities of the district—"Picts'," or "Earth Houses," "Laws," "Cairns," &c. — have attracted the attention of high authorities, says :—

The tumulus called Maryton Law stands about twenty feet higher than the level of the surrounding surface. Its lower portion seems to be a natural knob on the summit of the eastern extremity of the hill-range of Carcary, upon which has been raised a considerable cairn of rather large stones mixed with earth, near whose top, and exactly in the centre, the ancient interment has been made. . . . In the vicinity of that fine spring the "Lady Well," stands, at the side of the Arbroath and Brechin road, the elevation termed Green Law—a tumulus of unusual height and circumference. Many years ago I excavated this mound. No signs of ancient work appeared, but pretty far down we encountered a ponderous misshapen stone embedded in clayey soil—proof that the mound was not artificial, for what people would laboriously carry a huge boulder merely to throw it anyhow into an earth heap they were raising? My conclusion is, that if ever there was an interment at Green Law, it was made in a comparatively shallow deposit on the top of the natural elevation, as at Maryton Law. Some forty or fifty years ago, a small earthenware pot and other remains (now in the Montrose Museum) were discovered in the rising ground within a stone's throw to the south. . . . The Ardovie "Three Laws," the Bertie's Den hillock, where the pot-bottom was found, several hillocks near it, and, lastly, the Green Law itself, run all on a continuous west to east line, and are apparently moraines deposited by a glacier in its progress to the sea, many large boulders of a sort differing from the old red sandstone of the district being found at intervals in the same track—notably one of huge dimensions lying close to the road at the foot of Green Law. Monrommon (or Montreathmont) Moor, now wooded but formerly a wide heathery waste, has probably been the scene of many a battle and many a burial, but few traces of these now remain. Such burial-mounds as are visible have been long ago explored, as the only battle relic known to me is a man's wrist bone, severed from the arm at one stroke, which was found by Mr Carnegie of Redhall and myself among the roots of a prostrated spruce tree within a few yards of the "Battle Well"—a portion perhaps of some warlike Lindsay or Ogilvy shorn off during the retreat and pursuit after the Battle of Arbroath. It may be more ancient—but bronze or flint could not cut so clean. . . . In this Deer Park of Kinnaird, not far from the Brechin Lodge, there is a low rise known as the Corbie Hillock. Hearing, some years ago, that sandstone slabs had been found near the base when drainage was going on, I made excavations in the mound itself, and on the south side, about half way up, discovered a group of five or six cists. Some showed deposits of black, burnt matter; in one was a coarse, half-baked earthenware vase with "herring bone pattern" markings. At the bottom of one of the cists was a large block of white quartz.* This may have been deposited significantly—there is reason and precedent for thinking so—quartz as a fire stone, a spark-maker, was viewed by some of the old races as a type of divine creative force. .

. . My other most notable excavations were at Fithie. The first of these consisted in removing the remainder of the soil accumulated in a "Pict's House," or "Earth House," which had been discovered and partly opened by the tenant of the farm many years ago. This burrow, like others of its class, formed a narrow strongly-curved tunnel, gradually descending from the surface entrance to a point seventy or eighty feet distant, where the depth attained to about ten feet. The first portion of this passage was walled with large standing slabs (two of which now do duty as field gate-posts near the farm steading), then for a short way came a casing of rubble work, but for the rest of the distance the natural shaley clay was left unlined. Whether burrows of this type were used as winter dwellings, as temporary hiding places, or as granaries, is uncertain; they are pretty numerous in Angus and other Pictish territories. Many yet retain their roofing of stone slabs; in the Fithie example the roof seems to have been formed of planks, as socket holes for supporting posts had at intervals been cut in opposite pairs into the solid floor. . . . The second excavation in that neighbourhood was at Fithie Law, which occupies a commanding position near the Farnell and Renmuir road, in a southerly direction from the farm buildings of Fithie and the site of the ancient castle of the Fithies of that ilk. This must have been a grand tumulus, the tomb of some chieftain of importance.

Bonnyton or Bonnington was once the seat of the family of Wood. "The foundation of the castle they inhabited," says the "Statistical Account" of the parish, "is still to be seen; and of a moat or broad ditch by which it was fortified, the vestige still remains."

King William the Lion paid two visits to the northern part of Scotland, and each of them was to quell a rebellion. The King in his journeyings on these expeditions had probably rested with his troops at Montrose, where there was a royal castle, as he dated charters at it between 1178 and 1198. The gatekeeper of the castle was a man named Crane, for which he had the heritable fee of the lands of Iny-aney, situated on the south side of the South Esk, in what is now the parish of Maryton. His son Swayne, and grandson Simon, successively succeeded, and on the death of the latter without male issue, his five daughters made a joint claim to these lands. Their right was questioned, but an inquest was instituted in 1261-2, and an assize, consisting of eighteen of the chief barons of the county, gave decision in favour of the five co-heiresses.

Until a recent date the Den of Fullerton was called by the name of Ananie, but for many years the name has not been given to any lands in the parish, and it is now extinct. The Fullertons were proprietors of the third part of Ananie, which they sold to the Grahams of Old Montrose, and the Lady Magdalene Carnegie was life-rented in them, in Maryton, Old Montrose, &c., in terms of her marriage contract with the Earl of Montrose in 1629.

About 1640 Sir John Wood of Bonnyton married Lady Mary Ogilvy, third daughter of James, second Earl of Airlie. The old Castle of Bonnyton is supposed to have been erected in the year in which the baronetcy was created. Its site is well known, but no description of it is known to exist. It is said to have fallen down in 1785. It was surrounded by a moat. The only remains of the castle are two slabs, which are built into the farm offices. On one is a carving of the arms of Scotland, and on the other that of the family of Wood. Both are dated 1666. A parishioner of Maryton, whose grandmother was a cottager in Bonnyton, has heard her speak of a report, which was common in her younger days, that the Woods disappeared somewhat mysteriously from the parish. One evening they were known to have sat down to supper, and next morning they had disappeared, never again to be seen in the parish, and very little heard of until Sir James, as it has been stated, was found to be sojourning in another part of the county. This tradition so much resembles the story of the last descendants of the Murrays of Melgund that they probably have a common origin, and may be called legends.

The lands of Fullerton and Ananie were purchased by Sir David Carnegie in 1789, and since then they have remained in possession of the noble family of Carnegie of Kinnaird.

A small outlying section of the parish of Maryton is in the old Moor of Montreathmont, and there is a tradition that the union was formed in a romantic manner. When Lady Magdalene Carnegie was espoused to James Graham, the first Marquis of Montrose, she claimed from her father, the Earl of Southesk, something for pin money, in addition to her dowry, and he agreed to give her as much of the moor as she could walk round within a given time. The lady, perhaps with the view of getting a large slice of it, walked too far in a direct line, and found, when half the given time was almost gone, that to reach the starting point she could not make a long lateral diversion, and her perambulation, therefore, included a long narrow strip, which is the description of Grahamsfirth to the present time.

The lands of Fithie lie a little to the south-east of the Church of Farnell. In the first half of the thirteenth century, if not earlier, they belonged to a family who assumed a surname from them. Fithies of that Ilk appear to have been vassals of the Bishop of Brechin, to whom they paid feu for their lands. In early times there appears to have been a Castle of Fithie (referred to by the Earl of Southesk in the quotations we have given from his Lordship's "Notes"), the only part of which now remaining forms the back wall of a cottar's dwelling. An old gravestone which now covers the supposed grave of King William the Lion, in Arbroath Abbey, has a shield charged with the armorial bearings of the Fithies.

The Lyells, ancestors of the family of Lyall, farmed the lands of Carcary, on the Southesk estate, for upwards of two centuries. The same race farmed the lands of Fasque, Scotston, and Canterland, in the Mearns, in the 17th and 18th centuries.

Farnell Castle and Church.

> I do love these ancient ruins;
> We never tread upon them but we set
> Our foot upon some reverend history.

The old castle of Farnell is a fine stronghold on the north side of the picturesquely situated Parish Church

Farnell Cas.

(Rev. A. T. Cameron), about a mile from Kinnaird

Castle. Overlooking the Den of Farnell, and surrounded by grand old trees, the ancient pile is in a good state of preservation. Ochterlony, in 1685, describes Farnell as being then an "extraordinary sweet place, with delicate yards and much planting." The lands of Farnell belonged to the Cathedral of Brechin, and the castle was a palace or country residence of the Bishops of that Diocese. It was also at one time the seat of the Ogilvies of Airlie; and it is now kept in repair by the Earl of Southesk, as a comfortable almshouse for the old people and the poor connected with the estate and parish. To their sustenance and comfort the noble Earl and Countess administer, and the use to which the noble family of Southesk devotes this interesting old building reflects the highest honour upon them.

The Castle of Farnell was visited by Edward I. in his tour through the Kingdom, on 7th July, 1296. Long prior to this period, vassals of the Bishop of Brechin assumed their surname from the lands, and Duncan of Ferneyel (Farnell) is a witness to charters of the Earl of Angus from 1214 to 1227.

On 23rd May, 1570, and previous to the purchase of Farnell, Lord Ogilvy obtained a report by John Meldrum, vicar of Farnell, and others regarding the place of Farnell, and it was then in a very dilapidated condition, the great chalmer, the inner chapel, the chapel, and all the other apartments being utterly uninhabitable. The Airlie family retained the property until 1623, when James, Lord Ogilvy, sold it to David, Master of Carnegie. The Master of Carnegie died without male issue in 1633, when his father, David, Lord Carnegie, succeeded to Farnell, and these lands have ever since continued to form part of the Southesk estates.

The castle has not been occupied as a baronial residence for about a century. Lady Carnegie, grandmother of the present Earl, had it repaired and converted, as we have said, into a home for poor persons who had formerly been employed on the estate. The castle is a plain building of three storeys in height, with a circular staircase on the front, which faces the south.

Farnell Church is of unpretending, yet elegant design. Erected in 1806, it is altogether a more tasteful structure than most parish churches. ¶ The plans of the church (anciently Farneval, a deanery of Brechin Cathedral, the vicar holding the offices of Dean of the Church of Brechin) were designed by the Dowager Lady Carnegie. The name of the parish signifies "the burn of arns." Many alders still grow on the banks of the stream, which flows past the church on the north, and also of the Pow on the south side. With its pretty surroundings, it forms a most agreeable rural picture, and at once arrests the notice of the stranger. It is begirt with a kirkyard so green and quiet that one would almost wish to lie down in its verdant lap, and be at rest. Then there is the burn below, wimpling along its own little vale of flowers, with generally a group of urchins from the school close by, paidlin' in pursuit of the minnow, the eel, or the "beardie"—their gleeful voices falling with a fitful music on the ear.

In 1574 Farnell, Cuikston, and other four churches, were served by one minister. The present parish consists of the old parish of Farnell, and of part of Cuikston, afterwards Kinnaird, this addition having been made to it when that parish was suppressed. Near the end of the sixteenth century the church became ruinous, and a new one was built by David Carnegie of Kinnaird in the immediate vicinity of his Castle. David Carnegie died before the new church was completed, but in his will, made on 15th April, 1598, the day before his death, he ordained that his eldest son and successor should complete the "wark of the Kirk of Kinnaird." In 1870 the churchyard of Farnell was extended, and improvements made upon it. In these operations a line of coffins was discovered on the east side of the church. They had been carefully constructed of stone slabs. The heads of two crosses were also found, one of which was pierced with four holes, but the other was a plain cross in low relief on one side of a circle, and on the reverse was a similar figure, but in an unfinished state. There were also found two coffin slabs, the one having a smooth surface without ornamentation, and the other having on it a sword much defaced, the base of a cross incised, with some old English letters in relief. In the wall of the churchyard a dedication cross is built.

The foundations of the old Parish Church of Kinnaird can still be traced in an enclosure surrounded with trees a short distance in front of Kinnaird Castle. The burial place is not now used as such, but it still contains several well sculptured gravestones and other memorials of the past.

About a mile north from the church is a knoll called Rumes cross, and the church may have been dedicated to Saint Rumon or Rumold. A monument, with a representation of the Fall of Adam and Eve, and a beautifully interlaced cross, was found upon the site of the Old Church, and was presented to the Montrose Museum by the Earl of Southesk.

Kinnaird Castle.

Lo! princely mansion, hall and tower,
Proclaim the spell of beauty's power;
Here, ancient, modern art combine,
To raise a shrine almost divine.

Nothing can be more striking than the beauty of the canopy of grand old trees through which we attain to Kinnaird Castle. There are various stately avenues, with laced and interlaced branches meeting in a trellised archway above, where the lights and shadows are beautified, and the glimpses which anyone standing at the entrance to the great aisle of trees obtains is truly delectable. Perhaps the most striking approach to the lordly home of the universally esteemed Earl of Southesk is by the East Gate, from Bridge of Dun, although the scene by the Farnell Gate is one that will be admired by the ever welcome visitor. Indeed the Castle, with its rare delicacy and splendour of structure, forms the termination of many a beautiful vista, for Nature has been admirably seconded by art in the surrounding Deer Park, which is formed of beautifully diversified ground — shady neuks and verdant knowes, while clumps of great spreading trees dotted about here and there lend artistic boldness to the landscape. If in early summer, amid the gold of the oak twigs and the brown of the beech buds, there is a right-royal carolling of birds. "Thrush is heard calling to thrush." The cuckoo breathes its sweet plaintive note far and near. The low, gentle cooing of doves, and the melodious fluting of black-birds attunes one to all manner of placid thoughts. At one moment a pheasant whirrs through the undergrowth, and squirrels may be seen climbing the gnarled trunks to their nests in the oak hollows, while little white-tailed rabbits scamper across the road with a ridiculous affectation of alarm.

In the noble owner's own words, in one of his sweet little poems—

>   Now sweetly sound the cushat's notes,
>   And far around their softness floats,
>   While up on the top of the highest tree
>   The valiant thrush sings loud and free.

But the park has also its later beauties, which the Earl suggestively depicts in his "Winter Glories"—

>   'Tis in the winter of the year,
>   A silent, sad November day;
>   The beech is brown, the oak is sere,
>   The ash is sallow gray.
>
>   The blackbird on the balustrade
>   Beside the golden-olive moss,
>   His morning feast has yonder made
>   Where crimson berries cross.

> The shaggy cattle in the park
>   Move gently on like mystic dreams
> And o'er the herbage dun and dark
>   Their silvery softness gleams.
>
> And, through the orange fern, the deer
>   Among the fir-trees idly stray:
> The beech is brown, the oak is sere,
>   The fir is green alway.

The lands which form the territorial Earldom of Southesk extend from the basin of Montrose on the east to the western extremity of Montreathmont Muir on the west, a distance of fully eight miles. The southern division of the Kinnaird estates comprehends the lands of Baldovie, Fullerton, Bonnyton, part of Carcary, Upper and Lower Fithie, Bolshan, Kinnell, and others, comprehending the lands of Baldovie on the east, to the parish of Kinnell on the south-west, and is in length seven and a half miles. The northern division comprises the portion north of the river South Esk, and extends from Balwyllo on the east to Brechin on the west.

On 17th July, 1532, the lands of Kinnaird and Little Carcary were first erected into a barony by James V., by a charter under the Great Seal to Robert Carnegie of Kinnaird, on his own resignation, with the manor of Kinnaird, and the salmon fishing of the same on the water of the South Esk, and the commonty of the Muir of Montreathmont, with the exception of an eighth part of Kinnaird, and an eighth part and a sixth of Little Carcary to be called the barony of Kinnaird. The reddendo is a silver penny, if asked, and also the keeping of the King's ale cellar within the shire of Forfar, when he should happen to reside there. A new erection of the barony of Kinnaird was made by Queen Mary, by a charter under the Great Seal, 25th March, 1565.

Many interesting historical events have taken place

within the walls of Kinnaird Castle. We have already referred to the first visit King James paid to Kinnaird Castle, then in possession of David Carnegie, afterwards first Earl of Southesk. The time was spent by the King in hunting upon Montreathmont Muir, and he seems long to have remembered with pleasure the joys of the chase in which he shared during this brief holiday. David Carnegie received the honour of knighthood from the King, and in 1616 his own patriotic services and those of his father and grandfather were rewarded by a Royal Patent creating him Lord Carnegie of Kinnaird. The room in which the Chevalier slept in 1715, and which is probably the same as was occupied by King James VI. and Charles I. and II., on the occasion of their visits to Kinnaird, is still intact in the Castle. It was at the coronation of Charles I., in Holyrood (1633), that Lord Carnegie was raised to a higher dignity in the Peerage by the title of Earl of Southesk, as a reward for the faithful services performed by him and his forefathers to the reigning family. He died full of years and honours in 1658, his life having extended over the stormiest period in Scottish history. The last royal visitor to Kinnaird Castle was the hapless Chevalier de St George, the son of James VII.

There are few names that have been longer connected with Forfarshire or more honourably distinguished in history than that of Carnegie of Kinnaird. From information drawn from the "History of the Carnegies of Southesk"—printed for private circulation by the present Earl of Southesk in 1867—and also from charters and documents still in existence, we find that the family name in its present form of Carnegie dates from about 1340, when it was first assumed as a territorial title; and that the ancestors of the earliest Carnegie have been recorded from about

1210 under the name of De Balinhard. From the time of their first introduction to the estate of Kinnaird in the year 1401 the family seat of the Carnegies has been on or near the site of the present Castle; but the building has undergone frequent transmutations, and the existing structure, as shown in our illustration, cannot in any degree resemble its predecessors, though retaining many portions of them in the basement and elsewhere.

From charter evidence we find that a mansion-house existed in connection with the lands of Kinnaird in the fourteenth century, which appears to have belonged to a family designated De Kinnaird from that place, and quite distinct from the ancestry of the present Lord Kinnaird, whose designation was taken from another property of identical name. There is reason for supposing that about 1400 this family terminated in three co-heiresses, who seem to have held a joint proprietary in part of the estate for several years. One of these sisters, called Mariota de Kinnaird, is traditionally believed to have married Duthac de Carnegie, almost certainly brother of John de Carnegie, the first "of that Ilk." In 1409 Mariota resigned her portion of the property to the Regent, Robert, Duke of Albany, in transference of it to the above-mentioned Duthac, who had obtained a small portion of the estate in 1401 from Richard, son of Brice Ayre. By a charter dated 21st February 1409, the Regent conferred " the lands of the half the town of Kynnard and superiority of the brew-house thereof" upon " Duthac de Carnegie and his heirs [to be held] of our Lord and King and his heirs in fen and heritage for ever." Mariota expressly reserved to herself and her heirs "one house and one acre of land lying near the same and called 'lie chemyst,'" but no trace of this portion of her property can now be found, and in course of a few years this, with the whole of the lands of Kinnaird, came into the possession of the Carnegies. The estate has remained in the latter family, except during the short period of the attainder and forfeiture, from that time until now.

Sir John Carnegie of Kinnaird, Knight, took up arms under the Earl of Huntly in behalf of Queen Mary, and was in consequence deprived of his Castle of Kinnaird, which was committed to the charge of James Halyburton, Provost of Dundee, and by him was given over to the keeping of John, Lord Glamis, in obedience to an ordinance of the Regent Murray. The Queen was very grateful to Sir John for his sufferings on her behalf, and wrote him a very kind letter, dated from Chatsworth, 11th June, 1570.

After the Battle of Sheriffmuir Lord Southesk consistently adhered to his party. When the Pretender (King James VIII. of the Jacobites) landed in Scotland in the winter of 1715-16, with the view of supporting his pretensions to the British Throne, he visited the Earl of Southesk at his Castle of Kinnaird, at which he held a Court, and from which he issued manifestoes, warrants, and other documents to his adherents.

From the first acquisition of the lands of Kinnaird by the Carnegie family, the Castle of Kinnaird had been their principal residence. The House of Kinnaird is mentioned in a charter dated in 1409. In the four hundred and seventy-three years which have passed since then it has been enlarged again and again. It was burned to the ground by the Earl of Crawford (Beardie, the tiger Earl), in 1452, because Walter de Carnegie (who afterwards re-built it), had dared to support the King in the battle of Brechin.

In 1555 Sir Robert Carnegie, the fifth laird, made

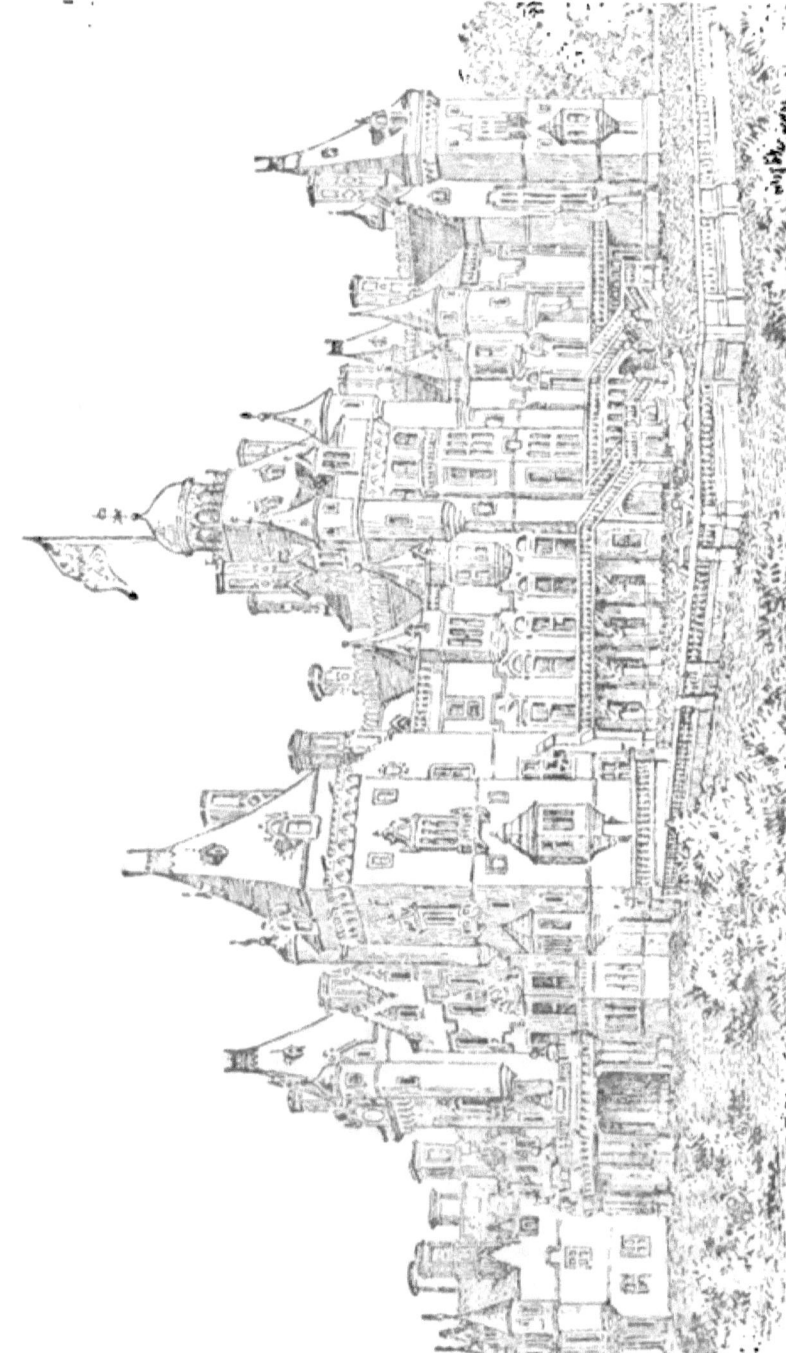

great additions to the Castle. David, first Earl of Southesk, made additions to it. Charles, the fourth Earl, intended to enlarge and renovate the mansion in 1698, but death prevented the work from being carried out. Then came the forfeiture of the estate, and the misfortunes which followed the support which Earl James had given the Pretender at Sheriffmuir in 1715. During the expatriation the Castle became decayed, and required to be repaired, but there was little done to it for many years.

About 1790 Sir David Carnegie began to make alterations and additions to the Castle which completely changed its appearance, and made it perhaps the largest mansion in Angus. He left it a huge, square building, with lofty square battlements. This plain though imposing structure, says Warden, did not satisfy the enlightened and classic taste of the present noble Earl, and a few years after his accession to the family honours and estate, he resolved to remodel the house within and without. Plans were obtained from Mr Bryce of Edinburgh; a beginning was made in 1854, and the work, carried on more or less vigorously during the intervening years, was brought to its completion in 1862. The Castle, as it now stands, forms a nearly perfect square; and very much presents the appearance of a French chateau of the olden time — with its massive towers capped by steep and lofty roofs; its long stretch of balustraded balconies and terrace walls; its many windows—mullioned and plain, dormer, bay, and oriel; its quaintly carved coats of arms, blazoning the alliances of its owners since, as already stated, the days of Duthac and Mariota.

The general effect of the building, says Mr A. H. Millar, in his "Castles and Mansions," viewed from any quarter, is very striking. It does not belong exclusively either to the Classic or Gothic styles of architecture, but may be classed with the numerous Scottish mansions, of which Glamis is a noble example, in which those styles are mingled with a greater or less predominance of the one or the other element. Kinnaird, however, bears a more distinctly French appearance than the older houses in Scotland of a kindred or similar type.

The position of the old gateway is now occupied by a fine stone staircase which rises from the terraced garden and gives access to the dining-room and drawing-rooms by a balustraded balcony upon which the windows of these apartments open. Much dignity is imparted to the flanking towers by the high sloping roofs which have been erected above the former towers, and these serve to give the whole building that quaint appearance which designedly recalls the French chateau of the sixteenth century.

The interior of the castle, with its rare and valuable art treasures, books, &c., is carefully and interestingly described by Mr A. H. Millar in his work already referred to. The pictures alone number nearly 200, including the Albert Dürer engravings, and are fairly representative of the principal Schools of Painting, many of them having special historical interest, in addition to their intrinsic value. In addition to over 40 portraits of members of the Carnegie family, the other paintings include notable productions of Italian, Dutch, Flemish, and other artists. A catalogue of the paintings is given in the "History of the Carnegies, Earls of Southesk."

From the platform of the central tower the view is enchanting, and we gaze with delight on the wide and varied expanse of land and sea which on either hand meet the admiring view. On the north the Grampian mountains form a noble background, and towards the front of the intervening undulations, the City of Brechin comes into sight. Stretching westwards, we descry the immense woods of Montreathmont Muir, once a barren, heath-covered plain. Its flat and monotonous outline, we observe, is picturesquely broken in the distance by the rocky heights of Turin. To the east from the foot of the Castle bank, extends a rich and level vale, along which, on the northern side, the river South Esk finds its way to the tidal lake commonly called the Basin; and bounding this estuary on the long promontory which shuts out the German Ocean, stands Montrose, with its lofty, well-proportioned steeple rising clear against the open sky. Immediately before the west and principal front of the Castle, lies the deer park stretching in one level sweep to woods which combine with those of Montreathmont Muir. At this part the deer park is a mile across, but it does not maintain an equal width in its whole north and south length of more than two miles. Within its area are contained 800 acres. Large woods of varying age and growth, and many young plantations shelter herds of red and fallow deer, in number generally limited to from 50 to 60 for the former, and from 400 to 500 for the latter, which, it may be noticed, are the direct descendants of those mentioned by Ochterlony in his account of the Castle.

In the conservatory, on the terraces in artistically arranged plots, and in numerous "borders" around the beautifully situated gardens a little below the Castle, are many rare specimens of exotic and indigenous plants in flourishing condition. The policies and deer park contain a space of 1314 acres in all, bounded on three sides, for over four miles, by a substantial wall, and on the fourth side by the river South Esk, the entire circuit being more than six miles. Every visitor cannot fail to be impressed by the immense size, fine symmetry, and great beauty of the numerous trees near the Castle (two of these of great age being known as "Adam" and "Eve," the former with a girth of 20 feet at 4 feet from the ground, though his top is now considerably decayed), as well as with the splendour of the house and gardens, and the picturesque beauty of the extensive policies by which they are surrounded.

The Carnegies of Southesk are not only famous as the inheritors of a very ancient name, but are equally distinguished by their brilliant talents and literary acquirements. Sir Robert Carnegie adopted, from choice, the law as a profession, and prosecuted it successfully while the Earl of Arran was Regent of Scotland, during the minority of Queen Mary. Arran, indeed, consulted Sir Robert, and relied on his advice and assistance during a great part of his regency. He made him a Senator of the College of Justice, and one of the Privy Councillors of the Regent. Notwithstanding the numerous important offices he held, he found leisure to write a work on the law of Scotland, which is quoted by Sir James Balfour in "Practicks of the Ancient Law of Scotland." Sir Robert married, in the year 1527, Margaret, daughter of Guthrie of Lunan. Of this marriage there were eight sons and eight daughters.

Mr David Carnegie of Colluthie and Kinnaird, who was also bred to the law, took a prominent part in the civil business of Scotland, and was appointed on many commissions by King James VI. David, first Earl of Southesk, inherited the talents of his father and grandfather for public business, and like them passed a long and active life in the service of his country. James, second Earl of Southesk, also took an active part in the civil and religious controversies which then occupied the attention of the country.

Tradition saith that his fame as an expert swordsman was attributed to the gift of supernatural power. He is said to have studied the *Black Art* at Padua, a place once famed for its seminaries of magic. There is also a tradition that at Earl James' death, the devil carried him away in a coach and six, and plunged with him into a well near the family burying-ground. The adjoining valley is still known as the "Deil's Den," and it is said that on stormy nights the Earl sometimes drives past his former home in the equipage provided for him by his Satanic Majesty!

James, fifth Earl of Southesk, is supposed to have been the brave Carnegie who is the hero of the popular song—" The Piper o' Dundee." The subject of the song appears to have been the proceedings of a private meeting held at Dundee for the purpose of favouring the Jacobite cause.

> There was Tullibardine and Burleigh,
> And Struan, Keith, and Ogilvie,
> And brave Carnegie, wha but he,
> The piper o' Dundee.

Sir David Carnegie, grandfather of the present Earl of Southesk, very early gave promising indications of literary talent and poetic genius. At the general election in 1784, he was elected Member of Parliament for the group of Burghs consisting of Montrose, Brechin, Aberdeen, Bervie, and Arbroath. Again, at the general election in 1796, Sir David was elected member for the county of Forfar. Sir David continued to represent Forfarshire till his death, which took place in 1805. At the early age of six years, Sir James Carnegie succeeded his father, having been born at Kinnaird in 1799. Like his father, Sir David, he became the representative of the Montrose district of Burghs.

Lady Charlotte Elliot, who was a sister of the present Earl, was one of the most accomplished and charming women of her time. She wrote some of our most popular sacred songs—including "Just as I am, without one plea"—and published several selections of her poems, under the titles "Stella, and other Poems, by Florenz" (1867); "Medusa, and other Poems" (1878), &c. These contained many productions of remarkable beauty.

James, sixth and present Earl of Southesk (and but for the attainder, ninth Earl), was born at Edinburgh on the 16th of November, 1827. He received the earlier part of his education at the Edinburgh Academy, and, in 1841, became a cadet at the Royal Military College at Sandhurst, where he passed examinations which entitled him to a commission without purchase. In 1845 he was gazetted to an ensigncy in the 92nd Highlanders; and on 23rd January, 1846, he obtained a commission in the Grenadier Guards, in which he remained for three years. It being the great ambition of his life to see his family reinstated in their ancient family honours, Sir James Carnegie, in the year 1853, renewed the claim originally made by his father and grandfather to the titles of Earl of Southesk and Lord Carnegie. The Committee of Privileges resolved that the claim to the titles had been established, and Lord Southesk was placed on the roll of Peers in Scotland, with the same precedency as if no forfeiture had taken place.

Although the Earl has never taken a very prominent part in public affairs, his published works—not to speak of his valuable and learned papers to antiquarian and scientific societies, pamphlets, &c.—are considerable, and prove that he has inherited the polished culture and literary genius of several of his distinguished ancestors. He has also distinguished himself as a traveller; for, during the year 1859 he travelled in the Far West of America, and in 1875 published a most interesting account of his adventures and experiences in a large volume, entitled "Saskatchewan, and the Rocky Mountains: a Narrative of Travel through the Hudson's Bay Territories." The work at once became popular, was admired for the easy and gracefully flowing style in which it was written, and became a standard book of modern travel. Attached to this volume are several very refined and enlightened critical articles on Shakespeare. A reverential student of Shakespeare, and an enlightened liberal patron of the drama and fine arts, he is considered an authority in literary and artistic circles.

In 1862 he published a romance bearing the title of "Herminius." "Britain's Art Paradise" appeared in 1871, being notes on pictures exhibited in the Royal Academy for that year. In rapid succession we have in 1876, "Jonas Fisher; a Poem in Brown and White," which soon went through two editions, and "Greenwood's Farewell, and other Poems." In 1877 his Lordship gave to the world "The Meda Maiden, and other Poems." The latter is the last published of his Lordship's effusions, and along with "Jonas Fisher" has perhaps secured the greatest amount of public favour.

These works show that the poet has thought deeply and justly on many things, the roots of which lie in us and around us, and that he has given utterance to ideas and fancies which will breed others in the minds of his readers. His fine, tender, cultured touches, refined subtlety of feeling, vigour, and pathos, have secured for him a good place among our present day poets. He finds poetry in all created existence—in man, and in every object that surrounds him; in the sweet and hallowed influences of Nature; in every leaf, bud, and flower; in the gentle influences of love and affection. He sings in pure language of the light ray that comes down upon the stream or hill; of the birks in the summer valleys; and in a low and mournful dirge he sings over the perishing flowers of summer. He feels the whispering of Divine love, and finds utterance of praise to the Creator in serenely calm and beautiful words.

Lord Southesk married, first, in 1849, the Lady Catherine Noel, third daughter of the first Earl of Gainsborough, who died in 1855. His Lordship married secondly (1860) the Lady Susan Catherine Mary Murray, eldest daughter of Alexander Edward, sixth Earl of Dunmore.

Charles Noel, Lord Carnegie, eldest son of the Earl of Southesk, was born in 1854, and married (1891) Ethel Mary Elizabeth, only daughter of the late Sir Alexander Bannerman of Elsick, Bart. Lord Carnegie is Colonel of the F. and K. Militia Artillery, and a Deputy Lieutenant of Forfarshire.

We leave Kinnaird Castle with the feeling that surely such a residence can well be called a "Meet nurse for a poetic child." Lord Southesk loves this quiet retreat. At the celebration of his 60th birthday, and in the course of his reply to the toast of his health, he said—"My greatest love is for the place of my birth. I wish to live here, and I love to live among you. I have a sincere desire to live on the kindliest terms with all with whom I have to do." From this, from his written works, and from his actions it is well known that Lord Southesk is a nobleman of universal humanity. His sympathies go forth to every form of human life. His is a beautiful and gentle nature, full of tenderness, and singularly imbued with sweetness and light.

We cannot fail to feel that his Lordship must often have felt inspired, when, raising his head from his manuscript to meditate over a more harmonious arrangement of a line, his eye would catch such a scene as the following, amongst many others, which he has graphically described —

> And the mellow green hillocks with flowerets were gay,
> And the song-birds sing softly their paradise lay,
> And quick gleams of delight on the water-waves play—
> > Sweet shrubs bedeck the strand;
> And the roses all glowing, the hills all fair,
> And the fruit trees of fragrancy rapture the air.
>
> . . . .
>
> 'Mong the hills and the rivers, the trees and the flowers,
> > Where all hath tender charms;
> Where the butterflies hover on opaline wing,
> And the birds, in descent, low melody sing,
> Where are lovely small creatures, most sweet to behold,
> In the tintings of ivory, and russet, and gold.

The burial vault of the Southesk family is on a rising ground to the south of the Castle of Kinnaird. It is surrounded by ivy-clad walls; the entrance is by a handsome gateway, flanked by stone panels. The Southesk arms are carved on the north panel, and the Southesk and Lauderdale arms impaled are on the south. The burial vault, having an arched roof, is near the centre of the enclosure, with an ornamental stone cross placed over the entrance. Several monuments and tablets with inscriptions in memory of members of the family are upon the walls. The present Earl had the walls and grounds put into a a state of good repair. An avenue of large trees leads from near the lake to the burying place, and while it is secluded, there are, as is the case throughout the beautiful grounds, "peeps" that afford a pleasant look out on smooth lawns and clustering thickets, cut up by the quiet footways which so lavishly adorn the surroundings of the Castle.

The Ancient Bridge of Brechin and its Surroundings.

We leave the ever charming Kinnaird grounds by the North, or Brechin Gate, and soon come in view of the approach to the Ancient City by the old bridge. As we purpose devoting the remainder of our trip to paying a visit to Brechin Castle, we turn to our left, and enter the grounds at the lodge, only a few yards distant. Before doing so, however, the Bridge and its surroundings might be referred to.

Distinguished visitors, ancient as well as modern, have expressed themselves as deeply interested not only in the historic associations and hoary antiquities of Brechin, but are also charmed with the beauty of its surroundings and approaches—the romantic dells and richly-clad braes, its fair sloping and fruitful gardens, and the South Esk winding along its skirts, pleasing to the eye, and investing it with a beauty all its own.

John Ochterlony of Guynd describes the city in 1682 as "a very pleasant place, a royal burgh, and extraordinaire good land about it. It lies very pleasantlie upon the north side of the water of South Esk, which runneth by the walls thereof, where there is a large well-built stone bridge of two arches."

Viewed from whatever quarter, the entrances to Brechin are extremely beautiful, while the Cathedral spires and Round Tower rising from amongst the trees present imposing and attractive objects. The city is picturesquely situated on the sunny slope of a richly-wooded valley, and thus, besides its antiquarian associations, the district possesses charms of a scenic

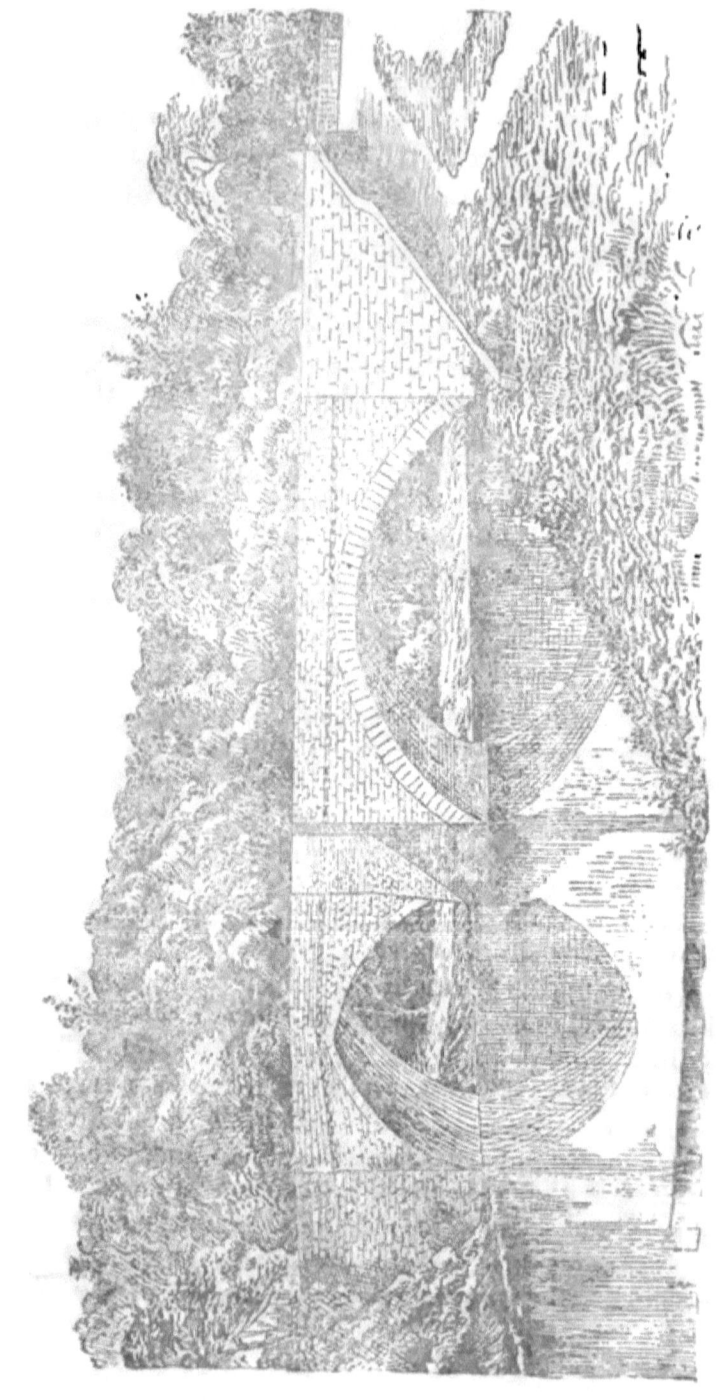

BRECHIN BRIDGE.

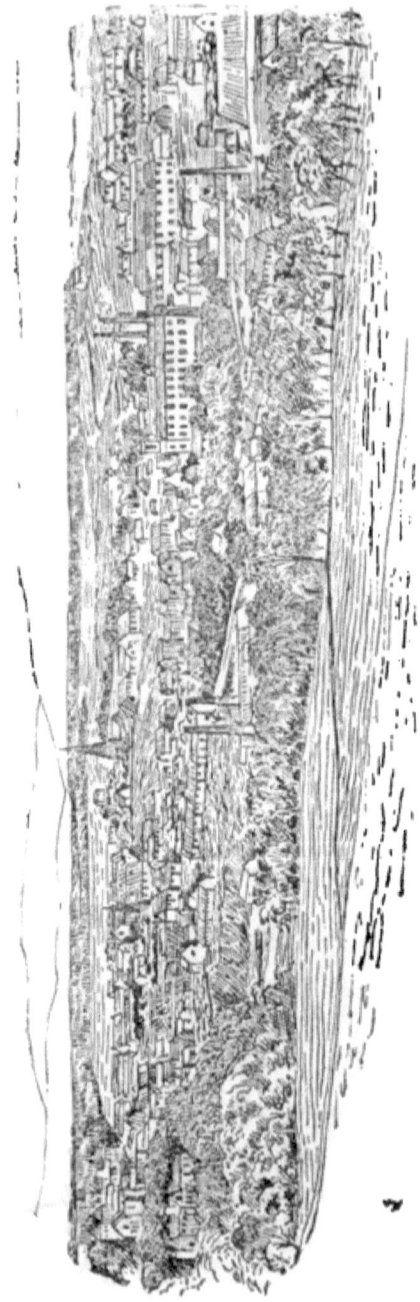

description which will abundantly repay a visit from the poet or the painter. From the "keystone o' the brig" you can at a glance take in the stretch of the river between you and the castle rock. Immediately to the right, and on a still higher elevation, rise the grey steeples of the cathedral, with the various spires and turrets of churches and schools peeping out among the trees. To the east, the tall smoking chimneys show the sites of the seats of industries. Above the Bridge, there are several pleasantly sheltered walks, either up the brae to Burghill, or by the low road to Stannochy and round to the west entrance to the town. The view from the "lee-side" of the "Hill-wood," or "Burghill," after walking among flickering shadows, presents many charms to the lover of landscape beauty. The town has the appearance of being built on terraces, with the everlasting hills as a solemn-looking and impressive background. We see the Castle, crowning the steep banks of the Esk, which here rises up suddenly as if for the special reception of the proud old fortress, with its weather-beaten walls and towers shadowed by noble trees, and wreathed about with twining ivy. This is a scene we can feast on under the delicious shade of the overhanging boughs, which spread their leafy arms, as if to screen us from the radiance of " the lord of day."

The Bridge of Brechin is supposed to be one of the most ancient stone bridges in Scotland, " but there is no tradition when or by whom it was built." It seems to have been in existence early in the thirteenth century, for amongst the records of Arbroath there is said to be a disposition granted by Stephen of Kinnardsley about 1220, in which he depones to Gregory, Bishop of Brechin, "for the sustenance of the Brechin Bridge." It has been the south entrance to the city for at least six or seven hundred years. Its praises were sung in Latin verse by a poet who wrote thus in 1642 (although modern poets and artists too have attempted to depict its situation in verse and on canvas)—

> This fertile town doth twixt two rivers stand,
> One to the north, one to the southward hand ;
> The waters down betwixt the rocks do glyde.
> Both Bridges have, and many Foords beside.

The poet, however, has here taken considerable license—the North Esk, evidently the other " river" referred to, being about six miles from Brechin. In 1786 the north arch was rebuilt, but we understand the other arch is the original one. The bridge is still a solid-looking structure, and it is likely to

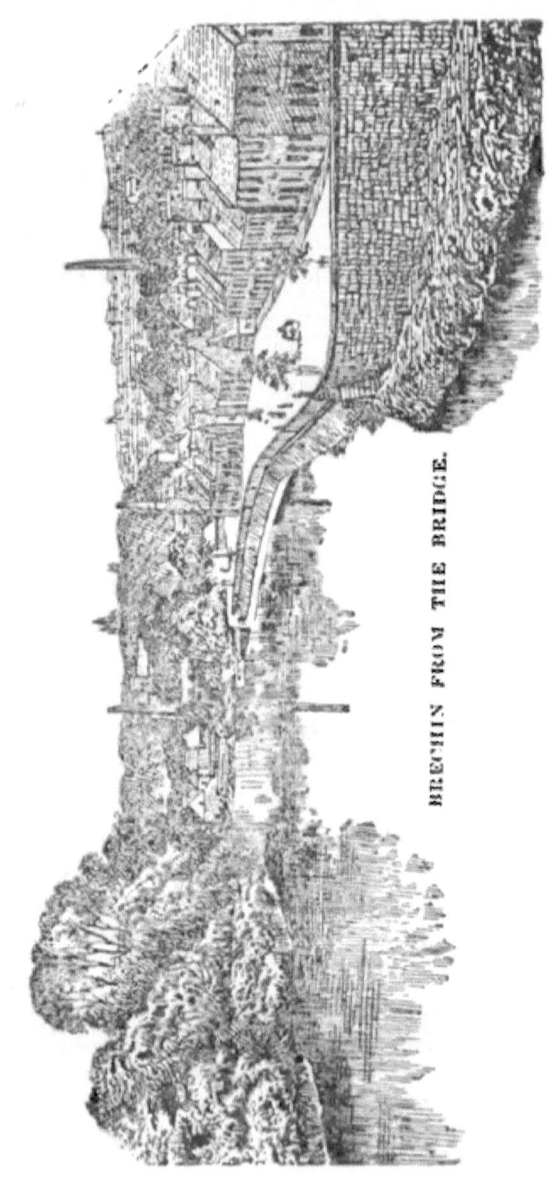

BRECHIN FROM THE BRIDGE.

stand for ages to come. During a long course of years it has been severely tried by many floods, but it has bravely withstood every assault, and calmly surveyed the torrent, while many more modern bridges on other parts of the stream have been swept away.

Above the bridge the river is overhung by the umbrageous trees, which are reflected as in a mirror on its unruffled surface. Below, however, the waters seem to become instinct with new life, and murmur sweetly among the channel stones as they pass with a fine sweep into the verdant recesses of the Kinnaird policies, giving and receiving beauty. No more charming woodlands could be wished for, and no more delightful seclusion could be found for long summer evening rambles. In speilin' the richly wooded braes, every change of position reveals a new picture to the gaze.

In the annals of witchcraft, the bridge is spoken of as the meeting-place of a noted witch and his Satanic Majesty. In 1650, a poor woman, named Jonat Coupar, was brought before the Brechin Kirk-Session charged with witchcraft, no fewer than nine witnesses giving evidence against her, one of these deponing that he saw a "branded dog meett Jonat Coupar whill shee was going alongst the bridge of Brechin, and that he lap upon her, but he could not tell if shee kissed the dog or not." Another deponed that "shee saw ane dog halsse Jonat Coupar upon the bridge of Brechin, and that she heard her say, 'What now, gòssip?'" She was afterwards imprisoned, and in her confession declared that "the grew hound which met her on the bridge was the Divell." The result was that "Jonat," either for her glib tongue, or her ignorant superstition, was burned at the Witch Den.

Brechin Castle.

> Our ancient castle rears its massive crest,
> And sweetly shades the winding streamlet's breast,
> Where noble Maule resisted Edward's laws,
> And fell, alas! in that eventful cause.
> Though now no war-sign from the turrets wave,
> Nor sound of trumpets gather forth the brave,
> Their lord is known for nobler acts and ways,
> And rich and poor alike resound his praise.

On the line of the carriage way leading to the Castle by the massive west entrance gate—cathedral-like in its shadowy grandeur—there is a luxuriant avenue of "green robed senators," through the dense umbrageousness of which the vertical radiance of noon sends with difficulty stray golden beams to fret the sweet mid-day gloaming. At the end of this picturesque vista the castle comes into view. Though, to some extent, devoid of architectural adornments, it is a princely looking structure. A circular tower at the north-western angle, a pediment in the centre, and another tower at the north west angle, rise over the west front. This is the principal facade; and in its centre, directly underneath the pediment, is the main entrance. Its numerous narrow windows bear undoubted evidence of antiquity, but although it has a distinctly "auld warl" aspect, it is not by any means a "howlet, haunted-looking biggin," with mere fragments of weather beaten walls showing the remains of a once lordly mansion, with weird stories and superstitions attached to its history. Neither does it contain a resident ghost, nor are there secret and tortuous vaulted passages connecting it with the Cathedral, as is stated by tradition to exist between the latter and Maisondieu ruins.

James, the fourth Earl of Panmure, gave the castle a new front, and upon the shields on the pediments are fine carvings of the bearings of the family, with crests and supporters. Above is the date 1711, and below are the initials of Earl James and his Countess, Margaret Hamilton. These refer to the fourth Earl, who was attainted in 1715. It was still further enlarged by the first Lord Panmure, whose favourite residence it was, and who died there in 1853. More recently both the interior and exterior were much improved—first under the direction of Colonel the Hon. Lauderdale Maule, and afterwards by his brother, the late Fox Maule, who was subsequently Earl of Dalhousie.

Five or six centuries ago, the castle, which then

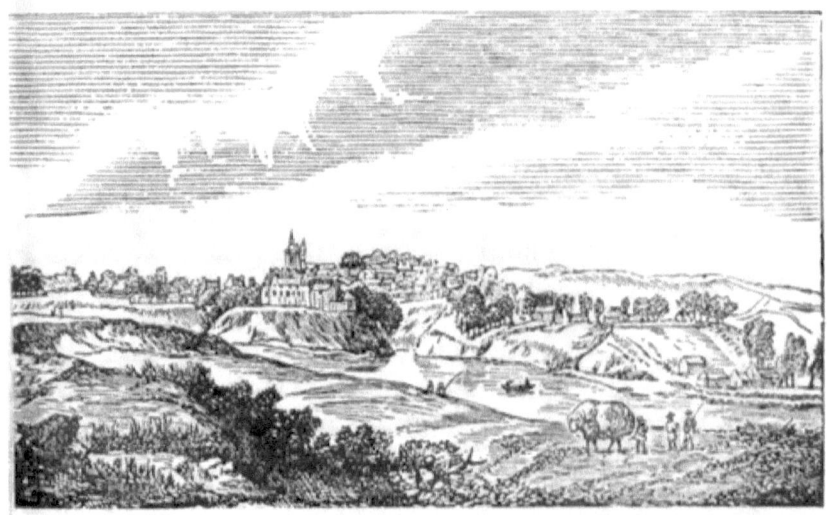

occupied almost the same site as the present noble building, was surrounded by water. The South Esk swept past on the south and east of the bottom of the perpendicular rock on which the structure still stands. On the west there was a natural or artificial ditch, as shown in our view engraved from Slezer's *Theatrum Scotiæ*, and on the north and east is a natural fosse, through which the Skinner's Burn runs, and which had evidently been converted into a moat in turbulent times.

The lawns of closely-cropped velvety turf are extensive, and they are beautifully studded with numerous tall ancestral trees—sylvan giants of lofty stature and goodly proportions. In the policies the visitor is charmed with a variety of landscape features of a most attractive nature. Indeed, with their suggestion of human care, and with interest at every step, they are in every way a fitting environment. The view from the battlemented wall facing the river, or from the tower, on which is the flagstaff from the Redan, presented to Fox Maule, who was Secretary of State during the Crimean War, is such as would take a summer day to describe. In close proximity is seen the grey old Round Tower and Cathedral spire uprearing their heads between openings in the dense mass of stately trees. Before you is the South Esk, meandering through rich alluvial meadows—now in sun, now in shadow—past mansions and comfortable farm houses, until it flows under a chaste bridge near the castle, known as the "Image Bridge," in the abutments of which there are fine statues, costing, it is said, £100 each. The river, flowing in majestic grandeur, is lost to view at the ancient Bridge of Brechin after several picturesque turnings. Looking from the tower, the whole city has a fine appearance, while the spires of Montrose glisten in the sun, and the German Ocean closes in the view to the south like a lake of crystal. The serrated ramparts of the Grampians to the north bound with their wild beauty the far stretching line of vision.

Altogether the circle of scenery from this "coigne of vantage" is of a rich and most varied description. Viewed from the north bank of the river, immediately below, or from the Bridge, as already stated, the castle forms an exceedingly picturesque object. It appears to rise out of a cluster of thick trees and shrubbery, over which its upper floors are seen, with the square tower rising in the centre—one of the finest sights on which the eye could wish to rest.

In the finely-situated gardens, approached from the castle by trimly-kept walks, things "rich and rare" seem to be collected from every country and clime, and the visitor is courteously shown all imaginable curiosities—indigenous and exotic plants in flourishing condition. Time would fail us to enumerate the leading features of the blooming wealth, to name which would puzzle a Linnæus. Away on the opposite rising ground is Burghill, the summit of which is thickly wooded, while its foreground is intersected with rich fields and picturesque clumps of trees. Indeed, there are hundreds in our own good city—admirers of nature too, in a fashionable way, and who travel far in search of the picturesque—who have never dreamed that such scenery exists almost at their own threshold.

Nature has greatly favoured the situation of the gardens. They are intersected with finely shaded walks and rich flower beds. There are several good specimens of the ancient Cedar of Lebanon in front of a line of well-stocked "greenhouses," while within the walls, in quiet secluded retreats, there are artistically laid out "rockeries," containing quaint-looking pieces of sculpture, and an aviary well-stocked with gaily plumaged birds.

Brechin Castle has a history that tells of

> Days when Scotland dealt in war,
> And wild her banners flew,
> And England drove her bloody car,
> Which thundered on the hills afar,
> In deep and deadly hue.

The castle was in 1296 occupied by Edward I., for a

purpose most humiliating to Scotland. On the 10th of July of that year he there received the homage of King John Baliol, and the resignation of the crown and kingdom.

> The English king to Brechin tower
>   Passed on in conquering state,
> Where Baliol stricken in his pride,
>   Stood singly at the gate.
>
> A suppliant for lands and life,
>   A beggar for the grace
> Of one that, as a rebel serf,
>   Now spurned him from his face.

His vassalage to Edward proving too galling to be tolerable, Baliol solemnly renounced his allegiance to him, sending to his Court Henry, Abbot of Arbroath, with the instrument of renunciation. This gave Edward the pretext waited for putting an end to the separate and independent existence of Scotland as a kingdom, and annexing it to his English dominions. He entered Scotland with an army to which it could offer no resistance, and when he had proceeded as far as Perth, Baliol felt himself reduced to the necessity of sending him a message offering submission, and imploring peace. Edward directed him to repair to Brechin Castle, where he would learn from the Bishop of Durham the terms on which mercy could be extended to him. He must not only abdicate his throne, but he must do so in a manner the most degrading. We are told that, "divested of his royal robes, and crown, and sceptre, he was compelled to stand as a criminal, with a white rod in his hand;" to "confess that, misled by evil and false council, as he averred, and through his own simplicity, he had grievously offended his liege lord;" to "recapitulate his various transgressions;" to "acknowledge the justice of the English invasion and conquest;" and to "resign his kingdom, its people, and their homage, into the hands of his liege lord, Edward." All this humiliation only saved his life; for he was forthwith sent a prisoner to the Tower of London, and thus ended his brief, inglorious, and wretched reign. In returning from the north, into which he had gone as far as Aberdeen and Elgin, Edward again visited Brechin Castle, and spent in it the night between the 4th and 5th of August, 1296. In 1297 Wallace drove the English from this stronghold, after which the castle was held in the Scotch interest by Sir Thomas Maule.

During the wars of the Independence, as well as the subsequent troubles of the times of Mary, the Castle was a place of note. It was besieged by the English under Edward I. in 1303, and was for twenty days gallantly defended by Sir Thomas Maule, an ancestor of the Panmure family.

> He livit quhen Briton's breach of faith
>   Wrought Scotland meikle wae,
> And aye his sword tauld to their cost
>   He was their deidly fae.
> Hie on a rock his castle stude,
>   With halls and touris a hicht,
> And gudly chambers fair to se,
>   Quhair he lodged mony a knicht.

Edward was on his way north to subdue Scotland. Finding the castle garrisoned, and the gates shut against him, he summoned Sir Thomas to surrender, but he refused, and the King, chagrined on account of this being the only opposition he met with in his march northward, at once laid siege to the building. The "War Wolf," capable of throwing stones of two or three hundred pounds weight, was brought against the besieged. The engine was planted on the east side of the deep ravine which then ran between the city and the castle. Notwithstanding this and the strong force the King had with him, Sir Thomas Maule made a gallant resistance for three weeks. At last, while he was standing on a bastion directing the defence, he was struck on the breast by a missile, and died on the evening of the same day. When his men saw that he was mortally wounded, they asked if they might surrender. He replied, "What, cowards, yield up the castle!" and then expired. Next day the garrison capitulated, and it appears to have then been destroyed.

The tower on which Sir Thomas stood is still pointed out, and near the spot there is now built a square tower, which adds much to the general appearance of the castle from this point. Though a Maule of Panmure happened to be military commander of Brechin at Edward's invasion, it was not until 1642 that the lordship of Brechin became the property of the Maules. In the interval it was in many different hands. For a while after the War of Independence it continued in the possession of Lords of the Huntingdon line.

The Earl of Panmure joined Mar in the revolt of which he raised the standard in 1715; and, at the Cross of Brechin, he proclaimed the Pretender King of Great Britain, as James VIII. of Scotland and III. of England. He and his brother Harry Maule of Kelly greatly distinguished themselves on the field of Sheriffmuir. The Earl, badly wounded, fell into the hands of the enemy, and owed his rescue to his brother's bravery:—

> "Brave Mar and Panmure
> Were firm I am sure;
>   The latter was kidnapped awa', man,
> With brisk men aboot,
> Brave Harry retook
>   His brother, and laugh'd at them a', man."

"Finding a little boat at Arbroath, he went off in it

BRECHIN CASTLE.

for France," and while there he made collections of charters and other muniments relating to his remote ancestors, and these documents were the basis of the *Registrum de Panmure* which form an authentic history of the family from 1066 to 1733.

The Maules have an unbroken descent in the male line for 760 years. Their history, for full particulars of which we refer the reader to our "History and Guide to Brechin," is traced as far back as the days of King Edgar. We are told that one Gaurin de Maule came from Normandy with the Conqueror in 1066, and that the family is in reality descended from him. The first of the old Lords de Brechin was Henry, son of the Earl of Huntingdon, who assumed the surname of Brechin; and it is thought that a fortress was erected by his father on the present site of the Castle.

By the marriage of Sir William, son of Walter de Maule of Panmure, who flourished in the reign of David II., to Marion, a grand-daughter of Sir David Barclay of Brechin, the Maules became related through the ancient Lords of Brechin to David, Earl of Huntingdon, and the Royal family of Scotland. The noble house have thus had long connection with the Ancient City.

In order to show how their interest in it originated, it is necessary to make some reference to the previous holders of the lordships of Brechin. Sir William de Brechin founded the Chapel of Maisondieu, "for the salvation of the souls of William and Alexander, Kings of Scotland . . . and for the welfare of his own soul." He was one of the most illustrious barons in the time of Alexander III., and his only child, David, married a sister of the Bruce. David, third in succession, entered into a conspiracy with William of Soules to deliver the town of Berwick to the English; but the plot was discovered, and he was executed for the crime in 1321. Some authorities have it that Sir David was only privy to the plot, and that he rather condemned the undertaking. Margaret, his sister and heir, married Sir David Barclay, who became Lord of Brechin, and was slain at Aberdeen in 1350. His son, David, succeeded to the lordship, and he is believed to have been murdered "by the contrivance" of Sir William Douglas of Leddisdale. His only daughter, Margaret, was married to the Earl of Athole, second son of Robert II., who kept possession of the lordship of Brechin after the death of his wife and their son. The Earl was executed for the part he took in the murder of James I. James III. granted "the whole lands" of the lordships of Brechin, Navar, &c., to his son, James Stewart.

The lordship of Brechin was purchased by Patrick, first Earl of Panmure; and although the property was lost to the family through forfeiture to the Crown on the execution of the Earl of Athole, it was again repurchased for the family, and has ever since been in their possession. Patrick, who died in 1671, wrote, in his old age, a "History of Sir William Wallace." George, third Earl, was a Privy Councillor to Charles II. and James VII. James, fourth Earl, bought a mansion in the Canongate of Edinburgh, and made improvements at Brechin. He was much opposed to the Union of Scotland and England. The Dowager Duchess, Jean, mother of Earls George and James, lived to see both of them in the possession of the honours of the family. The Pretender was entertained at Brechin Castle on 22nd January, 1716.

The Hon. Harry Maule married twice, but all his family by both wives died unmarried, with the exception of Jane, by his first wife, Mary Fleming, daughter of William, fifth Earl of Wigton. This daughter, in 1726, became the wife of George, Lord Ramsay, eldest son of the sixth Earl of Dalhousie, and from this marriage descended the Hon. William Ramsay Maule, afterwards Lord Panmure, and the late Fox Maule, and the present Earl of Dalhousie.

In 1764 Earl William purchased the family estates in Forfarshire for £49,157 18s 4d. The race of Maule ended, in the male line, with Earl William, who died in 1782, and the property thus descended to the family of Lady Jane as above. In this way the Ramsays acquired the large and beautiful estates of the Maules.

Here it might be stated that, after the attainder of 1716, the title having been conferred on the nephew of the forfeited Earl, he distinguished himself at the battle of Fontenoy, and in other engagements. He was remarkable in the senate for the liberality of his views during a somewhat illiberal period, and at home for kindness to his tenantry and servants, and his princely liberality to the poor. His Lordship, as was the custom of the time, had bakers and brewers of his own at Panmure House and at Brechin Castle, the gates of which were open " to all the vagrant train." To each poor wanderer he ordered a loaf of bread and a chopin of beer.

George, eighth Earl of Dalhousie, succeeded to the properties of his uncle, William Maule, Earl of Panmure, in the peerage of Ireland, at his death in 1782, and he retained possession of them during his lifetime. In terms of the entail created by his grand-uncle, Earl William Maule, the Panmure estates devolved in fee upon the Hon. William Ramsay, second son of George, Earl of Dalhousie, on the death of that nobleman in 1787. He was then in his sixteenth year, and assumed the name and arms of Maule of Panmure, and lived to possess them fully sixty-four years. He married, in 1794, Patricia

Heron, daughter of Gilbert Gordon of Halbeaths, and by her he had three sons and seven daughters. Of these the eldest, Patricia, was married to Gilbert Young; Elizabeth was married to Sir Alexander Ramsay of Balmain; Georgina, to W. H. Doubiggin; and Lady Christian Maule, who died a few years ago. The Hon. William Maule of Fearn, the youngest son, married Elizabeth, daughter of Thomas Binny of Fearn and Maulesden, to which properties he succeeded. He died in 1859, leaving several daughters—his only two sons having pre-deceased him. The second, Lauderdale Maule, while Assistant Adjutant-General in the Crimean War, died of cholera in 1854.

William, Lord Panmure, represented Forfarshire in Parliament from 1796 to 1831, when he was created a British Peer by the title of Baron Panmure of Brechin and Navar. Although he never shone as an orator, he was a nobleman of shrewd and discerning parts, had great tact in managing county business, was devoted to field sports, and was of a kind, social disposition, and fond of practical jokes. He was the helper of the poor and the friend of genius. His Lordship contributed an annuity of £50 to the widow of our national poet. He was the first to move in rewarding the heroic conduct of Grace Darling; and in our first tour we referred to his gift to the city of the Mechanics' Institution.

His convivial habits and love of amusement were often made the subject of scandal, and many stories are still current regarding his erratic doings. Some of these are doubtless mere oral traditions, exaggerated in their transmission from sire to son, having a modicum of truth garnished by the fanciful imagination of scandalmongers. The madcap freaks indulged in may appear incredible to modern ears.

We have only space to give one example, (details of his career, and many of his amusing escapades are given along with a portrait in our Almanac for 1894.) In Dundee one night he seized a waiter who had displeased him in some way, and threw him over a window into the backyard. Fortunately the poor fellow escaped with slight injuries, but he felt the indignity very keenly. He complained to his master, who mildly remonstrated with the lordly delinquent. "Is he dead?" said Maule. "No, your honour, he is not much hurt, but he considers that he has been insulted, and——" "Well, hang it, can't you put him in the bill at your own figure?" retorted his Lordship, waving him out of the room.

When it was resolved, in 1806, to modernise the Cathedral, an Edinburgh architect proposed to demolish the Round Tower, and utilise the stones in building the walls of the new aisles. No wonder that the Cathedral was quite disfigured by improvements (?) planned by an architect of this stamp. Fortunately, Lord Panmure and another heritor rejected the plans, and threatened to hang any one from the top of the Tower who removed a stone from it. Through the prompt action of his Lordship, we have still the glory of Brechin entire.

The records of almost every contemporary institution in Forfarshire which had for its object the alleviation of distress, or the improvement of the people, testify to the liberality of his gifts. The "Live and Let Live Testimonial" upon the hill of Downie, in Monikie, erected by his tenantry, shows their appreciation of him as a landlord; while the granite obelisk "erected by the People" over his grave, under the shadow of the graceful steeples of Brechin Cathedral, is a proof that the inhabitants were not unmindful of his kindness towards them.

His Lordship died on 14th April, 1852, in his 82nd year. He was in the eighteenth generation from the first Sir Peter Maule of Panmure and his wife Christian de Valoniis, and is believed to have been longer in possession of that property than any of his predecessors. The Hon. Fox Maule, eldest son of Lord Panmure, succeeded his father in 1852. In early life he retired from the army, and married the Hon. Lady Montague, daughter of Lord Abercromby. On the death, in 1860, of his cousin, the Marquis of Dalhousie, his Lordship, through the failure of heirs-male, became the 11th Earl of Dalhousie, and *Laird o' Cockpen*. Soon after, he resumed the family name of Ramsay in addition to that of Maule. He was long a member of the Privy Council, and held the offices of Vice-President of the Board of Trade, Under-Secretary for the Home Department, Secretary of State for War Department, and President of the Board of Control. As Secretary-at-War from 1855 to 1858, when the Crimean War and the Indian Mutiny engaged all his energies, the name of Lord Panmure was much before the public; in 1842 he was elected Lord Rector of Glasgow University. He had a rare combination of business talent, and was a very eloquent speaker. Dying in his 73rd year at Brechin Castle, in July, 1874, he was buried in the family vault at Panbride.

Leaving no issue, Fox Maule was the last Baron Panmure, but was succeeded by his cousin, the Hon. George Ramsay, C.B., second son of the Hon. John Ramsay, fourth son of the eighth Earl of Dalhousie. He was born at Kelly House, in 1805, entered the Royal Navy at the age of fourteen, and after seeing not a little service in all parts of the world, was appointed Admiral in 1875. In the same year he was elevated to the Peerage under the title of Baron

Ramsay of Glenmark. In 1845 he married Sarah Francis, daughter of William Robertson of Logan House, County of Edinburgh, who survives him—a highly-gifted lady, respected and esteemed for her ever kindly interest in all around her, and for her warm-hearted generosity. By her he had four sons —John William, born 1847, George Spottiswoode and Arthur Dalhousie, both deceased, and Hon. Charles Maule, born 1859. He died at Dalhousie Castle in July, 1880, and was buried in the family vault at Cockpen. Reference is made to his public career on page 181. In kindliness of heart, and the freedom of his intercourse with his tenants and others with whom he came in contact in the course of his rambles, he reminded old people much of his uncle, William, Lord Panmure.

Earl George was succeeded by his eldest son, the Hon. John William Ramsay, as thirteenth Earl of Dalhousie—Baron Ramsay of Dalhousie, and Lord Ramsay and Carrington in the Peerage of Scotland, and Baron Ramsay of Glenmark, County of Forfar, in the Peerage of the United Kingdom. His Lordship entered the navy at the age of fourteen. Having served in the Britannia, he passed out of the training ship at the top of his batch of cadets. After five or six years at sea as midshipman, he distinguished himself by passing the best examination of his year for the rank of Lieutenant. The next four years saw him on board H.M.S. Galatea, commanded by H.R.H. the Duke of Edinburgh, whom he accompanied twice round the world.

It was at this period that his determination and foresight came strongly to the front. Not content with the knowledge of the world which he had diligently stored up hitherto, he, at the age of twenty-seven, entered Oxford University. After two years' hard study (in 1877), at the earnest request of the Prince of Wales, he became commander of the training ship Britannia, at Dartmouth, on board of which the Prince's sons were to be educated. While there he married the Hon. Lady Ida Louisa Bennet, younger daughter of the Earl of Tankerville. When his Lordship stood for Liverpool, she proved herself a worthy descendant of the Lords of Chillingham and the Dukes of Gramont and Manchester. He often delivered as many as four speeches in one day, and then it was that her Ladyship was ubiquitous with a presence that attracted, and an influence that thrilled the bitterest opponent with admiration. While touching upon prospective legislation or other subjects, he did so with discreet and subdued eloquence. When raised to the Upper House, he at once came to the front, being appointed a Lord-in-Waiting and the representative of the Home Office. In 1881 his Lordship was placed on the roll of Knights of the Thistle, and invested by her Majesty with the insignia of the Order. It was said of him that while in the House of Commons he was one of the most popular members. He was the happy possessor of that gentlemanly frankness of manner which is somehow characteristic of sailors, and which in his case was the reflection of a singularly loveable nature. He had youth, cheerfulness, and shrewdness, with unaffected good sense, and seemed to " have a pleasant way of regarding the place as a sailor's mess, and all the members he came in contact with as shipmates ; yet he never gave the impression that he was for a moment unmindful of the important interests depending upon the proper navigation of the vessel of State." His speeches and actions on many and varied occasions showed breadth of vision, grasp of detail, and energetic administrative ability. He went out into life with the idea that his career would have to be of his own carving, and, given the talent of indomitable preseverance, he did everything well. Than the Earl and Countess no previous proprietors of the Castle could have been more popular, or identified themselves more with the welfare of the people. They thought more of the duties than of the privileges of the high position it was their lot for too short a period to fill. They were ever ready to give their aid and influence to every charitable object, and his lordship was a munificent supporter of the public institutions of Forfarshire. At all meetings with his tenantry distinct evidence was given of the excellent spirit which subsisted between them, and he showed this by a warm friendliness, goodness of heart, frank generosity, and an enlightenment that gave practical effect to the business truth that the interests of owners and occupiers are really one, and that prosperity, to be substantial, must be shared by both. In proof of this nobility of heart, it is only necessary to add that he on one occasion said that of all the money he had received from his tenants, he had spent much more than it all in improving their circumstances and surroundings, and had never expended a penny of it upon himself.

On the occasion of the opening of the City Hall, Brechin, on the 16th October, 1883, his Lordship was presented with the freedom of the Burgh. Provost Lamb appropriately referred to the close relations that had for centuries existed between the proprietors of the Castle and the town, and the hereditary and traditional ties that had so long united them, which had been strengthened since his Lordship's accession. In the course of an able and happy reply, the Earl referred to his high appreciation of the advantages of belonging to a community which has an undoubted history, and said that the burgh had a history nearly as old as the history of Scotland. He adverted to the wars of Edward I., and of the Covenanters in the seventeenth century, when Brechin was the headquarters of the Covenanting army. When that cause had finally triumphed, and was sullied by the surrender to the English of Charles I., among the four Commissioners who protested was the Commissioner for Brechin burgh. His Lordship was touched on the humiliating incident in Scottish history, of which the Castle was the scene—the surrender of Baliol, but, he added, " a few years afterwards the Castle had its revenge. Sir Thomas Maule—who seems to have been a very tough old gentleman—inflicted such a check on the English King as spoiled the enterprise on which he embarked. Your mode of evincing your kindly feeling to me in these days, though somewhat different to that employed by your predecessors, is none the less sincere, Looking over your burgess rolls I am proud to find that, since the beginning of the present century, of all the men who have had the honour of being admitted to that roll no less than one-third are of my own family. On the ground that you and your colleagues regard me as your hereditary friend, I am proud and grateful to accept the freedom of this burgh."

Lord Dalhousie's last public appearance in Brechin was on the 19th October, 1886, when he presided over a meeting held to promote the construction of a railway between Brechin and Edzell, when he indicated his desire to promote the undertaking as far as lay in his power. Particulars of the career of Lord and Lady Dalhousie, and of the esteem in which they were held throughout the country at large, are given in a memorial volume we issued, bearing the title " One in Life and in Death."

Two noble types of beauty and strength, and in the absence of external accident, an event so pathetically tragic as the death of the Countess in her 30th year—so lovely and accomplished, and of the Earl, twenty-four hours after, in his 40th year, so fruitful of usefulness and so full of promise—scarcely lives in the memory of man.

Two years before, Lord and Lady Dalhousie took a voyage to New Zealand for the benefit of his Lordship's health. Indeed, it may be said that he fell a victim to his high sense of public duty, for the illness which laid him aside from active work was induced by public labours, which overtaxed the energies of his body and mind. It was hoped that absence from political turmoil, residence at a health resort abroad, and, finally, a transatlantic tour would restore his vigour. On his return to this country it was understood that he had derived much benefit from the voyage: but fully a year before his death his health again gave way, and he joined Lord and Lady Brassey on board their yacht the Sunbeam, intending to accompany them on the voyage which for Lord Brassey had such a melancholy termination. Lord Dalhousie, however, was unable to go farther than the Mediterranean, where he left the Sunbeam and proceeded to Switzerland, remaining there for a considerable time, and next proceeded to visit his brother, the Hon. Charles M. Ramsay, in America, whence he was returning when the fatal illness overtook both himself and his Countess.

Lady Dalhousie, along with her husband, came ashore at Havre in very indifferent health. Her illness rapidly developed into blood-poisoning, and in a few days many were startled by the news of her death, which took place on 24th November, 1887. The lamentable illness and death of the Countess gave the Earl a shock which his system was unable to stand, and intense grief ended in an apoplectic attack which proved fatal only twenty four hours after. Thus the beautiful young mother and the devoted father, both in the hey-day of life, expired on a foreign shore, leaving five orphan children under the age of nine.

Under the fond care of his grandmother, and under the fostering guardianship of the Hon. C. M. Ramsay, his devoted and warm-hearted uncle, the young Earl, Arthur George Maule Ramsay (born 1878) affords in many ways clear proof that he will worthily represent the honoured name he bears, and that he has inherited much of the high sense of duty, kindness of heart, unswerving integrity, and guilelessness of disposition that were so marked characteristics of his much-loved father.

www.ingramcontent.com/pod-product-compliance
Lightning Source LLC
Chambersburg PA
CBHW021424300426
44114CB00010B/630